Ultimate Kubernetes for Cloud-Native Applications

Build, Scale, Secure, and Automate Enterprise Cloud-Native Applications Using Kubernetes, DevOps, and Multi-Cloud Strategies

Kamal Sharma

www.orangeava.com

First Published: January 2026
Published By: Orange Education Pvt Ltd, AVA®
Address: 9, Daryaganj, Delhi, 110002, India

275 New North Road Islington Suite 1314 London,
N1 7AA, United Kingdom

ISBN (PBK): 978-93-49887-86-2
ISBN (E-BOOK): 978-93-49887-73-2

Scan the QR code to explore our entire catalogue

www.orangeava.com

Dedicated To

This Book is Not Mine. It is a Humble Offering at the Feet of **Shri Bhagwan Narayan - The Supreme Lord**, *Eternal Master of All Creation, Knowledge, and Truth. Every Idea, Insight, and Clarity that has Manifested through These Pages is Merely a Reflection of His Divine Will and Grace. I Claim No Ownership - All Credit, Purpose, and Result of This Work Solely Belongs to Him.*

About the Author

Kamal Sharma is an accomplished Cloud Data Solutions Architect and visionary leader with over 16 years of experience in designing and implementing enterprise-grade cloud solutions and data architectures for global organizations. Specializing in cloud-native technologies, cloud migrations, DevOps, automation, and data engineering, Kamal is a Certified Cloud Solutions Architect (Azure, AWS, and GCP), and has been instrumental in delivering scalable, secure, and future-ready IT solutions across industries such as Healthcare, BFSI, Telecom, Retail, E-commerce, and Consulting Services.

He has consistently demonstrated a unique ability to align IT strategy with business goals, ensuring that complex technical challenges are met with innovative solutions that drive business growth and operational excellence. His expertise spans across building multi-tier, hybrid cloud architectures, data governance, and end-to-end data pipeline solutions, as well as leading complex projects leveraging AWS, Azure, GCP, and open-source technologies.

A strategic thinker, Kamal excels at leading cross-functional teams, defining long-term cloud strategies, and leveraging emerging technologies to drive business development, including GTM (Go-To-Market) strategies and presales support. With a proven track record in client-facing roles, Kamal has built and nurtured strong client relationships, and executed transformative cloud solutions that have resulted in measurable business impact and customer success.

Kamal has also played a key role in implementing CloudOps, DevOps practices, CI/CD, and FinOps, ensuring operational efficiency, cost-effectiveness, and security across enterprise infrastructures. He is an advocate of agile methodologies, and brings with him extensive experience in managing multi-cloud environments, overseeing large-scale distributed systems for complex, data-driven products.

His work has consistently been at the forefront of cloud transformation, helping organizations future-proof their infrastructure, and build resilient, adaptable IT ecosystems. Kamal's thought leadership in cloud-native and data architecture continues to inspire and influence organizations looking to embrace the full potential of digital transformation.

About the Technical Reviewer

Pramodh Kumar M is a seasoned DevSecOps consultant with over six years of hands-on industry experience. He specializes in designing, implementing, and optimizing secure, scalable automation solutions across modern cloud and enterprise platforms.

His expertise spans a broad ecosystem of tools and services, including GitHub Enterprise, ServiceNow, Azure DevOps, Launch Darkly, Octopus Deploy, SonarQube, the JFrog Platform, and the Atlassian stack. With a strong foundation in DevSecOps and automation best practices, Pramodh is known for delivering tailored solutions that drive efficiency, security, and measurable business value for today's hi-tech organizations.

Acknowledgments

I would like to express my heartfelt gratitude to everyone who supported me throughout this journey. A special thanks goes to my family - my wife, Dimple Kaushik, and my son, Joy Sharma - for their unwavering patience, love, and encouragement. I am also deeply grateful to my friends for their continued support. A sincere thanks to the reviewers, technical experts, and the publishing team at Orange Education Pvt. Ltd. for their invaluable contributions.

Preface

This book offers a comprehensive, hands-on journey into designing, building, and managing cloud-native applications using Kubernetes. It is crafted to help Cloud Engineers, DevOps professionals, Data Engineers, and Data Architects master real-world Kubernetes challenges and best practices.

The book begins by introducing cloud-native architecture, Kubernetes fundamentals, and container orchestration principles, laying the foundation for scalable, resilient applications. Readers will learn how to set up production-ready Kubernetes clusters across cloud (AWS, Azure, and GCP) and on-prem environments, ensuring robust and secure deployments.

As the book progresses, readers will dive into advanced topics such as microservices design patterns, CI/CD pipelines, Kubernetes security, observability, and workload automation. Special focus is given to real-world scenarios, including scaling distributed applications, monitoring cluster health, and securing workloads using DevSecOps best practices.

By the final chapters, the book will guide readers through troubleshooting Kubernetes clusters, debugging issues in production environments, and implementing Infrastructure as Code (IaC) with Terraform and Helm. It also explores emerging trends such as AI/ML workloads on Kubernetes, edge computing, and serverless container orchestration.

With step-by-step labs, expert insights, and real-world case studies, this book ensures that readers walk away with the skills and confidence to build, deploy, secure, and scale Kubernetes-powered cloud-native applications in any enterprise environment.

This book is divided into 13 chapters, each covering a deep dive into Kubernetes and cloud-native architectures. These chapters are exclusively designed to engage learners, and spark interest in cloud-native technologies. The details are listed as follows:

Chapter 1: Introduction to Cloud Native and Kubernetes

This chapter introduces the core concepts of cloud-native architecture, and explains why Kubernetes has become the de facto standard for container orchestration. The reader will learn how cloud-native applications address modern infrastructure challenges, and how Kubernetes fits into the DevOps ecosystem.

Chapter 2: Setting Up Kubernetes Clusters

This chapter provides a hands-on guide to setting up Kubernetes clusters in both on-premise and cloud environments. It covers installation methods, cluster configuration, and common setup challenges, while ensuring that readers understand how to create production-ready Kubernetes infrastructures.

Chapter 3: Kubernetes Architecture Deep Dive

This chapter offers a comprehensive exploration of Kubernetes architecture, detailing its internal components, and how they work together to orchestrate containerized applications seamlessly.

Chapter 4: Containers, Pods, and Microservices Patterns

This chapter dives deep into containerization concepts, pod management, and designing microservices patterns that thrive in Kubernetes environments.

Chapter 5: CI/CD Pipelines for Kubernetes

A practical guide to implementing CI/CD pipelines using Kubernetes-native tools, and integrating with Jenkins, GitHub Actions, and ArgoCD.

Chapter 6 (A/B): Scaling Applications Horizontally and Vertically

Learn how to scale Kubernetes applications efficiently, using horizontal pod autoscalers, vertical pod autoscalers, and custom metrics.

Chapter 7: Securing Kubernetes Workloads and DevSecOps

A hands-on exploration of Kubernetes security best practices, RBAC, and integrating DevSecOps pipelines.

Chapter 8: Networking Strategies and Service Mesh with Istio

This chapter introduces Kubernetes networking concepts, and explores how service meshes such as Istio enable secure, observable, and controlled microservices communication.

Chapter 9: Debugging Kubernetes

A practical guide to identifying and troubleshooting Kubernetes issues in real-world scenarios, including pod failures, performance bottlenecks, and networking glitches.

Chapter 10: Monitoring, Logging and Observability

This chapter covers the setup of a robust monitoring and logging stack to gain insights into cluster health and application performance. Hence, these processes are indispensable for monitoring ETL processes, and ensuring data integrity and performance.

Chapter 11: Automation with Helm, Terraform, and Ansible

Learn Infrastructure-as-Code practices to automate Kubernetes deployments, and manage cluster lifecycles efficiently.

Chapter 12: Emerging Trends in Cloud-native and Kubernetes

A forward-looking chapter that explores the latest trends and innovations shaping the future of Kubernetes and cloud-native technologies.

Chapter 13: Advanced K8s - StatefulSets and Multi-Cluster Management

This chapter covers advanced Kubernetes topics essential for managing complex, large-scale deployments across multiple environments. Readers will gain expertise in stateful workloads, optimized resource management, and multi-cluster federation, ensuring enterprise-grade scalability and resilience.

Get a Free eBook

We hope you are enjoying your recently purchased book! Your feedback is incredibly valuable to us, and to all other readers looking for great books.

If you found this book helpful or enjoyable, we would truly appreciate it, if you could take a moment to leave a short review with a 5 star rating on Amazon. It helps us grow, and lets other readers discover our books.

As a thank you, we would love to send you a free digital copy of this book, and a **30%** discount code on your next cart value on our official websites:

www.orangeava.com

www.orangeava.in (For Indian Subcontinent)

☑ **Here's how:**

Leave a review for the book on Amazon.

Take a screenshot of your review, and send an email to **info@orangeava.com** (it can be just the confirmation screen).

Once, we receive your screenshot, we will send you the digital file, within 24 hours.

Thank you so much for your support – it means a lot to us!

Downloading the code bundles and colored images

Please follow the links or scan the QR codes to download the ***Code Bundles and Images*** of the book:

https://github.com/OrangeAVA/Ultimate-Kubernetes-for-Cloud-Native-Applications

The code bundles and images of the book are also hosted on ***https://rebrand.ly/7a980f***

In case there's an update to the code, it will be updated on the existing GitHub repository.

Errata

We take immense pride in our work at **Orange Education Pvt Ltd,** and follow best practices to ensure the accuracy of our content to provide an indulging reading experience to our subscribers. Our readers are our mirrors, and we use their inputs to reflect and improve upon human errors, if any, that may have occurred during the publishing processes involved. To let us maintain the quality and help us reach out to any readers who might be having difficulties due to any unforeseen errors, please write to us at :

errata@orangeava.com

Your support, suggestions, and feedback are highly appreciated.

DID YOU KNOW

Did you know that Orange Education Pvt Ltd offers eBook versions of every book published, with PDF and ePub files available? You can upgrade to the eBook version at **www.orangeava.com** and as a print book customer, you are entitled to a discount on the eBook copy. Get in touch with us at: **info@orangeava.com** for more details.

At **www.orangeava.com**, you can also read a collection of free technical articles, sign up for a range of free newsletters, and receive exclusive discounts and offers on Print Books and eBooks.

PIRACY

If you come across any illegal copies of our works in any form on the internet, we would be grateful if you would provide us with the location address or website name. Please contact us at **info@orangeava.com** with a link to the material.

ARE YOU INTERESTED IN AUTHORING WITH US?

If there is a topic that you have expertise in, and you are interested in either writing or contributing to a book, please write to us at **business@orangeava.com**. We are on a journey to help developers and tech professionals to gain insights on the present technological advancements and innovations happening across the globe and build a community that believes Knowledge is best acquired by sharing and learning with others. Please reach out to us to learn what our audience demands and how you can be part of this educational reform. We also welcome ideas from tech experts and help them build learning and development content for their domains.

REVIEWS

Please leave a review. Once you have read and used this book, why not leave a review on the site that you purchased it from? Potential readers can then see and use your unbiased opinion to make purchase decisions. We at Orange Education would love to know what you think about our products, and our authors can learn from your feedback. Thank you!

For more information about Orange Education, please visit **www.orangeava.com**.

Table of Contents

CHAPTER 1

Introduction to Cloud Native and Kubernetes

Introduction

The world of software development has transformed significantly over the past decade. The adoption of **cloud-native architectures and enabling technologies** has been at the forefront of this transformation, enabling applications to be scalable, resilient, and easy to manage. Traditional deployment approaches, which rely on monolithic architectures, are now being replaced with microservices-based cloud-native applications. These applications fully leverage cloud computing capabilities and provide businesses with agility and flexibility.

At the heart of this transformation is Kubernetes, a powerful container orchestration platform that automates the deployment, scaling, and operation of containerized applications. Developed by Google and now an open-source project maintained by the Cloud Native Computing Foundation (CNCF), Kubernetes has become the de facto standard for managing cloud-native applications at scale.

This chapter explores the evolution of cloud-native applications, the benefits and challenges of traditional architectures, why Kubernetes is the industry-standard for containerized application management, and the fundamental components of Kubernetes that make it so powerful.

Structure

In this chapter, the following topics will be covered:

- Evolution of Cloud-Native Applications
- The Shift from Virtual Machines to Containers: The Rise of Kubernetes and Its Advantages
- Real-World Challenges of Monolithic Applications
- Kubernetes in the Modern DevOps Lifecycle
- Kubernetes for Data Engineers and Architects
- Security and Role-Based Access Control (RBAC) in Kubernetes
- Real-World Use Cases and Best Practices

Evolution of Cloud-Native Applications

The journey from traditional monolithic applications to modern cloud-native architectures has evolved through several stages, as illustrated in *Figure 1.1*:

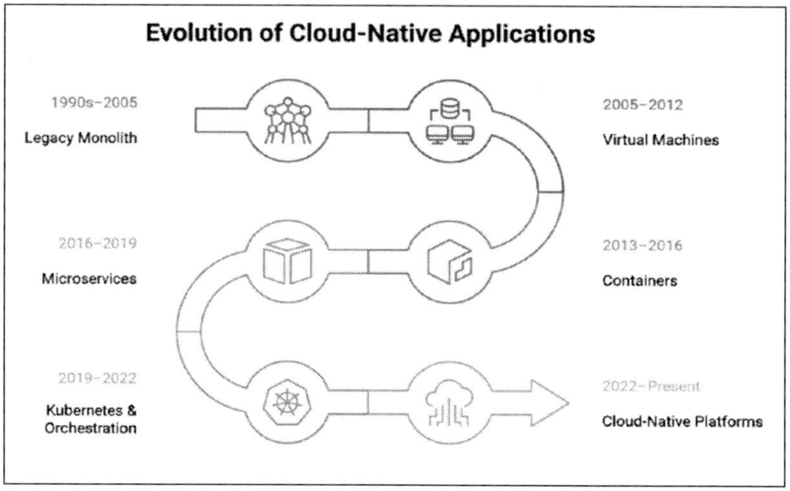

***Figure 1.1:** Evolution of Cloud-Native Applications*

Explanation: This visual timeline illustrates the major shifts in application deployment strategies. Starting from tightly-coupled monoliths, the industry progressed to virtualization, then embraced lightweight containers, eventually adopting Kubernetes-based orchestration, and now building fully cloud-native ecosystems.

Traditional Monolithic Applications

In Monolithic Architecture, all modules are tightly integrated, deployed as a single unit. A failure in one module may crash the entire application, and scaling must happen for the entire stack.

In Microservice Architecture, each service (frontend, business logic, and database access) is isolated and can scale, deploy, or fail independently. This enables fault isolation, CI/CD efficiency, and high agility across teams.

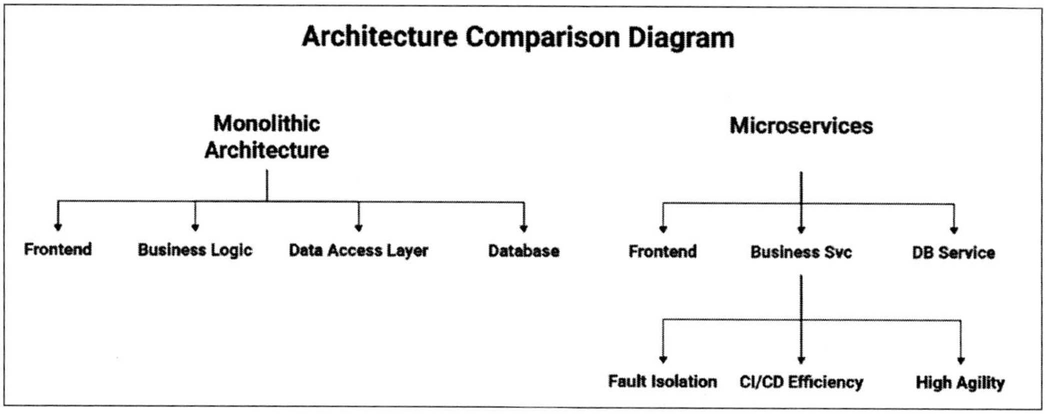

***Figure 1.2:** Architecture Comparison*

Why does this problem exist?

Earlier, applications were built using monolithic architectures, where all functionalities, such as business logic, UI, and database management, were tightly integrated into a single codebase. While this approach worked initially, it led to major bottlenecks in scaling, updating, and maintaining applications.

What is the core concept?

Monolithic applications are structured as a single large unit, making it difficult to modify or scale individual components independently.

When should this be applied?

This approach is typically used in legacy applications that require close integration between components but is now being phased out due to scalability limitations.

How do we implement this?

Example: A traditional banking application that handles account management, transactions, and customer support within the same codebase would require the entire application to be redeployed for a small update, leading to downtime.

Challenges of Monolithic Applications:

- **Difficult to Scale:** Scaling requires deploying the entire application, leading to inefficient resource usage.
- **Deployment Complexity:** Even minor updates necessitate redeploying the entire system.
- **Low Agility:** Teams struggle with parallel development due to tightly coupled dependencies.
- **Operational Challenges:** A failure in one module can affect the entire system.

The Shift to Virtual Machines (VMs)

Why did Virtual Machines become popular?

With the increasing need for scalability and isolation, organizations began shifting to Virtual Machines (VMs). A virtual machine allows multiple operating systems to run on the same physical server.

What problem do VMs solve?

They enable better resource utilization by allowing multiple instances to run on a single server, ensuring applications are isolated and independent.

When should this be applied?

VMs are useful when different applications require distinct environments but share the same hardware infrastructure.

How do we implement this?

Example: A travel booking company may deploy multiple VMs to handle different functions (booking, payments, user authentication). However, managing these VMs manually becomes complex as the system scales.

Advantages of Virtual Machines:

- **Better Resource Utilization:** Multiple VMs can run on a single server, optimizing resource allocation.
- **Security and Isolation:** VMs operate in their own environment, reducing conflicts.
- **Improved Flexibility:** VMs enable multi-OS environments within the same infrastructure.

However, VMs introduced new challenges:

- **Heavy Resource Consumption:** Each VM requires an entire OS, increasing overhead.
- **Slow Scaling:** Deploying new VMs takes time.

Containers and Microservices

Why were containers introduced?

To address VM limitations, containers emerged as a more efficient way to package and run applications. Unlike VMs, containers share the same OS kernel, making them lightweight and fast.

What problem do containers solve?

They provide a consistent, portable environment across multiple systems and significantly reduce the overhead of running applications.

When should this be applied?

Containers are ideal for microservices architectures, continuous deployment, and scalable applications.

How do we implement this?

Example: A ride-sharing application can be decomposed into separate microservices:

- **User Service:** Manages user authentication and profiles.
- **Ride Service:** Handles ride requests.
- **Payment Service:** Manages transactions securely.

Each microservice runs in its own container, allowing independent scaling and deployment.

Advantages of Containers:

- **Lightweight:** Containers share the OS kernel, reducing resource overhead.
- **Rapid Deployment:** Containers can start in seconds.
- **Portability:** Applications run consistently across different environments.
- **Microservices Architecture:** Enables breaking applications into independent services.

Kubernetes: The Game Changer

With the rise of containers, managing them efficiently became a challenge. Kubernetes provides a robust framework for automating container orchestration.

Why Kubernetes?

- **Automated Scaling:** Adjusts container instances based on demand.
- **Self-Healing:** Restarts failed containers.
- **Load Balancing:** Distributes traffic across multiple containers.
- **Multi-Cloud Support:** Runs on AWS, Azure, GCP, and on-premises.

When should Kubernetes be used?

When deploying applications that require dynamic scaling, high availability, and automated orchestration.

How do we implement Kubernetes?

Example: A video streaming service like Netflix uses Kubernetes to dynamically scale video processing workloads based on demand.

The Shift from Virtual Machines to Containers

Why was there a need to move from Virtual Machines to Containers?

Traditional Virtual Machines (VMs) revolutionized IT infrastructure by enabling multiple operating systems to run on a single physical machine. However, as applications grew more complex and cloud adoption increased, VMs started showing limitations, such as:

- **Resource Intensive:** Each VM requires its own OS, leading to high memory and CPU consumption.
- **Slow Boot Time:** VMs take several minutes to boot and initialize applications.
- **Limited Scalability:** Scaling applications with VMs often leads to inefficient resource utilization.
- **Complex Management:** Maintaining multiple VMs demands significant operational overhead.

These limitations led to the rise of **containers**, which offer a lightweight, portable, and efficient solution for application deployment.

What are Containers, and how do they work?

A container is a **lightweight, stand-alone, executable package** that includes everything needed to run an application: code, runtime, libraries, and dependencies. Unlike VMs, containers share the **host operating system kernel**, making them highly efficient.

Key Features of Containers:

- **Lightweight:** Containers do not require a full OS for each instance, reducing overhead.
- **Fast Boot Time:** Containers start in seconds compared to minutes for VMs.
- **Portability:** Containers run the same way across different environments (laptop, cloud, on-premises).
- **Isolation:** Each container runs in an isolated environment, ensuring application consistency.

When should you use Containers?

Containers are ideal for scenarios where:

- **Microservices Architectures:** Applications need to be broken into independent, scalable services.
- **Continuous Integration and Deployment (CI/CD):** Teams want to deploy applications quickly and efficiently.
- **Multi-Cloud Deployments:** Applications need to run seamlessly across AWS, Azure, and Google Cloud.
- **High Scalability Needs:** Businesses expect varying workloads that demand rapid scaling.

How to Implement Containers?

Step 1: Install Docker (A Popular Container Runtime)

Docker is the most widely used containerization platform. It enables developers to create, package, and distribute applications inside containers.

```
# Install Docker (Linux Example)
wget -qO- https://get.docker.com/ | sh
```

Step 2: Create a Simple Docker Container

Following is a basic **Dockerfile** for a simple Node.js application:

```
# Use an official Node.js runtime as a parent image
FROM node:14

# Set the working directory
WORKDIR /app

# Copy application files
COPY . .

# Install dependencies
RUN npm install

# Expose application port
EXPOSE 3000

# Start the application
CMD ["node", "app.js"]
```

Step 3: Build and Run the Docker Container

```
# Build Docker Image
docker build -t my-node-app .

# Run Container
docker run -d -p 3000:3000 my-node-app
```

The Role of Kubernetes in Managing Containers

Why was Kubernetes Developed?

While containers solve many application deployment challenges, managing them manually becomes complex. Kubernetes was introduced to automate container **orchestration**, ensuring:

- **Automatic Scaling:** Adjusts the number of containers based on demand.
- **Self-Healing:** Detects and restarts failed containers.
- **Load Balancing:** Distributes traffic across multiple containers.
- **Rolling Updates:** Deploys updates without downtime.

What is Kubernetes, and how does it work?

Kubernetes is an open-source **container orchestration platform** designed to automate deployment, scaling, and operations of containers across clusters.

Kubernetes Components:

- **Master Node:**
  - API Server: Manages cluster communication.
  - Scheduler: Assigns workloads to nodes.
  - Controller Manager: Maintains cluster state.
  - etcd: Stores configuration data.
- **Worker Nodes:**
  - Kubelet: Ensures containers are running.
  - Kube Proxy: Manages networking.

- Container Runtime: Runs containers (for example, Docker).

When should you use Kubernetes?

Kubernetes is beneficial when:

- You have multiple containers that need automated scaling.
- You require high availability and self-healing for applications.
- You deploy applications across multi-cloud environments.
- You want to streamline application rollouts and updates.

How to Deploy a Simple Kubernetes Application?

Step 1: Create a Kubernetes Deployment

```
apiVersion: apps/v1
kind: Deployment
metadata:
  name: my-app
spec:
  replicas: 3
  selector:
    matchLabels:
      app: my-app
  template:
    metadata:
      labels:
        app: my-app
    spec:
      containers:
      - name: my-app
        image: my-node-app
        ports:
        - containerPort: 3000
```

Step 2: Deploy the Application

```
kubectl apply -f deployment.yaml
```

Step 3: Expose the Application Using a Service

```
apiVersion: v1
kind: Service
metadata:
  name: my-app-service
spec:
  selector:
    app: my-app
  ports:
    - protocol: TCP
      port: 80
      targetPort: 3000
  type: LoadBalancer
kubectl apply -f service.yaml
```

Evolution of Application Deployment

- Virtual Machines were useful but inefficient for modern workloads.
- Containers revolutionized application deployment by being lightweight and portable.
- Kubernetes became the standard for managing containers at scale.

- Kubernetes enables automation, high availability, and multi-cloud deployments.

The Rise of Kubernetes as the Industry Standard

Kubernetes has rapidly become the de facto standard for container orchestration. But **why did Kubernetes emerge as the preferred choice?** The answer lies in the **challenges posed by traditional deployment methods and the inefficiencies of early container management solutions**.

The Need for a Kubernetes-Like Solution

Before Kubernetes, organizations struggled with managing containerized workloads at scale. Here are the key challenges that necessitated a robust orchestration system:

- **Manual Deployment and Scaling Issues:** Early containerized environments required engineers to manually deploy, start, and stop containers, making large-scale applications difficult to manage.
- **Inefficient Resource Allocation:** Containers were deployed without effective load balancing, leading to **resource wastage and performance bottlenecks**.
- **Service Discovery and Networking Complexities:** Communication between services running in different containers required extensive manual configuration.
- **Lack of Automated Fault Recovery:** When a container failed, there was no automated way to replace it or scale up based on demand.

Example: Imagine an **e-commerce website** running containers for different services, such as payments, inventory, and user authentication. If the payment service container crashes, **manual intervention** would be needed to restart it. This delay could lead to **failed transactions and revenue loss**.

Kubernetes solves these challenges by automating deployment, scaling, and self-healing of containers, ensuring reliability at scale.

Scaling with Kubernetes: Real-World Scenarios

In this section, we will explore how Kubernetes helps scale and manage applications dynamically, ensuring reliability and performance across various industries.

Example 1: E-commerce Payment Services Reliability

Why? In an e-commerce platform, different microservices including payments, inventory, and user authentication work together. If the **payment service** crashes, transactions fail, leading to revenue loss and poor user experience. Traditional approaches require manual intervention to restart the service, increasing downtime.

What? Kubernetes automates service recovery, restarts failed pods, and ensures high availability by distributing workloads across nodes.

When? This is critical during high-traffic sales events like **Black Friday** or **holiday shopping seasons** when thousands of transactions occur per second.

How? Kubernetes uses **Liveness and Readiness Probes** to monitor pod health and automatically restart crashed containers. **Horizontal Pod Autoscaler (HPA)** ensures more pods are added when traffic spikes.

Implementation: Example Code

```
apiVersion: apps/v1
kind: Deployment
metadata:
  name: payment-service
spec:
  replicas: 3
  template:
    spec:
      containers:
      - name: payment
        image: payment-service:v1
        livenessProbe:
          httpGet:
            path: /health
            port: 8080
        readinessProbe:
          httpGet:
            path: /ready
            port: 8080
```

Example 1.1: E-commerce Platform Handling High Traffic

Why? Traditional e-commerce platforms running on monolithic architectures struggle with sudden traffic spikes. Black Friday sales, product launches, and holiday seasons often lead to website crashes due to unscalable backend infrastructure.

What? Kubernetes helps e-commerce companies scale their services dynamically. It enables auto-scaling of microservices such as payment processing, inventory management, and user authentication.

When? Scaling is critical when traffic spikes unpredictably. Without auto-scaling, systems either overprovision resources (leading to cost inefficiencies) or underprovision (leading to downtime and revenue loss).

How? With Kubernetes, an e-commerce platform can:

- Use **Horizontal Pod Autoscaler (HPA)** to automatically increase or decrease the number of pods.
- Implement **Load Balancing** using Kubernetes Services.
- Deploy **Canary Deployments** to test new features without affecting live users.

Code Example: Horizontal Pod Autoscaler

```
apiVersion: autoscaling/v2beta2
kind: HorizontalPodAutoscaler
metadata:
  name: payment-service-hpa
spec:
  scaleTargetRef:
    apiVersion: apps/v1
    kind: Deployment
    name: payment-service
  minReplicas: 2
  maxReplicas: 10
  metrics:
    - type: Resource
```

```
      resource:
        name: cpu
        target:
          type: Utilization
          averageUtilization: 50
```

This ensures that Kubernetes automatically scales the payment service when CPU utilization exceeds 50%.

Why Kubernetes is the Ideal Solution

Kubernetes brings a **declarative approach** to managing containerized applications. Instead of manually defining which containers should run, you specify the **desired state**, and Kubernetes ensures that the system maintains it.

Key Features:

- **Automated Scaling**: Kubernetes can scale up or down **dynamically** based on real-time demand.
- **Self-Healing**: Failed containers are **automatically restarted**, ensuring minimal downtime.
- **Load Balancing**: Kubernetes efficiently distributes traffic between multiple instances.
- **Multi-Cloud Portability**: Run applications on **AWS, Azure, GCP, or On-Prem** without modification.

Example: Netflix uses Kubernetes to **scale video processing workloads dynamically**. When demand spikes during **prime-time streaming**, Kubernetes ensures that additional processing power is allocated without human intervention.

Example 2: Netflix Video Processing Scaling

Why? Streaming platforms like **Netflix** handle massive video workloads. During peak hours, millions of users stream simultaneously, increasing demand on video transcoding services. Without proper scaling, video buffering and poor-quality affect user experience.

What? Kubernetes dynamically scales video processing workloads using **Cluster Autoscaler and HPA**, allocating more nodes and pods as needed.

When? This is essential when streaming demand fluctuates—for example, during a **new movie release** or popular series premiere.

How? Kubernetes monitors CPU and memory usage, triggering auto-scaling policies to spin up additional processing instances.

Implementation: Example Code

```
apiVersion: autoscaling/v2
kind: HorizontalPodAutoscaler
metadata:
  name: video-transcoder-hpa
spec:
  scaleTargetRef:
    apiVersion: apps/v1
    kind: Deployment
    name: video-transcoder
  minReplicas: 2
  maxReplicas: 10
  metrics:
  - type: Resource
    resource:
```

```
        name: cpu
        target:
          type: Utilization
          averageUtilization: 75
```

Example 2.1: Video Streaming Services Like Netflix

Why? Video streaming services handle enormous amounts of data and require low-latency content delivery. Traditional architectures often struggle with real-time video processing and CDN scaling.

What? Kubernetes provides dynamic resource allocation for high-demand streaming content. It scales video encoding workloads and ensures failover mechanisms for smooth playback.

When? During peak hours, such as evening prime time, streaming services experience **10x the normal traffic**. Kubernetes ensures uninterrupted service.

How?

- **Dynamic Scaling:** Kubernetes automatically provisions GPU-based pods for encoding high-quality videos.
- **Self-Healing:** If a node fails, Kubernetes automatically shifts workloads to available nodes.
- **Multi-Region Load Balancing:** Kubernetes manages streaming servers across global data centers.

Ideal Use Cases for Kubernetes

Kubernetes is ideal for:

- **Microservices Architectures**: When applications are broken into independent, scalable services.
- **High-Traffic and Scalable Applications**: Websites, AI workloads, and real-time analytics.
- **Hybrid and Multi-Cloud Deployments**: Applications requiring seamless operation across cloud providers.
- **CI/CD Pipelines**: Automating software releases with minimal downtime.

Example: A **ride-sharing app** like Uber benefits from Kubernetes by dynamically **scaling ride-matching services** in real-time, ensuring smooth operations during peak hours.

Example 3: Uber Ride-Matching Optimization

Why? Ride-sharing platforms like **Uber** match drivers and passengers in real-time. During peak hours, an increased number of ride requests can overload backend services, causing delays in ride-matching and impacting user satisfaction.

What? Kubernetes ensures that ride-matching microservices scale automatically, handling peak demand effectively.

When? During events such as **concerts, sports games, or holiday seasons**, when demand for rides surges.

How? Kubernetes deploys new pods dynamically to process ride requests efficiently, ensuring fast matching between riders and drivers.

Implementation: Example Code

```
apiVersion: apps/v1
kind: Deployment
metadata:
```

```
  name: ride-matching-service
spec:
  replicas: 3
  template:
    spec:
      containers:
      - name: ride-matching
        image: ride-matching:v2
        resources:
          limits:
            cpu: "2"
            memory: "2Gi"
          requests:
            cpu: "0.5"
            memory: "512Mi"
```

Example 3.1: Ride-Sharing Apps Like Uber

Why? Ride-sharing applications must match users with drivers in real-time. A delay of even a few seconds can cause service failures.

What? Kubernetes ensures that ride-matching services scale instantly based on demand. It also integrates with event-driven architectures such as Apache Kafka for real-time processing.

When? Demand spikes during **rush hours**, special events, and bad weather conditions. Kubernetes ensures high availability for ride-matching algorithms.

How?

- **Kubernetes integrates with message queues** (Kafka) for real-time data streaming.
- **Pod Auto-Scaling** ensures sufficient compute resources for ride-matching.
- **Multi-Cloud Deployment** enables global availability.

Code Example: Kubernetes Deployment for Ride-Matching Service

```
apiVersion: apps/v1
kind: Deployment
metadata:
  name: ride-matching-service
spec:
  replicas: 3
  selector:
    matchLabels:
      app: ride-matching
  template:
    metadata:
      labels:
        app: ride-matching
    spec:
      containers:
      - name: ride-matching
        image: ridesharing-app:v1
        ports:
        - containerPort: 8080
```

This ensures Kubernetes keeps three replicas of the ride-matching service running at all times.

Example 4: Financial Services High Availability

Why? Banks and financial institutions process millions of transactions per second. If a failure occurs in the transaction processing system, it could lead to financial loss, regulatory violations, and customer distrust.

What? Kubernetes ensures transaction workloads run in multiple availability zones using **multi-region clusters** and **disaster recovery strategies**.

When? This is crucial for handling **stock market transactions, online payments, and banking operations** that require high availability.

How? Kubernetes distributes workloads across **multiple data centers** and automatically reroutes traffic to healthy instances in case of failure.

Implementation:

```
apiVersion: networking.k8s.io/v1
kind: Ingress
metadata:
  name: finance-ingress
spec:
  rules:
  - host: transactions.bank.com
    http:
      paths:
      - path: /
        pathType: Prefix
        backend:
          service:
            name: transaction-service
            port:
              number: 443
```

Example 4.1: Financial Transactions Processing

Why? Financial services companies process millions of transactions per second. Traditional database-driven architectures struggle with performance at scale.

What? Kubernetes provides fault-tolerant and globally distributed transaction processing capabilities.

When? During peak trading hours, financial institutions require **high throughput and low latency**. Kubernetes ensures transactions are not delayed due to hardware failures.

How?

- **StatefulSets for Databases:** Ensures transaction consistency.
- **Read-Replica Scaling:** Kubernetes scales database read replicas based on query loads.
- **CI/CD Pipelines:** Ensures zero-downtime updates for financial applications.

Kubernetes Architecture and Functionality

Kubernetes operates using a **master-worker architecture**, managing containerized workloads through the following components:

- **Control Plane (Master Node)**
    - **API Server**: Central hub for cluster communication.

    - **Scheduler**: Assigns workloads to worker nodes.
    - **Controller Manager**: Maintains system state.
    - **etcd**: Stores cluster configuration data.
- **Worker Nodes**
    - **Kubelet**: Ensures containers are running correctly.
    - **Kube Proxy**: Manages networking between containers.
    - **Container Runtime**: Runs the actual containers (for example, Docker, containerd).

Example: A financial services provider uses Kubernetes to process millions of transactions per second, ensuring high availability across global data centers.

Diagram: Kubernetes Architecture Overview

A high-level diagram showing the interaction between the control plane, worker nodes, and containers.

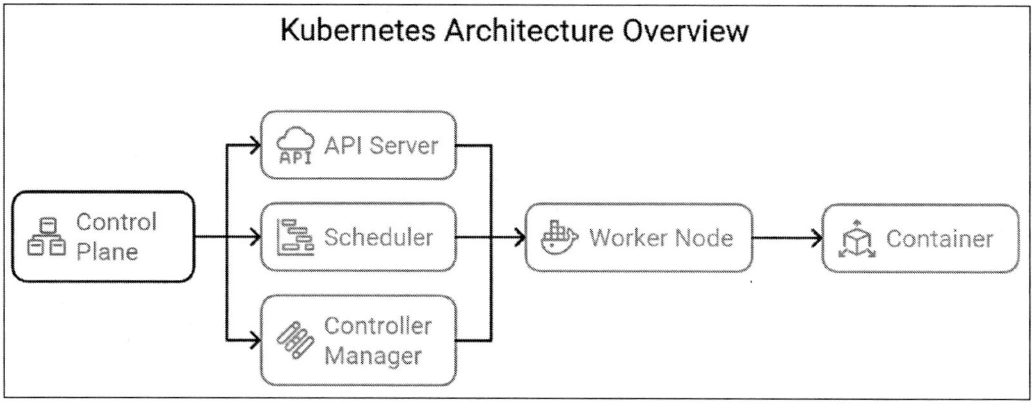

Figure 1.3: *Kubernetes Architecture Overview*

Kubernetes is not just a tool - it is a **game changer** in modern cloud-native application development. By understanding its capabilities and advantages, engineers can **build highly scalable, resilient, and automated deployments** that power some of the world's largest applications.

These real-world scenarios demonstrate how Kubernetes solves major scalability and reliability challenges. By leveraging **self-healing, auto-scaling, and multi-cloud deployments**, Kubernetes has become the backbone of modern cloud-native applications.

Real-World Challenges of Monolithic Applications

Modern applications are expected to be highly scalable, rapidly deployable, and resilient. However, traditional monolithic architectures pose significant challenges that prevent businesses from achieving these goals. This section explores the core limitations of monolithic applications, and how Kubernetes offers a path toward overcoming them.

Scaling Issues in Monoliths

Why is Scaling a Problem in Monoliths?

Monolithic applications are built as a single, large codebase where all components (UI, business logic, and database operations) are tightly coupled. As the user base grows, these applications become increasingly difficult to scale efficiently.

What are the Core Challenges?

- **Resource Wastage:** Scaling a monolith means replicating the entire application, even if only one component needs more resources.
- **Traffic Spikes Handling:** Monolithic applications struggle with sudden increases in user demand due to their rigid architecture.
- **Infrastructure Limitations:** Scaling a monolith requires provisioning larger VMs, leading to higher infrastructure costs and inefficient resource allocation.

When Does Scaling Become Critical?

- When a company experiences rapid user growth (for example, an e-commerce platform during Black Friday sales).
- When load spikes unpredictably, such as in event ticketing platforms handling sudden traffic surges.
- When application response time degrades due to increased concurrent requests.

How Kubernetes Resolves These Challenges?

- **Microservices and Independent Scaling:** Kubernetes allows breaking a monolith into smaller microservices, enabling independent scaling of specific components.
- **Auto-scaling and Load Balancing:** Kubernetes automatically adjusts resources based on demand, ensuring smooth operations.
- **Cost Optimization:** Kubernetes reduces infrastructure overhead by efficiently distributing workloads across nodes.

Example: A retail company using a monolithic e-commerce application faced major slowdowns during peak seasons. Moving to Kubernetes allowed them to break their application into microservices (cart, payments, search) and scale only high-demand services, improving performance while reducing costs.

Deployment Complexity and Slow Releases

Why do Monoliths have Deployment Issues?

Monolithic applications require deploying the entire codebase, even for minor changes, leading to slow and error-prone release cycles.

What are the Main Deployment Challenges?

- **Downtime Risks:** Deploying a new version often requires taking the entire system offline.
- **Limited CI/CD Capabilities:** Monolithic applications struggle with integrating modern DevOps practices, such as Continuous Integration and Continuous Deployment (CI/CD).
- **Rollback Complexity:** If a bug is introduced, rolling back requires redeploying the entire application, increasing the risk of failures.

When does Deployment become a Bottleneck?

- When frequent updates are needed, such as in SaaS-based applications requiring continuous feature enhancements.
- When downtime impacts business operations, leading to revenue loss.
- When application bugs require immediate hotfixes, but rollback is complicated.

How Kubernetes Helps?

- **Rolling Updates and Canary Deployments:** Kubernetes allows incremental updates without downtime, ensuring smooth rollouts.
- **CI/CD Integration:** Kubernetes supports automated deployments using tools such as Jenkins, ArgoCD, and GitOps methodologies.
- **Instant Rollbacks:** Kubernetes makes it easier to revert to previous versions in case of failures.

Example: A fintech company deploying updates to their payment gateway experienced frequent downtime. Kubernetes enabled them to implement rolling updates, ensuring zero downtime and improving deployment efficiency.

Migrating Monoliths to Kubernetes

Why Should Businesses Migrate to Kubernetes?

Migrating from a monolithic architecture to Kubernetes-based microservices improves scalability, agility, and fault tolerance.

What are the Key Migration Challenges?

- **Complex Refactoring:** Breaking down a monolith into microservices requires architectural redesign.
- **Data Consistency Management:** Ensuring smooth data flow between distributed services is critical.
- **Security Considerations:** Migration introduces new security challenges, such as API gateway authentication.

When is the Right Time to Migrate?

- When an application experiences performance bottlenecks and cannot scale efficiently.
- When deployment cycles are too slow, affecting business agility.
- When cloud-native strategies become a priority for IT transformation.

How to Migrate a Monolith to Kubernetes?

1. **Assess the Monolith:** Identify components that can be modularized.
2. **Adopt API-First Approach:** Implement API gateways to manage service interactions.
3. **Refactor Gradually:** Start by extracting high-impact services (for example, authentication, payments).
4. **Use Kubernetes Operators and Helm Charts:** Automate deployments and service orchestration.
5. **Monitor and Optimize:** Use observability tools such as Prometheus and Grafana to track performance.

Example: A healthcare provider with a monolithic patient management system struggled with slow performance. By gradually migrating to Kubernetes, they improved system reliability, enabling better patient data access and real-time processing.

Diagram: Migration Roadmap from Monolith to Kubernetes

Figure 1.4 outlines a step-by-step approach for migrating monolithic applications to Kubernetes-based microservices. It highlights refactoring strategies, API gateway implementation, and gradual adoption of cloud-native principles.

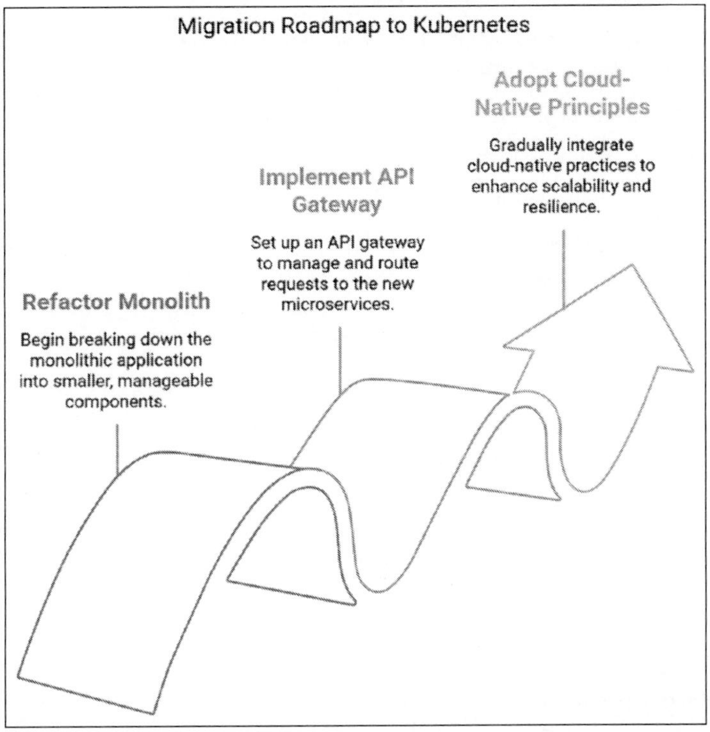

Figure 1.4: *Migration Roadmap to Kubernetes*

Kubernetes in the Modern DevOps Lifecycle

In the modern software development landscape, **Kubernetes plays a pivotal role in DevOps workflows** by streamlining deployment, scaling, and automation. Continuous Integration and Continuous Deployment (CI/CD) are at the core of DevOps, enabling faster software releases with minimal human intervention. In this section, we will explore how **Kubernetes integrates with CI/CD pipelines**, the role of **Infrastructure as Code (IaC) in Kubernetes automation**, and compare **Jenkins and GitHub Actions** to determine the best tool for automating Kubernetes workflows.

Kubernetes in CI/CD Pipelines

Before Kubernetes, **deploying applications was manual, time-consuming, and error-prone.** Teams had to manually configure servers, update applications, and manage dependencies. This approach was inefficient, leading to:

- **Long deployment cycles** causing slow software releases.
- **High failure rates** due to human error.
- **Inconsistent environments** leading to “it works on my machine” issues.

With Kubernetes, CI/CD automates:

- **Building container images** whenever code is committed.
- **Testing applications** in isolated Kubernetes environments.

- **Deploying updates** automatically to Kubernetes clusters.

Understanding Kubernetes CI/CD

CI/CD pipelines for Kubernetes automate the entire software delivery process, allowing teams to **build, test, and deploy** applications efficiently.

A Kubernetes CI/CD pipeline typically consists of:

- **Code Commit**: Developers push changes to GitHub/GitLab.
- **Automated Build**: Docker images are built using Jenkins or GitHub Actions.
- **Automated Testing**: Containers are tested in a staging environment.
- **Deployment to Kubernetes**: Updated containers are deployed using kubectl or Helm.

When to Implement Kubernetes CI/CD

- When teams **release software frequently** and need automated deployments.
- When applications **run in multiple environments (`dev`, `test`, `prod`).**
- When ensuring **high availability and zero-downtime deployments.**

How to Implement Kubernetes CI/CD

Using Jenkins for Kubernetes CI/CD

Jenkins is a well-established CI/CD tool that integrates with Kubernetes to automate deployments.

- **Install Jenkins** in a Kubernetes cluster.
- **Configure Jenkins pipelines** to build Docker images.
- **Push images** to a container registry (for example, Docker Hub, ECR, or GCR).
- **Deploy applications** using Helm or kubectl apply.

Example Jenkins file:

```
pipeline {
    agent any
    stages {
        stage('Build') {
            steps {
                sh 'docker build -t myapp:latest .'
            }
        }
        stage('Push') {
            steps {
                sh 'docker push myrepo/myapp:latest'
            }
        }
        stage('Deploy') {
            steps {
                sh 'kubectl apply -f deployment.yaml'
            }
        }
    }
}
```

Using GitHub Actions for Kubernetes CI/CD

GitHub Actions is a cloud-native CI/CD tool that integrates directly with GitHub repositories.

1. **Define a GitHub Actions workflow** (`.github/workflows/deploy.yaml`).
2. **Use pre-built Kubernetes and Docker actions.**
3. Deploy to Kubernetes using GitHub secrets for authentication.

Example GitHub Actions Workflow:

```
name: CI/CD Pipeline
on:
  push:
    branches:
      - main
jobs:
  build:
    runs-on: ubuntu-latest
    steps:
      - name: Checkout Code
        uses: actions/checkout@v2
      - name: Build Docker Image
        run: docker build -t myrepo/myapp:latest .
      - name: Push Image
        run: docker push myrepo/myapp:latest
      - name: Deploy to Kubernetes
        run: kubectl apply -f deployment.yaml
```

Jenkins versus GitHub Actions

Feature	Jenkins	GitHub Actions
Ease of Use	Requires setup and maintenance	Fully managed and easy to use
Flexibility	Highly customizable	Pre-built integrations with GitHub
Scalability	Requires own infrastructure	Scales automatically in the cloud
Cost	Self-hosted, requires server costs	Free for open-source, paid for private repos

Table 1.1: *Jenkins versus GitHub Actions*

Cost-Saving Insights

- **GitHub Actions is cost-effective** for GitHub-based projects as it eliminates the need for self-hosted CI/CD servers.
- **Jenkins provides more flexibility** but requires maintaining infrastructure, which increases costs.
- **For small teams, GitHub Actions is ideal.** For large, complex pipelines, Jenkins remains a strong choice.

Infrastructure as Code (IaC) with Kubernetes

Infrastructure as Code (IaC) automates **Kubernetes infrastructure provisioning** using tools such as Terraform and Helm.

Why IaC?

- **Consistency**: Avoid manual errors.
- **Scalability**: Automate resource creation.

- **Version Control**: Maintain infrastructure changes in Git.

Example: Terraform for Kubernetes

```
provider "kubernetes" {
  config_path = "~/.kube/config"
}
resource "kubernetes_deployment" "nginx" {
  metadata {
    name = "nginx"
    labels = {
      app = "nginx"
    }
  }
  spec {
    replicas = 3
    selector {
      match_labels = {
        app = "nginx"
      }
    }
    template {
      metadata {
        labels = {
          app = "nginx"
        }
      }
      spec {
        container {
          image = "nginx:latest"
          name  = "nginx"
        }
      }
    }
  }
}
```

Kubernetes and GitOps Workflows

GitOps applies DevOps principles to Kubernetes by using **Git as the single source of truth** for infrastructure and application deployments.

How GitOps Works:

- Developers push changes to a Git repository.
- CI/CD pipeline builds and tests the application.
- GitOps tools such as ArgoCD or Flux detect changes and apply them to Kubernetes.

Benefits of GitOps:

- Declarative and version-controlled deployments.
- Automated rollbacks and disaster recovery.
- Stronger security with auditable changes.

Diagram: Kubernetes in DevOps

Figure 1.5 illustrates how Kubernetes integrates with CI/CD pipelines, GitOps workflows, and Infrastructure as Code.

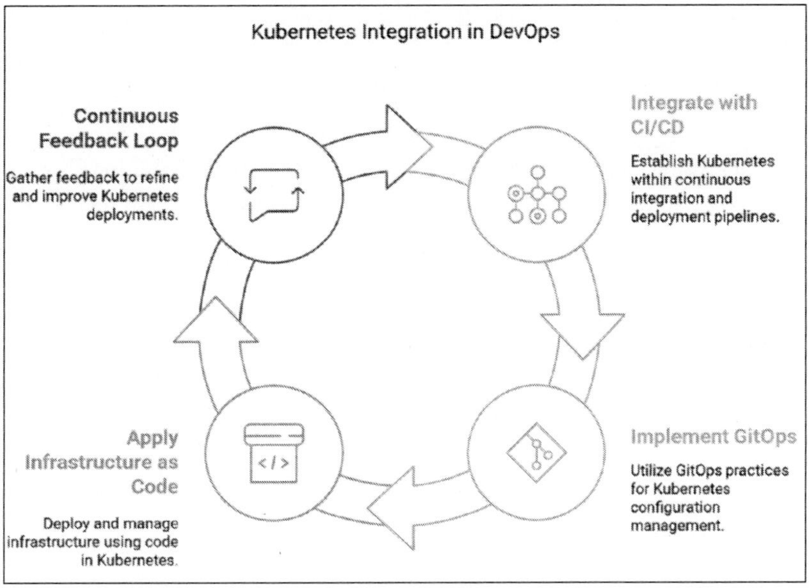

Figure 1.5: *Kubernetes Integration with CI/CD Pipelines, GitOps Workflows, and Infrastructure as Code*

In this section, we explored how Kubernetes revolutionizes **DevOps pipelines, CI/CD automation, and Infrastructure as Code.** We also compared **Jenkins and GitHub Actions, providing insights into their strengths, cost implications, and use cases.** Finally, we discussed **GitOps workflows for seamless Kubernetes automation.**

By mastering these concepts, teams can build **highly automated, scalable, and efficient DevOps pipelines** using Kubernetes.

Kubernetes for Data Engineers and Architects

This section explores the powerful intersection of **Kubernetes** and data-centric workloads. We will begin by focusing on how this container orchestration platform is specifically leveraged for running large-scale data tasks.

Big Data Processing with Kubernetes

Why?

Traditional big data processing systems rely heavily on on-premises Hadoop clusters or managed cloud services such as AWS EMR and Azure HDInsight. These approaches often face challenges such as **scalability limitations, operational complexity, and high costs**. Organizations need **a more flexible, cost-efficient, and scalable** way to process large datasets.

What?

Kubernetes provides a dynamic, containerized approach to big data processing. By leveraging Kubernetes, organizations can **run distributed workloads including Apache Spark, Presto, and Dask** with automatic scaling, self-healing, and efficient resource utilization.

When?

Kubernetes is the ideal choice for big data processing when:

- You need **elastic scalability** to process fluctuating data loads.

- Your team wants **vendor-agnostic solutions** instead of being locked into cloud-managed services.
- You require **high availability and resilience** in your data processing pipelines.

How?

- Deploy **Apache Spark clusters on Kubernetes** for distributed computing.
- Use **Kubernetes-native storage solutions** such as Ceph, Rook, or MinIO for persistent storage.
- Optimize cluster performance by tuning **Kubernetes resource requests and limits**.

ETL Pipelines and Streaming on Kubernetes

Why?

Legacy **ETL (Extract, Transform, Load)** workflows often run on heavyweight platforms like Informatica or Talend, which lack agility and require extensive infrastructure provisioning. **Real-time data streaming** is increasingly in demand, making traditional batch processing inefficient for modern data-driven applications.

What?

Kubernetes enables **containerized ETL pipelines and real-time streaming** using tools such as Apache Airflow, Kafka, and Flink. This approach provides **automation, orchestration, and scalability** to handle large-scale data ingestion and transformation.

When?

Use Kubernetes for ETL and streaming when:

- **Processing real-time event streams** (such as, financial transactions, IoT telemetry).
- Automating **complex workflows** using Apache Airflow.
- Scaling workloads dynamically **without over-provisioning resources**.

How?

- Deploy **Apache Kafka and Apache Flink** in Kubernetes for real-time event processing.
- Schedule **ETL jobs with Apache Airflow** running as Kubernetes Pods.
- Utilize **Kubernetes Operators** to simplify the management of streaming workloads.

Running Spark, Airflow, and Kafka in Kubernetes

Why?

Managing big data processing tools manually can be **operationally intensive**. Setting up and maintaining Spark clusters, Airflow DAGs, and Kafka topics requires **a high level of effort** when done without automation.

What?

Kubernetes simplifies the deployment and scaling of Spark, Airflow, and Kafka by leveraging **Helm charts, StatefulSets, and Operators**.

When?

- **Running distributed Apache Spark workloads** for data analytics and machine learning.
- **Automating batch jobs with Apache Airflow DAGs** running on Kubernetes.
- **Implementing real-time message streaming with Apache Kafka** in Kubernetes clusters.

How?

- Use **Spark-on-Kubernetes** to run distributed workloads efficiently.
- Deploy **Airflow with Kubernetes Executor** to dynamically schedule tasks.
- Run **Kafka on Kubernetes** with persistent storage (for example, EBS, Ceph, Rook).

Diagram: Kubernetes for Data Pipelines

A high-level architecture (*Figures* 1.6 and 1.7) illustrates:

- Data ingestion from multiple sources (for example, APIs, IoT, logs).
- Data transformation using Spark/Airflow.
- Data storage in distributed databases (for example, Cassandra, Snowflake).
- Real-time data streaming with Kafka.

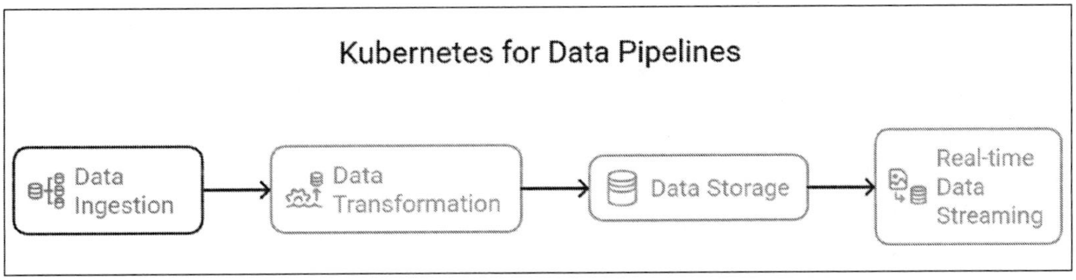

Figure 1.6: *Kubernetes for Data Pipelines*

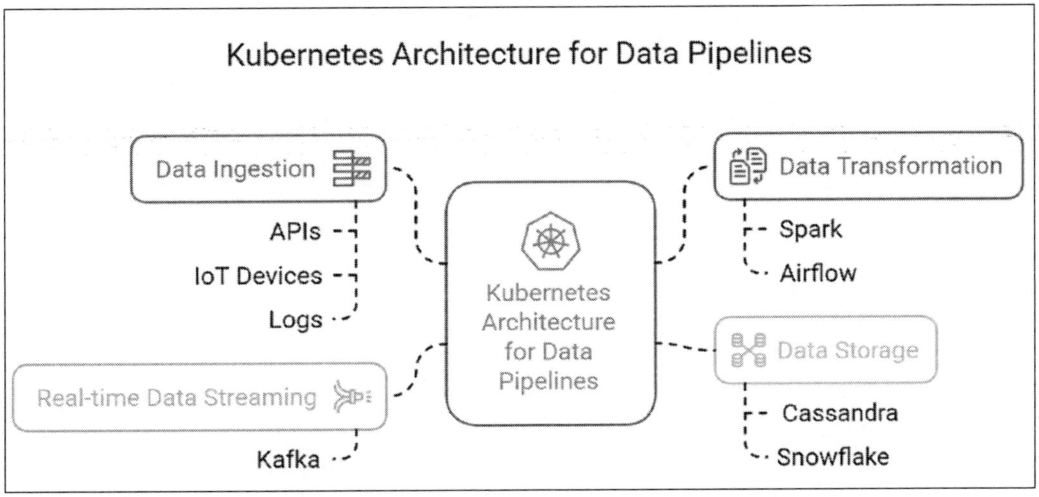

Figure 1.7: *Kubernetes Architecture for Data Pipelines*

How Kubernetes Enhances Data Engineering Workflows:

- **Orchestration:** Automated job scheduling with Apache Airflow.
- **Scalability:** Dynamic scaling of Spark executors.
- **Storage Flexibility:** Support for cloud and on-prem storage options.

Next Steps

- Kubernetes enables **big data processing** with scalability, automation, and cost efficiency.
- **ETL pipelines and streaming** workloads benefit from Kubernetes-native deployment.
- Running **Spark, Airflow, and Kafka on Kubernetes** simplifies complex data operations.
- The next chapter will dive into **Kubernetes security best practices for production workloads.**

This section provided **real-world use cases and implementation details** relevant to **Data Engineers and Architects**, making Kubernetes an integral part of modern data infrastructure.

Security and Role-Based Access Control (RBAC) in Kubernetes

Why is Kubernetes Security Critical?

Kubernetes has become the backbone of modern cloud-native applications, but with great power comes great responsibility. Security vulnerabilities in misconfigured clusters can expose businesses to risks such as data breaches, privilege escalation, and unauthorized access. Traditional security models struggle to provide granular access controls and centralized policy enforcement, leading to compliance issues and operational inefficiencies.

Example: The Cost of Poor Kubernetes Security

A fintech company using Kubernetes to manage its microservices architecture experienced an incident where an attacker exploited a misconfigured API server. The attacker gained unauthorized access, leading to the exposure of sensitive customer data. This resulted in compliance violations and reputational damage, forcing the company to invest heavily in security measures.

Understanding Kubernetes Security and the Role of RBAC

Kubernetes security is a multi-layered approach that includes network policies, Role-Based Access Control (RBAC), secrets management, and compliance enforcement. Among these, RBAC plays a pivotal role in defining who can access what within a cluster.

Key Security Concepts in Kubernetes

- **RBAC (Role-Based Access Control):** Provides fine-grained access control over Kubernetes resources.
- **Namespace Isolation:** Limits access between different teams or applications running in the same cluster.
- **Network Policies:** Restrict communication between pods based on predefined rules.
- **Secrets Management:** Securely stores sensitive information such as API keys, passwords, and certificates.
- **Pod Security Policies (PSP):** Enforce security settings for running containers.

Optimal Timing for Implementing Kubernetes Security and RBAC

From Day 1: Kubernetes security should not be an afterthought but an integral part of cluster setup.

- **Before Scaling Up:** Implementing RBAC and security measures early prevents unauthorized access when multiple teams and services interact.
- **For Compliance Requirements:** Organizations handling sensitive data (for example, finance, healthcare, and so on) must enforce strict security policies for regulatory compliance (GDPR, HIPAA, and PCI-DSS).
- **During Incident Response:** Security controls should enable quick identification and resolution of breaches.

Example: Implementing RBAC for a Multi-Tenant Kubernetes Cluster

A SaaS provider hosting multiple clients on a shared Kubernetes cluster faced challenges in isolating customer workloads. By implementing RBAC with namespace isolation, they restricted tenant access to only their assigned resources, preventing accidental data leaks.

Securing Kubernetes Clusters Using RBAC

Understanding Kubernetes RBAC Components

RBAC uses four primary API objects to enforce access controls:

- **Roles and ClusterRoles:** Define permissions for resources within a namespace or across the cluster.
- **RoleBindings and ClusterRoleBindings:** Associate users, groups, or service accounts with roles.

Creating an RBAC Policy Example

Step 1: Define a Role for Read-Only Access to Pods

```
apiVersion: rbac.authorization.k8s.io/v1
kind: Role
metadata:
  namespace: dev
  name: pod-reader
rules:
- apiGroups: [""]
  resources: ["pods"]
  verbs: ["get", "list", "watch"]
```

Step 2: Bind the Role to a User

```
apiVersion: rbac.authorization.k8s.io/v1
kind: RoleBinding
metadata:
  name: read-pods-binding
  namespace: dev
subjects:
- kind: User
  name: dev-user
  apiGroup: rbac.authorization.k8s.io
roleRef:
  kind: Role
  name: pod-reader
  apiGroup: rbac.authorization.k8s.io
```

Securing Secrets in Kubernetes

Secrets in Kubernetes store sensitive data securely. Instead of hardcoding credentials in configuration files, secrets provide a secure mechanism to inject them into pods.

Example: Storing a Database Password as a Secret

```
apiVersion: v1
kind: Secret
metadata:
  name: db-secret
  namespace: production
type: Opaque
data:
  password: c2VjdXJlcGFzc3dvcmQ=
```

The password is base64-encoded and can be accessed by pods securely.

Diagram: Kubernetes Security Layers

A comprehensive security model for Kubernetes includes multiple layers:

- **Infrastructure Security:** Secure cloud and on-prem infrastructure hosting Kubernetes.
- **Cluster Security:** RBAC, API server security, and network policies.
- **Workload Security:** Pod security policies, image scanning, and runtime monitoring.
- **Data Security:** Secrets encryption, compliance enforcement, and auditing.

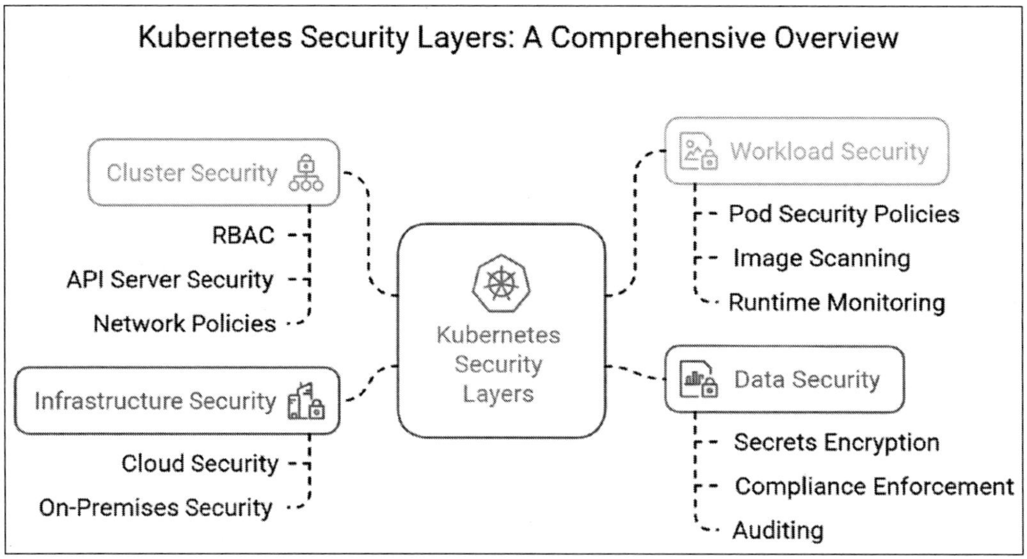

***Figure 1.8:** Kubernetes Security Layers*

Key Takeaways

- Kubernetes security should be implemented from the beginning, not as an afterthought.
- RBAC plays a crucial role in controlling access to Kubernetes resources.
- Namespace isolation prevents unauthorized access between workloads.

- Secrets management secures sensitive information such as passwords and API keys.
- Implementing a layered security approach enhances protection against cyber threats.

Thus, by following these best practices, organizations can safeguard their Kubernetes environments and ensure compliance with industry security standards.

Real-World Use Cases and Best Practices

Let us discuss real-world use cases and best practices for deploying and managing applications, culminating in a detailed case study demonstrating how large enterprises effectively leverage Kubernetes.

Case Study: How Enterprises Use Kubernetes?

Why?

As businesses scale, they face challenges in managing applications across **multiple cloud environments**, ensuring **high availability**, and **optimizing infrastructure costs**. Traditional on-premises systems **lack flexibility**, and enterprises struggle with **scalability** and **automation**. Kubernetes provides a **solution** to these challenges by offering **container orchestration, self-healing, and multi-cloud compatibility**.

What?

Kubernetes is **widely adopted** across industries to improve **application resilience, scalability, and efficiency**. Some **real-world use cases** include:

- **E-Commerce Giants (Amazon, Shopify):** Handling fluctuating traffic with auto-scaling.
- **Financial Institutions (Goldman Sachs, JPMorgan):** Ensuring compliance and security.
- **Streaming Services (Netflix, Spotify):** Managing microservices for uninterrupted streaming.
- **AI and Machine Learning (OpenAI, Tesla):** Running distributed AI workloads efficiently.

When?

- When enterprises need **high availability** across multiple locations.
- When businesses aim to **reduce infrastructure costs** by optimizing cloud resources.
- When adopting **DevOps and CI/CD** to improve deployment efficiency.
- When implementing **hybrid or multi-cloud architectures**.

How?

- **Use Kubernetes Clusters** across **AWS, Azure, and GCP** for **multi-cloud deployments**.
- **Leverage Auto-scaling** to adjust **compute resources** dynamically.
- **Implement Kubernetes Operators** for database and ML model orchestration.
- **Utilize Istio and Service Mesh** to improve **network security and observability**.

Performance Optimization and Cost Management

Why?

As Kubernetes scales, enterprises struggle with **resource wastage**, **over-provisioning**, and **performance bottlenecks**. Without proper cost control and optimization, **cloud bills skyrocket**.

What?

Optimizing Kubernetes workloads ensures **efficient resource utilization** and **cost savings**. The key strategies include:

- **Right-Sizing Pods:** Optimizing CPU and memory requests/limits.
- **Cluster Autoscaling:** Adjusting the number of nodes based on demand.
- **Load Balancing:** Efficient traffic routing via Ingress Controllers.
- **Spot and Preemptible Instances:** Using cost-effective cloud compute options.
- **Observability Tools:** Leveraging **Prometheus, Grafana, and OpenTelemetry**.

When?

- When cloud spending **exceeds budget**.
- When performance degradation **affects end-users**.
- When under-utilized resources lead to **inefficiency**.
- When large-scale deployments require **scalability without overspending**.

How?

- Enable Vertical and Horizontal Pod Autoscaling to optimize resource allocation.
- Implement Cost Visibility Tools such as Kubecost and AWS Cost Explorer.
- Monitor Cluster Health using Datadog and New Relic.
- Adopt Serverless Kubernetes (EKS Fargate, GKE Autopilot) to reduce operational overhead.

Future Trends in Kubernetes

Why?

As Kubernetes adoption grows, new **innovations and best practices** emerge, making it more **secure, scalable, and developer-friendly**.

What?

Key trends shaping Kubernetes' future include:

- **AI-Powered Kubernetes Management** (such as, AI-driven autoscaling, predictive analytics).
- **Edge Computing and Kubernetes** (5G deployments, IoT workloads at the edge).
- **Security Enhancements** (Zero Trust, Confidential Computing, Kubernetes Sandboxing).
- **Multi-Cloud Federation** (Seamless workload portability across cloud providers).

When?

- When managing **distributed workloads** across multiple cloud providers.
- When **AI-driven optimization** is required to improve performance.
- When **security and compliance** regulations demand tighter controls.
- When enterprises explore **serverless and edge computing solutions**.

How?

- **Integrate AI and Machine Learning** into Kubernetes cluster management.
- **Adopt Service Mesh Technologies** (Istio, Linkerd) for secure microservices communication.
- **Utilize Multi-Cloud Orchestration Tools** such as **Anthos and Azure Arc**.
- **Implement Zero Trust Security Models** in Kubernetes environments.

Diagram: Kubernetes in Multi-Cloud and Hybrid Environments

The following figure illustrates Kubernetes cluster deployment across AWS, Azure, and GCP, showing traffic routing, cost optimization, and security best practices:

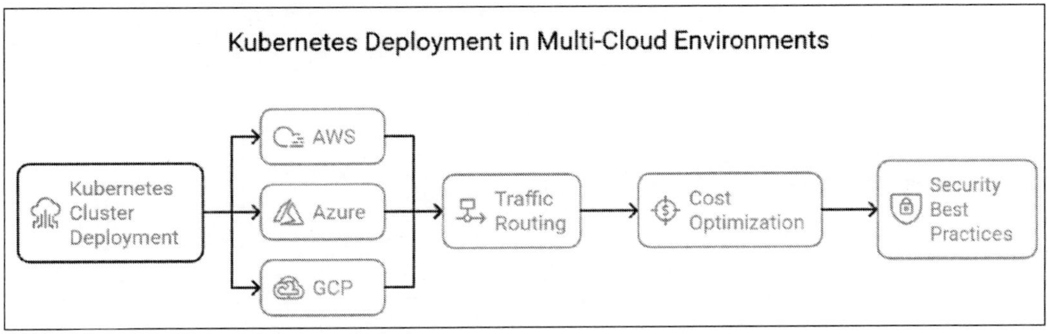

Figure 1.9: *Kubernetes Deployment in Multi-Cloud Environment*

Conclusion

In this chapter, we explored real-world enterprise use cases, performance tuning techniques, cost management strategies, and future trends shaping the Kubernetes landscape. With Kubernetes continuing to redefine cloud-native computing, organizations must stay ahead by implementing best practices, leveraging automation, and embracing multi-cloud strategies. This marks the conclusion of this chapter, having provided a comprehensive foundation in Kubernetes for the technical discussions ahead.

In the next chapter, we will move from foundational concepts to practical implementation. This hands-on guide will walk you through setting up Kubernetes clusters both on-premise and in the cloud. You will gain a strong understanding of installation methods, infrastructure provisioning, and troubleshooting techniques essential for building resilient, production-grade environments.

CHAPTER 2
Setting Up Kubernetes Clusters

Introduction

Kubernetes has become the de facto standard for container orchestration, enabling organizations to manage large-scale distributed systems efficiently. Setting up a Kubernetes cluster is the foundational step towards deploying cloud-native applications. The process involves choosing the right installation method, configuring networking, and ensuring security best practices.

In this chapter, we will explore multiple installation methods for Kubernetes, including **kubeadm, Minikube, and Kind**. We will also evaluate their advantages, limitations, and ideal use cases to help engineers and architects select the right approach for their needs.

Structure

In this chapter, we will cover the following topics:

- Importance of Kubernetes Installation
- Introduction and Kubernetes Installation Methods
- Setting Up Kubernetes on Cloud Platforms
- Cluster Networking and Storage Provisioning
- Troubleshooting Cluster Initialization and Node Issues
- Securing Kubernetes Setups and Best Practices
- Designing a Resilient Infrastructure for Data Pipelines

Importance of Kubernetes Installation

Before diving into installation methods, let us understand why setting up Kubernetes properly is crucial:

- **Scalability:** A well-configured cluster ensures efficient scaling of applications.
- **Reliability:** A robust setup minimizes downtime and ensures high availability.
- **Security:** Proper installation mitigates vulnerabilities and enhances cluster security.
- **Resource Efficiency:** The right configuration optimizes compute, storage, and networking resources.

Organizations that overlook these factors often face performance bottlenecks, security risks, and operational inefficiencies.

A structured Kubernetes setup is important because:

- A poorly configured cluster can lead to **scalability issues, performance bottlenecks, and security vulnerabilities**.
- Different use cases (testing, development, production) **require different installation methods**.
- **On-prem versus cloud deployments** have varying network, storage, and infrastructure requirements.

Common Challenges in Kubernetes Installation:

Challenge	**Impact**
Misconfigured Networking	Cluster components may fail to communicate
Incorrect Storage Setup	Persistent volumes may not work properly
Security Gaps	API server vulnerabilities, unauthorized access risks
Resource Misallocation	Poor scheduling leads to inefficient cluster utilization

Table 2.1: *Common Challenges in Kubernetes Installation*

By understanding these challenges, organizations can **select the best installation method** for their needs.

Kubernetes Installation Methods: Overview

There are multiple ways to install Kubernetes, each suited for different environments:

Method	**Best For**	**Pros**	**Cons**
kubeadm	Production and test environments	Highly configurable, integrates with cloud/on-prem	Requires manual networking and storage setup
Minikube	Local development	Easy setup, lightweight	Not suited for production workloads
Kind	CI/CD testing	Fast and simple setup	Limited to containerized Kubernetes clusters

Table 2.2: *Multiple Ways to Install Kubernetes*

Each method serves different purposes, so selecting the right one depends on your infrastructure and use case.

Installing Kubernetes Using Kubeadm

kubeadm is a tool that simplifies Kubernetes cluster setup by automating control plane configuration. It is a tool provided by Kubernetes to simplify cluster bootstrapping. It is widely used in production environments due to its flexibility. It focuses on setting up **only the cluster control plane**.

When should you use kubeadm?

- **Production-grade environments** where full control over configuration is needed.
- **Self-managed Kubernetes clusters** in data centers or cloud VMs.

Step-by-Step Installation Using kubeadm

Step 1: Prepare the Environment

Ensure that all nodes have the following requirements:

- **Operating System:** Ubuntu 20.04/CentOS 8

- **Minimum Hardware:** 2 CPUs, 4GB RAM, 20GB disk
- **Disable Swap:**

```
sudo swapoff -a
sed -i '/ swap / s/^/#/' /etc/fstab
```

Step 2: Install Dependencies

```
sudo apt update && sudo apt install -y apt-transport-https curl
curl -s https://packages.cloud.google.com/apt/doc/apt-key.gpg | sudo apt-key add -
cat <<EOF | sudo tee /etc/apt/sources.list.d/kubernetes.list
deb https://apt.kubernetes.io/ kubernetes-xenial main
EOF
sudo apt update
sudo apt install -y kubelet kubeadm kubectl
```

Step 3: Initialize the Master Node

```
sudo kubeadm init --pod-network-cidr=192.168.1.0/16
```

After initialization, configure `kubectl`:

```
mkdir -p $HOME/.kube
sudo cp -i /etc/kubernetes/admin.conf $HOME/.kube/config
sudo chown $(id -u):$(id -g) $HOME/.kube/config
```

Step 4: Deploy a Network Add-On (Flannel)

kubectl apply -f https://raw.githubusercontent.com/coreos/flannel/master/Documentation/kube-flannel.yml

Step 5: Join Worker Nodes

Run the following on worker nodes (token obtained from `kubeadm init` output):

```
sudo kubeadm join <master-ip>:6443 --token <token> --discovery-token-ca-
cert-hash sha256:<hash>
```

Pros and Cons of Kubeadm:

Pros	**Cons**
Suitable for production	Requires manual network and storage setup
More control over components	No GUI, CLI-based setup
Compatible with various infrastructures	Not ideal for local development

Table 2.3: *Pros and Cons of Kubeadm*

Installing Kubernetes Using Minikube

It is a lightweight tool for local Kubernetes development and testing. It is a tool for running Kubernetes locally on a single node. This is the best tool for **development, testing, and learning Kubernetes**. It runs a single-node Kubernetes cluster inside a VM or container.

When should you use Minikube?

- When developing and testing applications **without needing a full cluster**.
- For **learning Kubernetes basics** before moving to multi-node setups.

Step-by-Step Installation Using Minikube

Step 1: Install Minikube

```
curl -LO https://storage.googleapis.com/minikube/releases/latest/minikube-linux-amd64
sudo install minikube-linux-amd64 /usr/local/bin/minikube
```

Step 2: Start a Cluster

```
minikube start --driver=docker
```

Step 3: Verify Installation

```
kubectl get nodes
```

Minikube is ideal for development but lacks the multi-node capabilities of production clusters.

Pros and Cons of Minikube:

Pros	Cons
Easy to set up and use	Not suitable for production
Ideal for local testing	Single-node cluster only
Supports multiple drivers (Docker, KVM, VirtualBox)	Resource-intensive for large workloads

Table 2.4: *Pros and Cons of Minikube*

Installing Kubernetes Using Kind

Kubernetes-in-Docker (Kind) is a tool to **run Kubernetes clusters in Docker containers**. Kind is designed for testing Kubernetes clusters inside Docker containers. It is designed for **testing Kubernetes applications**. It is used mainly for CI/CD pipelines and quick Kubernetes testing.

When should you use Kind?

- Ideal for **CI/CD testing pipelines** where lightweight Kubernetes clusters are needed.
- When **you need multiple cluster environments quickly**.

Step-by-Step Installation Using Kind

Step 1: Install Kind

```
curl -Lo ./kind https://kind.sigs.k8s.io/dl/latest/kind-linux-amd64
chmod +x ./kind
mv ./kind /usr/local/bin/kind
```

Step 2: Create a Cluster

```
kind create cluster --name test-cluster
```

Step 3: Verify Cluster

```
kubectl cluster-info --context kind-test-cluster
```

Pros and Cons of Kind:

Pros	Cons
Fastest setup for testing	Not meant for production
Lightweight	Limited scalability
Easy integration with CI/CD pipelines	Requires Docker

Table 2.5: *Pros and Cons of Kind*

Choosing the Right Installation Method

Choosing the right installation method depends on scalability, ease of use, and production readiness.

Scenario	Recommended Method
Production Kubernetes cluster	kubeadm
Local development and testing	Minikube
CI/CD testing	Kind

Table 2.6: *Installation Method with Scenarios*

Next, we will explore **setting up Kubernetes clusters on AWS, Azure, and GCP**, ensuring the best practices for production workloads.

Setting Up Kubernetes on Cloud Platforms

Kubernetes adoption has skyrocketed due to its ability to run workloads seamlessly across multiple environments. As discussed previously, traditional Kubernetes cluster management is complex, requiring significant expertise in provisioning, scaling, networking, and security. Cloud providers offer **managed Kubernetes services** that simplify cluster setup, enhance security, and optimize costs.

Challenges in Traditional Kubernetes Deployments:

- **Infrastructure Overhead**: Setting up control planes, worker nodes, networking, and security.
- **Operational Complexity**: Managing upgrades, scaling, and high availability.
- **Security Risks**: Manual configurations often lead to vulnerabilities.
- **Resource Optimization**: Inefficient scaling can lead to overprovisioning and wasted costs.

Cloud providers such as AWS, Azure, and Google Cloud offer managed Kubernetes services–EKS, AKS, and GKE respectively–to simplify cluster deployment and management. This section explores setting up Kubernetes clusters on these cloud platforms, detailing their configurations, cost optimizations, and best practices.

AWS EKS, Azure AKS, and GCP GKE

Each cloud provider offers a managed Kubernetes service that abstracts away the complexities of setting up and maintaining a Kubernetes control plane, eliminating most administrative overhead. The three major managed Kubernetes services are:

- **AWS Elastic Kubernetes Service (EKS)**: AWS Managed Kubernetes Solution - Integrates with AWS networking, IAM, and auto-scaling features.
- **Azure Kubernetes Service (AKS)**: Microsoft's managed Kubernetes platform - Provides deep integration with Azure DevOps and security controls.
- **Google Kubernetes Engine (GKE)**: Google Cloud's enterprise-ready Kubernetes service - Offers automated cluster management with advanced networking and scalability.

These managed services handle control plane provisioning, patching, upgrades, and availability, allowing engineers to focus on deploying and managing applications.

Feature	AWS EKS	Azure AKS	GCP GKE
Managed Control Plane	Yes	Yes	Yes
Auto-Scaling	Yes (Karpenter)	Yes	Yes

Security Features	IAM, VPC CNI	RBAC, Azure AD	Workload Identity
Networking	AWS VPC CNI	Azure CNI	Google Cloud VPC
Cost Model	Pay per control plane and nodes	Pay per node only	Pay per node and per second

Table 2.7: *Cloud Provider offers a Managed Kubernetes Service*

When to Choose Each Cloud Provider?

Scenario	**Recommended Service**
Deep AWS Integration (for example, using S3, Lambda, DynamoDB)	AWS EKS
Enterprise Workloads on Azure (for example, Active Directory, Hybrid Cloud)	Azure AKS
AI/ML and Data Processing (for example, BigQuery, TensorFlow)	GCP GKE

Table 2.8: *When to Choose Cloud Providers Managed Kubernetes Service*

Benefits of Managed Kubernetes Services

Challenges and Complexity of Self-Managed Kubernetes Before managing Kubernetes, companies had to set up and manage their own clusters manually, which required expertise in networking, infrastructure, and security. The key challenges included:

- **Cluster Maintenance Overhead:** Upgrades, patching, and securing a self-managed cluster require significant effort.
- **Control Plane Management:** Handling API servers, etcd, and scheduling components can be complex.
- **Scalability Challenges:** Self-managed clusters require custom scaling logic.
- **Security and Compliance:** Companies need to configure RBAC, IAM, and compliance policies manually.

Challenges with Self-Managed Clusters:

- **Operational Overhead**: Managing Kubernetes control plane, networking, and security requires deep expertise.
- **High Maintenance**: Manual upgrades, patching, and monitoring add complexity.
- **Scaling Issues**: Dynamically adjusting infrastructure to traffic demands is non-trivial.

Benefits of Managed Kubernetes (EKS, AKS, GKE):

- **Automated Scaling and Maintenance**: Cloud providers handle upgrades, security patches, and scaling.
- **Integrated Security and Compliance**: Built-in role-based access control (RBAC) and compliance certifications.
- **Optimized Cost and Performance**: Pay-as-you-go model with auto-scaling capabilities.

Managed Kubernetes Services

Managed Kubernetes services provide fully managed control planes, automated scaling, and integrated security features.

When to Use Managed Kubernetes Service

- When you want to avoid managing Kubernetes control planes manually.

- When you need seamless integration with cloud-native services (for example, IAM, load balancers, storage).
- When scaling workloads dynamically is a priority.

The following sections cover how to set up Kubernetes clusters in AWS, Azure, and GCP.

Deploying Kubernetes on AWS EKS

Infrastructure Requirements:

- **VPC and Subnets**: AWS EKS requires a properly configured VPC with public and private subnets.
- **IAM Roles and Permissions**: Grant necessary permissions for EKS service to interact with AWS resources.
- **Worker Nodes**: EC2 instances or AWS Fargate to run workloads.

Step-by-Step Setup

Step 1: Prerequisites

a. AWS CLI installed and configured.

b. eksctl (simplifies cluster provisioning).

c. IAM permissions to create VPCs, IAM roles, and EKS clusters.

Step 2: Create an EKS Cluster

Run the following command to create an EKS cluster with `eksctl`:

```
eksctl create cluster --name my-eks-cluster \
--region us-west-2 \
--nodegroup-name worker-nodes \
--node-type t3.medium \
--nodes 3
```

Step 3: Verify Cluster Status

```
aws eks describe-cluster --name my-eks-cluster --query "cluster.status"
```

Expected Output: `ACTIVE`

Step 4: Deploy a Test Application

```
kubectl apply -f https://k8s.io/examples/application/deployment.yaml
```

Common Troubleshooting Issues:

- **IAM Role Issues:** Ensure that IAM roles for nodes and clusters are properly assigned.
- **Networking Problems:** EKS requires correctly configured VPCs and security groups.

Deploying Kubernetes on Azure AKS

Infrastructure Requirements:

- **Resource Group:** Required to organize Azure resources.
- **AKS Cluster:** Managed control plane with built-in security.
- **Node Pools:** Virtual Machine Scale Sets (VMSS) for workload deployment.

Step-by-Step Setup

Step 1: Prerequisites

a. Azure CLI installed (az command-line tool).

b. Azure subscription with permission to create resources.

Step 2: Create an AKS Cluster

```
az aks create --resource-group myResourceGroup \
--name myAKSCluster \
--node-count 3 \
--enable-addons monitoring \
--generate-ssh-keys
```

Step 3: Connect to the Cluster

```
az aks get-credentials --resource-group myResourceGroup --name myAKSCluster
kubectl get nodes
```

Step 4: Deploy an Application

```
kubectl apply -f https://k8s.io/examples/application/deployment.yaml
```

Common Troubleshooting Issues:

- **RBAC Authentication Issues:** Ensure that users have proper Azure RBAC assignments.
- **Networking Configurations:** Azure CNI must be correctly set up for pod networking.

Deploying Kubernetes on Google Cloud GKE

Infrastructure Requirements:

- **VPC and Firewall Rules**: Ensure proper network segmentation and security policies.
- **IAM and Service Accounts**: Assign least-privilege access policies.
- **Compute Instances**: Auto-scaling node pools for efficient workload management.

Step-by-Step Setup

Step 1: Prerequisites

a. Google Cloud SDK installed (gcloud command-line tool).

b. A GCP project with Kubernetes Engine API enabled.

Step 2: Create a GKE Cluster

```
gcloud container clusters create my-gke-cluster \
--zone us-central1-a \
--num-nodes 3
```

Step 3: Connect to the Cluster

```
gcloud container clusters get-credentials my-gke-cluster --zone us-central1-a
kubectl get nodes
```

Step 4: Deploy an Application

```
kubectl apply -f https://k8s.io/examples/application/deployment.yaml
```

Common Troubleshooting Issues:

- **Insufficient IAM Permissions:** Ensure that correct GCP IAM roles are assigned.
- **Node Pool Scaling Issues:** Adjust auto-scaling configurations.

Common Deployment Issues and Solutions

Issue	Solution
Authentication failures	Ensure correct IAM roles and permissions.
Networking issues	Verify VPC configurations and firewall rules.
Nodes not joining cluster	Check kubelet logs and API connectivity.
High pod scheduling times	Adjust resource requests and limits.

Table 2.9: *Common Deployment Issues and Solutions*

Best Practices for Secure Cluster Setup:

- **Least Privilege Access:** Use **RBAC policies** to limit cluster permissions.
- **Private Networking:** Enable **private clusters** to restrict public access.
- **Pod Security Policies:** Restrict container capabilities to minimize the attack surface.
- **Audit Logging:** Enable logging for cluster activity monitoring.
- **Regular Updates:** Apply **security patches** and Kubernetes upgrades.

The following table lists **Cost Optimization Strategies**:

Cloud Provider	Auto-Scaling	Spot Instances	Pricing Model
AWS EKS	Horizontal Pod Autoscaler (HPA), Cluster Autoscaler	EC2 Spot Instances	Pay-as-you-go, Savings Plans
Azure AKS	Virtual Machine Scale Sets	Spot VMs	Reserved Instances, Pay-as-you-go
Google GKE	Cluster Autoscaler, Node Auto-Provisioning	Preemptible VMs	Sustained Use Discounts

Table 2.10: *Cost Optimization Strategies*

Best Practices to Reduce Costs:

- **Use Auto-Scaling:** Adjust node count dynamically based on demand.
- **Leverage Spot Instances:** Cost-efficient alternative for non-critical workloads.
- **Monitor Resource Utilization:** Optimize pod requests/limits to avoid over-provisioning.

The following table lists when to choose which cloud provider:

Use Case	Best Cloud Platform
Heavy AWS Ecosystem	AWS EKS
Azure DevOps and AD Integration	Azure AKS
AI/ML and Big Data Workloads	Google GKE
Multi-Cloud Deployments	GKE and AKS

Table 2.11: *Brief about When to Choose Which Cloud Provider*

We explored the benefits of managed Kubernetes services, how to deploy clusters on AWS, Azure, and Google Cloud, and best practices for cost optimization. The next section will cover Kubernetes networking and storage provisioning to build a strong foundation for scalable applications.

Cluster Networking and Storage Provisioning

Kubernetes networking and storage provisioning are critical aspects of a well-functioning cluster. Understanding how networking works ensures seamless communication between services, while proper storage provisioning guarantees persistent and scalable data storage for workloads.

This section explores networking fundamentals such as **Container Network Interfaces (CNI), Service Mesh, and Kubernetes DNS**, along with **Persistent Volume Claims (PVC), StatefulSets, and Container Storage Interfaces (CSI)** for data storage.

Importance of Networking and Storage in Kubernetes

Networking Challenges without Kubernetes

Before Kubernetes, traditional networking and storage faced several challenges, including:

- **Manual IP Management:** Assigning and tracking IPs for containers was cumbersome.
- **Complex Service Discovery:** Traditional networks required load balancers for internal services.
- **Limited Scaling:** Network configurations did not automatically adjust with scaling applications.

Storage Challenges before Kubernetes:

- **Ephemeral Storage:** Containers lose data upon restart, if no persistent storage is attached.
- **Manual Volume Management:** Admins had to provision, attach, and manage storage manually.
- **Non-Portable Storage:** Traditional storage solutions tied applications to specific cloud vendors.

To overcome these issues, Kubernetes introduced **CNI for networking** and **Persistent Volumes (PV), Persistent Volume Claims (PVC), StatefulSets, and CSI for storage.**

Kubernetes Networking Fundamentals

Kubernetes networking ensures that all pods in a cluster can communicate seamlessly.

Introduction to Kubernetes Networking

Kubernetes networking is based on a **flat, non-overlapping IP model**, where every pod receives its own IP address, allowing direct communication without the need for **Network Address Translation (NAT).**

Key Networking Components:

- **Container Network Interface (CNI):** Handles pod networking within the cluster.
- **Kubernetes Services:** Manages internal and external communication.
- **Ingress Controllers:** Routes external traffic to internal services.
- **Service Mesh (Istio, Linkerd):** Enhances security, observability, and traffic control.
- **Network Policies:** Defines rules for inter-pod communication.

When is Kubernetes Networking Critical

- When deploying microservices that need **service discovery** and **load balancing.**
- When ensuring **secure communication** across namespaces.
- When implementing **multi-cloud and hybrid cloud** networking strategies.

Implementing Kubernetes Networking:

Step 1: Install a CNI Plugin (Flannel Example)

```
kubectl apply -f https://raw.githubusercontent.com/coreos/flannel/master/
Documentation/kube-flannel.yml
```

Step 2: Create a Kubernetes Service

```
apiVersion: v1
kind: Service
metadata:
  name: my-service
spec:
  selector:
    app: my-app
  ports:
    - protocol: TCP
      port: 80
      targetPort: 8080
```

Step 3: Configure Network Policies

```
apiVersion: networking.k8s.io/v1
kind: NetworkPolicy
metadata:
  name: allow-specific-pods
spec:
  podSelector:
    matchLabels:
      role: backend
  ingress:
    - from:
      - podSelector:
          matchLabels:
            role: frontend
      ports:
        - protocol: TCP
          port: 80
```

Kubernetes Storage Provisioning

Persistent storage is necessary for databases, logs, and any workload that requires data retention beyond container lifetimes.

Introduction to Kubernetes Storage

Kubernetes provides **Persistent Volumes (PVs)** and **Persistent Volume Claims (PVCs)** to handle stateful applications.

Key Storage Components:

- **Persistent Volume (PV):** A storage resource available to the cluster.
- **Persistent Volume Claim (PVC):** A request for storage by a pod.
- **Storage Classes:** Defines different storage types and policies.
- **StatefulSets:** Manages stateful applications with stable network identifiers.
- **Container Storage Interface (CSI):** Standard API for integrating third-party storage solutions.

When is Kubernetes Storage Critical

- When deploying **databases (MySQL, PostgreSQL, MongoDB).**
- When ensuring **persistent logging for compliance.**
- When running **stateful applications that require durable storage.**

Implementing Kubernetes Storage:

Step 1: Create a Persistent Volume (PV)

```
apiVersion: v1
kind: PersistentVolume
metadata:
  name: my-pv
spec:
  capacity:
    storage: 10Gi
  accessModes:
    - ReadWriteOnce
  persistentVolumeReclaimPolicy: Retain
  hostPath:
    path: /mnt/data
```

Step 2: Create a Persistent Volume Claim (PVC)

```
apiVersion: v1
kind: PersistentVolumeClaim
metadata:
  name: my-pvc
spec:
  accessModes:
    - ReadWriteOnce
  resources:
    requests:
      storage: 10Gi
```

Step 3: Attach PVC to a Pod

```
apiVersion: v1
kind: Pod
metadata:
  name: my-pod
spec:
  containers:
    - name: my-container
      image: nginx
      volumeMounts:
        - mountPath: "/data"
          name: storage
  volumes:
    - name: storage
      persistentVolumeClaim:
        claimName: my-pvc
```

Best Practices for Kubernetes Networking and Storage

Networking Best Practices:

- Use **Ingress Controllers** for managing external traffic.

- Implement **Network Policies** to restrict unauthorized access.
- Choose the right **CNI Plugin** based on workload needs.
- Enable **Service Mesh (Istio, Linkerd)** for microservices-based architectures.

Storage Best Practices:

- Choose the right **Storage Class** based on performance needs.
- Use **ReadWriteMany (RWX) volumes** for shared workloads.
- Enable **Backup and Disaster Recovery** for critical applications.
- Implement **Storage Security Policies** to prevent unauthorized access.

Next, we will explore **troubleshooting Kubernetes cluster initialization and node issues**, covering real-world scenarios and debugging techniques.

Troubleshooting Cluster Initialization and Node Issues

Kubernetes clusters form the foundation for containerized applications, but setting them up is not always smooth. Cluster initialization failures, node join issues, and pod misconfigurations can cause major disruptions. Understanding common problems and their solutions help engineers maintain a stable and resilient cluster.

This section provides a structured approach to troubleshooting Kubernetes cluster initialization and node failures, using real-world scenarios and debugging methodologies.

Common Causes of Initialization and Node Issues

Cluster setup issues arise due to several factors, such as:

- **Misconfigured Networking**: The control plane and worker nodes may not communicate properly.
- **Resource Constraints**: Insufficient CPU, RAM, or disk space prevents nodes from starting.
- **Missing Dependencies**: Required Kubernetes components (e.g., kubelet, container runtime) may not be installed or configured correctly.
- **Incorrect API Server Configuration**: Misconfigured certificates, ports, or authentication can cause API server failures.

In traditional IT setups, identifying such issues took hours or even days. Kubernetes provides diagnostic tools, but effective troubleshooting requires understanding how different cluster components interact.

Common Cluster Initialization and Node Issues

Kubernetes clusters form the foundation for containerized applications, but setting them up is not always smooth. Cluster initialization failures, node join issues, and pod misconfigurations can disrupt workloads and impact availability. Understanding common problems and their solutions enables engineers to build and maintain stable, resilient Kubernetes clusters.

This section provides a structured approach to troubleshooting control plane initialization and worker node onboarding issues. It focuses on real-world failure scenarios, common root causes, and practical debugging techniques to identify and resolve cluster setup problems effectively. The following table lists some common issues and their impact:

Issue	Impact
API Server Not Responding	Cluster control plane fails to initialize
Node Not Joining Cluster	Workloads cannot be scheduled
DNS Resolution Issues	Pods fail to communicate internally
Network Policy Misconfiguration	Services cannot communicate across nodes
Insufficient Resources	Cluster components crash due to resource exhaustion

Table 2.12: *Common Issues and Their Impact*

Diagnosing Issues Using Kubernetes Logs

Kubernetes logs are the best starting point for debugging issues:

- Check **kubelet logs** on worker nodes:
```
journalctl -u kubelet --no-pager | tail -n 50
```
- Verify API server logs on the master node:
```
kubectl logs -n kube-system etcd-master
```
- Inspect pod logs for failing workloads:
```
kubectl logs <pod-name> -n <namespace>
```

Indicators That Cluster and Node Issues are Critical

Cluster and node issues are critical in the following scenarios:

- **During Initial Cluster Setup:** If the master node fails to initialize, workloads cannot be deployed.
- **When Scaling Up:** If new worker nodes fail to join the cluster, scaling Kubernetes workloads becomes impossible.
- **During Network Policy Implementation:** Misconfigured policies can block inter-service communication.
- **When Upgrading Kubernetes:** Version mismatches and deprecations can break cluster components.

Troubleshooting Kubernetes Cluster and Node Issues

Debugging Cluster Initialization Issues

Issue: API Server Fails to Start

Steps to Fix:

1. Verify if the API server is running:
```
kubectl get pods -n kube-system | grep apiserver
```
2. Check API server logs:
```
kubectl logs -n kube-system kube-apiserver-master
```
3. Restart the API server if necessary:
```
systemctl restart kube-apiserver
```
4. Check certificate validity:
```
openssl x509 -in /etc/kubernetes/pki/apiserver.crt -text -noout
```

Debugging Node Issues

Issue: Worker Node Not Joining Cluster

Steps to Fix:

1. Check node status:
```
kubectl get nodes
```
2. Verify that kubelet is running:
```
systemctl status kubelet
```
3. Ensure the node can communicate with the API server:
```
curl -k https://<master-ip>:6443
```
4. Rejoin the cluster using kubeadm:
```
kubeadm reset
kubeadm join <master-ip>:6443 --token <token>
```

Fixing Network and DNS Issues

Issue: Pods Cannot Resolve DNS

Steps to Fix:

1. Check CoreDNS logs:
```
kubectl logs -n kube-system coredns-<pod-id>
```
2. Verify DNS service configuration:
```
kubectl get svc -n kube-system | grep kube-dns
```
3. Restart CoreDNS if needed:
```
kubectl rollout restart deployment/coredns -n kube-system
```

Real-World Example: Troubleshooting a Production Cluster

Scenario:

A financial services company noticed that their Kubernetes cluster failed to schedule new pods. Developers reported that newly launched applications were stuck in a "Pending" state.

Investigation and Resolution:

- **Checked node status:** Found that new nodes were in a "NotReady" state.
- **Examined kubelet logs:** Logs showed "failed to start container runtime" errors.
- **Fixed container runtime:** Restarted Docker and rejoined the node.
- **Validated node registration:** After resetting kubeadm and rejoining the cluster, workloads started scheduling correctly.

Outcome:

- Reduced cluster downtime from **4 hours to 30 minutes**.
- Created automated alerts for node failures.
- Implemented cluster auto-scaling for future resilience.

Securing Kubernetes Setups and Best Practices

Security in Kubernetes is paramount as misconfigurations can lead to breaches, data leaks, and compromised infrastructure. Kubernetes provides multiple security layers, but improper implementation can expose critical vulnerabilities. This section dives deep into securing Kubernetes clusters by implementing Role-Based Access Control (RBAC), network policies, securing API servers, and best practices for securing Kubernetes nodes in multi-cloud environments.

The Need for Kubernetes Security

Kubernetes security is critical because of the following reasons:

- **Multi-Tenancy Risks:** Kubernetes clusters often host multiple applications, increasing security threats.
- **Complex Networking:** Kubernetes networking requires proper segmentation to prevent unauthorized access.
- **RBAC Misconfigurations:** Improper role definitions can lead to privilege escalation.
- **Exposure to the Public Internet:** Misconfigured API servers can expose clusters to cyber threats.
- **Container Vulnerabilities:** Running outdated or vulnerable container images can lead to exploits.

Common Security Challenges in Kubernetes:

Security Issue	**Impact**
Over-privileged Users	Unauthorized access and privilege escalation.
Unrestricted API Access	Potential data breaches and system compromise.
Weak Network Policies	Unsecured pod-to-pod communication.
Container Escapes	Attackers gaining access to the host system.
Lack of Audit Logging	Difficulty in tracing security incidents.

Table 2.13: *Common Security Challenges in Kubernetes and Impacts*

Key Security Mechanisms in Kubernetes

Role-Based Access Control (RBAC)

RBAC restricts user permissions based on roles. It ensures that only authorized users and processes can access specific Kubernetes resources.

Implementing RBAC

1. Create a **Role** (Restricts actions within a namespace):

```
apiVersion: rbac.authorization.k8s.io/v1
kind: Role
metadata:
  namespace: dev
  name: pod-reader
rules:
- apiGroups: [""]
  resources: ["pods"]
  verbs: ["get", "watch", "list"]
```

2. Bind the role to a **User or Group** using a **`RoleBinding`**:

```
apiVersion: rbac.authorization.k8s.io/v1
kind: RoleBinding
metadata:
  namespace: dev
  name: read-pods-binding
subjects:
- kind: User
  name: dev-user
  apiGroup: rbac.authorization.k8s.io
roleRef:
  kind: Role
  name: pod-reader
  apiGroup: rbac.authorization.k8s.io
```

Network Policies

Network policies control traffic flow between pods and external services, preventing unauthorized access.

Example: Restricting Traffic Between Namespaces

```
apiVersion: networking.k8s.io/v1
kind: NetworkPolicy
metadata:
  name: deny-cross-namespace
  namespace: production
spec:
  podSelector: {}
  policyTypes:
  - Ingress
  ingress:
  - from:
    - podSelector: {}
      namespaceSelector:
        matchLabels:
          name: development
```

This policy blocks all ingress traffic from the **`development`** namespace to the **`production`** namespace.

Securing the API Server

The Kubernetes API server is a central control point and must be secured properly.

Best Practices:

- Restrict API server access using authentication and authorization mechanisms.
- Enable **Audit Logging** to track all API requests.
- Use **TLS Certificates** to encrypt API server communications.

Example: Enforcing API Authentication

```
kube-apiserver --authorization-mode=RBAC --audit-log-path=/var/log/k8s-audit.
log
```

Protecting Kubernetes Nodes

Nodes run workloads and need strict security configurations to prevent unauthorized access.

Best Practices:

- Enable automatic security updates.

- Use container runtime sandboxes such as gVisor.
- Restrict SSH access and enforce firewall rules.

When Should These Security Measures Be Applied

Security Measure	When to Apply
RBAC	During user and service account creation.
Network Policies	Before deploying applications in production.
API Hardening	During cluster setup and regular security audits.
Node Security	Before launching workloads and continuously.

Table 2.14: *When to Apply Security Measures in Kubernetes*

Securing Kubernetes Effectively

Implementation steps:

Step 1: Enable Role-Based Access Control (RBAC)

a. Ensure all users have the **least privilege** permissions.

b. Regularly review and audit roles.

Step 2: Implement Network Policies

a. Define **pod-to-pod** and **namespace-level** network rules.

b. Block unauthorized ingress/egress traffic.

Step 3: Secure API Server

a. Restrict API exposure to public networks.

b. Enable authentication and authorization modules.

c. Use **OIDC-based authentication** for improved security.

Step 4: Harden Kubernetes Nodes

a. Disable unused ports and protocols.

b. Enforce kernel security modules (SELinux, AppArmor).

c. Regularly update Kubernetes versions and patches.

Kubernetes Security Layers

The following figure illustrates Kubernetes security layers, including RBAC, Network Policies, API Security, and Node Hardening:

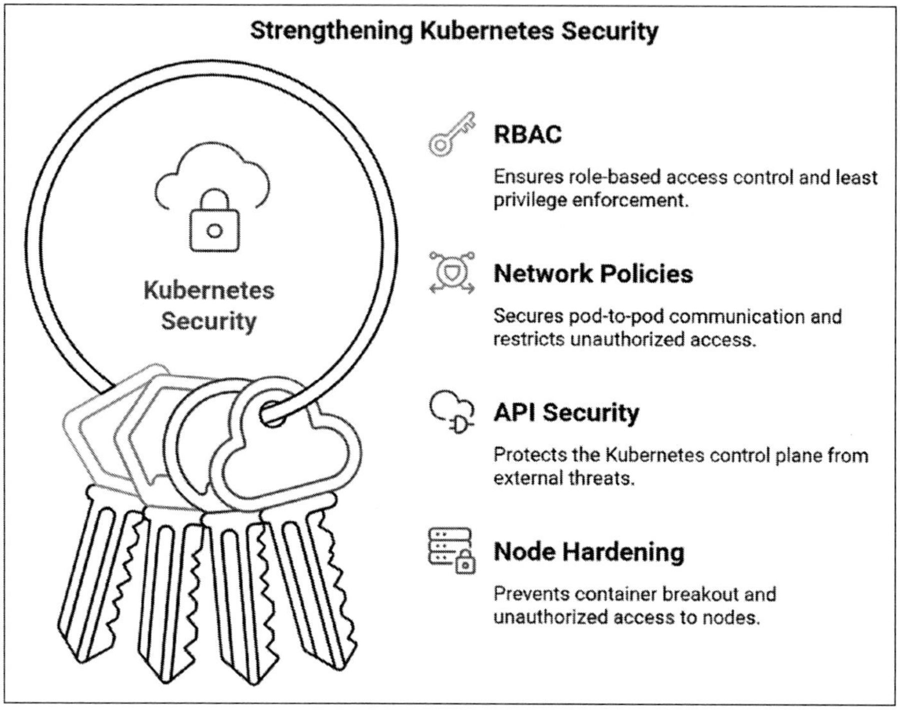

Figure 2.1: *Kubernetes Security Layers*

Kubernetes security requires a multi-layered approach to ensure infrastructure protection.

Key takeaways include:

- **RBAC** ensures role-based access control and least privilege enforcement.
- **Network Policies** secure pod-to-pod communication.
- **API Hardening** protects the Kubernetes control plane.
- **Node Security** prevents container breakout and unauthorized access.
- **Continuous Security Audits** are necessary to maintain a secure environment.

By following these best practices, organizations can effectively mitigate security risks and build resilient Kubernetes clusters.

Designing a Resilient Infrastructure for Data Pipelines

Building a fault-tolerant and scalable Kubernetes infrastructure is critical for ensuring high availability, optimized performance, and seamless operations of large-scale data pipelines. In modern enterprises, data engineering workloads involve ingesting, processing, and analyzing petabytes of data in real-time, requiring a resilient architecture that can handle failures gracefully.

This section covers best practices for designing a resilient infrastructure on Kubernetes, optimizing high-volume data pipelines, and real-world use cases where distributed data processing is critical.

The Need for Resilient Infrastructure

Challenges in Traditional Data Pipelines

Before Kubernetes, traditional data architectures had multiple challenges, such as:

- **Single Points of Failure**: If a server crashes, the entire pipeline could be disrupted.
- **Scalability Issues**: Data workloads often spiked unpredictably, leading to overprovisioning or failures.
- **Manual Recovery and Maintenance**: System admins had to manually recover from failures, leading to downtime.
- **High Latency**: Processing large datasets sequentially increased response times.

A resilient infrastructure solves these challenges by **automating failovers, dynamically scaling workloads, and ensuring data integrity** even under high loads.

Resilient Kubernetes Architecture

A resilient Kubernetes infrastructure is designed to provide **high availability, automated fault recovery, and optimized resource utilization** for big data workloads. The core components include:

- **Multi-Node Clusters**: Workloads are distributed across multiple worker nodes to avoid single points of failure.
- **Auto-Scaling Mechanisms**: Horizontal and vertical scaling ensure optimal resource usage.
- **Stateful Workload Management**: StatefulSets ensure persistence in distributed systems.
- **Fault Tolerance and Self-Healing**: Kubernetes automatically restarts failed pods and reschedules workloads.
- **Multi-Cloud and Hybrid Deployments**: Ensures disaster recovery and business continuity across cloud providers.

The following figure depicts a high-level resilient Kubernetes architecture:

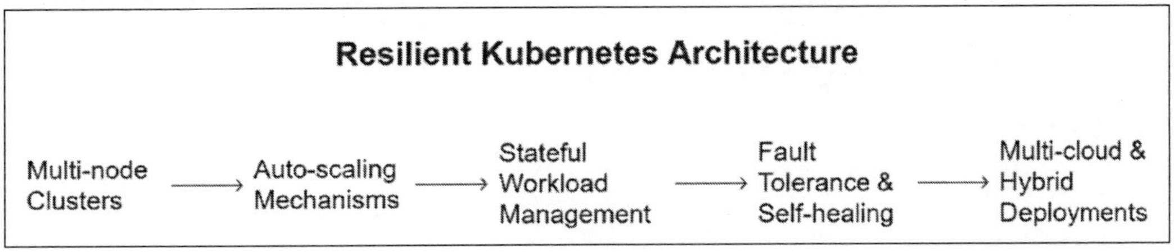

Figure 2.2: *Resilient Kubernetes Architecture*

Implementing a Resilient Architecture

Resilient architectures are crucial when dealing with:

- **Real-Time Streaming Workloads**: Applications such as Apache Kafka or Spark Streaming require continuous data ingestion and processing.
- **Batch Processing Pipelines**: Large-scale data processing (such as, ETL pipelines in Apache Airflow) must not fail due to node crashes.
- **Machine Learning Pipelines**: AI/ML workloads rely on GPUs and require auto-scaling and fault recovery.
- **Multi-Region Deployments**: Disaster recovery strategies need Kubernetes to run across multiple data centers or cloud regions.

- **Compliance and Security Requirements**: Industries such as finance and healthcare need high availability and data integrity.

Designing a Resilient Infrastructure

Key Principles:

- **Multi-Master Node Setup**: Prevents single points of failure in the control plane.
- **Multi-Zone Deployments**: Distributes workloads across different availability zones.
- **Auto-Scaling Configuration**: Implements both **Horizontal Pod Autoscaler (HPA)** and **Cluster Autoscaler**.
- **Service Mesh Implementation**: Tools such as Istio ensure traffic reliability and security.
- **Observability and Monitoring**: Implement **Prometheus + Grafana** for real-time insights.

Code Example: Enabling Horizontal Pod Autoscaler (HPA)

```
apiVersion: autoscaling/v2beta2
kind: HorizontalPodAutoscaler
metadata:
  name: data-pipeline-hpa
spec:
  scaleTargetRef:
    apiVersion: apps/v1
    kind: Deployment
    name: data-processing-app
  minReplicas: 3
  maxReplicas: 10
  metrics:
  - type: Resource
    resource:
      name: cpu
      target:
        type: Utilization
        averageUtilization: 60
```

Architecting High-Volume Data Pipelines on Kubernetes

Choosing the Right Data Processing Framework

Popular frameworks for Kubernetes-based data processing are:

- **Apache Spark**: Distributed batch and stream processing.
- **Apache Flink**: Low-latency real-time data processing.
- **Airflow DAGs on Kubernetes**: Orchestrating complex ETL workflows.

Code Example: Running Apache Spark on Kubernetes

```
kubectl apply -f spark-master-deployment.yaml
kubectl apply -f spark-worker-deployment.yaml
```

spark-master-deployment.yaml

```
apiVersion: apps/v1
kind: Deployment
metadata:
  name: spark-master
```

```
  labels:
    app: spark
    role: master
spec:
  replicas: 1
  selector:
    matchLabels:
      app: spark
      role: master
  template:
    metadata:
      labels:
        app: spark
        role: master
    spec:
      containers:
        - name: spark-master
          image: bde2020/spark-master:latest
          ports:
            - containerPort: 7077
            - containerPort: 8080
          env:
            - name: SPARK_MODE
              value: "master"
---
apiVersion: v1
kind: Service
metadata:
  name: spark-master
spec:
  type: ClusterIP
  ports:
    - port: 7077
      name: spark-master
    - port: 8080
      name: spark-ui
  selector:
    app: spark
    role: master
```

Explanation:

Spark Master Deployment: Runs a single instance of Spark Master.

Ports:

- `7077` → Used by worker nodes to connect.
- `8080` → Spark Master Web UI.

Service: Exposes Spark Master within the cluster.

spark-worker-deployment.yaml

```
apiVersion: apps/v1
kind: Deployment
metadata:
  name: spark-worker
  labels:
    app: spark
```

```
    role: worker
spec:
  replicas: 2  # You can adjust the number of worker replicas
  selector:
    matchLabels:
      app: spark
      role: worker
  template:
    metadata:
      labels:
        app: spark
        role: worker
    spec:
      containers:
        - name: spark-worker
          image: bde2020/spark-worker:latest
          ports:
            - containerPort: 8081
          env:
            - name: SPARK_MODE
              value: "worker"
            - name: SPARK_MASTER
              value: "spark://spark-master:7077"
---
apiVersion: v1
kind: Service
metadata:
  name: spark-worker
spec:
  type: ClusterIP
  ports:
    - port: 8081
      name: spark-worker-ui
  selector:
    app: spark
    role: worker
```

Explanation:

Spark Worker Deployment:

- Deploys **two worker replicas** (can be adjusted).
- Connects to **Spark Master** at spark://spark-master:7077.
- Exposes **port 8081** for Spark Worker UI.

Service:

- Exposes Spark Worker UI **within the cluster**.

Storage Considerations:

- **Persistent Volumes (PV) and Persistent Volume Claims (PVC):** Ensure long-term data storage.
- **Object Storage (S3, GCS, Azure Blob):** Offloads large data processing workloads.
- **HDFS on Kubernetes:** Suitable for Hadoop-based applications.

Example: Kubernetes Persistent Volume Configuration

```
apiVersion: v1
kind: PersistentVolumeClaim
metadata:
  name: data-pipeline-pvc
spec:
  accessModes:
    - ReadWriteOnce
  resources:
    requests:
      storage: 500Gi
```

Real-World Case Studies of Resilient Data Processing on Kubernetes

Case Study 1: Netflix's Data Infrastructure on Kubernetes

Netflix processes **tens of petabytes of data daily**, requiring a resilient infrastructure. They use:

- Kubernetes clusters with auto-scaling and fault tolerance.
- Apache Kafka for streaming analytics.
- Istio Service Mesh for secure traffic routing.

Case Study 2: Financial Services – Fraud Detection Pipelines

A leading bank runs fraud detection on Kubernetes with:

- **Apache Spark for real-time analytics**.
- **Multiple Availability Zone clusters** for failover protection.
- **RBAC security policies** to protect sensitive data.

Conclusion

Setting up a **Kubernetes cluster**, whether **on-premises or in the cloud**, is the **foundation of modern cloud-native architectures**. A well-configured cluster ensures **scalability, high availability, security, and cost efficiency**, making it an essential skill for **DevOps engineers, data architects, and cloud professionals**.

This chapter provided a **hands-on, structured approach** to deploying Kubernetes across different environments, covering **installation, networking, security, and infrastructure best practices** to create **production-ready, resilient clusters**.

In the next chapter, we will deep dive into the core components of the Kubernetes control plane and node architecture.

Chapter 3
Kubernetes Architecture Deep Dive

Introduction

Understanding Kubernetes at an architectural level is crucial for building, operating, and troubleshooting modern cloud-native applications. While Kubernetes abstracts much of the orchestration complexity, its internal architecture comprises multiple components that work in harmony to manage containerized workloads at scale. This chapter provides a deep dive into the core components of the Kubernetes control plane and node architecture, explaining how the system maintains state, schedules pods, and ensures high availability. Hence, whether you are an architect, DevOps engineer, or platform operator, mastering the internals of Kubernetes will empower you to design more resilient and efficient systems.

Structure

In this chapter, we will cover the following topics:

- Kubernetes Control Plane and Its Components
- Node components: Kubelet, Kube-Proxy, and Container Runtime
- etcd: The Brain of Kubernetes Clusters
- Pod Lifecycle and Scheduling Internals
- Multi-Master and HA (High Availability) Kubernetes Setups

Kubernetes Control Plane and Its Components

Kubernetes is a highly scalable, distributed system designed to orchestrate containerized applications. At the heart of Kubernetes lies the **Control Plane**, which manages cluster operations, schedules workloads, and maintains the desired state of applications. Understanding how the Control Plane works is essential for engineers, architects, and DevOps professionals who design and maintain Kubernetes clusters.

This section provides a deep dive into the **Control Plane components**, explaining how they interact to ensure efficient and reliable cluster management.

Importance of Control Plane

Challenges in Managing Distributed Applications

- **Manual Container Management:** Orchestrating multiple containers across distributed nodes is complex.
- **Workload Scheduling Issues:** Without a centralized scheduler, workloads may be unevenly distributed.

- **Scalability Challenges:** Manually scaling workloads leads to inefficiencies and downtime.
- **Configuration Drift:** Maintaining consistency across environments becomes difficult.

To address these issues, Kubernetes introduces the **Control Plane**, which automates and streamlines cluster operations.

Defining Kubernetes Control Plane

The Control Plane is the **brain of Kubernetes**, responsible for managing the cluster's lifecycle and ensuring the desired state is maintained. The following table lists the core components of Control Plane:

Component	Description
API Server	The entry point for all Kubernetes commands and communications.
Controller Manager	Monitors and reconciles the actual cluster state with the desired state.
Scheduler	Assigns workloads (Pods) to suitable worker nodes.
etcd	Stores all cluster configurations and state information.

Table 3.1: *Core Components of Control Plane*

The following table lists critical scenarios of Control Plane:

Scenario	Importance of Control Plane
Scaling Applications	Ensures workloads scale up/down efficiently.
Handling Failures	Self-heals failed Pods and reschedules them.
Multi-Cluster Management	Enables centralized control across multiple Kubernetes clusters.
Security and Access Control	Enforces RBAC and authentication policies.

Table 3.2: *Control Plane Critical Scenarios*

Understanding the Kubernetes Control Plane Architecture

API Server - The Communication Hub

The **API Server (kube-apiserver)** is the gateway for all Kubernetes operations. It exposes the Kubernetes API, handles authentication, and validates requests.

Example: Querying Cluster Nodes via API Server

```
kubectl get nodes --output=json
```

This command queries the API Server, which fetches node information from etcd.

Controller Manager: The Reconciler

The **Controller Manager (kube-controller-manager)** ensures that the cluster always matches the desired state by running multiple controllers:

- **Node Controller:** Detects failed nodes and replaces them.
- **Replication Controller:** Maintains the correct number of running Pods.
- **Endpoint Controller:** Manages Pod-to-Service networking.

Scheduler: Assigning Workloads

The **Scheduler (kube-scheduler)** places new workloads onto the most suitable nodes based on available resources.

Example: Viewing Scheduled Pods

```
kubectl get pods -o wide
```

This command retrieves Pod placement information, showing which nodes they are assigned to.

Etcd: The Kubernetes Database

etcd is a highly available key-value store used to store all cluster data, including:

- Node states
- Pod configurations
- Authentication and RBAC rules

Example: Retrieving Cluster Configuration from etcd

```
ETCDCTL_API=3 etcdctl get /registry/pods --prefix --keys-only
```

This command lists all stored Pod configurations.

Flow Diagram: Kubernetes Control Plane Communication

The following is a high-level overview of how the Control Plane components interact:

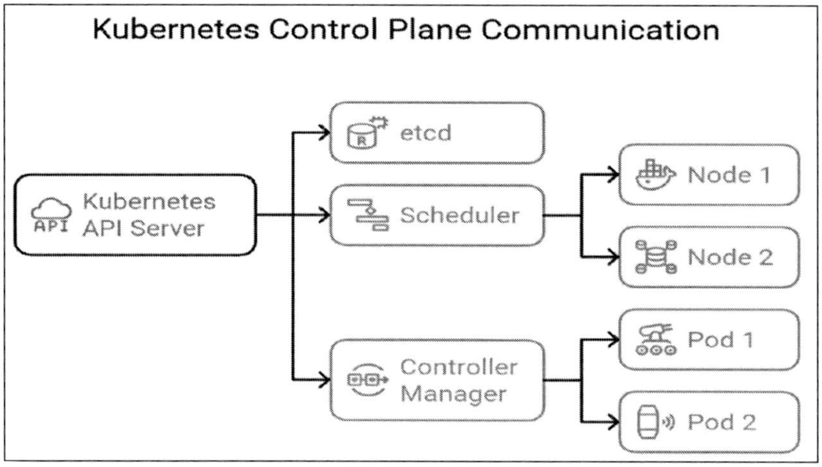

***Figure 3.1:** Kubernetes Control Plane Communication – Detailed Explanation*

This figure represents a **high-level flow of communication** between various core components of the Kubernetes **Control Plane**. These components are essential for maintaining the desired state of the cluster, orchestrating containers, and ensuring reliability and scalability.

Let us discuss each component in detail:

- **Kubernetes API Server**
    - **Role:** Acts as the *central management entity* of the cluster.
    - **Function:** All operations – whether user-initiated (via kubectl, CI/CD tools, dashboards) or internal – pass through the API Server.

  - **Communication Hub:** Serves as the *entry point* for all control plane components and external requests. It ensures secure and validated communication using RESTful API endpoints.

- **etcd**
  - **Role:** The *key-value store* that maintains the cluster state.
  - **Function:** Stores all Kubernetes objects, configurations, and secrets (such as, deployments, pod specs, service definitions).
  - **Interaction:**
    - The API Server writes to and reads from etcd.
    - Only the API Server communicates directly with etcd to ensure data consistency and security.
- **Scheduler**
  - **Role:** Determines *where* newly created Pods should run.
  - **Function:** Based on current cluster utilization, node capacity, affinity/anti-affinity rules, and other constraints, the Scheduler assigns Pods to Nodes.
  - **Interaction:**
    - Listens to the API Server for unscheduled Pods.
    - Makes decisions and updates the Pod specs with node information via the API Server.
    - The decisions affect Nodes (for example, Node 1, Node 2) where Pods will run.
- **Controller Manager**
  - **Role:** Ensures the actual state of the system matches the desired state.
  - **Function:** Manages various controllers, including:
    - Replication Controller
    - Node Controller
    - Deployment Controller
    - ServiceAccount Controller
  - **Interaction:**
    - Watches objects through the API Server.
    - For example, if a Pod fails, it triggers the creation of a replacement.
    - Communicates indirectly with Pods (for example, Pod 1, Pod 2) by pushing updates via the API Server.
- **Nodes**
  - **Role:** The *worker machines* (physical or virtual) where actual container workloads run.
  - **Function:** Host containers inside Pods, monitored and managed by kubelet.
  - **Interaction:**
    - Receive instructions from the Scheduler via the API Server.
    - Each node runs a local agent (kubelet) which pulls the Pod specs from the API Server and manages container runtime (like Docker or containerd).
- **Pods**
  - **Role:** The *smallest deployable units* in Kubernetes.
  - **Function:** Encapsulate one or more containers, storage, IP, and configuration.

- **Interaction:**
    - Managed and monitored by the Controller Manager.
    - Run on Nodes as assigned by the Scheduler.
    - Report health/status back via the kubelet to the API Server.

Summary of Flow

1. Users/devs submit configurations via the API Server.
2. API Server stores this desired state in etcd.
3. Scheduler assigns Pods to Nodes.
4. Controller Manager ensures that Pods are running as intended.
5. Nodes execute workloads and report back via kubelet.
6. API Server remains the central brain, facilitating all communication.

Next, we will explore **Node Components (Kubelet, Kube-Proxy, and Container Runtimes)**, explaining their role in managing containerized workloads at the node level.

Node Components and Their Roles

In Kubernetes, worker nodes are responsible for running containerized applications. Each node comprises multiple components that ensure seamless orchestration and management of workloads. The key components of a Kubernetes node include:

- **Kubelet:** Ensures containers are running in a Pod.
- **Kube-Proxy:** Manages network communication between nodes and services.
- **Container Runtime:** Runs and manages containers using tools such as Docker, containerd, or CRI-O.

This section provides an in-depth exploration of these components, their interactions, and their significance in Kubernetes cluster operations.

Importance of Node Components

Before Kubernetes, containerized applications ran on individual virtual machines or bare-metal servers, often leading to:

- **Inconsistent Deployments:** Manual container management caused discrepancies across environments.
- **Scalability Issues:** No automated mechanism to distribute workloads efficiently.
- **Resource Utilization Problems:** Some nodes remained underutilized while others were overburdened.

What is the Modern Approach

Kubernetes introduced an automated way to manage and scale workloads using worker nodes. The key node components ensure:

- **Efficient resource allocation** by dynamically scheduling workloads.
- **Seamless networking** through kube-proxy.
- **Reliable container execution** via container runtimes.

When should this be Applied

Understanding node components is critical in scenarios such as:

- **Setting up a production-ready Kubernetes cluster.**
- **Troubleshooting pod scheduling failures.**
- **Scaling applications dynamically.**

How do we Implement this

We will explore each node component in detail, followed by practical examples and a step-by-step guide for configuring them.

Understanding Worker Nodes and Their Components

Each Kubernetes cluster consists of multiple worker nodes responsible for executing application workloads. These nodes interact with the control plane to receive instructions and report their status.

Kubelet: The Node Agent

- Kubelet is a crucial component that runs on every worker node.
- It ensures that containers inside a pod are running as expected.
- It communicates with the API Server to receive workload assignments.

Workings of **Kubelet**

1. Registers the node with the control plane.
2. Watches the API Server for assigned pods.
3. Ensures pod health and restarts failed containers.
4. Reports node health and metrics to the control plane.

Example: Checking Kubelet Status

```
systemctl status kubelet
```

The following table lists common Kubelet issues and fixes:

Issue	Possible Cause	Fix
Node Not Ready	API server unreachable	Restart Kubelet and check network
Pods Not Scheduling	Resource constraints	Scale up node capacity
Kubelet Crash Loop	Misconfigured certificates	Regenerate TLS certificates

Table 3.3: *Common Kubelet Issues and Fixes*

Kube-Proxy: Managing Kubernetes Networking

Defining Kube-Proxy

- Kube-Proxy runs on each node and manages service networking.
- It ensures seamless communication between services within the cluster.
- It supports **iptables**, **IPVS**, and **userspace** networking modes.

Workings of **Kube-Proxy**

1. Watches the API Server for new services/endpoints.
2. Updates routing rules to enable pod-to-pod and pod-to-service communication.
3. Implements **load balancing** between pods.

Example: Checking Kube-Proxy Configuration

```
kubectl get configmap -n kube-system kube-proxy -o yaml
```

Flow Diagram: Node Communication in Kubernetes

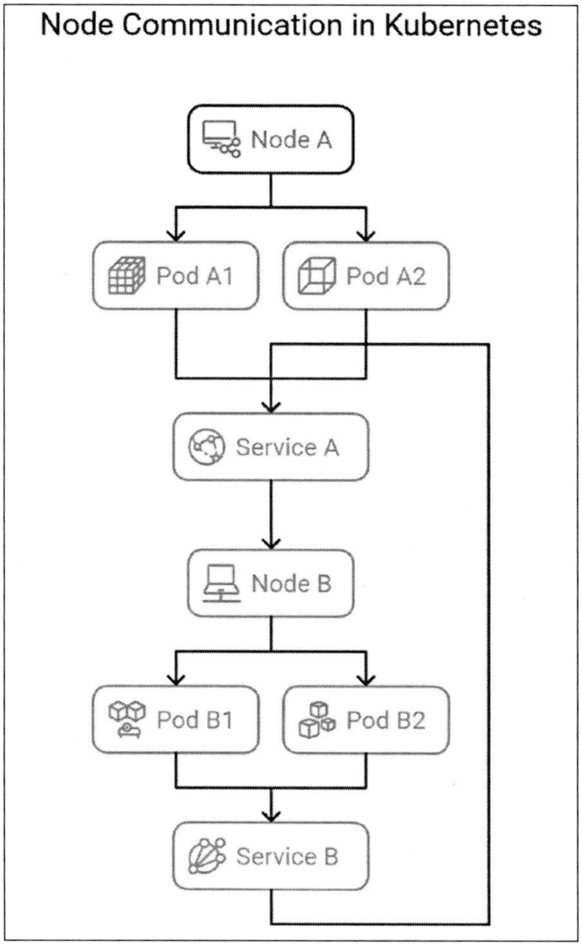

Figure 3.2: *Node Communication in Kubernetes (Flow-Based Representation)*

This flow diagram represents inter-node and intra-node communication in Kubernetes, showing how different components interact in a distributed environment.

Components and Flow Explanation

- **Node A:**
  - A physical or virtual machine in the Kubernetes cluster that runs containerized workloads.
  - Hosts multiple **Pods (Pod A1 and Pod A2)**.

- **Pod A1 and Pod A2:**
    - Smallest deployable units in Kubernetes, each running one or more containers.
    - They can communicate with each other directly if they belong to the same **Kubernetes Service**.
    - These pods send requests through **Service A** to route traffic efficiently.
- **Service A:**
    - Kubernetes **Service** provides an abstraction over multiple pods, exposing them as a **single network endpoint**.
    - Ensures that even if pods restart or get rescheduled, traffic is routed correctly.
- **Node B:**
    - Another node in the Kubernetes cluster.
    - Receives traffic from **Service A** and directs it to **Pod B1 and Pod B2**.
- **Pod B1 and Pod B2:**
    - Similar to Node A's pods, they run application workloads.
    - Receive requests from **Service A** and further process them.
- **Service B:**
    - Exposes Pod B1 and Pod B2 to external or internal consumers.
    - Ensures consistent access to pods despite potential changes in pod IPs.

Key Takeaways

- The diagram represents a **multi-node Kubernetes cluster** where services are used to manage pod communication.
- Communication can happen **within the same node (intra-node)** or across different nodes (inter-node).
- **Services** enable seamless communication and load balancing.

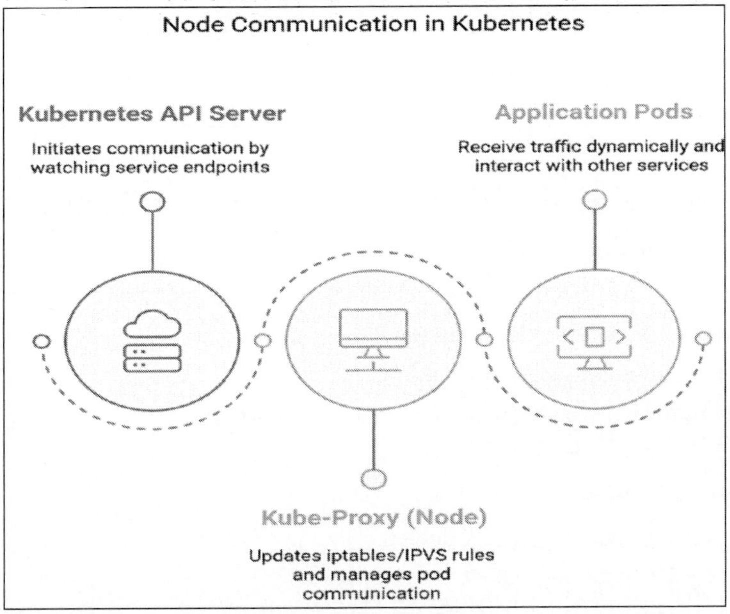

***Figure 3.3:** Kubernetes Node Communication (Concept-Based Representation)*

This conceptual diagram illustrates the three major components responsible for network communication in a Kubernetes cluster.

Components and Flow Explanation

- **Kubernetes API Server (Control Plane Component):**
  - Acts as the **main entry point** for all interactions with the cluster.
  - Continuously watches Kubernetes objects, including services and pods.
  - Helps in **initiating** communication by updating relevant service endpoints when pods change.
- **Kube-Proxy (Node-Level Component):**
  - Runs on each node to manage network rules.
  - Uses **iptables or IPVS** to route requests to the correct pod.
  - Ensures that incoming traffic is properly forwarded to the appropriate **Service and Pods.**
- **Application Pods (Workload Component):**
  - Receive traffic dynamically and interact with other services.
  - Depending on the networking model (for example, **CNI plugins such as Calico, Flannel, Cilium**), they can communicate with other pods across different nodes.

Key Takeaways:

- The diagram highlights **how the control plane, network routing, and workload components interact.**
- Kubernetes API Server maintains **service endpoints**, which are used by kube-proxy to **route network traffic.**
- Kubernetes networking is abstracted, allowing pods to **communicate seamlessly** across nodes.

The following table lists common Kube-Proxy issues and fixes:

Issue	Possible Cause	Fix
Service Unreachable	Incorrect iptables rules	Restart Kube-Proxy and check logs
Load Balancer Not Working	Misconfigured network plugin	Validate CNI configuration
Network Latency	High traffic load	Optimize pod-to-pod communication

Table 3.4: *Common Kube-Proxy Issues and Fixes*

Container Runtime: Running Containers in Kubernetes

Defining Container Runtime

- A container runtime is software responsible for running containers.
- Kubernetes supports multiple runtimes:
  - **Docker:** Traditional container runtime.
  - **containerd:** Lightweight, optimized for Kubernetes.
  - **CRI-O:** Designed specifically for Kubernetes.

Working of **Container Runtime**

1. Receives pod specifications from Kubelet.
2. Pulls the required container image.
3. Creates and runs containers inside the pod.

Example: Checking Installed Container Runtime

```
kubectl get nodes -o wide
```

Configuring containerd as the default runtime

```
cat <<EOF | sudo tee /etc/containerd/config.toml
[plugins."io.containerd.grpc.v1.cri"]
  sandbox_image = "k8s.gcr.io/pause:3.5"
EOF
systemctl restart containerd
```

The following table lists common container runtime issues and fixes:

Issue	Possible Cause	Fix
Containers Not Starting	Image pull failure	Check container runtime logs
High CPU Usage	Inefficient resource allocation	Optimize pod resource limits
Networking Issues	CNI misconfiguration	Verify CNI plugin status

Table 3.5: *Common Container Runtime Issues and Fixes*

Summary

- Kubernetes nodes host application workloads and interact with the control plane.
- Key node components include Kubelet, Kube-Proxy, and the container runtime.
- Kubelet manages pod lifecycle, Kube-Proxy handles networking, and the container runtime runs containers.
- Understanding these components helps in troubleshooting performance and connectivity issues.

In the next section, we will explore **etcd: The Brain of Kubernetes Clusters**, covering its architecture, data storage mechanisms, and best practices for high availability.

etcd: The Brain of Kubernetes Clusters

In a Kubernetes cluster, etcd serves as the **single source of truth** for all cluster configurations and states. It is a distributed key-value store that ensures **consistency, high availability, and fault tolerance**. Without etcd, Kubernetes would not be able to maintain the desired state of the cluster, store critical metadata, or coordinate workloads across nodes.

This section dives deep into **how etcd functions, why it is crucial for Kubernetes, its architecture, performance optimization techniques, and real-world deployment best practices.**

Importance of etcd in Kubernetes

Before understanding the internals of etcd, let us explore why it plays a **critical role** in a Kubernetes cluster:

- **State Management:** Kubernetes stores all cluster information in etcd, including nodes, pods, services, and network policies.
- **Cluster Coordination:** Ensures all nodes receive updates and changes instantaneously.
- **Fault Tolerance:** If a node fails, Kubernetes can rebuild the cluster using the data in etcd.
- **High Availability (HA):** Enables multi-master Kubernetes deployments to function efficiently.
- **Security and Access Control:** Stores **secrets, ConfigMaps**, and sensitive data securely with encryption.

Why is the Old Approach Inefficient

- **Lack of Consistency:** Legacy approaches struggled to maintain a **single source of truth** across distributed environments.
- **Manual State Tracking:** Traditional deployments required **manual intervention** to maintain cluster state and configurations.
- **No Automated Failover:** If a master node failed, **state corruption or data loss** was a common issue.

The following table lists common challenges without a well-configured etcd:

Challenge	Impact
Data Loss	Cluster state may become inconsistent, leading to service disruptions.
Performance Bottlenecks	Slow read/write operations affect Kubernetes API response times.
Single Point of Failure	Without a replicated etcd setup, cluster downtime increases.
Security Vulnerabilities	Unauthorized access to etcd can expose critical secrets.

Table 3.6: *Common Challenges without a Well-Configured etcd*

Etcd: The Core of Kubernetes State Management

etcd is an open-source, **strongly consistent, distributed key-value store** designed to handle **highly available and highly concurrent workloads**. Originally developed by **CoreOS** (now part of Red Hat), etcd is a fundamental component in Kubernetes.

Key Features of etcd include:

- **Consistency and High Availability:** Uses the **Raft consensus algorithm** to ensure data consistency across multiple nodes. Designed to handle **leader elections** and **failovers** automatically.
- **Fast Read and Write Performance:** Optimized for real-time cluster state updates.
- **Snapshot and Backup Support:** Regular snapshots prevent data loss.
- **Secure Communication:** Supports **TLS encryption** to prevent unauthorized access.
- **Horizontal Scalability:** Can be deployed across multiple nodes to enhance cluster resilience.

etcd Data Storage Model in Kubernetes

etcd stores Kubernetes data as key-value pairs. An example of how etcd stores information is as follows:

```
/kubernetes.io/nodes/<node-name> -> Node configuration & metadata
/kubernetes.io/pods/<pod-name> -> Pod state, resource allocations
/kubernetes.io/services/<service-name> -> Service definitions, load balancing details
/kubernetes.io/configmaps/<configmap-name> -> Configurations for applications
```

Criticality of etcd in a Kubernetes Cluster

Focusing on etcd health and scaling becomes non-negotiable under the following conditions:

- **Cluster Size Increases:** As the Kubernetes cluster grows, etcd **must scale** to handle thousands of objects.
- **High Availability Requirements:** In mission-critical applications, etcd **needs redundancy** to prevent failures.

- **Performance Bottlenecks Appear:** Slow API responses or frequent cluster failures indicate **etcd performance issues**.

The following table lists when to scale etcd:

Scenario	Action to Take
Cluster has **more than 500 nodes**	Scale etcd horizontally
Frequent **API server timeouts**	Optimize etcd read/write operations
High network latency	Ensure etcd cluster is deployed **closer to master nodes**
etcd leader failures are frequent	Enable **automatic failover and backup strategies**

Table 3.7: *Scenarios when to Scale etcd with Action*

The following table outlines the key use cases for **etcd** within a Kubernetes cluster:

Use Case	Description
Multi-Master Kubernetes Setup	etcd ensures consistency across multiple control plane nodes.
High Availability Clusters	If one master node fails, etcd allows seamless failover.
Secure Data Storage	Stores Kubernetes secrets and sensitive configurations securely.
Cluster Recovery and Backups	Enables restoring Kubernetes clusters in case of failure.

Table 3.8: *etcd in Kubernetes Cluster with Use Cases*

Working of etdc: Deep Dive into Architecture and Data Flow

etcd operates on a **leader-follower architecture**, ensuring consistency across nodes through the **Raft Consensus Algorithm**. Implementation:

- **etcd is the data store** for Kubernetes API server.
- It runs as a **separate process** on Kubernetes master nodes.
- The **Kubernetes API server communicates with etcd** to read and write cluster state.

The following table lists **key etcd operations in Kubernetes:**

Operation	Description
Create	Stores new objects like Pods, Deployments, and ConfigMaps
Read	Retrieves current cluster state (example, kubectl get nodes)
Update	Modifies existing objects (example, changing pod labels)
Delete	Removes objects from the cluster

Table 3.9: *Key etcd Operations in Kubernetes Cluster*

etcd Cluster Architecture

A typical etcd cluster consists of:

- **Leader Node:** The primary node responsible for handling all read/write requests.
- **Follower Nodes:** Replicate data from the leader and participate in the consensus process.
- **Clients:** Components like the Kubernetes API Server interact with etcd to read/write data.

Data Flow in etcd for Kubernetes

1. **Kubernetes API Server Requests Data:** The API server queries etcd for cluster state information.
2. **etcd Leader Processes the Request:** The leader node validates the request and updates the state.
3. **Data Replication to Followers:** Changes are synchronized across all follower nodes.
4. **Clients Receive Updated Data:** The API server retrieves the updated state, and reflects it in the cluster.

The following figure represents API server interactions with etcd, leader election, and follower synchronization:

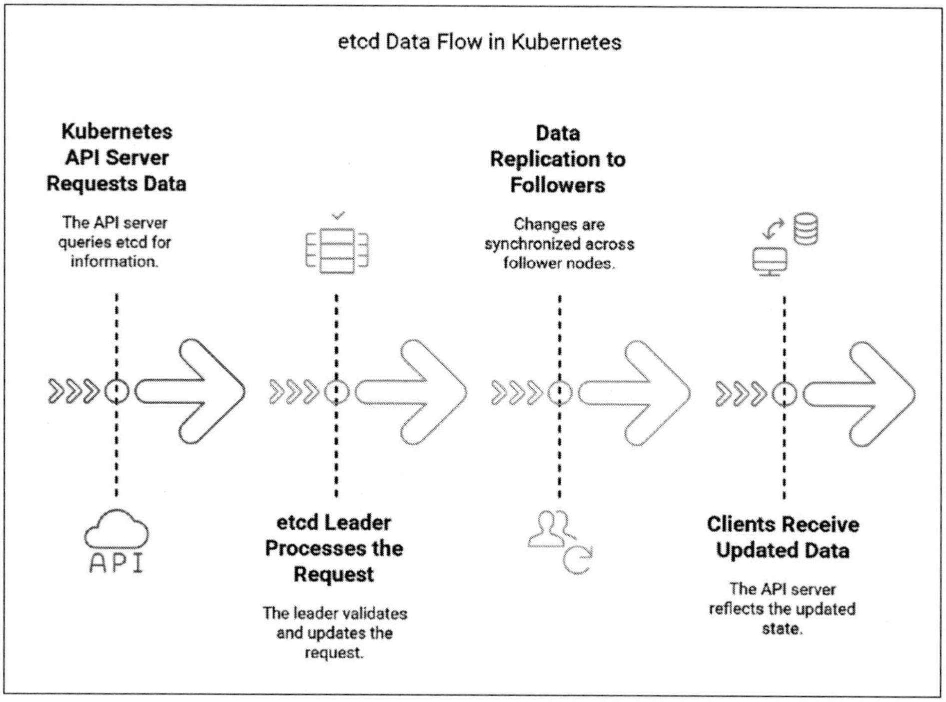

***Figure 3.4:** etcd Data Flow in Kubernetes Clusters*

In Kubernetes, **etcd** plays the critical role of a key-value store that acts as the **single source of truth** for the entire cluster state. The control plane components depend on etcd to retrieve and persist cluster configuration and runtime state. This flow diagram illustrates the step-by-step lifecycle of how data is requested, processed, replicated, and eventually served back to clients via the Kubernetes API server.

The detailed process is explained as follows:

1. **Kubernetes API Server Requests Data**

   Everything in Kubernetes begins with the **API Server**, which acts as the primary communication hub for all cluster operations. When any client (for example, kubectl, internal controller, or another system) requests cluster data or initiates a change, the API Server queries etcd for the required information.

Role of API Server: Acts as the front door of the cluster. Validates, authenticates, and routes requests to the etcd datastore.

2. **etcd Leader Processes the Request**

   In an etcd cluster, a **leader node** is elected among peers. All write operations go through this leader to maintain strong consistency.

   - The API Server's request is forwarded to the etcd leader.
   - The leader **validates the request**, ensuring that the data conforms to cluster policies and expected formats.
   - Once validated, the request is **persisted into the leader's local copy** of the etcd store.

   Leader Responsibility: Central decision-maker. Ensures consistency, applies change, and initiates replication.

3. **Data Replication to Follower Nodes**

   After the leader stores the change:

   - It replicates the new state **asynchronously to all follower nodes**.
   - Replication ensures **high availability** and **resilience**.
   - Even if the leader fails, a new one can be elected without data loss, thanks to the synchronized replicas.

   Replication Purpose: Maintains quorum and consistency. Prevents data loss or divergence during leader failure or node crashes.

4. **Clients Receive Updated Data**

   Once the change is committed:

   - The etcd leader sends an acknowledgment back to the Kubernetes API Server.
   - The API Server then reflects this change in the cluster state.
   - Finally, the updated data is available to clients or controllers monitoring that resource.

Final Outcome: The change is live, and other components (such as, controllers, schedulers, pods) can now react based on the new state.

Real-World Insight

A misconfigured etcd cluster is one of the top reasons for **control plane instability** in large-scale Kubernetes environments. That is why production-grade clusters use **TLS, snapshots, RAFT consensus, and regular backup strategies** to ensure data durability and fault tolerance.

Best Practices for Running etcd in Production

Configuring a Highly Available etcd Cluster

A **Highly Available (HA) etcd setup** ensures cluster resilience. The following are the **recommended best practices** for production environments:

1. **Deploy etcd as a Cluster:** Use an **odd number of nodes** (3, 5, or 7) for **high availability**.
2. **Enable Encryption and Authentication:** Secure communications with TLS and restrict API access.
3. **Regular Snapshots and Backups:** Use the `etcdctl` command to regularly save the database:
   ```
   ETCDCTL_API=3 etcdctl snapshot save /backup/etcd-snapshot.db
   ```

4. **Tune Performance Parameters:** Optimize `--quota-backend-bytes` and `--heartbeat-interval` for faster responses.
5. **Monitor etcd Health:** Use Prometheus and Grafana to track key metrics such as `etcd_server_leader_changes_seen_total`.

Real-World Use Cases: etcd in Action

Example 1: High Availability Kubernetes Cluster

Scenario: A financial institution running Kubernetes needs 24/7 uptime for its trading platform.

- **Why:** A single etcd node risks data loss and downtime.
- **What:** Deployed a 5-node etcd cluster to maintain **99.99% availability**.
- **When:** Required for critical services handling real-time transactions.
- **How:** Implemented **multi-region etcd replication** and automated backups to S3.

Example 2: Multi-Cloud Disaster Recovery

Scenario: An e-commerce company wants **multi-cloud Kubernetes failover**.

- **Why:** Cloud outages cause revenue losses during peak sales.
- **What:** Cross-cloud etcd replication across **AWS, GCP, and Azure**.
- **When:** Required for handling traffic surges and infrastructure failures.
- **How:** Configured **cross-region etcd syncing** with encrypted storage.

Example 3: Securing Kubernetes Secrets

Scenario: A healthcare company stores **patient data in Kubernetes secrets**.

- **Why:** Regulatory compliance (HIPAA, GDPR) requires **encrypted data storage**.
- **What:** Enabled **TLS encryption and RBAC policies** for etcd API access.
- **When:** Implemented before handling sensitive data workloads.
- **How:** Restricted etcd API access using IAM roles and Kubernetes RBAC.

Key Takeaways

- **etcd is the core datastore of Kubernetes**, storing all cluster state and configuration, with consistency maintained via the Raft consensus algorithm.
- **High availability and security of etcd** are crucial—regular backups, strict access controls, and performance tuning ensure a stable and resilient Kubernetes control plane.

In the next section, we will explore **Pod Lifecycle and Scheduling Internals**, diving deeper into how Kubernetes assigns workloads, and optimizes resource allocation across the cluster.

Pod Lifecycle and Scheduling Internals

In Kubernetes, Pods are the smallest deployable units. In other words, Pods are the most fundamental unit of deployment in kubernetes. Understanding how Pods are scheduled, created, managed, and destroyed is crucial for designing stable, performant, and highly available systems. But behind the simplicity of kubectl apply lies a highly dynamic, orchestrated engine handling container execution, networking, volumes, scheduling, lifecycle transitions, failure recovery, and more.

This part is crafted to help engineers move beyond the surface, and understand **how Pods are orchestrated under the hood**, and **how scheduling logic actually impacts their performance and**

availability in real-world clusters. Additionally, it also explores the internals of Pod lifecycle, and scheduling from a practical and architectural perspective.

Relevance in Real-World Systems

In modern production environments:

- Workloads must dynamically scale and self-heal.
- Scheduling impacts performance, cost, and availability.
- Mismanaged Pod lifecycles lead to instability and outages.

Mastering Pod internals means mastering the very foundation of Kubernetes orchestration.

Deep Dive into Pod Lifecycle and Scheduling

Let us understand the **Pod Lifecycle Stages (Pending → Running → Succeeded/Failed → Terminating)** in detail.

Each Pod goes through a well-defined lifecycle:

1. **Pending:** Kubernetes accepts the Pod but cannot yet schedule it to a node.
2. **Running:** The Pod has been bound to a node and containers are running.
3. **Succeeded/Failed:** Containers have terminated either successfully or with error.
4. **Terminating:** The Pod is being gracefully shut down (via SIGTERM and grace periods).

Realistic Insight: If a Pod is stuck in the **Pending** state, it is often due to insufficient node resources (CPU/Memory), affinity/taint rules, or network/storage issues.

Example:

```
kubectl describe pod my-app
```

Look for `Events:` section to debug lifecycle transitions.

When you deploy an application to Kubernetes, what happens next. Let us break down each lifecycle phase with theoretical depth:

1. Pending
   a. This is the initial state of any Pod.
   b. The Pod definition is accepted by the API server and stored in **etcd**, but it hasn't been assigned to a node.
   c. It stays in Pending until the **Scheduler** binds it to a suitable node.

Reasons a Pod may remain in Pending:

- No node has enough resources.
- Misconfigured affinity rules.
- Taints not tolerated.
- PVCs-PersistentVolumeClaims cannot be provisioned due to missing or misconfigured StorageClasses, unavailable PersistentVolumes, unsupported access modes, or insufficient underlying storage capacity. When a PVC remains in the Pending state, pods that depend on it cannot be scheduled, and therefore, remain in the Pending phase.

Example: A 16GB RAM request might stay pending on nodes with only 8GB free.

2. Running
   a. The Scheduler selects a node.
   b. The **Kubelet** on the node pulls the image and starts the container(s).
   c. The Pod transitions to Running once all containers are up and **Readiness Probes** pass.
3. Succeeded/Failed
   a. A Pod is **Succeeded** if all containers exit with exit code 0.
   b. A Pod is **Failed** if any container exits with a non-zero code, and the restart policy does not restart it.
4. Terminating
   a. On deletion or scale-down, Pods enter this phase.
   b. Kubernetes sends a **SIGTERM** signal.
   c. The container has a **grace period** to finish cleanup.
   d. If it does not finish in time, it receives **SIGKILL.**

Industry Best Practice: Use a preStop hook to gracefully release resources (for example, database connections).

Working of Kubernetes Scheduler (Affinity, Taints, Resource Fit)

The Scheduler is responsible for placing Pods on appropriate nodes. This is not a random process–it follows a deterministic pipeline:

- **Filtering Phase**

  Removes all nodes that cannot accommodate the Pod. Reasons might include:
  - Not enough CPU or memory.
  - Mismatched node selectors.
  - Unsatisfied affinity rules.
  - Node is cordoned or tainted without a matching toleration.
- **Scoring Phase**

  Scores all eligible nodes using algorithms such as:
  - **Least Requested Resources**
  - **Balanced Resource Allocation**
  - **Topology Spread**

Kubernetes chooses the node with the highest score.

Real-World Considerations:

- In large environments, poor scheduling can lead to latency, underutilization, or even cascading failures.
- Affinity rules should be used carefully to avoid unintentional node locking.

YAML Sample:

```
affinity:
  nodeAffinity:
    requiredDuringSchedulingIgnoredDuringExecution:
      nodeSelectorTerms:
      - matchExpressions:
        - key: disktype
          operator: In
          values:
          - ssd
```

The Scheduler decides *where* to run a Pod. Its decisions are based on:

- **Resource requests/limits** (cpu, memory)
- **NodeSelector**, **Affinity/AntiAffinity** rules
- **Taints and Tolerations**
- **Node availability** (cordoned, unschedulable, draining)

Real-world example: If your workload requires a GPU and nodes are labeled with `accelerator=nvidia-tesla`, use:

```
nodeSelector:
  accelerator: nvidia-tesla
```

Scheduling logic:

- **Filtering Phase:** Excludes nodes that don't satisfy constraints.
- **Scoring Phase:** Prioritizes among remaining nodes using weight-based functions (least utilized, balanced, and more)

Pod Template Internals and Controller Ownership

A Pod is rarely created in isolation. Instead, it is part of a **controller-managed workload** such as:

- **Deployment** (for stateless apps)
- **StatefulSet** (for apps needing persistent identity)
- **Job/CronJob** (for finite or scheduled tasks)
- **DaemonSet** (one per node, such as, logging agents)

Why this matters:

- **Controllers manage Pods declaratively.**
- If a Pod dies, the controller automatically recreates it.
- Pod Templates define how Pods look and behave:
  - Containers
  - Images
  - Ports
  - Volumes
  - Probes
  - Resource Limits

Note: *Treat controllers as source-of-truth, not individual Pods. Update controllers, and let Kubernetes manage the rest.*

Real-World Insight: In regulated industries such as finance and healthcare, Pod templates must comply with security, audit, and governance policies (for example, base image versions, volume encryption).

Each uses a **Pod template** (metadata, spec, containers, and volumes) to generate Pods dynamically.

Industry Practice: Avoid managing standalone Pods. Always use a controller for:

- Auto-healing
- Declarative updates
- Rollback/versioning

Code Example – Basic Deployment:

```
yaml

apiVersion: apps/v1
kind: Deployment
metadata:
  name: nginx-deploy
spec:
  replicas: 3
  selector:
    matchLabels:
      app: nginx
  template:
    metadata:
      labels:
        app: nginx
    spec:
      containers:
        - name: nginx
          image: nginx:1.24
```

Termination Lifecycle and Readiness Checks

When you delete a Pod or reduce a replica count, the process is not instant.

What Happens during Termination

- Kubernetes sends a `SIGTERM` to each container.
- It waits for a **grace period** (`terminationGracePeriodSeconds`, default 30s): this allows cleanup.
- If containers don't exit in time, a `SIGKILL` is sent, the Pod is forcefully terminated.

Best Practices

- Define a `preStop` hook to close DB connections, flush logs, and more.
- Use readiness probes to avoid routing traffic to terminating Pods.

Sample Hook

```
lifecycle:
  preStop:
    exec:
      command: ["/bin/sh", "-c", "echo Terminating...; sleep 5"]
```

Readiness versus Liveness

- **Readiness Probe:** Determines if the Pod can receive traffic.

- **Liveness Probe:** Determines if the Pod should be restarted.

Example:

```yaml
yaml

readinessProbe:
  httpGet:
    path: /healthz
    port: 8080
  initialDelaySeconds: 5
  periodSeconds: 10
```

Industry Tip: Use **readiness probes** to gracefully remove Pods from service mesh/load balancer before termination to prevent 500 errors during deployments.

In-Depth Explanation of the Diagram: Pod Lifecycle and Scheduler Interaction

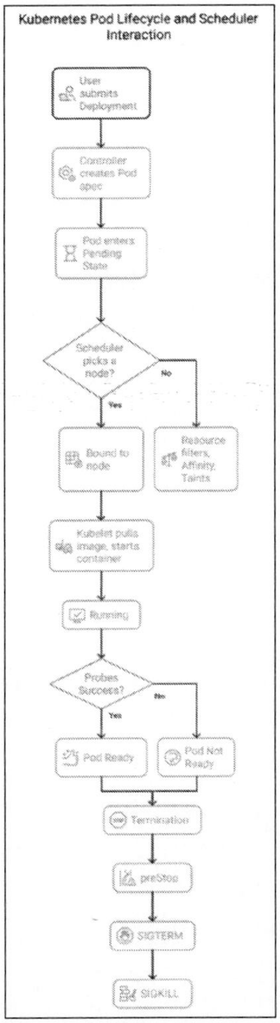

***Figure 3.5:** Kubernetes Pod Lifecycle and Scheduler Interaction*

Step-by-step Flow Explanation:

1. **Deployment Submission:**
    a. User applies YAML using `kubectl apply`.
    b. The object is stored in `etcd` via the API server.
2. **Controller Activity:**
    a. The relevant controller (for example, Deployment) notices the desired replica count.
    b. It creates a Pod template and issues Pod creation requests.
3. **Pod Enters Pending:**
    a. Pods without assigned nodes are in Pending.
    b. Scheduler detects them and adds them to its queue.
4. **Scheduler Executes:**
    a. Filtering removes unsuitable nodes.
    b. Scoring selects the most suitable node.
5. **Pod Gets Bound:**
    a. Scheduler writes a "binding" object back to the API server.
    b. Pod is assigned to a node.
6. **Kubelet Activity:**
    a. Kubelet on the chosen node pulls the container images.
    b. It sets up volumes, networking, and runs the containers.
7. **Running State:**
    a. If liveness and readiness probes pass, the Pod enters Running.
    b. Services can now route traffic to it.
8. **Termination:**
    a. On deletion or scaling, termination starts.
    b. `preStop` hooks run, followed by `SIGTERM`, then `SIGKILL` if needed.

Additional Real-World Considerations

- **Restart Policies:**
    - Always: for Deployments
    - OnFailure: for Jobs
    - Never: manual cleanup required
- **Probe Failures** (Readiness/Liveness) can auto-restart containers
- **Evicted Pods:** Triggered by resource pressure (disk, memory)

Final Thoughts: Pod Lifecycle is Where Stability Starts

Most Kubernetes failures are rooted in mismanaged lifecycle events:

- Probes misconfigured → traffic hits broken Pods.
- No `preStop` → dropped DB connections.
- Resource overcommitment → Pods OOMKilled and restarted repeatedly.

By deeply understanding the internals, you can:

- Optimize scaling and recovery.
- Minimize downtime during rolling updates.
- Build production-grade systems with zero surprises.

Key Learnings

- Pods are the core execution unit; every failure, scale-up, or deployment revolves around them.
- Scheduling decisions affect latency, availability, and cost.
- Controllers bring declarative orchestration and auto-healing to Pod lifecycles.
- Proper lifecycle management (preStop, probes, graceful termination) ensures system stability.

We will now elevate the discussion to **Multi-Master and High Availability (HA) Kubernetes Setups**, exploring real-world patterns for fault tolerance, leader election, and robust cluster design.

Multi-Master and High Availability Kubernetes Setups

As Kubernetes adoption matures in enterprises, so does the need for resilient, fault-tolerant, and highly available architectures. For mission-critical systems, a **Single Master Node** design is a potential point of failure. In this section, we will explore the theory, practice, and real-world deployment of **Multi-Master Kubernetes Clusters**.

This part is explained in the structured format as follows:

1. Core Components of HA Kubernetes Cluster
2. Building and Operating Multi-Master Setups
3. Load Balancing and etcd Redundancy
4. Hands-On YAML Lab + Architectural Flow Diagram + Case Study

Let us explore each section with detailed explanations, practical examples, and industry-aligned deployment strategies.

Core Components of HA Kubernetes Cluster

A **Highly Available (HA) Kubernetes Cluster** is designed to ensure that the critical services responsible for managing the cluster—such as scheduling, cluster state, and API communication—remain operational even in the face of node, network, or service failures. This architecture is essential for production-grade deployments where downtime can have severe operational or financial consequences.

Control Plane Nodes

The Control Plane is the "brain" of Kubernetes. For High Availability, you deploy multiple replicas of the control plane components across separate nodes:

- **API Server:**
  - The only component that all other components communicate with.
  - It serves as the gateway for all cluster operations (for example, `kubectl` commands, internal communication).
  - Must be horizontally scalable and stateless to allow for load-balanced access.
- **Scheduler:**
  - Watches for newly created pods without a node assigned, and assigns them to suitable nodes.
  - Though typically one active instance is sufficient, redundant passive schedulers can be deployed for failover.
- **Controller Manager:**
  - Runs various controllers (`ReplicationController`, `NodeController`, and more).
  - Only one leader is active at a time; the rest are on standby, ready to take over if needed.

HA Strategy: Deploy 3 or 5 control plane nodes behind a load balancer to ensure fault tolerance.

etcd Cluster

- **etcd** is the **distributed key-value store** that stores all cluster state data: node statuses, pod specs, secrets, configurations, and more.
- It is **critical** to Kubernetes operations, and its failure can paralyze the entire cluster.

Key Characteristics:

- Strong consistency (uses the Raft consensus algorithm).
- Requires **quorum** to make updates (majority of nodes must agree).
- Supports **leader election** for write operations.

Cluster Design Guidelines:

- **3-node etcd cluster** can tolerate **1 failure**.
- **5-node etcd cluster** can tolerate **2 failures**.
- Always use an **odd number** of etcd nodes to maintain quorum.

Note: *Never use an even number of etcd nodes – it reduces the fault tolerance, and may result in split-brain or data unavailability.*

Load Balancer

- Acts as a **single entry point** for API server access.
- Can be external (for example, AWS ELB, F5, HAProxy) or internal (for example, kube-vip, MetalLB) depending on the deployment environment.
- Distributes traffic evenly across all healthy API server instances.

  HA Best Practices:

  - Deploy multiple load balancers for redundancy.
  - Use health checks to ensure traffic is only sent to active API servers.

Worker Nodes (with Kubelet and Kube-Proxy)

- **Kubelet:** Agent running on each worker node. Ensures containers are running as expected.
- **Kube-Proxy:** Handles network routing for services on each node.

Though not part of the control plane, worker node availability impacts **pod scheduling and application uptime**. Worker nodes should also be **redundant**, and **spread across zones or racks** to avoid localized failures.

Key Attributes of a Highly Available Kubernetes Cluster

- **No Single Point of Failure (SPOF):**
  - Multiple instances of control plane components.
  - Redundant etcd nodes and load balancers.
  - Stateless components wherever possible.
- **Leader Election:**
  - For etcd and some controller components, only one active instance acts as leader.
  - Failover mechanisms promote standby nodes automatically upon failure.
- **Quorum-based Decision Making:**
  - etcd ensures data consistency through quorum; without majority agreement, writes are rejected.
  - This ensures consistency even during partial failures.
- **Zonal or Regional Redundancy:**
  - Best practice is to distribute master and worker nodes across **multiple availability zones** or **data centers**.
  - Prevents downtime in case of zone-level outages (for example, cloud provider zone failure).
- **Self-Healing and Resilience:**
  - Kubernetes automatically tries to maintain the desired state (for example, reschedules pods, if a node fails).
  - Liveness and readiness probes ensure unhealthy workloads are removed and replaced.

Real-World Insight

In a production-grade Kubernetes deployment, a typical HA setup might consist of:

- 3 control plane nodes
- 5 etcd nodes (separate from control plane for performance and security)
- 2 or more load balancers
- N worker nodes across multiple availability zones

Example Failure Tolerance:

- A **3-node etcd cluster** can survive **1 node failure**.
- A **5-node etcd cluster** can survive **2 node failures**.
- If **3 out of 5 etcd nodes are available, quorum is preserved and the cluster continues to function**.

Building and Operating Multi-Master Kubernetes Setups

Setting up a **multi-master Kubernetes cluster** is a cornerstone of achieving High Availability (HA) and fault-tolerance in cloud-native infrastructure. This approach ensures that the **control plane** does not become a **single point of failure**, enabling resilient workload orchestration even during node outages or maintenance events.

Key Principles of Multi-Master Design

A Kubernetes control plane typically includes:

- **kube-apiserver:** The front door to your cluster.
- **etcd:** A distributed key-value store that holds the cluster state.
- **kube-scheduler:** Assigns pods to worker nodes.
- **kube-controller-manager:** Runs core control loops.
- **cloud-controller-manager** *(optional in cloud)*: Interfaces with the cloud provider.

In a **multi-master setup**, these components are either **replicated (for example, API server)** or **elected (for example, scheduler, controller-manager)** using leader-election mechanisms to ensure seamless failover.

Deployment Approaches:

- **Kubeadm HA** (most popular for manual setups): Flexible and widely used in private and hybrid environments.
- **Managed Services** (for example, GKE, AKS, EKS handle HA internally): Fully abstracted HA; control plane is managed by the cloud provider.
- **Custom Automation with Ansible/Terraform:** Kubespray or RKE allow full automation and flexibility.

Cluster Setup Options:

- **Stacked etcd topology:**
  - etcd is co-located with other control plane components.
  - Simpler to manage for small or resource-constrained clusters.
  - Easier for **single-node test setups, lab environments**, or **edge deployments.**
- **External etcd topology:**
  - etcd runs on a dedicated node pool (separate from masters).
  - Recommended for production, large-scale, and mission-critical environments.
  - Improves security isolation, resource contention, and upgrade safety.

Industry Note: While stacked topology offers easier setup, it can create risks in resource-starved or overcommitted nodes, where API responsiveness depends on etcd health. External etcd clusters reduce such coupling and make it easier to scale and monitor.

Security and Operational Considerations

- **etcd** is the brain of your Kubernetes cluster–**encrypt all communication** using **mutual TLS (mTLS)**.

- Use **Role-Based Access Control (RBAC)** to restrict who can access or modify control plane components.
- Protect etcd with:
  - **Firewall rules**
  - **Audit logging**
  - **Regular backups**
- Protect kube-apiserver endpoints with:
  - **TLS certificates**
  - **API authentication layers** (OIDC, service accounts)
  - Ingress whitelisting

YAML Sample: Static Pod Manifest for kube-apiserver

In a kubeadm-based HA cluster, the control plane components are often run as **static pods,** managed directly by the `kubelet`. Here is a simplified example:

```
yaml


apiVersion: v1
kind: Pod
metadata:
  name: kube-apiserver
  namespace: kube-system
spec:
  containers:
  - name: kube-apiserver
    image: k8s.gcr.io/kube-apiserver:v1.27.0
    command:
    - kube-apiserver
    - --advertise-address=192.168.10.10
    - --etcd-servers=https://192.168.10.11:2379,https://192.168.10.12:2379
    - --client-ca-file=/etc/kubernetes/pki/ca.crt
    - --tls-cert-file=/etc/kubernetes/pki/apiserver.crt
    - --tls-private-key-file=/etc/kubernetes/pki/apiserver.key
    - --authorization-mode=Node,RBAC
    volumeMounts:
    - mountPath: /etc/kubernetes/pki
      name: k8s-certs
      readOnly: true
  volumes:
  - name: k8s-certs
    hostPath:
      path: /etc/kubernetes/pki
```

This config ensures:

- Secure communication with etcd.
- API server advertising the right endpoint.
- Enabling RBAC for access control.

Best Practice: Always secure etcd communication with TLS, and use RBAC to restrict access to API server endpoints.

Category	Recommendation
Availability	Deploy 3 or 5 masters in separate AZs or failure domains.
etcd	Always use **odd numbers** of nodes (e.g., 3, 5) to maintain quorum.
Security	Enable **TLS encryption** and **API server audit logging**.
Automation	Use kubeadm with **certificate-key sharing** to join control planes.
Load Balancing	Deploy **external load balancer** (HAProxy, ELB) to route traffic to API server
Monitoring	Integrate **Prometheus** to monitor etcd latency, disk I/O, and leader changes.
Backup and Recovery	Automate etcd snapshots and verify restore processes regularly.

Table 3.10: *Best Practices: etcd Communication in Kubernetes Cluster*

Deep Dive: Failover Mechanics

- The **API server** is **stateless** and can run on all master nodes simultaneously.
- The **scheduler** and **controller-manager** run **only one active leader** per cluster.
- Kubernetes uses **lease-based leader election** (`configmapsleases` in recent versions).
- When a master fails, **standby schedulers/controllers** automatically take over leadership.

Operations Insights

Scenario	Handling Approach
Master node crash	New leader elected; workloads continue unaffected.
etcd node failure	If quorum remains (for example, 2 of 3 nodes up), cluster remains operational.
Control plane upgrade	Use **kubeadm upgrade plan/apply** in rolling fashion.
Load balancer misconfiguration	Can cause complete access loss; always have **out-of-band kubectl access**.

Table 3.11: *Operations Insights: With Scenarios*

Load Balancing and etcd Redundancy

HA control plane depends on redundant etcd nodes and a robust load balancer in front of the API servers. In Other words, High Availability (HA) in a Kubernetes cluster is heavily dependent on the robustness of the control plane, which in turn relies on two major components: redundant **etcd** nodes and a **load balancer** that evenly distributes traffic to multiple API servers. If either fails, the cluster's availability, state consistency, and orchestration logic are at risk.

Load Balancer Requirements

The Kubernetes API server is the primary communication point for both external clients (kubectl, CI/CD pipelines) and internal components (kubelets, controllers). To avoid a single point of failure, multiple API servers must be fronted by a load balancer.

Core Requirements:

- **Health Checks:** The load balancer must continuously probe each API server to ensure traffic is only routed to healthy nodes.
- **Layer-4 (TCP) or Layer-7 (HTTP) Routing:** Layer-4 is preferred for performance and simplicity, as the Kubernetes API is primarily TCP-based.
- **Session Persistence:** Not usually required for Kubernetes API traffic, but can be useful in edge cases with long-lived connections.

- **Redundancy:** Use multiple load balancers (active-passive or active-active) to eliminate single points of failure at the Load Balancer (LB) level.

Popular Load Balancer Choices

- **HAProxy:** Lightweight, configurable, open-source.
- **NGINX:** Versatile with Layer-7 capabilities.
- **Cloud-native options:** AWS ELB, Azure Load Balancer, GCP Load Balancer provide integrated failover and scaling features.

Use multiple load balancers (active-passive or active-active) to eliminate single points of failure at the LB level.

Load Balancer Sample (HAProxy Configuration Example)

```
frontend kubernetes
  bind *:6443
  default_backend kube_apiservers

backend kube_apiservers
  balance roundrobin
  server master1 192.168.10.10:6443 check
  server master2 192.168.10.11:6443 check
  server master3 192.168.10.12:6443 check
```

Best Practice: Use check directive to enable health checks on each backend server to prevent routing to unresponsive API servers.

etcd Clustering

`etcd` is a key-value store that acts as the **brain of Kubernetes**—storing all cluster state data such as configurations, secrets, nodes, and workloads. Therefore, ensuring its availability and integrity is mission-critical.

Key Concepts:

- **Odd Number of Nodes:** etcd uses Raft consensus algorithm, which requires a quorum (majority) to operate. An odd number (for example, 3, 5) avoids split-brain scenarios and optimizes decision-making.
- **Peer-to-Peer Communication:** etcd nodes must discover and maintain communication with each other to replicate state changes reliably.
- **Cluster State Replication:** Any change to Kubernetes (such as, creating a Pod or updating a ConfigMap) is written to etcd. This ensures high reliability and allows state recovery during failures.

Note: *Always backup etcd regularly It is the single source of truth for your cluster. It can be done using `etcdctl snapshot save`. In a disaster recovery scenario, restoring etcd is the fastest way to recover cluster state.*

etcd YAML Manifest (Minimal Sample):

```
spec:
  containers:
  - name: etcd
    image: k8s.gcr.io/etcd:3.5.0
    command:
    - etcd
    - --name=etcd1
```

```
    - --initial-cluster=etcd1=https://192.168.10.11:2380,etc-
d2=https://192.168.10.12:2380
    - --initial-cluster-state=new
```

Case Study, Lab, and Architecture Diagram

Case Study: Building a Production-Grade High Availability (HA) Kubernetes Cluster for a FinTech

Scenario Overview:

A FinTech company offering real-time fraud detection and analytics needed a **zero-downtime Kubernetes platform**. Any service interruption could impact financial transactions, risk scoring models, and SLA-bound third-party services. Therefore, building an **HA control plane** with robust observability, failover handling, and seamless upgrades was a critical business requirement.

Solution Highlights:

- **3 Master Nodes (Stacked etcd):** Each master node runs both the Kubernetes control plane components and its own local etcd instance. This "stacked" architecture is simpler to deploy and works well in tightly coupled setups.
- **External HAProxy as Load Balancer:** A single-entry point for the Kubernetes API that distributes traffic to healthy master nodes. Critical for both kubectl operations and kubelet authentication.
- **Floating IP with keepalived:** A Virtual IP managed by keepalived ensures the load balancer remains reachable even if one HAProxy node fails. This helps eliminate any single point of failure at the LB level.
- **External Monitoring with Prometheus and Loki:** Centralized metrics (Prometheus) and logs (Loki) ensure observability. Useful for alerting, debugging, and capacity planning–crucial for production systems.

Outcome:

- **Zero Impact During Rolling Updates and Failovers:** Upgrades to master components and temporary node failures did not affect API access or application pods.
- **Achieved 99.99% Uptime SLA:** The combination of HA master nodes, load balancing, and monitoring delivered strong fault tolerance and availability guarantees.

Key Lesson: Building HA is not just about redundancy–observability, proactive failover, and smooth upgrades matter just as much.

YAML Lab: Provisioning Control Plane with kubeadm (Stacked etcd Architecture)

In a stacked etcd architecture, the etcd database runs **on the same node** as the control plane components. This is common in smaller HA deployments, and acceptable for many production use cases.

Bootstrap the First Master:

```
kubeadm init \
  --control-plane-endpoint "LOAD_BALANCER_DNS:6443" \
  --upload-certs \
  --pod-network-cidr=192.168.0.0/16
```

- `--control-plane-endpoint`: DNS or VIP of the HA load balancer.
- `--upload-certs`: Allows secure certificate sharing with other control plane nodes.

Copy the generated cert-key and join command to other master nodes using:

```
kubeadm join LOAD_BALANCER_DNS:6443 \
  --token <token> \
  --discovery-token-ca-cert-hash sha256:<hash> \
  --control-plane \
  --certificate-key <cert-key>
```

Note: *Always verify that certificate distribution uses secure channels and private IPs where possible.*

Effectiveness of This Architecture

- **Load Balancer:** Acts as the single access point for all API operations—clients never need to know which master node is active.
- **Stacked etcd Model:** Reduces external dependency footprint and is easier to manage in small to mid-sized clusters. Each node contributes to quorum.
- **Quorum and Fault Tolerance:** With 3 etcd members, the system can tolerate 1 failure, while maintaining consensus and availability.
- **Failover:** With proper health checks and floating IP failover (via keepalived), both API server and etcd traffic can continue flowing during node outages.
- **Observability:** Without metrics and logs, HA is blind. Prometheus and Loki allow teams to pre-empt issues before they escalate.

Diagram: High Availability Kubernetes Cluster Design

High Availability (HA) is a foundational principle for production-grade Kubernetes deployments. It ensures that control plane services remain operational and responsive even in the face of node failures, network disruptions, or maintenance activities. *Figure* 3.6 illustrates how Kubernetes achieves this through a well-architected combination of redundancy, consensus, secure communication, and observability.

- **Load Balancer:** Directs kubectl or internal requests to any healthy API server. Ensures seamless interaction regardless of which master is currently available.
- **Master Nodes:** Run kube-apiserver, controller-manager, scheduler, and etcd locally (stacked setup). Contribute to etcd quorum.
- **Worker Nodes:** Register with API via the load balancer. Workload Pods run here, managed by kubelet and controlled by master.
- **etcd Cluster:** Communicates over encrypted TLS channels. Uses Raft consensus to replicate changes and elect leaders.

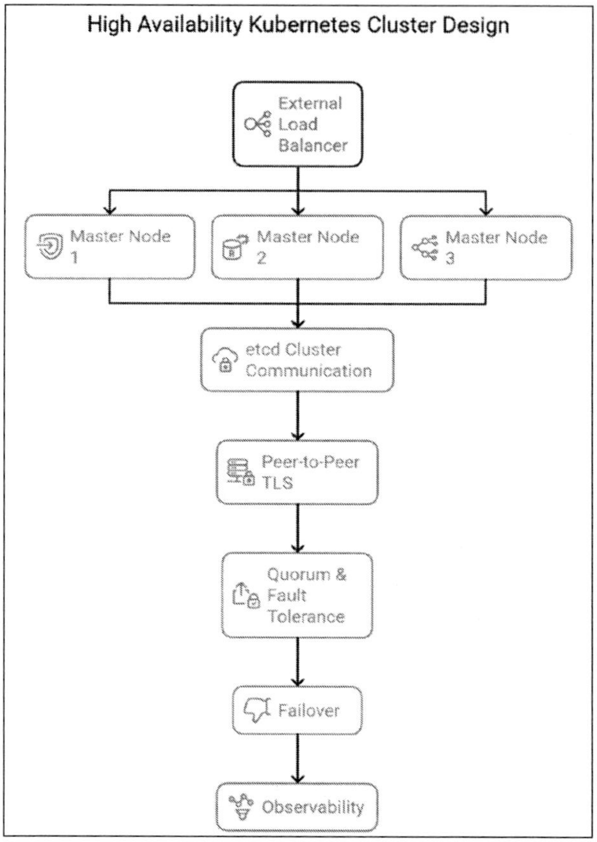

Figure 3.6: *High Availability Kubernetes Cluster Design*

External Load Balancer

At the top of the architecture lies the **External Load Balancer**, which serves as the entry point for all client requests to the Kubernetes API server. This component is responsible for:

- **Distributing incoming traffic** evenly across all master nodes.
- Detecting node health and **automatically rerouting traffic** away from any failed or unresponsive master node.
- Ensuring that from the user's perspective, there is always a seamless connection to the Kubernetes control plane, regardless of the underlying node health.

This mechanism is the first layer of defense in maintaining high availability.

Master Nodes (1, 2, 3)

The architecture includes **three master nodes**, which is a common pattern for HA to ensure quorum in distributed consensus systems such as etcd. Each master node runs the full suite of **Kubernetes control plane components**, including:

- **`kube-apiserver`:** Handles all API requests.
- **`kube-scheduler`:** Assigns workloads (pods) to worker nodes.
- **`kube-controller-manager`:** Runs controller loops for managing cluster state.
- **`cloud-controller-manager` (optional):** Manages cloud-specific resources.

Each of these nodes is **active and synchronized**, meaning the cluster does not rely on a single point of failure. The load balancer ensures that traffic reaches any of the healthy master nodes.

etcd Cluster Communication

At the heart of the control plane lies the **etcd cluster**, a distributed, consistent key-value store that acts as the **single source of truth** for all cluster state data. Master nodes communicate with etcd to:

- Persist the current state of the cluster.
- Retrieve real-time configuration and status information.
- Coordinate updates to the desired state.

This communication is bidirectional and **synchronous**, making etcd's performance and stability crucial for the cluster's reliability.

Peer-to-Peer TLS (Secure Communication)

All communication between etcd nodes and between etcd and master components is **secured using TLS (Transport Layer Security)**. This ensures:

- **Encryption** of data in transit to prevent eavesdropping.
- **Authentication** of peers to prevent spoofed or rogue nodes.
- **Integrity** of messages to guard against tampering or replay attacks.

Mutual TLS (mTLS) ensures that both clients and servers verify each other's certificates, providing a robust trust boundary.

Quorum and Fault Tolerance

The **Raft consensus algorithm** underpins etcd's distributed nature. It ensures that even when a subset of nodes fail, the remaining nodes can still reach consensus and serve data. This is governed by a **quorum**, which is defined as:

- A **majority** of nodes in the cluster (for example, 2 out of 3, 3 out of 5).

By maintaining quorum:

- The cluster **continues to operate** even during partial failures.
- **Split-brain scenarios** are avoided, where conflicting cluster states could be written.

This fault tolerance mechanism is a key enabler for high availability.

Failover Handling

In the event where one or more master nodes become unreachable:

- The **load balancer automatically reroutes traffic** to the remaining healthy nodes.
- The etcd cluster remains operational as long as quorum is maintained.
- Kubernetes continues to schedule and manage workloads without manual intervention.

Failover is thus both **automatic and transparent**, minimizing downtime and operator involvement.

Observability

No HA system is complete without visibility. Kubernetes provides deep observability via integrations with tools, such as:

- **Prometheus:** For metrics collection and alerting.

- **Grafana:** For dashboard visualizations.
- **ELK Stack / Loki:** For centralized logging.
- **Jaeger or OpenTelemetry:** For distributed tracing.

These tools help administrators:

- Detect issues proactively.
- Analyze system performance.
- Respond to anomalies with precision.

Observability is essential for long-term stability, compliance, and operational excellence in Kubernetes environments.

Key Notes and Real-World Advice: This setup ensures that even if a master or etcd node fails, the cluster remains functional.

- A **3-node master/etcd cluster** is ideal for HA. Add more only if the workload grows, and ensure it is always an odd number for consensus.
- Use **network policies and firewalls** to secure etcd communication (port 2380) and API access (port 6443).
- Use **taints on master nodes** to keep workloads off them unless necessary: NoSchedule taints help preserve control plane stability.
- Always **test failover scenarios** (for example, stop etcd on one node, reboot master, simulate network partitions).

Conclusion

This chapter gave a solid foundation in building **highly available Kubernetes clusters**. You learned about multi-master setups, etcd quorum, load balancing, and real-world deployment patterns. With practical labs and architecture diagrams, you are now equipped to design **resilient, production-ready Kubernetes environments** that can withstand failures and ensure uptime.

In the next chapter, we will shift our focus to the core units of Kubernetes - containers and pods - and explore how to design efficient microservices architectures. You will learn how to leverage StatefulSets, DaemonSets, and ReplicaSets to build scalable, cloud-native applications tailored for modern data workloads and real-time processing.

CHAPTER 4

Containers, Pods, and Microservices Patterns

Introduction

In modern cloud-native architectures, Docker containers are the building blocks of deployment. Their lightweight, portable, and consistent nature allows developers, DevOps engineers and data engineers to package, test, and ship applications seamlessly across environments. Kubernetes, as the orchestration layer, relies heavily on container images for deploying and scaling workloads. Before diving into Kubernetes pods and services, it is essential to thoroughly understand Docker's internal workings, advanced capabilities, and best practices, especially for large-scale data engineering scenarios.

Structure

In this chapter, we will cover the following topics:

- Docker Deep Dive for Kubernetes
- Pods and Multi-Container Patterns
- Deployments, ReplicaSets and Scaling
- StatefulSets, DaemonSets, and Static Pods
- Microservices Design Patterns in Kubernetes
- Containerizing ETL Pipelines and Stateful Workloads

Docker Container Concepts

Docker containers standardize how applications are developed and deployed. At the heart of Docker lies its image-based architecture.

Core Concepts:

- **Images**: Read-only templates used to create containers. They include the application code, dependencies, libraries, and configuration files.
- **Layers**: Each Docker image consists of layers. Each instruction in a Dockerfile (for example, `RUN`, `COPY`) creates a new layer. Docker uses a union file system to manage and cache layers efficiently.
- **Containers**: Running instances of Docker images. Containers add a read-write layer on top of the image's read-only layers.
- **Registries**: Storage for Docker images. Docker Hub is the default public registry, but private registries such as Harbor or AWS ECR are used for enterprise-level deployments.

Example: Minimal Dockerfile for a Python Data App

```
FROM python:3.10-slim
WORKDIR /app
COPY requirements.txt .
RUN pip install -r requirements.txt
COPY . .
CMD ["python", "main.py"]
```

This builds an image for a Python-based ETL job with lightweight dependencies.

Understanding the Minimal Dockerfile for a Python Data App

In modern data engineering workflows, **containerizing ETL jobs and data pipelines** is critical for portability, reproducibility, and simplified deployment. The following example demonstrates a minimal yet powerful Dockerfile that can be used to package and run a Python-based data processing application:

```
Dockerfile

# Base image with Python pre-installed
FROM python:3.10-slim

# Set working directory inside the container
WORKDIR /app

# Copy dependency list to the container
COPY requirements.txt .

# Install dependencies
RUN pip install -r requirements.txt

# Copy all project files into the container
COPY . .

# Define the command to run the app
CMD ["python", "main.py"]
```

Line-by-Line Breakdown of the Preceding Dockerfile

```
FROM python:3.10-slim
```

This line sets the **base image** for your container.

- **`python:3.10-slim`** refers to an official Python image, with version 3.10.
- The **`slim` tag** is a stripped-down version of the full image, optimized for smaller sizes and faster builds.
- Using a slim image reduces:
  - **Attack surface area** (security benefit),
  - **Build time** and **image size** (performance and cost-benefit),
  - Unnecessary packages that are not needed for most data applications.

Note: *Always specify the exact Python version (for example, **`3.10`**), to avoid unexpected version upgrades.*

`WORKDIR /app`

This instruction sets the **working directory** inside the container to `/app`.

- Every command (for example, **`RUN`**, **`CMD`**, **`COPY`**) after this line will be **executed relative to this path**.
- This simplifies the file structure and keeps the container organized.

Why it matters: It is equivalent to **`cd /app`** inside the container - helping maintain clarity and structure.

```
COPY requirements.txt .
```

This line **copies only the `requirements.txt` file** from your local project directory to the **`/app`** directory inside the container.

- This is a **layered optimization trick**.
- By copying **`requirements.txt`** first (before copying all files), Docker can **cache the dependency installation** in intermediate layers.
- If you change your Python source code but not the dependencies, Docker will not re-run **`pip install`**, which saves build time.

Smart Docker Layering: Small change = fast rebuild.

```
RUN pip install -r requirements.txt
```

This installs the Python dependencies listed in the **`requirements.txt`** file.

- Uses **`pip`**, Python's package manager.
- Installs dependencies inside the container's environment, isolated from the host machine.
- These packages are required for your data app or ETL job to run (for example, **`pandas`**, **`numpy`**, **`sqlalchemy`**, and so on).

Note: *Always pin versions in your `requirements.txt` file to avoid breaking changes (for example, **`pandas==1.5.3`**).*

`COPY . .`

This command **copies the entire contents of the local directory** (including source code, config files, and assets) into the container's working directory (**`/app`**).

- Now the container has access to everything needed to run your application, such as:
  - **`main.py`**
  - Any Python modules or utilities
  - JSON/CSV configs, logging config, and so on.

Note: *Use a **`.dockerignore`** file to exclude unnecessary files such as **`.git`**, **`.DS_Store`**, test logs, and so on.*

`CMD ["python", "main.py"]`

This is the **default command** that will be run when the container starts.

- Runs your main application logic, typically your **ETL script** or **data processing job**.
- The array syntax (**`exec form`**) is preferred because it avoids running the command through a shell, which is more secure and signals correctly to Docker how to manage the process.

Note: *Consider using **`ENTRYPOINT`** if you want to always run **`python main.py`**, regardless of passed arguments.*

Real-World Application Scenarios

This Dockerfile is ideal for:

- ETL pipelines processing data from cloud storage or databases.
- Scheduled batch jobs using Apache Airflow, Prefect, or cron.
- Data transformation and cleansing scripts.
- Microservices exposing ML models or analytics APIs (if extended further).

You can build and run the container as:

```
bash

docker build -t python-etl-app .
docker run python-etl-app
```

Advanced Tips and Enhancements:

- **Slim but Compatible**
  - If you need system libraries (for example, for `psycopg2` or `opencv`), you might need `python:3.10-slim-buster` or explicitly install build tools such as `gcc`.
- **Non-root user**
  - For security, create a non-root user in the Dockerfile and run the app with limited privileges.
- **Add Health Checks**
  - Add `HEALTHCHECK` to ensure your data app is behaving as expected (especially for services or long-running ETL daemons).
- **Logging and Observability**
  - Mount logs to a shared volume or push logs to a centralized logging system.

Real-World Insight:

Using a base image such as `python:3.10-slim` significantly reduces image size, which is crucial for faster pulls in Kubernetes pods.

Advanced Docker Usage

As projects scale, advanced Docker techniques help optimize builds, enforce security, and support complex pipelines.

Multi-Stage Builds

Allows separating build and runtime environments to reduce final image size.

```
# Stage 1 - Build
FROM golang:1.19 AS builder
WORKDIR /app
COPY . .
RUN go build -o server .

# Stage 2 - Run
FROM alpine:3.17
COPY --from=builder /app/server /server
CMD ["/server"]
```

Volume Mounts

Enable sharing files and data between host and container.

```
docker run -v /host/data:/app/data my-etl-image
```

Used in **`dev`** workflows to persist data or mount code changes.

Networking

Docker provides bridge networks, overlays, and host networking.

- **`docker network create analytics-net`** for isolated communication
- Microservices can use Docker DNS to refer to each other by container name.

Security Best Practices:

- Use non-root users in containers,
- Scan images using tools such as Trivy or Clair,
- Sign and verify images with Docker Content Trust or Notary.

Best Practices for Data Engineering Containers

Containers in data engineering should support consistency, reproducibility, and fault tolerance.

- **Lean Base Images**
  - Use minimal base images such as **`alpine`** or **`slim`** to reduce the attack surface and image size.
  - Example: **`python:3.10-slim`** over full **`python:3.10`**
- **Immutable Builds**
  - Use version-pinned requirements files.
  - Example: **`pandas==1.5.3`** to avoid breaking updates.
- **Data Volume Strategy**
  - Avoid writing to container file systems.
  - Use mounted volumes or object storage APIs (for example, S3, GCS).
- **Observability and Logging**
  - Direct logs to **`stdout`** and **`stderr`** for collection via Fluentd or Loki.
  - Example:

    ```
    import logging
    logging.basicConfig(level=logging.INFO)
    ```

Case Study: Containerizing a Streaming ETL Pipeline

Scenario: A data engineering team at a logistics firm wants to build a streaming pipeline using Apache Kafka and process it with a Python-based ETL job. They need to containerize the solution to run on Kubernetes.

Solution Architecture:

- Kafka Cluster (on cloud)
- Python container with:
  - **`kafka-python`** library
  - Batch logic and checkpointing
  - Configurable via environment variables

Dockerfile:

```
FROM python:3.10-slim
WORKDIR /etl
COPY requirements.txt .
RUN pip install -r requirements.txt
COPY . .
CMD ["python", "etl_consumer.py"]
```

Kubernetes YAML Lab:

```
apiVersion: apps/v1
kind: Deployment
metadata:
  name: etl-kafka-consumer
spec:
  replicas: 2
  selector:
    matchLabels:
      app: kafka-etl
  template:
    metadata:
      labels:
        app: kafka-etl
    spec:
      containers:
      - name: etl-container
        image: myrepo/kafka-etl:1.0
        env:
        - name: KAFKA_BROKER
          value: "kafka-cluster:9092"
        - name: TOPIC_NAME
          value: "logistics"
```

Architecture Diagram: Containerized ETL on Kubernetes

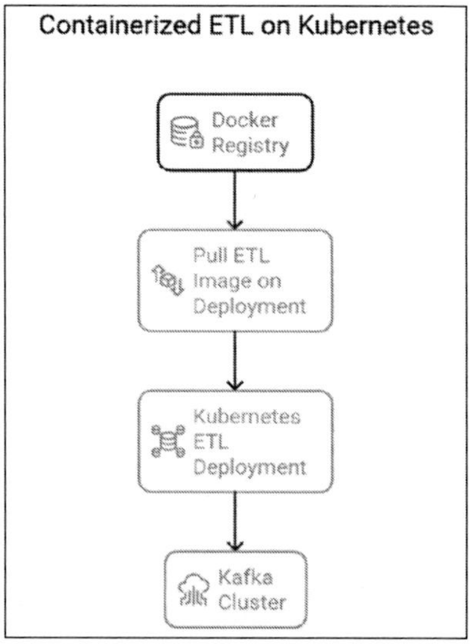

Figure 4.1: *Containerized ETL on Kubernetes*

This architecture illustrates a modern, cloud-native approach to running **ETL (Extract, Transform, Load)** processes using **containerized microservices on Kubernetes**, integrated with a **Kafka cluster** for scalable and real-time data ingestion.

- **Docker Registry**: Stores built ETL images, version-controlled and secure.
- **ETL Deployment**: Kubernetes pulls and runs the ETL containers. Scaling replicas ensures parallel processing.
- **Kafka Cluster**: External event source for the streaming pipeline.

Docker Registry

At the top of the pipeline is a **Docker Registry** (such as Docker Hub, AWS ECR, or Azure Container Registry), which stores the **containerized ETL images**. These images include the application logic and all required dependencies bundled together. This allows for version-controlled, repeatable, and portable deployment of ETL applications.

Key Role: Acts as the central repository for storing and retrieving ETL container images.

Pull ETL Image on Deployment

When a deployment is initiated (either manually, scheduled, or triggered via CI/CD), the Kubernetes cluster **pulls the ETL image** from the Docker registry. This is the first step in creating pods for the ETL workload.

Key Role: Ensures that the most recent and validated ETL application image is fetched from the registry before execution begins.

Kubernetes ETL Deployment

Once the image is pulled, Kubernetes handles the deployment using **Deployment manifests** or **Helm charts**, spinning up one or more pods to run the ETL workload. These ETL containers are scheduled and orchestrated by Kubernetes, allowing the system to:

- Automatically restart failed pods,
- Scale ETL workloads based on demand,
- Monitor and manage resources (CPU, memory),
- Provide environment isolation for different jobs.

Key Role: Ensures high availability, scalability, and lifecycle management of ETL jobs in a distributed, containerized environment.

Kafka Cluster

The containerized ETL application connects to a **Kafka Cluster**, which acts as the **real-time data backbone** of the system. It can:

- **Ingest streaming data** from upstream systems (IoT, apps, logs, and so on.)
- **Serve as a buffer** for incoming data before processing
- **Emit transformed data** to downstream systems such as Data Warehouses, Data Lakes, or other Kafka topics

Key Role: Acts as the data transport layer for both input and output of the ETL application, enabling real-time data pipeline capabilities.

Why Does This Architecture Matters?

This design offers several modern data engineering advantages:

- **Scalability**: Easily handles changing data volumes.
- **Resilience**: Kubernetes ensures automatic recovery and self-healing.
- **Reusability**: ETL code packaged in containers can be reused across environments.
- **Real-Time Readiness**: Kafka integration supports event-driven processing.
- **DevOps Friendly**: CI/CD pipelines can automate the image build and deployment process.

Real-World Use Case

Imagine a retail company collecting clickstream data from its e-commerce site:

- The data is streamed into Kafka in real-time.
- A Kubernetes-managed ETL service pulls this data, transforms it (for example, sessionizing, aggregating), and pushes the processed data back into Kafka or a Data Lake for analytics and reporting.

Containerized ETL on Kubernetes: Practical Implementation

After understanding the architecture, let us now look at how to **actually implement** this pattern using real-world artifacts.

Minimal Dockerfile for ETL Job

This Dockerfile packages your ETL logic (typically in Python) into a lightweight image ready for deployment on Kubernetes.

```
dockerfile

# Minimal Dockerfile for a Python-based ETL Application
FROM python:3.10-slim

# Set working directory inside container
WORKDIR /app

# Install Python dependencies
COPY requirements.txt .
RUN pip install --no-cache-dir -r requirements.txt

# Copy the ETL source code into the container
COPY . .

# Define default command to run the ETL job
CMD ["python", "main.py"]
```

Best Practices:

- Use **`slim`** base image to reduce the size.
- Always pin versions in **`requirements.txt`** to ensure reproducibility.
- Use **`--no-cache-dir`** to save image space.

Kubernetes Deployment YAML for ETL Job

This YAML deploys the ETL container as a managed workload in Kubernetes.

```
yaml


apiVersion: apps/v1
kind: Deployment
metadata:
  name: etl-job
  labels:
    app: etl
spec:
  replicas: 2
  selector:
    matchLabels:
      app: etl
  template:
    metadata:
      labels:
        app: etl
    spec:
      containers:
      - name: etl-container
        image: your-dockerhub-username/etl-job:latest
        imagePullPolicy: Always
        env:
        - name: KAFKA_BROKER
          value: "kafka.kafka-namespace.svc.cluster.local:9092"
        - name: KAFKA_TOPIC
          value: "raw-events"
        resources:
          requests:
            memory: "512Mi"
            cpu: "250m"
          limits:
            memory: "1Gi"
            cpu: "500m"
        restartPolicy: Always
```

Key Highlights:

- Set **`replicas`** for horizontal scaling.
- Inject Kafka config using environment variables.
- Define resource limits for cost and scheduling efficiency.
- Use the internal service DNS name to connect to Kafka in-cluster.

Kafka Connection Example in Python (main.py)

```
python


from kafka import KafkaConsumer

import json
import os
```

```
KAFKA_BROKER = os.getenv("KAFKA_BROKER")
KAFKA_TOPIC = os.getenv("KAFKA_TOPIC")

consumer = KafkaConsumer(
    KAFKA_TOPIC,
    bootstrap_servers=KAFKA_BROKER,
    auto_offset_reset='earliest',
    enable_auto_commit=True,
    group_id='etl-consumer-group',
    value_deserializer=lambda m: json.loads(m.decode('utf-8'))
)

for message in consumer:
    event = message.value
    # ETL transformation logic goes here
    print("Processed:", event)
```

Note: *Use **confluent_kafka** or **aiokafka** for better performance in production setups.*

CI/CD Integration for ETL on Kubernetes

To fully automate the workflow, CI/CD can:

- Build the Docker image
- Push it to the Docker Registry
- Deploy updated version to Kubernetes

Example: GitHub Actions Workflow

```
yaml


name: CI/CD Pipeline for ETL

on:
  push:
    branches: [main]

jobs:
  build-deploy:
    runs-on: ubuntu-latest

    steps:
    - name: Checkout Code
      uses: actions/checkout@v3

    - name: Set up Docker
      uses: docker/setup-buildx-action@v2

    - name: Login to DockerHub
      run: echo "${{ secrets.DOCKER_PASSWORD }}" | docker login -u "${{ se-
crets.DOCKER_USERNAME }}" --password-stdin

    - name: Build and Push Image
      run: |
        docker build -t your-dockerhub-username/etl-job:latest .
        docker push your-dockerhub-username/etl-job:latest

    - name: Deploy to Kubernetes
```

```
      uses: appleboy/ssh-action@master
      with:
        host: ${{ secrets.K8S_HOST }}
        username: ${{ secrets.K8S_USER }}
        key: ${{ secrets.SSH_PRIVATE_KEY }}
        script: |
          kubectl rollout restart deployment etl-job
```

Highlights:

- Automatically triggers on every push to `main`
- Builds and pushes Docker image
- Connects securely via SSH to trigger redeploy using `kubectl`

With this implementation:

- You build reproducible and lightweight ETL containers using Docker.
- Deploy and scale them on Kubernetes with resilience and ease.
- Use Kafka as your data streaming backbone.
- Automate everything using CI/CD pipelines for faster and safer releases.

In the next section, we will dive deep into Kubernetes **Pods and Multi-Container Patterns**. We will explore how containers truly operate within Kubernetes, covering pod lifecycle, initContainers, sidecars, and real-world communication patterns. Through hands-on YAML labs, we will learn to design both single and multi-container pods and understand how they collaborate to power real-time workloads.

Pods and Multi-Container Patterns

Pods are the foundational execution unit of Kubernetes. They encapsulate one or more containers, shared storage, network, and a specification on how to run the containers. This section explores pod lifecycles and multi-container use cases using **`initContainers`** and **`sidecars`** and dives deep into communication patterns for real-time workloads.

Understanding Pods in Depth

Pod Lifecycle: From Creation to Termination

In Kubernetes, a **Pod** is the smallest deployable unit and acts as the execution environment for one or more tightly coupled containers. Understanding the lifecycle of a Pod is critical when designing scalable, resilient, and observable data systems.

Lifecycle Phases

Kubernetes manages pods through a well-defined sequence of lifecycle phases, listed as follows:

- **Pending:** Pod is accepted but not all containers are created. In other words, the pod has been accepted by the Kubernetes control plane but one or more containers are yet to be scheduled or pulled. This phase often reflects image pull delays or unsatisfied resource requirements.
- **Running:** All containers are created, at least one is still running/ actively executing. This is the operational state where the pod is serving workloads, participating in traffic, or consuming/ producing data.

- **Succeeded:** All containers have terminated successfully. In other words, all containers in the pod have terminated successfully (exit code 0), and no restart policy is configured for reruns. This is typical in batch ETL workloads or data processing jobs.
- **Failed:** All containers have terminated successfully or failed. In other words, one or more containers have exited with a non-zero code, indicating a failure. Depending on restart policies, Kubernetes might attempt a recovery.
- **Unknown:** State cannot be determined due to node communication failure. In other words, the pod state cannot be reliably determined due to a lost connection between the node and the control plane - common in infrastructure issues or node crashes.

Container Lifecycle and Probes

Within a pod, **each container follows an independent lifecycle**, governed by:

- **Readiness Probes:** Determines if the container is ready to receive traffic.
- **Liveness Probes:** Detects if the container is still running properly.
- **Startup Probes (optional):** Designed for applications with long initialization times.

These probes work in tandem with **restart policies** (**`Always`**, **`OnFailure`**, **`Never`**) to help Kubernetes maintain application availability.

Industry Insight

Lifecycle **hooks** such as **`PostStart`** (triggered after container starts) and **`PreStop`** (triggered before termination) are essential in **data engineering pipelines** for actions, such as:

- Initializing runtime environments,
- Flushing in-memory buffers,
- Notifying downstream systems of shutdowns,
- Ensuring graceful shutdown of streaming consumers (for example, Kafka, Spark jobs).

`InitContainers` and `Sidecar` Patterns

`InitContainers` are special containers that run before the main container. They are useful when you need to:

- Wait for a service dependency to be available (such as a database).
- Pull sensitive credentials or schema validation before startup.
- Load data from a remote source.

Sidecars are helper containers that run alongside the main application in a pod. Common sidecar use cases include:

- Logging agents such as Fluentd or Vector.
- Monitoring agents such as Prometheus exporters.
- Data transformation or message queuing interfaces.

Example Use Case:

- A pod running a Python ETL app has a sidecar that syncs data to AWS S3 every 5 seconds.

Hands-On YAML Lab: Single versus Multi-Container Pod

Single-Container Pod YAML

```
apiVersion: v1
kind: Pod
metadata:
  name: single-container-pod
spec:
  containers:
  - name: app
    image: python:3.11
    command: ["python3", "-m", "http.server"]
```

Multi-Container Pod with Sidecar

```
apiVersion: v1
kind: Pod
metadata:
  name: multi-container-pod
spec:
  containers:
  - name: etl-processor
    image: myrepo/etl-engine:v1
    ports:
    - containerPort: 8080
  - name: sync-agent
    image: myrepo/s3-sync-agent:v1
    args: ["--interval=5"]
```

This pod includes two containers sharing the same network space and volume mount. The **`etl-processor`** runs the core data workload, while the **`sync-agent`** pushes processed files to object storage periodically.

Pod-to-Pod Communication Patterns in Real-Time Workloads

In a dynamic Kubernetes environment, **pods are ephemeral**—they can be rescheduled, recreated, or migrated at any time. Each pod is assigned a **unique IP address** from the Kubernetes cluster network, allowing **direct IP-level communication**. However, relying on raw pod IPs is considered an anti-pattern due to volatility. Instead, Kubernetes provides built-in mechanisms to ensure **stable, discoverable, and resilient communication** across pods. In Kubernetes, each pod gets its own IP address. Pod-to-pod communication happens via:

Key Communication Mechanisms:

- **DNS-Based Discovery (Cluster DNS)**: Direct DNS-based access using Kubernetes internal DNS, Kubernetes runs an internal DNS server (typically **CoreDNS**) that allows pods to discover each other using Fully Qualified Domain Names (FQDNs).

  Format:

  `(<service-name>.<namespace>.svc.cluster.local)`

  This eliminates hardcoded IPs and supports dynamic resolution even as pods restart or scale.

- **Kubernetes Services as Stable Frontends:** Kubernetes Services abstract a group of pods and expose them under a single virtual IP address. These are critical for achieving stable, load-balanced communication:
    - **ClusterIP (default):** Accessible only within the cluster; used for internal service-to-service communication.
    - **NodePort:** Exposes service on a static port on every node; enables limited external access.
    - **LoadBalancer:** Integrates with cloud provider load balancers for full external exposure.
- **Headless Services for Direct Pod Access:**

  Created by setting `clusterIP: None` in the Service definition.

  Rather than routing traffic through a virtual IP, a headless service returns DNS A records of individual pod IPs behind the service.

  Use Cases and Ideal Scenarios

  Headless Services are **ideal for peer-to-peer or leader-follower communication models**. They are used when applications (such as **Spark, Kafka, or Cassandra**) need to know individual Pod addresses for direct, deterministic networking.

  While services like **ClusterIP, NodePort, and LoadBalancer** function as stable frontends, the Headless Service provides the direct network details required for stateful, distributed applications.

Real-World Scenario: (Spark ETL Pipeline)

A Spark driver pod communicates with Spark executors dynamically using a headless service. This enables the driver to discover each executor IP in a high-throughput ETL job.

Let us say you are running a real-time Spark job inside a Kubernetes cluster:

- The Spark Driver needs to coordinate tasks and shuffle data with multiple Spark Executor pods.
- These executors are dynamically launched and have ephemeral IPs.
- A Headless Service exposes the executor pods, allowing the driver to resolve each executor's IP using DNS lookups.
- This pattern enables the Spark Driver to dynamically discover all executors—ensuring high-throughput, low-latency communication during complex ETL jobs.

Best Practices for Production-Grade Design

Always rely on Services, not raw pod IPs, for communication. Services provide abstraction and stability.

- **Always use Kubernetes Services** to abstract communication:
    - They provide automatic load balancing, service discovery, and resiliency.
    - Avoid direct pod IPs, as they are not guaranteed to persist.
- Use **Headless Services** when:
    - Each pod must be addressable (for example, for stateful applications such as databases, brokers, and distributed compute engines).
    - You need to integrate with Service Mesh or custom DNS-aware components.
- For **secure communication**, implement:
    - `NetworkPolicies` to restrict which pods/services can talk to each other.
    - `mTLS` via Service Meshes (such as Istio or Linkerd) to encrypt inter-pod traffic.

Bonus Design Insight

In modern **event-driven architectures**, a producer pod (such as, streaming ETL source) might publish to a Kafka topic, and consumer pods might scale dynamically to process the load. Kubernetes services and DNS-based communication enable **resilient scaling and zero-downtime upgrades**, crucial for real-time pipelines.

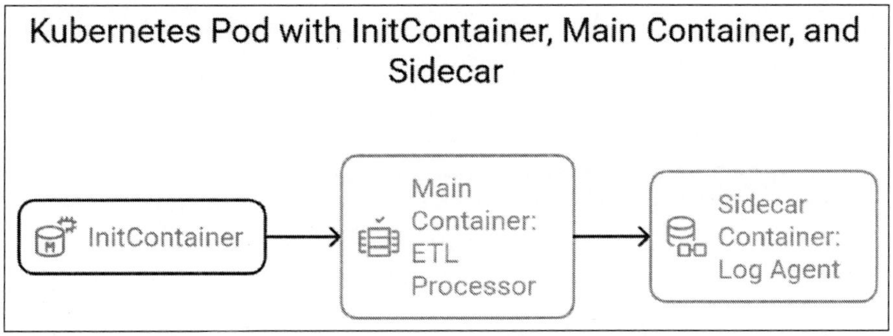

***Figure 4.2:** Multi-Container Pod with Sidecar and InitContainer*

Diagram Explanation:

- The **`InitContainer`** initializes the environment before the actual ETL container starts.
- The **`Main container`** does the actual transformation logic.
- The **`Sidecar`** streams the pod logs continuously to an external ELK stack.

This pattern enables a clean separation of responsibilities and supports microservices scalability. This architectural pattern showcases a **Kubernetes Pod** composed of three distinct containers, each with a clearly defined role:

`InitContainer` – "Prepares the Stage":

- **Purpose:** Executes *before* the main container starts. It is ideal for setup tasks that must be completed successfully prior to the workload's execution.
- **Real-World Role:** In this ETL pipeline, the **`InitContainer`** is responsible for pulling the latest **schema definitions or configurations** from a centralized Git or artifact repository.
- **Behavior:** Kubernetes ensures all **`InitContainers`** run **sequentially** and **to completion**, before any main or sidecar containers begin. This guarantees the environment is correctly initialized, reducing errors in downstream data processing.

`Main Container` – "ETL Workhorse":

- **Purpose:** Executes the primary business logic of the pod–in this case, data extraction and transformation.
- **Real-World Role:** The **`etl-processor`** container connects to various data sources (for example, Kafka, databases), extracts event data, applies transformation rules (filtering, aggregations, formatting), and prepares it for downstream consumption or loading.
- **Execution:** Starts only after the **`InitContainer`** completes successfully. It works independently of the Sidecar container but shares the same network and storage volumes if defined.

`Sidecar Container` – "The Observer":

- **Purpose:** Provides auxiliary functionality such as logging, monitoring, or syncing–without interfering with the main container logic.

- **Real-World Role:** The `log-agent` container continuously collects logs from the ETL processor and ships them to an external **ELK (Elasticsearch, Logstash, Kibana)** stack or similar observability system.
- **Benefit:** It allows the decoupling of observability logic from business logic. This promotes reuse across teams and reduces duplication.

Why This Pattern Matters in Real-World Data Engineering:

- **Separation of Concerns:** Each container does one job well—initialization, transformation, or observability. This improves maintainability and testability.
- **Better CI/CD Pipelines:** Updating the log-agent or schema pull logic does not affect the ETL logic. You can roll out changes independently.
- **Enhanced Reliability:** Using `InitContainers` ensures all prerequisites are met before the core logic runs, which is critical for schema-dependent jobs or runtime secret injection.
- **Microservices Alignment:** `Sidecar` and `initContainer` patterns are fundamental to service mesh and microservices architecture, enhancing scalability and fault isolation.

Case Study: Building Real-Time Data Pods for Fraud Analytics

Scenario: A FinTech startup processes Kafka events in real time to detect transaction fraud.

Pod Design:

- The `main container` runs a Scala-based stream processor.
- The `Sidecar` container manages real-time metrics streaming to Prometheus.
- The `InitContainer` ensures the secret token for API access is fetched before processing begins.

Outcome:

- Improved start-up reliability and traceability.
- Allowed team to decouple log and metrics handling from application logic.
- Enabled high-frequency deployments with minimal risk.

Deployments, ReplicaSets, and Scaling

Modern distributed applications must be scalable, resilient, and able to deploy updates with minimal or no downtime. Kubernetes enables this through `Deployments`, `ReplicaSets`, and **`auto-scaling capabilities`**, which work together to deliver production-grade application availability and speed.

For data platforms and real-time pipelines, this means deploying microservices that can handle high throughput, recover from failures, and scale elastically based on system load. This section explores the core building blocks of Kubernetes deployment strategies, explains how replica control maintains the desired state and introduces scaling policies to meet dynamic demand.

You will also learn industry-grade patterns such as high-throughput design and resilient microservice rollouts. These concepts are foundational for modern data platforms that demand 24/7 availability and real-time processing.

Decision Framework

The following table provides an explanation to the decision framework in Kubernetes:

Dimension	Explanation
Why	Why are Deployment strategies, ReplicaSets, and scaling mechanisms critical for high-availability systems? Because they ensure application uptime, zero-downtime rollouts, and dynamic adaptation to traffic without manual intervention.
What	What are Deployments and ReplicaSets? These are Kubernetes abstractions for managing stateless applications, scaling them, and controlling their rollout across clusters.
When	When do we use these features? During application updates, when traffic patterns change, or when building resilient microservices that must remain available at all times.
How	How do we implement them? Through Kubernetes, YAML manifests, autoscalers (HPA/VPA), deployment strategies such as Rolling, Blue-Green, and Canary, and robust pod health checks.

Table 4.1: *Decision Framework in Kubernetes*

Problem-Solving Framework:

- Understand Deployment Mechanics
- Explore Progressive Delivery Strategies
- Apply Autoscaling in Real Workloads
- Design High-Availability for Data Microservices

Understanding Deployments and ReplicaSets

Deployment

A **Deployment** in Kubernetes describes the desired state of an application. It manages the creation and replacement of Pods using underlying ReplicaSets.

In other words, Kubernetes Deployment automates the rollout and lifecycle of Pods. It abstracts the complexity of managing ReplicaSets and ensures declarative, versioned, and self-healing operations.

Key Functions:

- **Declarative Updates:** Modify a deployment YAML, and Kubernetes updates the Pods gradually.
- **Rollbacks:** Easily revert to previous revisions.
- **Scaling:** Adjust the number of replicas based on load or resource needs.

Real-World Application:

Imagine a **real-time fraud detection microservice** that needs to be updated without taking down the existing flow. A Rolling Update strategy would replace old Pods incrementally while continuing to serve traffic, ensuring uninterrupted analysis.

ReplicaSet

A ReplicaSet ensures that a specified number of identical Pods are always running. If a Pod crashes, Kubernetes will automatically schedule a new one to maintain the desired replica count.

ReplicaSet Benefits:

- **High Availability:** Ensures a minimum number of instances are always available.

- **Fault Tolerance:** Recovers from node or Pod failures automatically.
- **Horizontal Scalability:** Can be adjusted dynamically to match traffic load.

YAML Example: ReplicaSet

```
yaml
apiVersion: apps/v1
kind: Deployment
metadata:
  name: data-ingestion-deployment
spec:
  replicas: 3
  selector:
    matchLabels:
      app: ingestion
  template:
    metadata:
      labels:
        app: ingestion
    spec:
      containers:
      - name: ingestion-service
        image: myregistry/data-ingestor:1.0
        ports:
        - containerPort: 8080
```

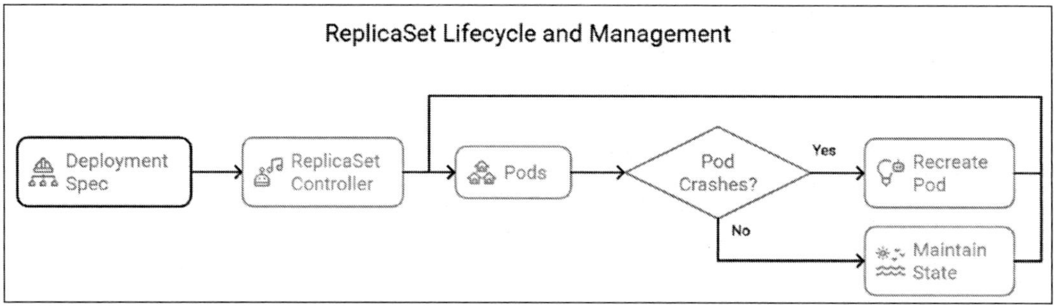

***Figure 4.3:** Deployment and ReplicaSet Lifecycle*

Figure 4.3 illustrates the **lifecycle and self-healing behavior of ReplicaSets in Kubernetes**, showcasing how Pods are managed from the moment a Deployment is created, all the way through crash recovery and state maintenance.

- A Deployment describes the desired state.
- ReplicaSet enforces that state.
- If a Pod crashes, the ReplicaSet recreates it instantly.

Deployment Spec

This is the **declarative configuration** written by the user (usually in a YAML or JSON format) that defines:

- The **desired state** of the application.
- Number of replicas (Pods) to run.
- Container specifications (image, ports, environment variables).
- Update strategy, selectors, and more.

Think of this as the **blueprint** that guides Kubernetes in maintaining application consistency.

ReplicaSet Controller

Once the Deployment is applied, it hands over control to the **ReplicaSet Controller**.

- This controller's job is to **ensure that the number of Pods** matches what is specified in the Deployment.
- If Pods are missing or extra, it **creates or deletes them** accordingly.
- It **keeps watching** the actual state of the system and constantly tries to reconcile it with the desired state.

Pods

The **ReplicaSet** spawns and manages **identical Pods** based on the template in the Deployment Spec.

- Each Pod is an instance of the application.
- Kubernetes uses these Pods to distribute workloads and scale the app.

Pod Crashes (Health Check)

This decision node checks whether **a Pod crashes or exits unexpectedly**.

- Kubernetes continuously **monitors Pod health** using readiness and liveness probes (if configured).
- If a Pod is found to be unhealthy or unresponsive, it is marked for recovery.

Recreate Pod (If Yes)

If a Pod crashes or becomes unresponsive:

- The **ReplicaSet Controller automatically recreates** a fresh Pod instance.
- This is part of Kubernetes' **self-healing mechanism**, ensuring service availability without manual intervention.

This behavior is one of the reasons Kubernetes is considered **highly resilient**.

Maintain State (If No Crash)

If the Pod is healthy:

- Kubernetes does **nothing extra**; it maintains the running state.
- The ReplicaSet continues to **watch and manage** the Pod as part of its normal operations.

This is the **stable state** where the system is running as expected.

Glance for Readers

ReplicaSets are the **backbone of fault tolerance and availability** in Kubernetes. This lifecycle ensures that:

- Applications are **always running the right number of instances**.
- Crashed Pods are **automatically recreated**.
- System integrity is **continuously monitored and restored**, making Kubernetes ideal for modern production-grade workloads.

Exploring Progressive Delivery Strategies

In traditional deployment models, new application versions were often released all at once, risking downtime, performance issues, or broken functionality. With microservices and container orchestration platforms such as **Kubernetes**, we now use **Progressive Delivery Strategies**—a modern approach that allows safer, controlled, and observable rollouts of new features or services.

Progressive delivery is especially **crucial in data engineering workloads** (ETL pipelines, stream processors, analytics APIs), where **data correctness, uptime, and performance** are non-negotiable.

Deployment Strategies for Data Workloads:

Strategy	*Description*
Rolling Update	Default strategy. Replaces pods incrementally with minimal downtime.
Blue-Green	Two environments (blue = old, green = new). Route traffic only after green is validated
Canary	Gradually shifts traffic to new pods. Allows testing with a small user base first.

Table 4.2: *Deployment Strategies for Data Workloads*

Real-World Use Case: A fintech company updates its **payment microservice** using **Canary deployment**. Initially, 5% of users got the new version. Metrics and logs are monitored, and only upon successful validation is traffic ramped up to 100%.

Rolling Update (Kubernetes Default): Gradually replaces old Pods with new ones. Overview: Kubernetes performs a **rolling update** by gradually terminating old pods and creating new ones, maintaining the **desired number of replicas** throughout the process.

When to Use:

- Minor application updates.
- Patches and bug fixes.
- Scenarios with low risk and minimal functional change.

Advantages:

- Built-in and simple to configure.
- Avoids full downtime during updates.

Risks:

- If not monitored, faulty pods may go unnoticed until full rollout.
- No traffic control during deployment; all users are impacted at the same time.

Rolling Update: Step-by-Step Pod Replacement

Step 1:

```
[v1 Pod]   [v1 Pod]      ← All Pods are old version
Step 2:
[v1 Pod]   [v2 Pod]      ← One new Pod deployed
Step 3:
[v2 Pod]   [v2 Pod]      ← All old Pods replaced
```

- Rolling Update is Kubernetes' default deployment strategy.
- It gradually replaces old Pods with new versions, ensuring minimal downtime.

- Kubernetes controls the update process using two key parameters:
    - **`maxUnavailable`:** Maximum number of unavailable Pods during the update.
    - **`maxSurge`:** Extra Pods allowed above the desired count during the update.

Ideal for: Patching services, minor releases, and environments needing high uptime.

Sample YAML Snippet:

```
yaml

strategy:
  type: RollingUpdate
  rollingUpdate:
    maxUnavailable: 1
    maxSurge: 1
```

Best Practice: Use **`readinessProbes`** to prevent routing traffic to pods that are not fully ready.

Blue-Green Deployment

Overview: Two identical environments run in parallel:

- **Blue:** Current stable version (live traffic)
- **Green:** New version (staging/testing)

After full validation in Green, traffic is **switched** from Blue to Green in one step.

Architecture Flow:

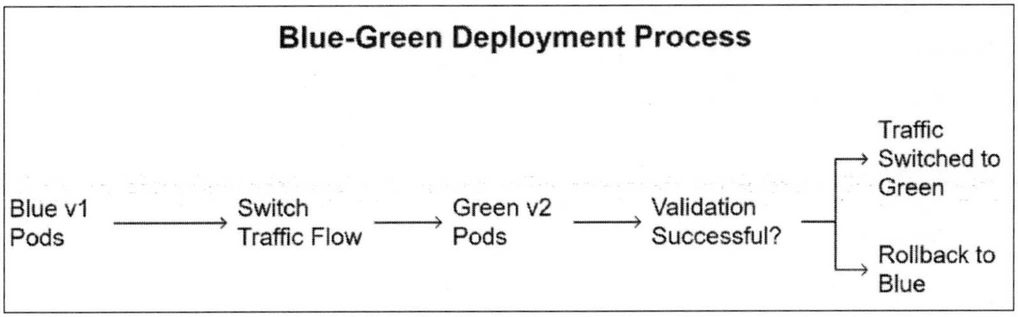

***Figure 4.4:** Architecture Flow - Blue-Green Deployment Process*

- **Blue v1 Pods:** These are the currently running production Pods receiving 100% of live traffic.
- **Switch Traffic:** After validation, traffic is routed to the Green Pods. Blue Pods remain for quick rollback if needed.
- **Green v2 Pods:** These are the new version Pods deployed in parallel and thoroughly tested in staging.

When to Use:

- Data pipelines where consistency, schema compatibility, or state management are critical.
- Workloads with complex downstream dependencies (example, Spark, Kafka consumers).

Advantages:

- Fast rollback to the Blue version.
- Clear traffic control and isolation.
- Enables full testing in a production-like environment.

Canary Deployment: Release a small percentage of traffic to new Pods.

Overview: Only a small percentage of users are exposed to the new version first. Based on **telemetry (logs, metrics, alerts)**, the traffic is gradually increased until full adoption.

Canary Deployment: Gradual Traffic Shift Strategy

```
Initial State:
[v1 Pod]  [v1 Pod] [v1 Pod]    ← 100% Traffic to v1

Canary Step 1:
[v1 Pod]  [v1 Pod] [v2 Pod]    ← 10% Traffic to v2 (Canary)

Canary Step 2:
[v1 Pod]  [v2 Pod] [v2 Pod]    ← 50% Traffic to v2

Final State (Success):
[v2 Pod]  [v2 Pod] [v2 Pod]    ← 100% Traffic to v2
```

Explanation: Canary Deployment is a progressive release strategy used to reduce risk by introducing a new version (v2) to a small subset of users before full rollout.

Key Concepts:

- **Incremental Traffic Shift**: Start with a low percentage (for example, 5–10%) of live traffic to the canary (new version).
- **Monitoring Phase**: Observe system metrics, errors, and logs for issues.
- **Stepwise Promotion**: If stable, increase traffic until full deployment.
- **Rollback Safety**: If issues are found, quickly revert without impacting all users.

When to Use:

- Real-time data streaming microservices.
- Services with unpredictable performance impact.
- AI/ML inference APIs where model behavior must be tested under real usage.

Advantages:

- Controlled rollout with built-in observability.
- Fast rollback with minimal exposure.

Industry Example:

A fintech company updating its fraud detection API uses a **Canary Deployment**:

- 5% of user traffic is routed to **`fraud-detector:v2`**.
- Logs are **monitored** via ELK and alerts are managed via Prometheus.
- Traffic is increased to 100% only after validation.

Popular Tools:

- **Flagger:** Progressive delivery operator for Kubernetes.
- **Istio:** Layer 7 traffic management.
- **Argo Rollouts:** Declarative progressive delivery for Kubernetes.

Strategy Comparison Table

Deployment Strategy	Rollback Ease	Infrastructure Cost	Use Case Fit
Rolling Update	Moderate	Low	General application updates
Blue-Green	Excellent	Medium/High	State-sensitive data pipelines
Canary	Excellent	Low to Medium	Risk-prone microservices and APIs

Table 4.3: *Deployment Strategy Comparison*

Best Practices for Progressive Delivery in Data Workloads

Area	Best Practice
Observability	Use Prometheus + Grafana dashboards and alerts for rollout monitoring
Metrics	Track latency, throughput, error rate, and schema validation
Rollbacks	Automate rollback triggers via health thresholds (for example, 5xx error spike)
Testing	Integrate synthetic and load tests in Canary or Green environments
Change Validation	Use A/B testing or shadow deployments for experimental features

Table 4.4: *Best Practices for Progressive Delivery in Data Workloads*

Applying Autoscaling in Real Workloads

Modern cloud-native applications are dynamic in nature – traffic varies, workloads spike unpredictably, and services must stay highly available. Kubernetes solves these real-world demands through **powerful autoscaling mechanisms** that not only scale application Pods but also the underlying compute infrastructure.

This section dives deep into **three core autoscaling techniques**:

- Horizontal Pod Autoscaler (HPA)
- Vertical Pod Autoscaler (VPA)
- Cluster Autoscaler
- Custom Metrics Autoscaler

Each of these plays a vital role in handling real-world production workloads efficiently.

Auto-scaling Techniques in Kubernetes

Kubernetes supports multiple layers of scaling mechanisms. These work either **independently** or **in combination**, depending on how your application behaves under different types of stress (CPU, memory, queue depth, and more).

Horizontal Pod Autoscaler (HPA)

The **Horizontal Pod Autoscaler** adjusts the number of running Pods in a Deployment, StatefulSet, or ReplicaSet based on **observed CPU utilization**, **memory usage**, or **custom metrics** (for example, number of requests per second, Kafka lag).

This is the most **commonly used** autoscaler in Kubernetes-based microservices because:

- It responds quickly to traffic spikes.
- It is easy to configure.
- It is suitable for stateless or loosely stateful services.

Example: Horizontal Pod Autoscaler (HPA) YAML

```
yaml

apiVersion: autoscaling/v2
kind: HorizontalPodAutoscaler
metadata:
  name: ingestion-hpa
spec:
  scaleTargetRef:
    apiVersion: apps/v1
    kind: Deployment
    name: data-ingestion-deployment
  minReplicas: 2
  maxReplicas: 10
  metrics:
  - type: Resource
    resource:
      name: cpu
      target:
        type: Utilization
        averageUtilization: 60
```

In this example:

- If the average CPU utilization across Pods exceeds **60%**, the HPA automatically **adds more Pods** (up to 10).
- If the utilization drops, it will **scale down** to a minimum of **2 Pods**.
- The `scaleTargetRef` links the HPA to the actual workload (data-ingestion-deployment).

Best Practices for HPA:

- **Always use readiness and liveness probes.** Without them, Kubernetes might route traffic to **unhealthy Pods** during scale-up.
- Set **realistic min and max replica limits** to prevent over-scaling or under-scaling.
- Combine with **Cluster Autoscaler** to ensure node capacity exists to accommodate additional Pods.
- Use **custom metrics** when CPU/memory is not enough (for example, API throughput, Kafka lag).

Vertical Pod Autoscaler (VPA)

While HPA adjusts the **number of Pods**, **Vertical Pod Autoscaler** modifies the **resource requests and limits** (CPU, memory) of each Pod.

This is particularly useful for:

- Applications with **varying resource usage over time**.
- Optimizing workloads for **cost and performance**.
- Services that cannot horizontally scale (such as, single-threaded apps).

How VPA Works:

1. Monitors the actual resource usage of running Pods.
2. Provides **recommendations** or directly **applies adjustments** to resource configurations.
3. Automatically restarts Pods to apply new settings.

VPA is generally **not recommended to run with HPA (CPU/memory)** together unless HPA is configured using **custom metrics**.

Cluster Autoscaler

Cluster Autoscaler operates on the **infrastructure level**, scaling the **underlying worker nodes** (EC2, VM, and so on) based on unschedulable Pods.

What it does:

- Detects when there are not enough resources (CPU/memory) to schedule new Pods.
- Works with cloud providers' compute groups:
  - AWS Auto Scaling Groups (ASG)
  - GCP Managed Instance Groups (MIG)
  - Azure Virtual Machine Scale Sets (VMSS)
- Automatically **adds new nodes** to the cluster.
- Scales down **idle nodes** when they are no longer needed.

It ensures that HPA and VPA can actually work by **providing compute capacity** on demand.

Custom Metrics Autoscaler

Sometimes, CPU and memory metrics are **not enough** to capture application demand.

Let us take an example:

- Your application reads from a **Kafka topic**.
- CPU is low, but **Kafka lag is increasing**, meaning it is not able to keep up.

In such cases, you can use **Custom Metrics Autoscaler** (an extension of HPA) that:

- Pulls data from **Prometheus** or **custom APIs**.
- Scales Pods based on **business/application-specific metrics**.

Examples:

- Kafka consumer lag
- Queue depth
- HTTP request rate
- Database connection pool usage

Real-World Use Case: Data Ingestion Pipeline

Consider a real-time data ingestion pipeline using Apache Kafka.

Scenario:

- The number of incoming Kafka messages varies during the day.
- During business hours, Kafka lag spikes.
- After hours, traffic dies down.

Solution:

- Deploy HPA based on **Kafka lag (custom metric)**.
- Combine with Cluster Autoscaler to provision nodes on demand.
- Add readiness probes to avoid routing traffic to unready Pods.

This setup ensures that:

- No manual intervention is needed during traffic spikes.
- Cost optimization through downscaling.
- High reliability and throughput.

Design High-Availability for Data Microservices

Modern data-intensive applications demand low-latency, scalable, and highly available architectures. When data workloads such as ETL pipelines, event processors, streaming consumers, or ML inference services are deployed as microservices, high availability and throughput become critical design goals. Kubernetes provides a robust platform for building and operating such data microservices reliably at scale.

High-Throughput and High-Availability Patterns for Data Microservices:

Modern data-intensive applications demand **low-latency, scalable, and highly available architectures**. Kubernetes offers the ideal foundation for building such systems, especially when dealing with real-time or high-throughput data microservices (such as ETL engines, event processors, ML inference services, or streaming data consumers).

This section focuses on key **design principles and architectural patterns** for building **stateless, scalable, and fault-tolerant** data microservices on Kubernetes.It explains how to handle state, distribute workloads efficiently, and ensure resilience under high data volumes and failure conditions.

Design Considerations for High-Throughput and HA

Let us break down the core design considerations:

- **Stateless Processing with External Stores**

  Kubernetes works best with **stateless containers**, especially for horizontal scaling. Instead of persisting state within pods (which are ephemeral), offload state to **external and resilient systems**, such as:

  - **S3/Cloud Blob Storage:** For storing batch job outputs, model files, and checkpoints.
  - **Kafka:** For ingesting and consuming streaming data in real-time.
  - **Redis:** For caching, ephemeral state, or pub/sub messaging.
  - **PostgreSQL/NoSQL DBs:** For durable metadata or transactional data.

Why: Stateless services are easier to scale, failover, and update. The externalizing state ensures resiliency and performance.

- **Affinity and Anti-Affinity Rules**

  Use **pod affinity and anti-affinity** rules to intelligently spread workloads:

  - **Anti-affinity** ensures pods from the same workload are not co-located on the same node or availability zone. This prevents **single points of failure**.
  - **Affinity** allows co-locating dependent services (for example, colocating Kafka consumers with Kafka brokers in the same zone for low latency).

Why: It improves availability and fault isolation by minimizing the blast radius of a node or AZ failures.

- **Probes for Fault Detection and Isolation**

  Implement **liveness** and **readiness probes** in your data microservices:

  - **Readiness Probes**: Ensure that traffic-only routes to healthy pods that are fully initialized and ready to serve.
  - **Liveness Probes**: Automatically restart pods that enter a broken or non-responsive state.

Why: Probes protect the system from cascading failures by isolating unhealthy pods proactively.

Architectural Pattern: High-Throughput Data Microservices

Figure 4.5 illustrates a **logical flow of traffic** and system components in a high-throughput, stateless data microservice architecture:

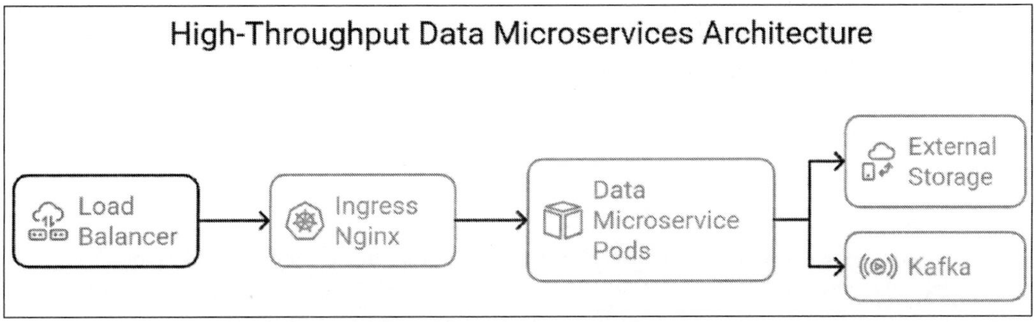

Figure 4.5: *High-Throughput Data Microservices Architecture*

Let us break down each component and its role:

- **Load Balancer**
  - This is typically a **cloud-native or on-prem load balancer** (for example, AWS ALB, Azure Application Gateway).
  - It routes external HTTP(S) traffic to your Kubernetes cluster securely.
  - In cloud-native setups, this is usually **provisioned automatically** when you expose an Ingress controller.
- **Ingress Nginx**
  - Acts as the **entry point** into the Kubernetes cluster.
  - Performs:
    - **Path-based routing** (for example, `/etl/v1`, `/ingest`)
    - **Rate limiting**
    - **TLS termination**
    - **Authentication and authorization**
  - Configurable with annotations or CRDs to handle **caching**, **timeouts**, and more.

Example: You expose `data-api.mycompany.com/ingest` via Ingress that routes to internal pods.

- **ReplicaSet with 3 Data Microservice Pods**
  - A **ReplicaSet** ensures that there are always N number of pod replicas running.

- In our pattern, 3 pods are used to:
  - Handle concurrent incoming data requests
  - Improve fault tolerance (if 1 pod fails, 2 remain active)
- These microservice pods perform stateless processing–data transformations, enrichment, validation, and so on.

These pods may consume data from Kafka, apply logic, and write to S3 or a data warehouse.

- **Autoscaler (not shown in the figure but important)**
  - Attach a **Horizontal Pod Autoscaler (HPA)** to this deployment.
  - Scales pods up/down based on:
    - CPU usage
    - Memory
    - Custom metrics (for example, Kafka lag, request count)

Helps maintain throughput under peak loads without over-provisioning.

- **External Storage and Kafka**
  - **External Storage:** Could be cloud buckets, object stores, or distributed filesystems (such as Ceph, HDFS).
  - **Kafka:** Acts as the event backbone for streaming microservices.
    - Producer apps send messages.
    - Your microservices consume them asynchronously.
  - These external systems ensure the **persistence and durability** of the data pipeline.

Real-World Use Case

Let us consider a **real-world data ingestion and transformation pipeline**:

- A retail company processes clickstream data in real-time.
- Raw events are ingested via **Kafka**.
- Microservice pods process events, enrich them with metadata, and store them in **Amazon S3**.
- The system runs **24x7**, auto-scales during Black Friday, and routes traffic via Ingress.
- Failures are handled using **probes**, and no data is lost because the state is handled externally.

StatefulSets, DaemonSets, and Static Pods

As Kubernetes has matured, it has evolved from stateless microservice orchestration to support stateful applications, cluster-wide daemons, and critical control-plane workloads. This section explores three powerful controllers that make such workloads manageable and resilient: **StatefulSets**, **DaemonSets**, and **Static Pods**.

Each has a unique role:

- **StatefulSets** manages stable, unique network identities and storage for each Pod, perfect for databases and distributed systems.
- **DaemonSets** ensures that a copy of a Pod runs on every (or selected) node, useful for logging, monitoring, and security agents.
- **Static Pods** are directly managed by the kubelet and used for essential control-plane services in self-hosted Kubernetes environments.

Why Do These Patterns Matter in Real-World Kubernetes Deployments?

Traditional Deployments (such as Deployments or ReplicaSets) work well for stateless apps. However, they fall short for workloads requiring **data persistence**, **node-specific scheduling**, or **early-boot initialization**.

Use Case Breakdown:

Pattern	When to Use
StatefulSets	Databases, messaging queues, distributed stateful apps
DaemonSets	Log shippers (Fluentd), monitoring agents (Prometheus Node Exporter), CNI plugins
Static Pods	kube-apiserver, etcd, core DNS in bare-metal HA setups

Table 4.5: *When to Use StatefulSets, DaemonSets, and Static Pods*

StatefulSets: Managing Stateful Applications

What is a StatefulSet?

A controller that manages the deployment and scaling of Pods with persistent identity and stable storage.

Why Does This Exist?

Traditional Deployments randomly assign Pod names and do not guarantee persistent volume identity. StatefulSets solve that by creating predictable names and volumes (such as, kafka-0, kafka-1) for each Pod.

When Should You Use This:

- When each Pod must have a **stable hostname**.
- When each instance requires a **persistent disk**.
- For apps such as Cassandra, MongoDB, Kafka, and Zookeeper.

How Does It Work?

StatefulSets ensure:

- Stable DNS and hostname (for example, **`zookeeper-0.zk-hs.default.svc.cluster.local`**)
- Stable PVC per Pod
- Ordered deployment, scaling, and deletion

Sample YAML: StatefulSet for Kafka Broker

```
apiVersion: apps/v1
kind: StatefulSet
metadata:
  name: kafka
spec:
  serviceName: "kafka"
  replicas: 3
  selector:
    matchLabels:
      app: kafka
  template:
    metadata:
      labels:
        app: kafka
```

```
      spec:
        containers:
        - name: kafka
          image: wurstmeister/kafka
          ports:
          - containerPort: 9092
          volumeMounts:
          - name: kafka-data
            mountPath: /kafka/data
  volumeClaimTemplates:
  - metadata:
      name: kafka-data
    spec:
      accessModes: ["ReadWriteOnce"]
      storageClassName: "standard"
      resources:
        requests:
          storage: 10Gi
```

DaemonSets: Ensuring Per-Node Workload Deployment

What is a DaemonSet?

It ensures that **exactly one copy** of a Pod runs on every node (or a selected group of nodes).

Why Does This Exist?

Some workloads must exist on every node to collect system-level data, logs, or monitor resources. These cannot be scheduled like regular apps.

When Should You Use This:

- Log collection (for example, Fluentd, Logstash).
- Metrics collection (for example, Node Exporter, Telegraf).
- Networking components (for example, Calico, Cilium).

How Does It Work?

As nodes join the cluster, the DaemonSet ensures that Pods are created there automatically.

Sample YAML: Node Exporter DaemonSet

```
apiVersion: apps/v1
kind: DaemonSet
metadata:
  name: node-exporter
spec:
  selector:
    matchLabels:
      app: node-exporter
  template:
    metadata:
      labels:
        app: node-exporter
    spec:
      containers:
```

```
      - name: node-exporter
        image: prom/node-exporter
        ports:
        - containerPort: 9100
```

Static Pods: Core Components in Self-Hosted Clusters

What is a Static Pod?

It is a Pod defined directly in a file and managed by the kubelet. It is not associated with a Kubernetes controller such as Deployments or DaemonSets.

Why Does This Exist?

In bare-metal or bootstrapping scenarios, kubelet must run critical components **before** the API server is even operational.

When Should You Use This:

- To run etcd or API server in custom cluster builds.
- During kubeadm or custom installations.

How Does It Work:

- kubelet watches a directory (for example, **`/etc/kubernetes/manifests`**).
- Any Pod YAML added there is automatically started.

Sample YAML: Static Pod for etcd

```
apiVersion: v1
kind: Pod
metadata:
  name: etcd
  namespace: kube-system
spec:
  containers:
  - name: etcd
    image: k8s.gcr.io/etcd:3.5.0
    command:
    - etcd
    - --name=etcd1
    - --data-dir=/var/lib/etcd
    - --initial-cluster-state=new
```

Real-World Example: Kafka with StatefulSet + DaemonSet

Scenario: A real-time data platform uses Kafka for stream ingestion. Each Kafka broker must maintain logs on a per-node basis for audit compliance.

Architecture Solution:

- Kafka runs as a **StatefulSet** with persistent volumes.
- A **DaemonSet** runs Fluent Bit on each node to stream logs to Elasticsearch.
- Kafka metrics are exposed on port 9100 and collected by Prometheus running as a DaemonSet.

Diagram Explanation:

This setup ensures both data persistence and observability across the stateful Kafka cluster.

```
                                    +--------------------------------+
                                    | Fluent Bit (DaemonSet)         |
                                    | Log shipping to ELK stack      |
                                    +--------------------------------+
                                                        |
                                                        v
+-------------+    +-------------+    +-------------+
| Kafka-0     |<--->| Kafka-1     |<--->| Kafka-2     |
| PVC: 10Gi   |    | PVC: 10Gi   |    | PVC: 10Gi   |
+-------------+    +-------------+    +-------------+
```

Figure 4.6: *Kafka with StatefulSet and DaemonSet*

Overview of the Architecture

This diagram illustrates a **distributed log ingestion pipeline** commonly used in **cloud-native environments** to handle logs at scale. It integrates:

- **Fluent Bit** as a lightweight log forwarder.
- A highly available **Kafka cluster** for log buffering and streaming.
- An implied backend like the **ELK stack** (Elasticsearch, Logstash, Kibana) for centralized analysis and visualization (though not shown in the diagram).

Let us break it down layer by layer.

Fluent Bit DaemonSet – Log Shipping Layer

```
+--------------------------------+
| Fluent Bit (DaemonSet)         |
| Log shipping to ELK stack      |
+--------------------------------+
```

Figure 4.7: *Kafka with StatefulSet and DaemonSet*

- **Fluent Bit** is deployed as a **DaemonSet** in Kubernetes. A DaemonSet ensures that **one Fluent Bit Pod runs on every node** in the cluster.
- Fluent Bit **reads logs directly from each node's filesystem**, commonly under **`/var/log/containers/`**, and processes logs from all Pods running on that node.
- It **parses, filters, and forwards logs** to external systems such as **Kafka** or directly to the **ELK Stack**.
- It is highly efficient, uses low memory, and is ideal for edge log processing.

Key Functions:

- Collects logs from multiple container runtimes (Docker, containerd, CRI-O).
- Supports parsing of structured logs (JSON).
- Ships logs to multiple destinations: Kafka, Elasticsearch, S3, and so on.
- Ensures that logs are offloaded from nodes to avoid disk bloat.

Best Practice:

Use Fluent Bit as a **lightweight agent** for log shipping in large-scale Kubernetes clusters to minimize performance overhead.

Apache Kafka Cluster – Log Buffering and Streaming Layer

```
+-------------+      +-------------+      +-------------+
| Kafka-0     |<--->| Kafka-1     |<--->| Kafka-2     |
| PVC: 10Gi   |      | PVC: 10Gi   |      | PVC: 10Gi   |
+-------------+      +-------------+      +-------------+
```

Figure 4.8: *Kafka with StatefulSet and DaemonSet*

- The **Kafka Cluster** consists of **three brokers** (`Kafka-0`, `Kafka-1`, `Kafka-2`) to ensure **high availability**, **partition tolerance**, and **data replication**.
- Each broker is connected in a **peer-to-peer manner** and can serve as a **leader** or **follower** for different partitions of topics.
- The **`PersistentVolumeClaims` (PVCs)** of 10Gi per broker ensure the **durability** of logs even during restarts or failures. This means Kafka can **retain logs on disk**, replay them, or redistribute them as needed.

Why Kafka in the Middle:

- Kafka serves as a **decoupling layer** between Fluent Bit (producer) and ELK (consumer).
- This allows buffering during traffic spikes and adds **fault tolerance** and **backpressure handling**.
- Enables replaying logs for downstream consumers (such as Logstash or Flink).

How It All Works Together:

1. **Fluent Bit** on every Kubernetes node collects and forwards logs.
2. Logs are streamed into the **Kafka cluster**, and partitioned for parallel processing.
3. Kafka stores logs durably, ready for consumption by tools such as **Logstash**, **Elasticsearch**, or **Apache Flink** for indexing, visualization, and anomaly detection.

Production Use Case Example

In a microservices-based e-commerce platform running on Kubernetes, each microservice generates logs that must be centrally monitored. Fluent Bit collects these logs, Kafka buffers them, and Elasticsearch indexes them for real-time monitoring in Kibana.

Scalability and Reliability Features

Component	**Scalability Feature**	**Reliability Feature**
Fluent Bit	DaemonSet runs on every node	Low resource usage, supports retries
Kafka Cluster	Topic partitioning, broker scaling	Data replication, persistent storage
Storage (PVC)	Scales per node with StatefulSet	Durable storage even across Pod restarts

Table 4.6: *Production Use Case Examples and Features - Scalability and Reliability*

Next, we will explore **microservice architecture patterns** and how Kubernetes enables scalable design using Deployments, Services, and Service Meshes.

Microservices Design Patterns in Kubernetes

As cloud-native applications grow in complexity, traditional monolithic designs become difficult to scale, test, and maintain. Kubernetes, with its modular container orchestration model, has revolutionized how microservices are deployed and managed.

This section focuses on designing efficient, scalable microservice patterns in Kubernetes. We will explore modern patterns such as Service Mesh, API Gateway, and inter-service communication strategies using gRPC, REST, and event-driven models. In addition, we will study common anti-patterns to avoid in production.

Why Microservices Patterns Matter in Kubernetes?

Why: Microservices introduce flexibility but also complexity. Without a proper communication and governance model, services can become tightly coupled, leading to inconsistent APIs, performance bottlenecks, and operational nightmares.

What: Microservice patterns are design blueprints that help define interaction models, fault tolerance strategies, observability, and interconnectivity between distributed services.

When: These patterns become essential as your application scales beyond a handful of services or when adopting DevOps, CI/CD, or multi-team collaboration.

How: Kubernetes provides core primitives (Services, Ingress, ConfigMaps, Secrets) and integrations (Istio, Linkerd, Envoy) to implement these patterns effectively.

Cloud-Native Microservice Patterns

Service Mesh Pattern

Overview: A service mesh manages service-to-service communication transparently via a sidecar proxy (for example, Envoy) deployed alongside application containers.

Key Capabilities:

- Load balancing
- Mutual TLS (mTLS)
- Retry policies
- Observability and tracing
- Circuit breaking

Popular Tools: Istio, Linkerd, Kuma

Flow Diagram: Service Mesh Architecture:

```
 +-------------+            +--------------+
 |  Service A  |<------------ |  Service B   |
 |(App + Envoy)|            | (App + Envoy |
 +-------------+            +--------------+
        |                          |
+---------------+          +---------------+
|     Istiod    | <-------> |    Metrics    |
| Control Plane |          |  and Tracing  |
+---------------+          +---------------+
```

Figure 4.9: *Service Mesh Architecture*

Diagram Explanation:

- Each microservice runs with a sidecar proxy (Envoy).
- All traffic between services is intercepted and routed by these proxies.
- Istiod configures policies, collects telemetry, and enforces security.

Best Practice: Offload non-business logic (auth, retries, TLS) to the mesh to keep microservices lightweight.

API Gateway Pattern

Overview: An API Gateway acts as the single entry point for external clients. It routes, authenticates, and transforms requests before forwarding them to services.

Features:

- Path-based routing
- Rate limiting
- Authentication (JWT/OAuth)
- Traffic splitting for canary releases

Popular Tools: NGINX Ingress, Kong, Ambassador, Traefik

YAML Lab: Sample NGINX Ingress Gateway

```yaml
apiVersion: networking.k8s.io/v1
kind: Ingress
metadata:
  name: api-gateway
spec:
  rules:
  - host: myapp.example.com
    http:
      paths:
      - path: /user
        pathType: Prefix
        backend:
          service:
            name: user-service
            port:
              number: 80
      - path: /order
        pathType: Prefix
        backend:
          service:
            name: order-service
            port:
              number: 80
```

Best Practice: Place authentication and traffic policies at the gateway level to decouple them from individual microservices.

Inter-Service Communication Models

REST

Pros:

- Language agnostic
- Easy to test with tools such as Postman or curl

Cons:

- Higher latency due to HTTP overhead
- Less efficient for internal service calls

gRPC

Pros:

- High-performance protocol based on HTTP/2
- Strong typing using Protocol Buffers (Protobuf)
- Ideal for service-to-service communication

Cons:

- Steeper learning curve
- Difficult to debug with browser tools

YAML Lab: gRPC Deployment with Health Probes

```
apiVersion: v1
kind: Service
metadata:
  name: grpc-service
spec:
  ports:
  - name: grpc
    port: 50051
    protocol: TCP
    targetPort: 50051
  selector:
    app: grpc-server
```

Event-Driven (Kafka/NATS)

Use Case: Asynchronous workloads, decoupling of producers and consumers

Pros:

- Loose coupling
- Easy to scale consumers independently

Cons:

- Complex message delivery semantics
- Debugging event flows can be tricky

Event-Driven Flow with Kafka:

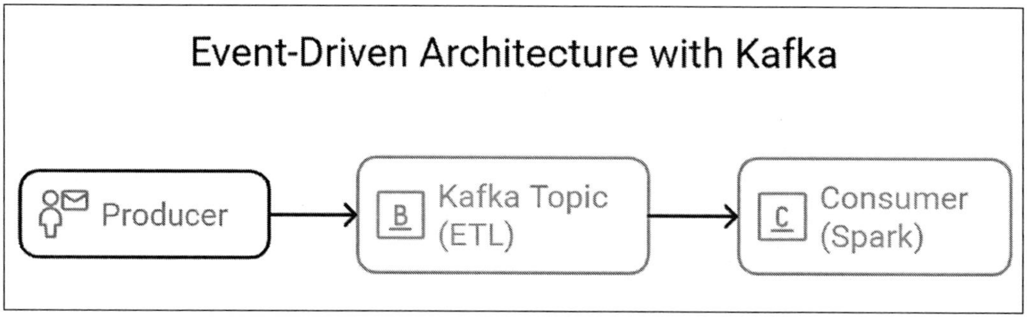

Figure 4.10: *Kafka Topic as a Central Pipeline for ETL with Apache Spark*

This simple yet powerful diagram showcases a **streaming ETL pipeline** using **Apache Kafka and Apache Spark**–two cornerstone technologies in modern data engineering.

It illustrates the **producer-Kafka-consumer** pattern where real-time data flows continuously from a data source (producer) through Kafka (topic) and is processed by a consumer (Apache Spark). Let us break it down.

Producer – Real-Time Data Source:

- The **Producer** is any service or application that generates or emits data, and sends it to a **Kafka topic**.
- Producers can be:
  - o Microservices emitting application logs.
  - o IoT sensors generating telemetry data.
  - o APIs sending transactional events (orders, payments, and so on).
  - o Databases using **CDC (Change Data Capture)** tools such as Debezium.

Key Technical Aspects:

- Kafka producers write to specific **topics**, and optionally, partitions, ensuring high throughput.
- Producers are usually stateless and retry-capable.
- Can use Kafka client libraries (Java, Python, Golang, and more) or log shippers such as **Fluent Bit** or **Logstash**.

Real-World Example:

A retail application's **order service** sends every purchase event (order ID, user ID, item ID, amount) into a Kafka topic for real-time downstream analytics.

Kafka Topic (ETL) – Real-Time Event Buffer:

- A **Kafka Topic** is a **distributed, append-only log** where events are written by producers and consumed by downstream systems.
- This acts as a **durable buffer**, making it the centerpiece of **streaming ETL pipelines**.
- The (`ETL`) label here implies that the topic is part of a real-time ETL (Extract-Transform-Load) workflow.

Why Kafka in ETL:

- **Extract:** Kafka gathers raw data from multiple producers.
- **Transform:** Data is cleaned, enriched, or joined using tools such as Spark/Flink.
- **Load:** Transformed data is pushed to downstream sinks such as Data Lakes, Data Warehouses, or NoSQL stores.

Design Considerations:

- Topics can be **partitioned** to enable parallelism and scalability.
- Topics retain data based on time or size policies (for example, 7 days, 10GB).
- Supports **exactly-once semantics** when integrated with tools such as Kafka Streams or Spark Structured Streaming.

Consumer (Apache Spark) – Stream Processing Layer

- The **Consumer** is responsible for **reading events** from Kafka and performing **stream processing**.
- In this case, **Apache Spark** is used–one of the most powerful distributed data processing engines.

What Spark Does:

- Reads from Kafka topics in **micro-batches or continuous mode** using Spark Structured Streaming.
- Performs **ETL transformations**: filtering, mapping, joining, and aggregating.
- Pushes output to:
  - Data Lakes (for example, S3, HDFS)
  - Databases (for example, Cassandra, PostgreSQL)
  - Dashboards (via Elasticsearch or OLAP systems)

Key Features:

- Spark ensures **fault tolerance** via checkpointing.
- Can **scale horizontally** across a Kubernetes cluster or YARN/Mesos.
- Supports **stateful stream processing** and **windowed aggregations**.

Real-World Example:

Apache Spark consumes real-time order data from Kafka, joins it with user metadata from a database, calculates the user's lifetime value in real-time, and writes the result into a Delta Lake for further BI analysis.

Full Data Flow (End-to-End):

1. **Producer** extracts or generates data (for example, user signups and orders).
2. Sends events to the **Kafka Topic**, which buffers and retains them.
3. **Spark Streaming** reads events, transforms them, and loads them into storage or analytics platforms.

Advantages of This Architecture:

Benefit	Description
Decoupling	Producers and consumers evolve independently.
Scalability	Kafka handles millions of messages per second.
Fault Tolerance	Kafka and Spark both provide durability and recovery.
Real-time Insight	Enables real-time decisions and analytics.

Table 4.7: *Advantages of Event-Driven Flow with Kafka*

Anti-Patterns to Avoid:

- **Shared Databases across Services**
  - Leads to tight coupling
  - Causes data ownership issues
- **Direct Service Calls without Gateway or Mesh**
  - Increases code complexity
  - No centralized control or observability
- **Synchronous Chaining of Too Many Services**
  - Introduces latency and cascading failures

- **Ignoring Circuit Breakers and Retry Logic**
  - o Services may crash or get stuck waiting
- **Over-Reliance on REST for Internal Calls**
  - o Can slow down inter-service communication

Summary

Kubernetes enables scalable microservices architecture through modular and flexible patterns. A well-architected system should:

- Use API Gateways for ingress control.
- Implement Service Mesh for internal service communication.
- Choose the right communication protocol per use case.
- Avoid tight coupling and embrace observability.
- Rely on YAML configuration to enforce standards across environments.

With thoughtful application of these patterns, teams can build cloud-native microservices that are resilient, maintainable, and ready for production.

Next, we will explore how to containerize complex ETL pipelines and manage stateful data workloads on Kubernetes, with hands-on YAML examples, data volume management, and real-time architecture use cases.

Containerizing ETL Pipelines and Stateful Workloads

Modern Extract, Transform, Load (ETL) pipelines and stateful workloads are evolving beyond traditional server-bound data processing. With the adoption of containerization and Kubernetes, organizations can now run scalable, fault-tolerant, and portable ETL workflows. This section covers how to containerize ETL workloads, persist state effectively using Kubernetes-native tools, and orchestrate batch and real-time pipelines using Kubernetes.

Why Traditional ETL Workflows Struggle in Cloud-Native Environments?

Why:

- Traditional ETL jobs often run as scheduled scripts or monoliths on VMs or physical servers, tightly coupled to infrastructure.
- Scaling, failure recovery, or resource optimization becomes complex without automation.
- Difficult to integrate with CI/CD pipelines or respond to real-time data ingestion requirements.

Containerized ETL

What: Containerized ETL encapsulates data workflows inside portable, reproducible Docker containers. These containers are orchestrated using Kubernetes jobs, CronJobs, or streaming platforms (such as Apache Kafka or Flink) and managed with cloud-native best practices.

Core Design Elements:

- **Dockerized ETL Code:** Written in Python, Java, or Spark, packaged as Docker images.
- **Kubernetes Jobs:** One-time batch workloads.
- **Kubernetes CronJobs:** Scheduled pipelines.
- **Volumes and Secrets:** Manage persistent state, credentials, and configuration.

When to Containerize ETL Pipelines?

When:

- When you need **high availability** and **horizontal scalability** of batch pipelines.
- When ETL jobs need to be integrated into **CI/CD workflows** or triggered via events.
- For **hybrid cloud** or **multi-cloud** environments where portability is essential.
- In real-time or near-real-time data ingestion and transformation use cases.

How to Containerize ETL Pipelines in Kubernetes?

How:

Step 1: Dockerize the ETL Code (Python Example)

```
dockerfile

# Dockerfile for ETL
FROM python:3.10-slim
WORKDIR /app
COPY requirements.txt .
RUN pip install -r requirements.txt
COPY etl_job.py .
CMD ["python", "etl_job.py"]
```

Step 2: Create a Kubernetes CronJob YAML

```
yaml

apiVersion: batch/v1
kind: CronJob
metadata:
  name: etl-daily-cronjob
spec:
  schedule: "0 2 * * *"  # Daily at 2AM
  jobTemplate:
    spec:
      template:
        spec:
          containers:
          - name: etl-job
            image: your-registry/etl:latest
            volumeMounts:
              - name: etl-volume
                mountPath: /data
          restartPolicy: OnFailure
          volumes:
            - name: etl-volume
              persistentVolumeClaim:
                claimName: etl-pvc
```

Managing State in Kubernetes

Managing state requires careful volume and configuration separation.

Volumes for Storage:

- Use **PersistentVolumeClaims (PVCs)** for intermediate files, large datasets, or temporary states.

- **StatefulSets** are ideal for stateful engines such as Kafka, Cassandra, or Zookeeper.

Secrets and ConfigMaps:

- Store DB credentials, S3 keys, or pipeline configs securely.
- Secrets are base64 encoded; always mount them securely in volumes or environment variables.

Use Cases

Component	Purpose
PVC	Store intermediary CSV, Avro, and Parquet files
Secrets	Credentials to DB, S3, Kafka, and so on.
ConfigMap	Pipeline config such as schema, table names

Table 4.8: *Managing State in Kubernetes - Component Use Cases*

Example: Real-Time Streaming ETL with Kafka and Spark on Kubernetes

Scenario: You want to process clickstream data in real-time and aggregate events for dashboards.

Architecture Flow:

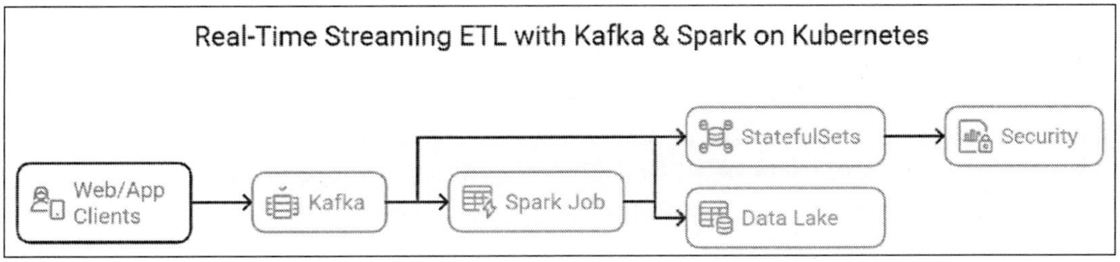

Figure 4.11: *Real-Time Streaming ETL with Kafka and Spark on Kubernetes*

The following explanation breaks down the logic of *Figure* 4.9:

- **Kafka** acts as a buffer between data producers and Spark.
- **Spark** reads streaming data via structured streaming.
- Results are dumped into a **data lake** (S3, GCS, HDFS).
- Kafka and Spark use **StatefulSets** for persistent state.
- Security is handled via **TLS** and **RBAC** in Kubernetes.

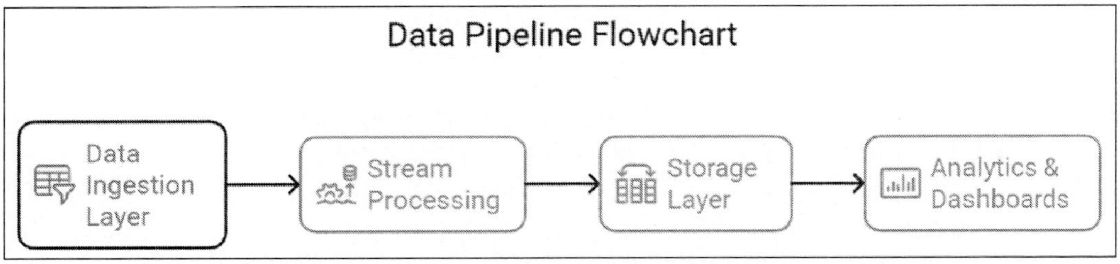

Figure 4.12: *Flow Diagram of Batch + Real-Time Data Pipelines on Kubernetes*

Diagram Explanation:

- **Data Ingestion Layer:** Ingests real-time or batch data via Kafka and REST APIs.
- **Processing Layer:** Spark/Flink/Beam processes both batch and stream jobs using Kubernetes Jobs or StatefulSets.
- **Storage Layer:** Uses cloud buckets (S3, GCS, HDFS or PVCs) for durability.
- **Visualization Layer:** Connects to processed output for business reporting (Superset, Grafana).

Best Practices for ETL on Kubernetes

Best Practice	Description
Stateless by Default	Containerize ETL logic to be stateless; use PVCs for intermediate data
Batch + Stream Split	Isolate real-time from batch for fault-tolerance
Environment Isolation	Use namespaces, labels, and RBAC for job segmentation
Versioned Pipelines	Tag images and config versions for reproducibility
Monitoring and Alerts	Use Prometheus, Grafana, and logging sidecars for observability

Table 4.9: *Best Practices for ETL on Kubernetes*

Case Study: ETL on Kubernetes for Financial Fraud Detection

Why: A fintech company processed large CSV dumps for fraud detection using monolithic cronjobs on EC2, which often failed silently.

What: They moved to a containerized pipeline using Spark on Kubernetes, managed with CronJobs and StatefulSets, leveraging cloud-native logging and monitoring.

When: Migrated during Black Friday surge prep for fault tolerance.

How:

- Dockerized Spark ETL in a reproducible pipeline.
- Used Flink for real-time scoring.
- Data landed in S3 for analytics, exposed via Redash.

Outcome: 60% cost savings, auto-recovery from crashes, 2x faster throughput.

Conclusion

In this chapter, we explored how containers and pods form the foundation of Kubernetes workloads. We covered advanced Docker techniques, pod patterns such as sidecars and initContainers, and effective deployment strategies for high availability. From managing stateful workloads using StatefulSets and DaemonSets to designing cloud-native microservices and containerized ETL pipelines, this chapter provided a practical blueprint for real-world implementation. By applying these patterns, engineers can build scalable, resilient, and production-grade Kubernetes applications.

In the next chapter, we turn our attention to automating these workloads through CI/CD pipelines. It focuses on implementing continuous integration and delivery using Kubernetes-native tools such as ArgoCD and Flux, along with integrations for Jenkins and GitHub Actions. Cloud and DevOps engineers, data teams, and architects will gain hands-on knowledge to streamline deployments, enable GitOps workflows, and fully automate the data pipeline lifecycle across cloud and on-prem environments.

CHAPTER 5
CI/CD Pipelines for Kubernetes

Introduction

Continuous Integration and Continuous Delivery (CI/CD) are at the heart of modern software development, enabling faster, safer, and more reliable deployments. In Kubernetes-native environments, CI/CD pipelines must not only build and test code but also handle containerization, orchestration, and Git-based automation workflows. This chapter dives deep into building robust CI/CD pipelines tailored for Kubernetes, covering popular tools such as Jenkins, GitHub Actions, ArgoCD, and Flux. You will also explore GitOps principles, deployment strategies, and CI/CD practices for data engineering workloads. Whether you are running microservices or large-scale data pipelines, this chapter equips you to automate, secure, and scale your Kubernetes delivery lifecycle.

Structure

In this chapter, we will cover the following topics:

- Introduction to CI/CD in Kubernetes
- Setting Up Jenkins with Kubernetes
- GitHub Actions for Kubernetes CI/CD
- GitOps with ArgoCD and Flux
- CI/CD for Data Engineering Pipelines
- Rollback, Versioning, and Best Practices
- Automating Data Ingestion, Transformation, And Deployment Cycles

Understanding the Role of CI/CD in Kubernetes Environments

In modern cloud-native environments, teams must release features rapidly, securely, and reliably. Without automation, deployments are error-prone and time-consuming. Traditional CI/CD pipelines often fall short when scaling to microservices and containerized applications.

The problem with manual deployments

Before automation, engineering teams relied on manually building, testing, and deploying applications across environments. This led to:

- Inconsistent deployments
- Manual errors
- Delayed releases

- Difficult rollback strategies
- Zero traceability

In a world of microservices and fast-paced feature development, such manual processes break under pressure. Hence, Continuous Integration/Continuous Deployment (CI/CD) emerged as the industry standard.

What is CI/CD?

CI/CD stands for Continuous Integration and Continuous Delivery/Deployment. It is a set of practices and tools that automate every stage of your software delivery process:

- **Continuous Integration (CI):** Automatically builds and tests your code every time changes are pushed to the version control system.
- **Continuous Deployment (CD):** Automatically deploys successfully built applications into the target environment.

CI/CD bridges the gap between development and operations by delivering tested code frequently, reliably, and with high confidence. In Kubernetes, this means automating the build, test, deploy, and monitor cycle for containers across clusters.

CI/CD should be used:

- In microservices-based applications that need frequent updates or when deploying multiple microservices across environments.
- When you want to ensure repeatability, rollback, and auto-scaling or when manual deployments introduce risk, downtime, or delays.
- When supporting multiple environments (dev, staging, and production).
- For teams working across geographies with high commit velocity.
- When building data engineering pipelines that need scheduled and automated runs.

Implementing CI/CD in Kubernetes

CI/CD becomes even more powerful when paired with Kubernetes:

- Infrastructure-as-code practices
- Container registries (Docker Hub, ECR, GCR)
- Orchestrators (Kubernetes controllers, Helm)
- Declarative deployment tools (ArgoCD, FluxCD)
- Auto-scaling test environments
- Rollback and versioned deployments

Together, they bring GitOps, DevSecOps, and container-native deployment strategies into one ecosystem.

Traditional CI/CD versus Kubernetes-Native CI/CD Workflows

Traditional CI/CD struggles in Kubernetes:

- CI servers run on VMs or bare metal.
- Deployment involves Scripting and Secure Shell (SSH) access to servers.
- Highly coupled to infrastructure.

- Pipeline scripts are tightly coupled to infrastructure.
- Poor container awareness (for example, missing health probes).
- No GitOps support, leading to drift between code and infra.

Kubernetes-Native CI/CD excels:

- Pipelines run in pods within Kubernetes itself.
- CI/CD tools use Kubernetes APIs and Controllers.
- Built for autoscaling, versioned deployments, and GitOps.
- Pipelines are infrastructure-agnostic and declarative.
- Configurations are version-controlled via Git.
- Built-in support for autoscaling, secrets, and observability.

The following table compares Traditional CI/CD with Kubernetes-Native CI/CD workflows:

Feature	**Traditional CI/CD**	**Kubernetes-Native CI/CD**
Infrastructure	Static VMs or Bare Metal	Containers and Pods
Pipeline Control	Jenkins/TeamCity	ArgoCD, Flux, Tekton
Rollbacks	Manual or scripted	Declarative (via Git)
Monitoring	External tools	Prometheus, Grafana
Scaling	Difficult and manual	HPA, KEDA integration
Observability	External tools	Native metrics/logging
Deployment Strategy	Manual/Scripted	Declarative (YAML, Helm, GitOps)
Tool Execution	External agent	Inside Kubernetes

***Table 5.1:** Traditional CI/CD vs. Kubernetes-Native CI/CD Workflows*

Tools Comparison – Jenkins, GitHub Actions, ArgoCD, Flux

This section analyzes and compares the tools Jenkins, GitHub Actions, ArgoCD, and Flux.

Jenkins (CI):

- Mature and widely adopted
- Plugin-driven
- Can be deployed inside Kubernetes
- Requires persistent storage for configuration
- Works with Jenkinsfiles (pipeline as code)

Example:

```
pipeline {
  agent any
  stages {
    stage('Build') {
      steps { sh 'docker build -t myapp .' }
    }
    stage('Test') {
      steps { sh 'pytest tests/' }
    }
```

```
        stage('Deploy') {
          steps { sh 'kubectl apply -f k8s.yaml' }
        }
      }
    }
```

GitHub Actions (CI/CD):

- GitHub-native CI/CD
- YAML-based workflows
- Seamless integration with GitHub repos
- Supports building, testing, pushing images, and deploying to Kubernetes

Example:

```
name: CI/CD Pipeline
on:
  push:
    branches: [ main ]

jobs:
  build-deploy:
    runs-on: ubuntu-latest
    steps:
      - name: Checkout
        uses: actions/checkout@v2
      - name: Build Docker Image
        run: docker build -t myapp .
      - name: Push to DockerHub
        run: docker push myapp
      - name: Deploy to K8s
        run: kubectl apply -f k8s.yaml
```

ArgoCD (GitOps - CD):

- Kubernetes-native CD tool
- Pull-based model (sync from Git to K8s)
- Version-controlled deployments
- Visualization dashboards

FluxCD (GitOps - CD):

- Lightweight GitOps operator
- Declarative infrastructure syncing
- Supports Helm, Kustomize

The following table provides a comprehensive comparison of all tools:

Tool	Purpose	Pros	Limitations
Jenkins	General-purpose CI/CD	Mature ecosystem, plugin-rich	Steep learning curve, heavyweight
GitHub Actions	Cloud-native CI/CD	Built into GitHub, YAML-based, fast to start	Limited visibility into K8s
ArgoCD	GitOps delivery	Real-time syncing, rollback, visual UI	Needs Git + Kubernetes literacy

FluxCD	GitOps automation	Lightweight, scalable, integrates with Helm	Steeper learning for new teams

Table 5.2: *Tools Comparison*

The following figure represents CI/CD Integration in Kubernetes:

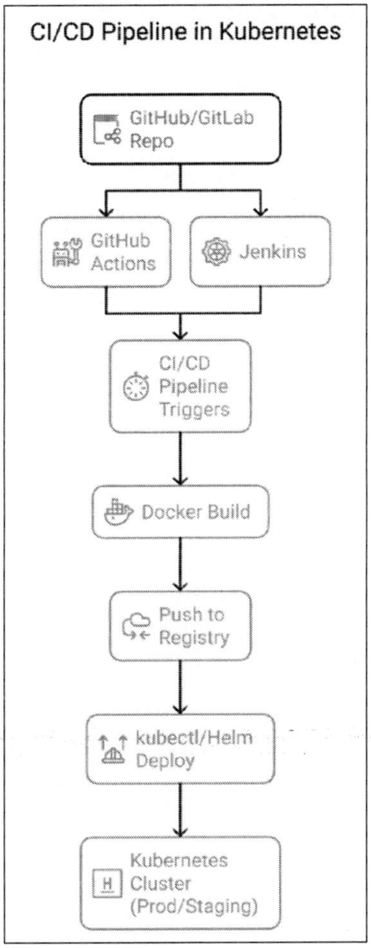

Figure 5.1: *Flow Diagram - CI/CD Pipeline in Kubernetes*

Architecture explanation: CI/CD Workflow in Kubernetes

Figure 5.1 represents a modern DevOps workflow designed to automate the software build, test, and deployment lifecycle using Kubernetes as the deployment target. It integrates source control, automation tools, containerization, and orchestration in a streamlined manner.

- **Code Commit** triggers pipeline via GitHub Actions or Jenkins.
- **CI/CD job** builds a Docker image and pushes it to a registry.
- **Deployment tools** such as kubectl/Helm apply updated YAML.
- ArgoCD/Flux can watch for Git changes and auto-deploy via GitOps.

Here is a detailed walkthrough of each component in the pipeline:

- **GitHub/GitLab Repo**

  At the top of the pipeline lies the **Source Code Repository**—either GitHub or GitLab.

  - This is where developers push code changes.
  - It serves as the single source of truth.
  - Commits or Pull Requests (PRs) trigger downstream CI/CD actions.

  Example: A developer pushes code to the main branch of a GitHub repository.

- **GitHub Actions/Jenkins**

  The figure supports two popular CI/CD tools:

  - **GitHub Actions:** GitHub's native CI/CD service that runs workflows based on events such as push, pull request, and so on.
  - **Jenkins:** An open-source automation server widely used for more customizable CI/CD pipelines.

  These tools act as the orchestrators for the build and deployment processes. You can use either one, depending on project requirements.

  Example: A GitHub Action runs a pipeline when a new PR is created; Jenkins could be configured to poll the repo periodically or respond to webhooks.

- **CI/CD Pipeline Triggers**

  This stage signifies the automated **triggering mechanism** for the CI/CD workflow.

  - Triggered by events such as:
    - Code commit
    - PR merge
    - Scheduled jobs
  - Initiates the entire CI/CD flow downstream, including building and testing the code.

  Think of it as the ignition switch that starts the engine.

- **Docker Build**

  Once the pipeline is triggered:

  - A **Docker image** of the application is built.
  - This image packages the application code, runtime, libraries, and dependencies.
  - Dockerfiles define how this image should be constructed.

  This encapsulates the app in a portable unit that can run consistently across environments.

- **Push to Registry**

  After a successful Docker build:

  - The image is pushed to a **Docker image registry**, which could be (depending on your business/environment use case):
    - Docker Hub
    - GitHub Container Registry
    - Amazon Elastic Container Registry (AWS ECR)
    - Google Cloud Artifact Registry (GCP Artifact Registry)

    - Azure Container Registry

  This acts as a centralized storage for container images, accessible during deployment.

- **kubectl/Helm Deploy**

  This step is responsible for **deploying the image to Kubernetes**:

  - **kubectl**: The Kubernetes CLI tool used to apply YAML manifests (for example, deployments, services).
  - **Helm**: A package manager for Kubernetes that uses **Helm Charts** to manage application releases.

  This step uses the newly pushed Docker image tag to deploy or update workloads in the Kubernetes cluster.

- **Kubernetes Cluster (Prod/Staging)**

  Finally, the application gets deployed to a **Kubernetes Cluster**, which could be:

  - A **Staging** environment (for QA/testing)
  - A **Production** environment (for real user traffic)

  Kubernetes manages the containers, ensures the desired state, performs auto-scaling and handles service discovery.

Key benefits of this CI/CD Workflow are:

- **Automation:** Removes manual intervention, increasing efficiency.
- **Consistency:** Ensures the same process runs every time code is pushed.
- **Scalability:** Easily supports multiple environments and microservices.
- **Observability:** Tools such as Prometheus, Grafana, or ELK stack can be added for monitoring/logging.

Real-World Scenario 1: CI/CD in Action for a FinTech App on Kubernetes

A leading FinTech startup is building a **payment gateway platform** that must be highly available, secure, and scalable. Their product team releases multiple microservices every week, ranging from transaction handling and fraud detection to customer onboarding.

To manage this velocity without compromising quality or uptime, they adopted a **CI/CD pipeline integrated with Kubernetes**, following GitOps principles and best practices.

The following figure provides an illustration of the CI/CD process for a FinTech app on Kubernetes:

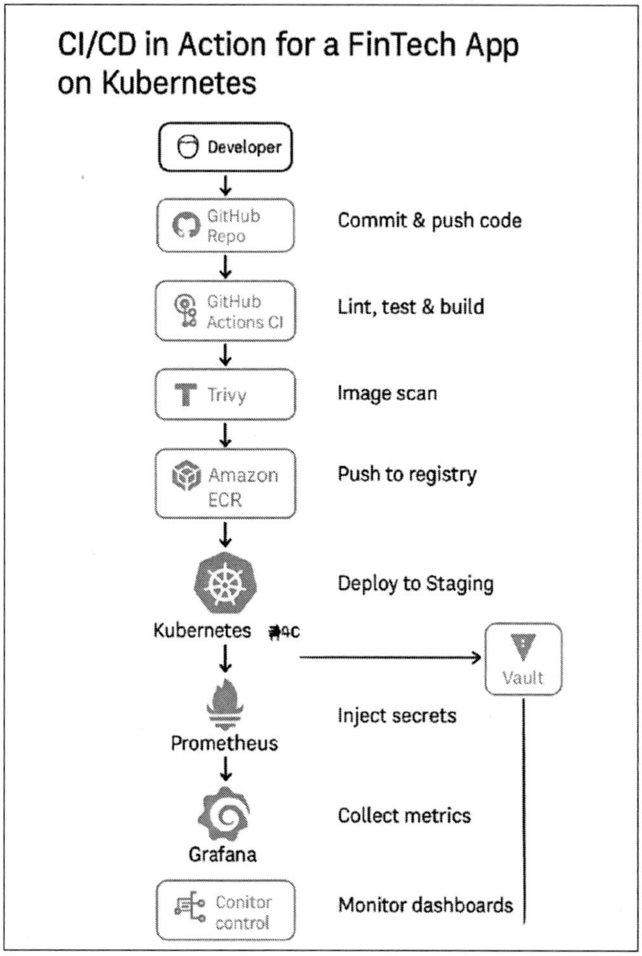

Figure 5.2: *Real-World Scenario 1: CI/CD in Action for a FinTech App on Kubernetes*

How the Pipeline Works in Practice:

1. **Developer Workflow**
    a. A backend developer commits code for a new fraud detection algorithm.
    b. The code is pushed to GitHub, triggering a GitHub Actions workflow.
2. **CI Pipeline Triggered**
    a. GitHub Actions lints the code, runs unit tests, and builds a Docker image.
    b. The image is tagged and pushed to **Amazon ECR** (Elastic Container Registry).
    c. **Trivy** scans the image for known vulnerabilities.
3. **Configuration in GitOps Repo**
    a. A corresponding Helm chart is updated with the new image tag in a separate Git repository (used for infra and deployment).
    b. This update triggers **ArgoCD**, which continuously watches the Git repo for changes.

4. **CD via GitOps**
   a. **ArgoCD** fetches the updated chart and applies it to the **Staging Kubernetes Cluster**.
   b. A canary deployment rolls out 10% of the traffic to the new fraud detection logic.
   c. If Prometheus metrics remain healthy for 15 minutes, the rollout continues automatically to 100%.
5. **Secrets and Security**
   a. Sensitive values such as API keys are pulled securely from **HashiCorp Vault** and injected into the pods at runtime.
   b. Role-based access ensures developers do not have direct access to production secrets.
6. **Monitoring, Logging, Alerts**
   a. **Prometheus** scrapes metrics from each pod.
   b. **Grafana** dashboards show latency, success rate, and transaction volume.
   c. Logs are centralized in the **ELK stack**, while anomalies trigger Slack alerts.
7. **Feedback Loop**
   a. Within 30 minutes of pushing the code, the new feature is live.
   b. QA teams receive real-time alerts if the service misbehaves.
   c. If any issues are detected, **ArgoCD** supports one-click rollback via Git revert.

Key Benefits:

- **Deployment frequency increased by 5x.**
- **Mean Time to Recovery (MTTR) reduced by 60%.**
- **No downtime deployments** even during peak business hours.
- Full traceability and auditability of changes across teams.

Takeaway:

This real-world example demonstrates how a modern CI/CD pipeline—backed by Kubernetes and GitOps—empowers DevOps teams to **move fast without breaking things**. With automation, observability, and version control at the center, engineering teams can innovate rapidly while maintaining stability, security, and confidence in their releases.

Real-World Scenario 2: CI/CD Pipeline for a Healthcare Platform on Kubernetes

A healthcare technology company is building a **telemedicine platform** used by clinics and hospitals to manage patient appointments, digital prescriptions, and real-time doctor consultations. The system must adhere to Health Insurance Portability and Accountability Act **(HIPAA) regulations**, ensure zero downtime for mission-critical services, and support frequent feature updates.

To meet these goals, they implemented a **CI/CD pipeline integrated with Kubernetes**, with secure automation, GitOps-driven deployments, and audit-ready workflows.

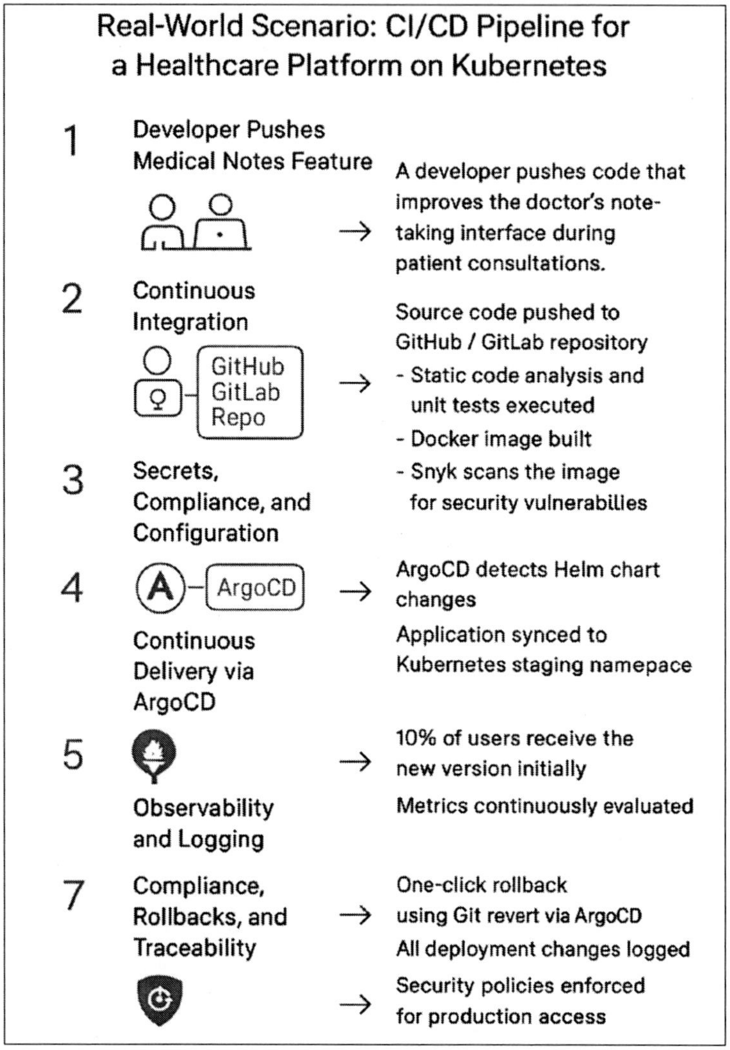

Figure 5.3: *Real-World Scenario 2: CICD Pipeline for a Healthcare Platform on Kubernetes*

How the Pipeline Works in Practice:

1. **Developer Pushes Medical Notes Feature**
    a. A developer pushes code that improves the **doctor's note-taking interface** during consultations.
    b. The push goes to a secured Git repository (for example, GitLab or GitHub Enterprise), triggering a CI pipeline.
2. **Continuous Integration**
    a. GitHub Actions runs:
        i. Static code analysis and unit tests.
        ii. A Docker image build for the updated microservice.
    b. **Snyk** scans the image for security vulnerabilities.

   c. The image is pushed to **Azure Container Registry** (ACR), with versioning based on commit SHA.

3. **Secrets, Compliance, and Configuration**

   a. Helm values (deployment config) are updated in a GitOps repo.

   b. Environment secrets (for example, access tokens for Electronic Health Record (EHR) APIs) are securely managed in the **HashiCorp Vault.**

   c. All audit logs are stored in **immutable storage** to meet compliance standards.

4. **Continuous Delivery via ArgoCD**

   a. **ArgoCD** detects the Helm chart update in the GitOps repo.

   b. It syncs the deployment to a **staging namespace** in Kubernetes (AKS or EKS).

   c. Automated health checks ensure the service boots correctly, meets response SLAs, and passes HIPAA-related checks.

5. **Production Rollout with Canary Strategy**

   a. Using **progressive delivery**, 10% of users (clinics in non-critical regions) get the new version first.

   b. Prometheus monitors latency and error rates.

   c. If metrics stay within safe thresholds, the rollout continues gradually.

6. **Observability and Logging**

   a. **Prometheus** + **Grafana** tracks API response time, CPU/memory usage, and patient session duration.

   b. All logs flow into a **HIPAA-compliant ELK stack** with alerts sent to the DevSecOps team via Microsoft Teams.

   c. A custom dashboard visualizes doctor-patient video uptime and prescription generation errors in real-time.

7. **Compliance, Rollbacks, and Traceability**

   a. ArgoCD offers a **one-click rollback** through Git revert if errors are found.

   b. Every deployment and access event is **logged for compliance audits**.

   c. Security policies ensure that only authorized teams can deploy to production.

Business Impact:

- **Compliance built into the pipeline**, not as an afterthought.
- **The deployment cycle reduced from 2 weeks to 1 day**, accelerating innovation in patient care.
- **Zero downtime** for critical systems such as appointment scheduling and EMR access.
- Developers push code confidently, with **automated safety nets and observability baked in.**

Takeaway

For healthcare organizations, **CI/CD in Kubernetes with GitOps and secure automation** is more than a tech upgrade–it is a strategic necessity. By building trust into the pipeline through secrets management, compliance tracking, and gradual rollouts, healthcare tech teams can innovate safely while protecting patient data and delivering life-changing digital care.

Setting Up Jenkins with Kubernetes

Why Jenkins on Kubernetes?

Organizations that rely on continuous integration and delivery (CI/CD) require a powerful and scalable automation system. Jenkins, a widely adopted CI/CD tool, provides flexibility to define complex pipelines. However, when run on traditional infrastructure, Jenkins can become a bottleneck due to limited scalability, plugin issues, or mismanagement of build agents.

What changes in Kubernetes- Deploying Jenkins on Kubernetes allows dynamic provisioning of agents (build pods), isolation of workloads, autoscaling based on load, and containerized builds. It eliminates the need for static agent machines and brings observability, fault tolerance, and cloud-native efficiency to the CI/CD ecosystem.

This should be applied when:

- Teams managing multiple microservices with independent pipelines.
- Data engineering and DevOps teams working with containerized workflows.
- Organizations requiring scalable, self-healing CI/CD environments.

How does it solve the problem- By containerizing Jenkins and provisioning agents as Kubernetes pods, you get elasticity, lower costs, and automated failure recovery. Kubernetes-native constructs can also monitor, restart, and auto scale Jenkins components.

The following figure illustrates the Jenkins Architecture on Kubernetes:

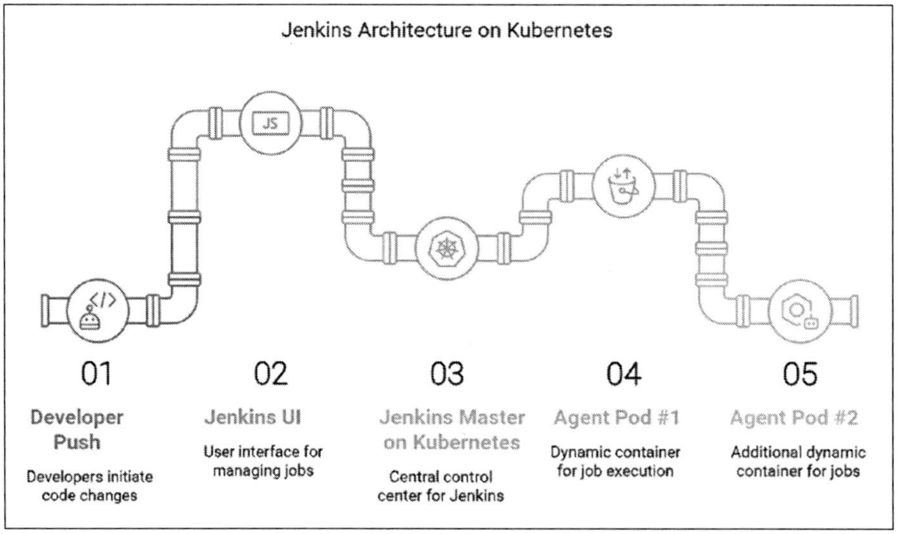

Figure 5.4: *Jenkins Architecture on Kubernetes*

This process outlines the modern, Kubernetes-native architecture for Jenkins, which leverages the cluster for elastic scaling and job isolation:

- Jenkins master is deployed as a StatefulSet in Kubernetes.
- When a job is triggered, the Kubernetes plugin requests an ephemeral agent pod.
- Jenkins executes the pipeline on the agent and discards it post-build.

Core Components:

- **Jenkins Master:** The control center that manages jobs and user interfaces.

- **Jenkins Agent Pods:** Dynamically launched containers for executing jobs.
- **Persistent Volume:** Stores job configurations, logs, and plugins.
- **Helm:** Simplifies deployment of Jenkins with custom values.
- **Kubernetes Plugin:** Enables dynamic provisioning of agents on-demand.

The following figure illustrates how Jenkins, a widely used automation server, is deployed in a Kubernetes-native architecture to enable scalable, resilient, and dynamic CI/CD pipelines:

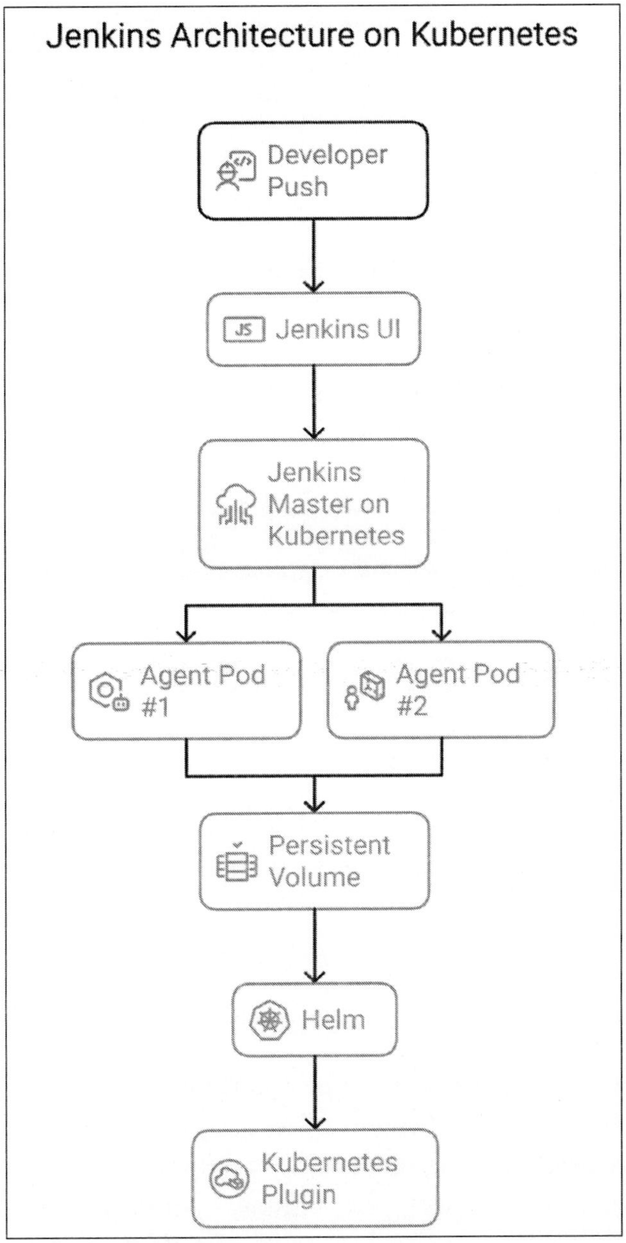

***Figure 5.5:** Deployment of Jenkins Architecture on Kubernetes*

Here is a breakdown of each component and their roles in the workflow:

- **Developer Push**
    - The CI/CD process begins with a developer pushing code changes to a version control system (for example, GitHub, GitLab).
    - This action serves as a trigger for Jenkins to begin pipeline execution via a webhook or polling mechanism.
- **Jenkins UI**
    - Jenkins provides a **web-based user interface** through which users can configure jobs, manage pipelines, monitor builds, and access logs.
    - Hosted inside the Kubernetes cluster, the Jenkins UI is typically exposed via an Ingress or LoadBalancer service.
- **Jenkins Master on Kubernetes**
    - The **Jenkins Master** orchestrates the pipeline execution. It is deployed as a **Kubernetes Deployment**, ensuring high availability and scalability.
    - Responsibilities of the Jenkins master include:
        - Managing the job queue,
        - Allocating build tasks to agents,
        - Storing plugin configurations and credentials,
        - Communicating with Kubernetes API to dynamically launch build agents (pods).
- **Agent Pods (Ephemeral Build Workers)**
    - When a job is triggered, Jenkins Master provisions **Agent Pods** on-demand using the Kubernetes Plugin.
        - **Agent Pod #1** and **Agent Pod #2** represent concurrent builds.
    - These pods are **ephemeral**–they spin up, run the pipeline tasks, and terminate after the job is completed.
    - Isolation between pods enhances security, resource control, and fault tolerance.
- **`PersistentVolume`**
    - Jenkins often needs persistent storage for job history, workspace data, and plugin state.
    - A **`PersistentVolume` (PV)** is mounted to the Jenkins master (and optionally agents), managed by Kubernetes' native storage class provisioning.
    - Ensures state is preserved even if the Jenkins pod is restarted or rescheduled.
- **Helm**
    - Jenkins can be deployed and managed on Kubernetes using **Helm**, the Kubernetes package manager.
    - Helm simplifies the installation, upgrade, and configuration of Jenkins by using pre-defined charts.
    - Also useful for deploying plugins and configuring storage, Ingress, and RBAC.
- **Kubernetes Plugin**
    - The **Kubernetes Plugin** in Jenkins connects the Jenkins master to the Kubernetes cluster.
    - Enables Jenkins to dynamically launch pods as build agents with custom Docker images and resource limits.
    - Configuration defines how each pod should behave (such as, container image, namespace, service account).

Why This Architecture?

Deploying Jenkins on Kubernetes unlocks a wide range of benefits, including:

- **Dynamic Scaling**: Auto-creation of agents based on demand.
- **Cost-Efficiency**: No idle agents consuming resources.
- **High Availability**: Leveraging Kubernetes' self-healing and scaling features.
- **Cloud-Native Agility**: Integrates seamlessly with other cloud-native tools (Helm, Vault, Prometheus).

Real-World Use Case

In modern microservices and DevOps workflows, Jenkins on Kubernetes fits perfectly to:

- Run parallel pipelines across isolated environments.
- Support multiple developer teams without resource contention.
- Ensure high availability of CI/CD operations with auto-scaling agents.

Installing Jenkins on Kubernetes using Helm

To leverage the scalability and reliability of Kubernetes for your CI/CD, here is the step-by-step deployment process using Helm:

Prerequisites:

- Helm installed on your system.
- A running Kubernetes cluster (Minikube, GKE, EKS, and so on)

Step 1: Add Jenkins Helm Chart Repository

```
helm repo add jenkins https://charts.jenkins.io
helm repo update
```

Step 2: Create a Namespace for Jenkins

```
kubectl create namespace jenkins
```

Step 3: Install Jenkins

```
helm install jenkins jenkins/jenkins \
  --namespace jenkins \
  --set controller.serviceType=LoadBalancer \
  --set controller.adminPassword=admin123 \
  --set persistence.enabled=true \
  --set persistence.size=10Gi
```

Step 4: Access Jenkins UI

```
kubectl --namespace jenkins port-forward svc/jenkins 8080:8080
```

Kubernetes Plugin and Agent Auto-Discovery

Why Use Kubernetes Plugin?

This plugin enables Jenkins to provision agent pods dynamically instead of relying on pre-created nodes.

Steps to Configure Kubernetes Plugin:

1. Navigate to `Manage Jenkins > Manage Plugins` and install the Kubernetes plugin.
2. Go to `Manage Jenkins > Configure Clouds`.

3. Add a new Kubernetes cloud with:
   i. Kubernetes API URL: https://kubernetes.default
   ii. Jenkins URL: http://jenkins.jenkins.svc.cluster.local:8080
   iii. Credentials (**`ServiceAccount`** token)
4. Define Pod Templates for agents:
   i. Add container name **`jnlp`** with image **`jenkins/inbound-agent:latest`**.
   ii. Set resource requests and environment variables if needed.

Building and Deploying with Jenkins Pipelines

To begin building and deploying your application, here is a simple declarative Jenkinsfile defining the pipeline workflow:

Simple Declarative Pipeline - Jenkinsfile:

```
pipeline {
  agent {
    kubernetes {
      yaml '''
apiVersion: v1
kind: Pod
spec:
  containers:
  - name: maven
    image: maven:3.6.3-jdk-11
    command:
    - cat
    tty: true
'''
    }
  }
  stages {
    stage('Build') {
      steps {
        container('maven') {
          sh 'mvn clean package'
        }
      }
    }
    stage('Deploy') {
      steps {
        sh 'kubectl apply -f deployment.yaml'
      }
    }
  }
}
```

Real-World Example: Containerized ETL Pipeline with Jenkins

Why: A data team wanted to orchestrate ETL pipelines using Jenkins while ensuring each transformation ran in an isolated, reproducible container.

What: Each ETL job was defined as a separate stage using Dockerized Spark jobs.

When: Jenkins jobs were triggered nightly via cron or on-demand with Git triggers.

How:

- Jenkins agent spun up Spark-based containers on Kubernetes.
- Each job pulled data from S3, applied transformations, and wrote to a data lake.
- Logs and metrics were collected using Fluentd and Prometheus.

Best Practices for Jenkins on Kubernetes:

- Use **`StatefulSet`** for Jenkins master to ensure persistence.
- Store credentials in Kubernetes Secrets, not hardcoded.
- Use separate namespaces per environment (dev/test/prod).
- Integrate with Prometheus for monitoring build health and duration.
- Keep builds stateless; store artifacts in external repositories (for example, Nexus, Artifactory).

GitHub Actions for Kubernetes CI/CD

GitHub Actions has rapidly emerged as a leading CI/CD automation platform for modern DevOps workflows, especially within Kubernetes ecosystems. With its deep integration with GitHub repositories, GitHub Actions allows developers to build, test, and deploy containerized applications directly from source code pushes.

Unlike legacy CI/CD platforms that require complex plugin installations and external servers, GitHub Actions provides a fully managed, scalable, and event-driven approach to cloud-native delivery pipelines. For Kubernetes users, this results in lightweight, declarative, and GitOps-friendly automation.

Why GitHub Actions for Kubernetes: Legacy CI/CD platforms such as Jenkins often require separate infrastructure and do not offer native version control integration. Manual secret management and external triggers slow down deployments.

What: GitHub Actions is a fully integrated CI/CD solution with GitHub. It automates workflows using .yml files and supports native Kubernetes deployments via kubectl, Helm, Kustomize, and GitOps-based approaches.

When: Ideal for projects already hosted on GitHub, especially microservices, APIs, or event-driven data pipelines targeting Kubernetes clusters in dev, staging, or production.

How:

- Define a GitHub Actions workflow (**`.github/workflows/deploy.yml`**).
- Configure build and deployment jobs using Docker, **`kubectl`**, and Helm.
- Manage secrets via GitHub Secrets.
- Trigger pipeline on push, PR, or tag events.

GitHub Actions follows an event-driven architecture that responds to GitHub events (push, PR, release) to trigger workflows. These workflows consist of jobs that run in containers (called runners), executing steps such as build, test, and deploy.

Architecture Flow:

1. Code push to GitHub triggers a CI/CD workflow.
2. Workflow builds Docker image and pushes to DockerHub or GitHub Container Registry (GHCR).

3. Deployment job runs **kubectl** apply or Helm chart to deploy to Kubernetes cluster.
4. Monitoring or rollback steps follow if configured.

The following figure illustrates GitHub Actions to Kubernetes Pipeline:

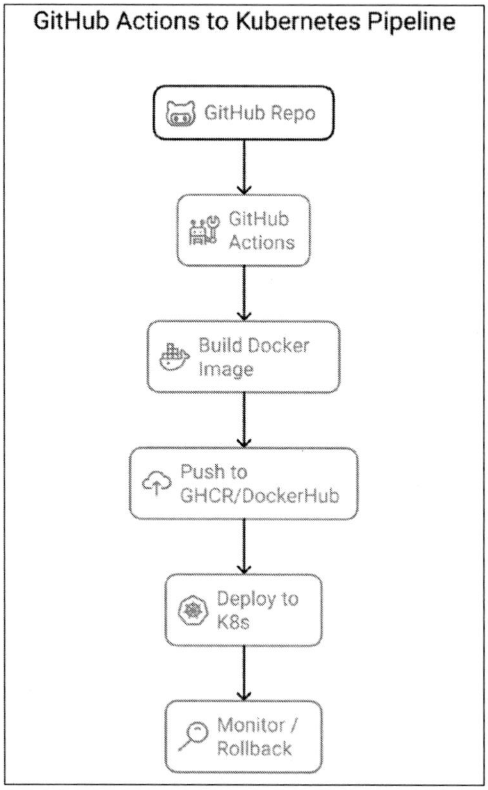

Figure 5.6: *GitHub Actions to Kubernetes Pipeline*

The detailed explanation of the figure is provided as follows:

- **GitHub Repo:** Holds source code, YAMLs, and GitHub Actions workflow.
- **GitHub Actions Workflow:** Triggered on commit or PR.
- **Build Step:** Builds a Docker image using GitHub-hosted runners.
- **Registry Step:** Authenticates and pushes the image to DockerHub or GitHub Container Registry.
- **Deployment Step:** Uses kubectl, helm, or kustomize to deploy the app to Kubernetes.
- **Post-Deploy Step:** Observability, alerting, or rollback logic.

This figure illustrates a modern CI/CD pipeline where **GitHub Actions** orchestrates the automation of building, packaging, and deploying applications to a **Kubernetes cluster**. This workflow ensures continuous integration and continuous deployment (CI/CD) by minimizing manual intervention, promoting DevOps best practices, and enabling rapid iteration.

GitHub Repository (Source of Truth)

The journey begins with a **GitHub repository** that contains the application source code, Dockerfile, and Kubernetes manifests or Helm charts. This repository acts as the **single source of truth**, where any changes in the codebase (for example, commits or pull requests) serve as triggers for the automation pipeline.

Key Concepts:

- Version control with Git
- Branching strategies (for example, `main`, `develop`, feature branches)
- Webhooks to trigger workflows on `push` or `pull_request` events

GitHub Actions (CI/CD Orchestration)

GitHub Actions is a powerful automation tool natively integrated into GitHub. It uses YAML-based workflows to define jobs and steps. Once a code is committed, GitHub Actions triggers the pipeline.

- **Typical Actions:**
    - Run unit tests
    - Lint the code
    - Execute security scans
    - Build the Docker image
- **Example Workflow File**: `.github/workflows/deploy.yml`

Build Docker Image

In this stage, the application code is **containerized** using a Dockerfile. GitHub Actions runs steps to build the Docker image using Docker CLI or buildx.

- **Dockerfile** defines the environment, dependencies, and runtime.
- **Build output** is a tagged Docker image (for example, `myapp:v1.0.3`).
- **Benefits**:
    - Consistent environments
    - Dependency isolation
    - Easier debugging and replication

Push to GHCR/DockerHub

After the Docker image is built, it is pushed to a **container registry**:

- **GitHub Container Registry (GHCR)**: A GitHub-native registry.
- **DockerHub**: Widely used public/private registry.

This step ensures that the image is stored in a central location from where Kubernetes can later pull it.

- **Authentication is required**, typically via GitHub secrets (for example, `DOCKER_USERNAME`, `DOCKER_PASSWORD`).

Deploy to Kubernetes

Next, the pipeline deploys the application to a **Kubernetes (K8s)** cluster. This step can use:

- kubectl applied with raw YAML manifests.
- Helm for templated deployments.
- Kustomize for customized overlays.

The deployment typically includes:

- Deployments
- Services
- ConfigMaps/Secrets
- Ingress controllers

Deployment strategies such as **RollingUpdate** or **Blue-Green** may be configured to ensure zero downtime.

Monitor/Rollback

Post-deployment, the application is monitored using observability tools (for example, Prometheus, Grafana, Loki, or external monitoring services). If a deployment fails health checks or metrics degrade, rollback strategies can be applied.

- **Rollback Methods:**
  - **`kubectl rollout undo deployment/<app>`**.
  - Automated rollback using GitHub Actions + Kubernetes health probes.
- **Goals:**
  - Minimize MTTR (Mean Time to Recovery).
  - Maintain application stability.
  - Alert DevOps teams in real time.

Summary: Value for Engineering Roles

This automated pipeline delivers high value for:

Role	Benefit
Cloud Engineers	Manage scalable, cloud-native workloads
DevOps Professionals	Automate and standardize CI/CD
Data Engineers	Deploy services for ETL/ELT pipelines with speed
Data Architects	Ensure governed, reliable deployments
Software Architects	Align application delivery with microservices and DevOps principles

***Table 5.3**: Value of Engineering Roles and Benefits*

Sample GitHub Actions Workflow (YAML)

```
name: CI/CD Pipeline for Kubernetes

on:
  push:
    branches:
      - main

jobs:
  build-and-deploy:
    runs-on: ubuntu-latest

    env:
      IMAGE_NAME: ghcr.io/your-org/your-app:${{ github.sha }}

    steps:
```

```
      - name: Checkout code
        uses: actions/checkout@v3

      - name: Set up Docker
        uses: docker/setup-buildx-action@v2

      - name: Log in to GitHub Container Registry
        uses: docker/login-action@v2
        with:
          registry: ghcr.io
          username: ${{ github.actor }}
          password: ${{ secrets.GITHUB_TOKEN }}

      - name: Build & push Docker image
        run: |
          docker build -t $IMAGE_NAME .
          docker push $IMAGE_NAME

      - name: Set up Kubeconfig
        run: |
          echo "$KUBECONFIG_CONTENT" > kubeconfig.yaml
          export KUBECONFIG=$PWD/kubeconfig.yaml
        env:
          KUBECONFIG_CONTENT: ${{ secrets.KUBECONFIG }}

      - name: Deploy to Kubernetes
        run: |
          kubectl apply -f k8s/deployment.yaml
          kubectl rollout status deployment your-app
```

Secrets and Multi-Environment Strategy Secrets Management:

- Use GitHub Secrets to securely store `KUBECONFIG`, Docker credentials, and tokens.
- Reference them in workflows using `${{ secrets.YOUR_SECRET_NAME }}`.

Environment Strategies:

- Use separate workflow files or environment contexts for dev, staging, and prod.
- Use branching (`main`, `release/*`, `feature/*`) to conditionally trigger environment deployments.

Example: Automated Data Pipeline Deployment Using GitHub Actions.

This example demonstrates how GitHub Actions can be used to automatically build, package, and deploy a real-time Kafka-based streaming pipeline on Kubernetes.

- Push code to `main`.
- GitHub Actions builds Kafka microservice Docker image.
- Pushes to GHCR.
- Deploys Kafka producer pod to K8s.
- Validates
- delivery with a test consumer.

Breakdown:

- **Why:** Traditional CI/CD for data pipelines requires a manual release or Jenkins agents.
- **What:** GitHub Actions simplifies this using a few lines of declarative YAML.
- **When:** For any microservice or batch job with frequent iteration.

- **How:** Docker + GitHub Actions + Kubernetes YAML = fast, secure, GitOps-style delivery.

Best Practices:

- Use reusable workflows (`workflow_call`) to standardize builds across teams.
- Keep workflows in sync with Helm/kustomize values.
- Rotate secrets regularly.
- Enable branch protection and signed commits.
- Set `imagePullPolicy` to Always for the latest updates.

GitOps with ArgoCD and Flux

Introduction to GitOps principles

GitOps is a modern deployment paradigm where **Git is the single source of truth** for declarative infrastructure and application state. This model aligns perfectly with Kubernetes' declarative design.

Core principles of GitOps:

- **Declarative Infrastructure:** All configurations (Kubernetes YAMLs, Helm charts, and so on) are stored in Git.
- **Automated Sync:** Tools such as ArgoCD and Flux watch Git repositories and sync changes to the cluster.
- **Versioned Changes:** Every change is auditable and traceable via Git commit history.
- **Pull-Based Deployments:** GitOps agents pull changes from Git rather than pushing from CI.

Why GitOps matters in Kubernetes:

- Reduces human error in production deployments.
- Offers built-in rollback via Git history.
- Enforces compliance and auditability.

In traditional CI/CD workflows, pipelines push changes directly to the Kubernetes cluster using imperative commands (`kubectl apply`, `helm upgrade`, and more). While this worked in earlier DevOps stages, it posed critical challenges for large-scale, production-grade systems:

- **Lack of Auditability:** No clean history of what and when something changed.
- **Security Risks:** Direct CI/CD access to cluster credentials.
- **Manual Drift Handling:** When changes are made outside of automation, clusters diverge from the Git state.
- **Complex Rollback:** Rolling back meant re-running pipelines or manually reconfiguring services.

GitOps addresses all these challenges by enforcing declarative state and pull-based deployment principles.

GitOps (Core Concept)

GitOps is a methodology where Git acts as the single source of truth for all infrastructure and application configurations. It follows declarative infrastructure and automated synchronization practices.

- Git stores Kubernetes YAML, Helm charts, or Kustomize templates.
- A GitOps operator (ArgoCD or Flux) runs inside the cluster and **pulls** the desired state from the Git repo.

- The operator compares the current live state of the cluster with the Git state and **automatically applies changes**.
- Drift detection and rollback become seamless by reverting Git commits.

When to use GitOps?

GitOps is critical when:

- You need strong auditability and change history (for example, finance, healthcare).
- You manage multi-environment deployments (`dev` → `test` → `staging` → `prod`).
- You want RBAC-enforced operations with least-privilege Git-based workflows.
- Your clusters are deployed across multi-cloud or hybrid infrastructure.
- You need to **onboard developers quickly** with minimal Kubernetes expertise.

How GitOps works with ArgoCD?

ArgoCD GitOps Workflow

An end-to-end automation flow showing how ArgoCD detects changes in Git, syncs to the Kubernetes cluster, monitors for drift, and ensures continuous reconciliation with the declared configuration.

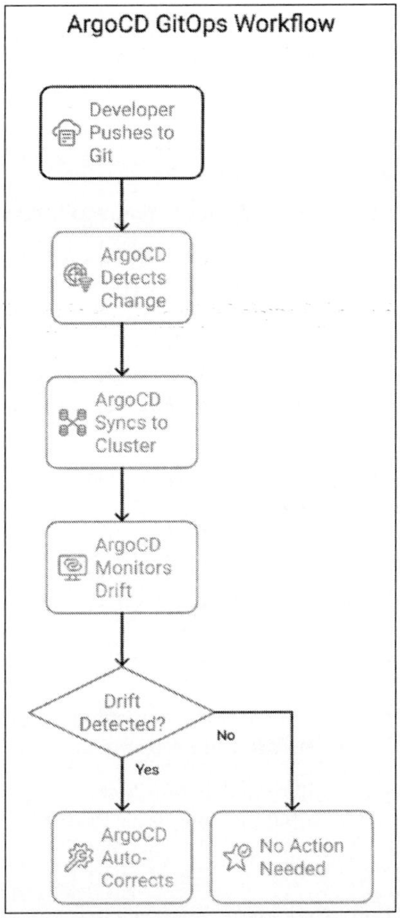

Figure 5.7: *GitOps Workflow with ArgoCD*

The preceding figure represents the lifecycle of deploying and managing Kubernetes resources using **ArgoCD**, a declarative, GitOps-based continuous delivery tool. It outlines how changes pushed to a Git repository are automatically detected, synchronized, and monitored by ArgoCD to ensure cluster state consistency.

Developer Pushes to Git

What Happens: A developer makes changes to Kubernetes manifests or Helm charts (for example, new deployments, config changes, resource scaling) and commits them to a Git repository.

Why It Matters: Git is the single source of truth in the GitOps paradigm. Any desired state of the Kubernetes environment is declared and version-controlled in Git, ensuring traceability and auditability.

ArgoCD Detects Change

What Happens: ArgoCD continuously polls or listens for webhook notifications from the Git repository. Once a change is detected in the tracked branch or path, it marks the application as "OutOfSync."

Why It Matters: This detection mechanism ensures **immediate awareness** of updates, enabling faster and automated propagation of changes to the Kubernetes cluster.

ArgoCD Syncs to Cluster

What Happens: ArgoCD compares the declared state (from Git) with the live state (in the cluster). If they differ, ArgoCD performs a **sync operation**, applying the new manifests to the cluster to align it with Git.

Modes of Sync:

- **`Manual Sync`:** Triggered by the user.
- **`Automatic Sync`:** Automatically applied without human intervention.

Why It Matters: Syncing bridges the gap between Git and the cluster. This is the core of the GitOps principle, ensuring **declarative synchronization.**

ArgoCD Monitors Drift

What Happens: ArgoCD continuously monitors the live state of Kubernetes resources and compares it with the Git state to detect **drift** – any unauthorized or manual changes made directly in the cluster.

Why It Matters: This ensures **configuration integrity**. Any changes outside Git are considered non-compliant, prompting reconciliation to restore the declared state.

Drift Detected?

- **Decision Point:** ArgoCD checks if there is a mismatch between the desired (Git) and actual (cluster) state.

If Yes - ArgoCD Auto-Corrects

What Happens: If drift is detected and auto-sync is enabled, ArgoCD automatically reapplies the manifests from Git to bring the cluster back to the desired state.

Why It Matters: This **self-healing** capability maintains cluster fidelity, eliminates configuration drift, and reduces operational risks due to manual interventions.

If No - No Action Needed

What Happens: If no drift is detected, the cluster is in the desired state, and ArgoCD takes no further action.

Why It Matters: This confirms that the system is **compliant and healthy**, aligned with the Git-defined configuration.

Key Benefits of This Workflow:

- **Declarative Management:** Every desired configuration is stored in Git.
- **Auditability and History:** Full traceability of changes.
- **Security:** Prevents unauthorized changes by continuously reverting them.
- **Automation:** Reduces manual operations and human errors.
- **Consistency:** Multiple clusters can be managed uniformly from a central Git repo.

ArgoCD and Flux

ArgoCD and **Flux** are the two most popular GitOps tools for Kubernetes.

Feature	ArgoCD	Flux
UI	Full-featured web UI and CLI	CLI-focused, optional UI (Weave UI)
Sync Method	Pull-based (automated or manual)	Pull-based (fully automated)
Helm Support	Native	Native + Helm Controller
Kustomize Support	Native	Native
Multi-Tenancy	Supported with RBAC	Supported via Git repositories
Notifications	Webhooks, Slack, Email	Event-driven via Flux controllers

Table 5.4: *Features of ArgoCD and Flux*

Hands-on Lab: ArgoCD + GitHub Integration

The key phases of setting up ArgoCD are listed as follows:

1. **Install ArgoCD**

```
kubectl create namespace argocd
kubectl apply -n argocd -f https://raw.githubusercontent.com/argoproj/argo-cd/
stable/manifests/install.yaml
```

2. **Expose ArgoCD UI (Dev Only):**

```
kubectl port-forward svc/argocd-server -n argocd 8080:443
```

3. **Login to ArgoCD CLI:**

```
argocd login localhost:8080
```

4. **Create `Application.yaml`:**

```
yaml

apiVersion: argoproj.io/v1alpha1
kind: Application
metadata:
  name: my-k8s-app
  namespace: argocd
spec:
  destination:
    namespace: default
    server: https://kubernetes.default.svc
  project: default
  source:
```

```
      repoURL: https://github.com/your-org/your-repo
      targetRevision: HEAD
      path: manifests/
    syncPolicy:
      automated:
        prune: true
        selfHeal: true
```

5. **Apply Application:**

   ```
   kubectl apply -f application.yaml -n argocd
   ```

This connects the Kubernetes cluster to the Git repository and automatically deploys manifests from the **`manifests/`** folder.

Advanced Use: Helm and Kustomize with ArgoCD

- **Helm:** Supports **`values.yaml`** overrides for environment-specific deployments.
- **Kustomize:** Lets you patch base resources without forking YAML.

Real-World GitOps Setup:

- Repo Structure:

  ```
  k8s-manifests/
    └── base/
    └── overlays/
          ├── dev/
          ├── staging/
          └── prod/
  ```

- ArgoCD syncs each overlay to different clusters/namespaces using one repo.

Deep-Dive Example: ArgoCD for ML Model Deployment

Scenario: A data science team wants to deploy retrained ML models using GitHub.

Why: Manual deployments are slow, error-prone, and difficult to track.

What: Use GitOps to automate model deployment YAMLs via ArgoCD.

When: Every time a new model version is pushed to Git (via CI).

How:

- Push model-serving manifest to Git.
- ArgoCD detects the change.
- Syncs changes to deploy the model on K8s.
- Enables rollback to the previous version via Git commit.

Flux as an Alternative GitOps Tool:

- **Flux** uses controllers such as **source-controller**, **kustomize-controller**, and **helm-controller**.
- Designed for GitOps pipelines and lightweight environments.

Flux Setup Sample:

```
flux install
flux create source git app-repo \
--url=https://github.com/myorg/k8s-manifests --branch=main
flux create kustomization app-deploy \
--source=app-repo --path="./prod" --interval=1m
```

Real-World GitOps Example: Multi-Environment Deployment

Case Study: Multi-Stage Deployment with GitOps

Scenario: A fintech company wants to deploy a payment API across dev, staging, and prod.

- Branch-based Git strategy (**`dev` → `staging` → `main`**).
- ArgoCD watches each branch and syncs respective clusters.
- Application version promotion is done by **merging PRs**, not running scripts.

Outcome:

- Clear audit trails.
- RBAC control over who merges to production.
- Developers can deploy by pushing to Git.

Anti-Patterns to Avoid:

Anti-Pattern	**Why It is Bad**
GitOps controller pushing to Git	Breaks pull model
Storing Secrets in Git	Serious security issue
Manual changes to live cluster	Causes Git drift
Large YAML duplication	Use Kustomize or Helm

***Table* 5.5**: *Anti-Patterns to Avoid and Why it is Bad*

Final Thoughts and Key Takeaways:

- GitOps transforms Kubernetes deployment into a **secure, version-controlled, and auditable** process.
- ArgoCD and Flux provide flexible GitOps automation; choose based on team maturity and ecosystem needs.
- The best practice is to separate environments (**`dev/staging/prod`**) with branch-based or path-based strategies.
- A well-structured GitOps system reduces outages, improves DevOps velocity, and boosts confidence in deployment automation.

ArgoCD and Flux are foundational GitOps tools that enable secure, automated, and scalable deployments in Kubernetes. They simplify complex delivery pipelines, reduce errors, and empower teams to manage infrastructure like code. Choosing the right tool depends on visibility needs, team workflows, and environment constraints. Both offer powerful integrations with GitHub, Helm, and Kustomize to drive continuous delivery in the modern DevOps lifecycle.

Versioning, Rollbacks, and Deployment Automation

Modern cloud-native systems demand not only fast deployments but also safe rollbacks and tight control over versioning. Kubernetes supports all these capabilities natively, and when combined with CI/CD pipelines, teams can deliver software faster while maintaining high reliability.

In this section, we will explore versioning strategies, rollback mechanisms, and various automation techniques for Kubernetes deployments. These practices ensure your workloads remain stable and recoverable, even in complex production environments.

Why are Versioning and Rollback Critical in CI/CD?

Why: In traditional environments, rollback often meant restoring a VM snapshot or redeploying an older build manually. In Kubernetes, failures can be mitigated instantly using declarative version control.

What: Kubernetes deployments allow automated tracking of revisions. This includes:

- Image versioning (tagging)
- Configuration versioning (**`ConfigMaps`**, **`Secrets`**)
- Deployment revisions (via **`ReplicaSets`**)

When: Rollbacks become critical:

- After failed canary/blue-green rollouts.
- During incident response (bugs, regressions).
- When infra/config changes break compatibility.

How: Kubernetes enables rolling deployments and maintains a history of ReplicaSets, which can be instantly rolled back using **`kubectl rollout undo`** or via GitOps.

Deployment Strategies

Kubernetes supports multiple deployment techniques that align with automation and safety.

- **Rolling Update (default)**
  - Updates Pods in batches
  - Minimizes downtime
  - Can auto rollback on failure (using readiness probes)
- **Blue-Green Deployment**
  - Deploys new version alongside the existing one
  - Routes traffic to new deployment after validation
  - Rollback is a simple DNS switch
- **Canary Deployment**
  - Routes partial traffic to new Pods
  - Gradual rollout based on metrics (error rate, latency)
  - Suitable for high-risk changes

YAML Lab: Safe Rolling Deployment with Revisions

```
apiVersion: apps/v1
kind: Deployment
metadata:
  name: payment-service
spec:
  replicas: 3
  selector:
    matchLabels:
      app: payment
  strategy:
```

```
      type: RollingUpdate
      rollingUpdate:
        maxUnavailable: 1
        maxSurge: 1
    template:
      metadata:
        labels:
          app: payment
      spec:
        containers:
        - name: payment-container
          image: registry.example.com/payment:v1.0.3
          ports:
          - containerPort: 8080
```

After applying this:

To check history, use:

- `kubectl rollout history deployment/payment-service`

To rollback, use:

- `kubectl rollout undo deployment/payment-service`

Automating Rollbacks Based on Health Checks

Example Scenario: During a deployment, new Pods fail health checks. Kubernetes marks them as unready. Monitoring tools (Prometheus, Argo Rollouts) detect the issue and initiate rollback.

Tool Integration:

- **`Prometheus Alert`** > **`Argo Rollouts`** > **`Trigger rollback`** via webhook
- Jenkins pipeline **`detects failure`** > triggers **`kubectl rollout undo`**

Real-World Case Study: Rollback in Production

Company: FinServe Inc. (a fintech company handling live financial transactions)

Problem: A config error in v1.2.4 of payment-service caused 5% payment failures.

Approach:

- Canary deployment detected high latency on new pods
- Alert triggered rollback via Jenkins pipeline
- Switched back to v1.2.3 within 3 minutes

Outcome:

- No full outage
- 95% of users unaffected
- Confidence in CI/CD and GitOps processes increased

The following figure represents the Automated Rollback Architecture:

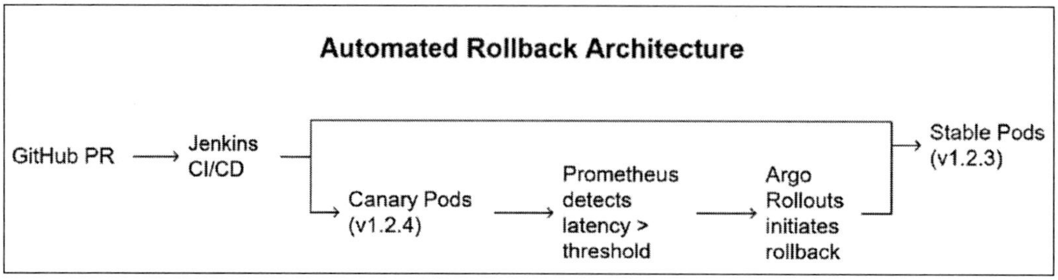

Figure 5.8: *Automated Rollback Architecture*

Figure 5.8 illustrates a **self-healing deployment pipeline** where **automated rollbacks** are triggered in case of performance degradation in canary releases. This is a modern DevOps pattern combining **progressive delivery**, **observability**, and **deployment orchestration** to minimize risk in production environments.

Step-by-Step Explanation:

1. **GitHub PR (Pull Request)**
    a. The process begins when a developer raises a Pull Request in **GitHub** to merge new code into the main branch.
    b. This triggers the **CI/CD pipeline**, initiating the build and deployment sequence.
    c. This ensures the new version (for example, v1.2.4) goes through automated validation steps such as linting, testing, and building.
2. **Jenkins CI/CD Pipeline**
    a. **Jenkins**, a popular automation server, executes the CI/CD pipeline triggered by the GitHub PR.
    b. The pipeline builds the application, runs tests, and then prepares it for deployment.
    c. Instead of deploying the new version to all users, it first deploys to a small subset via **canary deployment**.
3. **Canary Pods (v1.2.4)**
    a. **Canary Pods** are lightweight instances of the new version (v1.2.4) deployed alongside the existing stable version (v1.2.3).
    b. Only a small percentage of live traffic is routed to these canary pods.
    c. This strategy allows real-user feedback and performance monitoring on the new release without exposing all users to potential failures.
4. **Prometheus Detects Latency > Threshold**
    a. **Prometheus**, an open-source monitoring tool, continuously scrapes metrics (for example, request latency, error rate) from the canary pods.
    b. If it detects that **latency exceeds a defined threshold**, it flags the release as potentially unstable.
    c. Prometheus is usually integrated with **Alert manager** to trigger alerts or custom actions.

5. **Argo Rollouts Initiates Rollback**
   a. **Argo Rollouts** is a Kubernetes controller for managing progressive delivery strategies such as canary, blue-green, and more.
   b. Upon receiving the alert from Prometheus (through metrics-based checks), Argo Rollouts **automatically triggers a rollback**.
   c. It halts the deployment of the new version and reverts to the last known stable version.
6. **Stable Pods (v1.2.3)**
   a. The system is rolled back to the **stable pods running version v1.2.3**.
   b. These pods continue serving all user traffic while issues with v1.2.4 are investigated.
   c. This rollback is seamless, and minimizes downtime or user disruption.

Best Practices:

- Always tag container images (v1.0.5), and avoid using latest.
- Store YAMLs and Jenkinsfiles in Git with proper versioning.
- Use health checks and monitoring to automate rollbacks.
- Limit downtime using blue-green or canary techniques.
- Rollback should be treated as a first-class citizen in pipeline design.

Key Benefits of this Architecture:

Feature	Description
Progressive Delivery	Deploys new versions to a small subset of users to reduce blast radius.
Observability-Driven	Relies on Prometheus metrics to validate deployment health in real-time.
Automation First	Jenkins, Prometheus, and Argo Rollouts work in harmony to eliminate manual intervention.
Risk Mitigation	Failures are auto-detected and rolled back without human involvement.
Faster Iteration	Enables rapid deployment cycles with confidence and built-in safety checks.

Table 5.6: *Key Benefits of Automated Role Back Architecture*

Automating Data Ingestion, Transformation, And Deployment Cycles

Continuous Integration with Container Image Builds and Automating Data Pipelines

In a modern DevOps and DataOps environment, Continuous Integration (CI) does not end with code commits and unit testing–it must also cover automated container image builds and end-to-end deployment of data ingestion and transformation pipelines.

For Kubernetes environments, this means ensuring that:

- Code is containerized in real-time with version control.
- Images are tested, tagged, scanned, and pushed to registries.
- Deployment is triggered with zero manual effort.
- Data pipelines (batch, micro-batch, streaming) are orchestrated in sync with CI/CD pipelines.

This section explores real-world approaches to automate container image builds and fully manage the data lifecycle—from ingestion to transformation to deployment—inside Kubernetes-native pipelines.

Why does this problem exist?

Traditional CI pipelines often stop after application build and testing. However, **data engineers and cloud architects** face new challenges:

- **No end-to-end automation** of data pipelines—ETL jobs are often deployed manually.
- **Delays in containerization** of code changes result in slower delivery.
- **Manual image versioning** and deployments increase risk in production.
- **Inconsistent environments** between dev, staging, and prod due to a lack of container orchestration.

Solution

A robust CI/CD setup should:

- Automate **container image builds** using GitHub Actions or Jenkins pipelines.
- Push signed and scanned images to secure registries (DockerHub, ECR, GCR).
- Trigger Kubernetes deployments or ArgoCD rollouts on image change.
- Containerize and deploy **data ingestion, transformation**, and orchestration tools such as:
  - Apache NiFi, Spark, Flink, Kafka Connect
  - Airflow DAGs for ETL pipelines

When should this be applied?

Apply CI for image builds and deployment automation when:

- You have **frequent code changes** in microservices or ETL logic.
- Teams need **zero-touch container rollout** across dev → test → prod.
- Real-time data processing and ingestion need consistent deployments.
- Image security, auditability, and rollback are mandatory.

How do we implement this?

Step 1: Automating Image Builds on Code Push

GitHub Actions Workflow – Auto-Build on Push

```yaml
yaml

name: Build and Push Container

on:
  push:
    branches:
      - main

jobs:
  build:
    runs-on: ubuntu-latest
    steps:
    - name: Checkout
      uses: actions/checkout@v3
```

```
    - name: Set up Docker
      uses: docker/setup-buildx-action@v2

    - name: Login to DockerHub
      uses: docker/login-action@v2
      with:
        username: ${{ secrets.DOCKER_USERNAME }}
        password: ${{ secrets.DOCKER_PASSWORD }}

    - name: Build and Push
      run: |
        docker build -t myrepo/data-etl:latest .
        docker push myrepo/data-etl:latest
```

Step 2: Containerizing Data Ingestion Pipeline (Kafka Connect Example)

```
Dockerfile

FROM confluentinc/cp-kafka-connect:latest

COPY connector-configs /etc/kafka-connect/

ENV CONNECT_BOOTSTRAP_SERVERS=kafka:9092
ENV CONNECT_GROUP_ID=etl-group

CMD ["connect-distributed", "/etc/kafka-connect/connect-distributed.properties"]
```

Step 3: Auto-Deploy on Image Push Using ArgoCD or Flux

ArgoCD **application.yaml** configured to watch for new tags:

```
yaml


apiVersion: argoproj.io/v1alpha1
kind: Application
metadata:
  name: etl-pipeline
spec:
  destination:
    server: https://kubernetes.default.svc
    namespace: data-pipelines
  source:
    repoURL: https://github.com/myorg/etl-deployment
    path: manifests/
    targetRevision: HEAD
  syncPolicy:
    automated:
      prune: true
      selfHeal: true
```

The following figure represents CI/CD Workflow for Data Pipeline Automation:

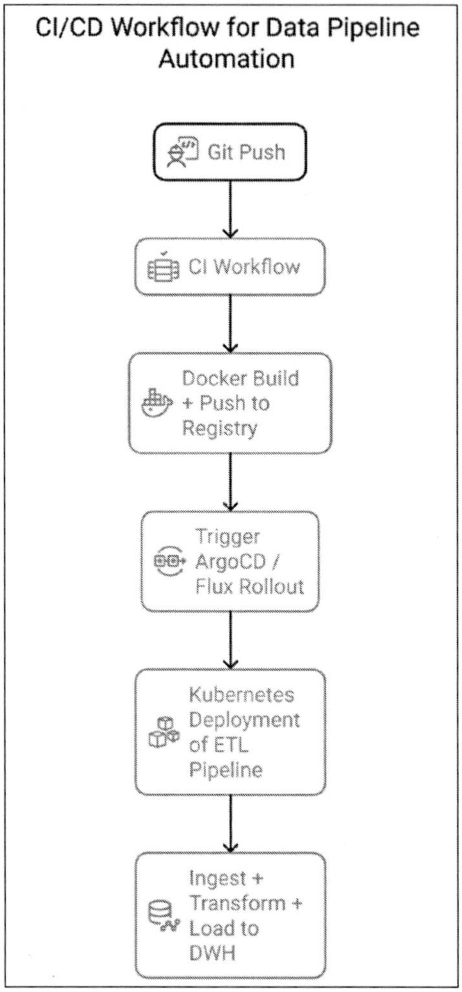

Figure 5.9: *CI/CD Workflow for Data Pipeline Automation*

CI/CD Workflow for Data Pipeline Automation

Figure 5.9 illustrates a modern, automated workflow for deploying and managing data pipelines using CI/CD practices. It integrates version control, containerization, orchestration, and continuous deployment to ensure reliable and repeatable data pipeline execution from code push to data warehouse ingestion.

Step-by-Step Explanation:

1. **Git Push**
    a. **Description:** The workflow begins when a developer or data engineer pushes code to a Git repository (for example, GitHub, GitLab, Bitbucket).
    b. **Purpose:** This code could include ETL logic, configuration files, or infrastructure-as-code scripts for data pipelines.
    c. **Significance:** Git serves as the **single source of truth**, enabling version control, traceability, and collaborative development.

2. **CI Workflow**
    a. **Description:** The Continuous Integration (CI) pipeline is automatically triggered upon a Git push. CI tools such as **GitHub Actions**, **GitLab CI**, **Jenkins**, or **CircleCI** come into play here.
    b. **Tasks Performed:**
        i. Linting and syntax validation
        ii. Unit and integration tests for data transformations
        iii. Code quality checks
    c. **Significance:** Ensures that only valid, tested code proceeds further in the pipeline. It enforces code hygiene and reduces the risk of runtime errors in production.
3. **Docker Build + Push to Registry**
    a. **Description:** Once the code passes all checks, it is containerized using Docker.
    b. **Process:**
        i. A Docker image is built from the ETL pipeline code.
        ii. The image is tagged with a unique version or commit hash.
        iii. It is then pushed to a Docker registry (for example, DockerHub, AWS ECR, Azure ACR, or GCP GCR).
    c. **Significance:**
        a. Containerization ensures environment consistency across development, testing, and production.
        b. Versioned images support rollback and reproducibility.
4. **Trigger ArgoCD / Flux Rollout**
    a. **Description**: The Continuous Deployment (CD) process begins here. Tools such as **ArgoCD** or **Flux** monitor Git repositories for changes to Kubernetes manifests or Helm charts.
    b. **Trigger Mechanism**:
        i. When the updated container image or configuration is pushed, ArgoCD/Flux detects the change.
        ii. It initiates a deployment rollout based on GitOps principles.
    c. **Significance**:
        i. This makes deployments declarative, auditable, and controlled.
        ii. Promotes a **GitOps-based deployment** model, minimizing manual intervention.
5. **Kubernetes Deployment of ETL Pipeline**
    a. **Description**: The ETL (Extract, Transform, Load) pipeline is deployed as Kubernetes workloads–typically as **Jobs**, **CronJobs**, or **Airflow DAGs**–depending on the orchestration design.
    b. **Infrastructure**:
        i. Kubernetes manages the container lifecycle, scalability, fault tolerance, and resource allocation.

c. **Significance**:

i. Provides scalability and resilience.

ii. Decouples compute and storage, enabling distributed and parallel data processing.

6. **Ingest + Transform + Load to DWH**

a. **Description:** Once deployed, the pipeline performs its core data tasks:

i. **Ingest:** Pull data from sources such as APIs, files, databases, or streams.

ii. **Transform:** Cleanse, enrich, and reshape the data using business logic.

iii. **Load:** Write the processed data into a Data Warehouse (DWH) such as **Snowflake**, **BigQuery**, **Redshift**, or **Azure Synapse**.

b. **Significance:**

i. The final stage ensures that data is ready for analytics, reporting, and ML workflows.

ii. Automation guarantees consistency and freshness of data without human intervention.

The following table lists the benefits of this CI/CD Workflow for Data Pipelines:

Benefit	**Description**
Automation	Reduces manual deployment steps and errors.
Consistency	Ensures reliable deployments across environments.
Observability	Each step is traceable, enabling better monitoring and auditing.
Rollback Capability	Failed deployments can be reverted quickly via Git tags or image versions.
Scalability	Kubernetes enables elastic scaling of data processing workloads.

Table 5.7: *Benefits of the CI/CD Workflow for Data Pipelines*

Note: *Integrating data quality checks and metadata logging into this CI/CD workflow can further enhance reliability and observability. Tools such as Great Expectations, OpenLineage, and DataHub can be embedded into the pipeline stages.*

Case Study: Automating a Streaming Data Pipeline in Production

Problem: A retail analytics company needed to **auto-deploy Spark and Kafka connectors** for ingesting streaming sales data from multiple regions in near real-time.

Solution:

- Developers pushed Spark logic and Kafka Connect config to GitHub.
- GitHub Actions built images, ran tests, and pushed them to DockerHub.
- ArgoCD monitored Git repo and applied deployment changes to GKE.
- Grafana and Loki used for centralized monitoring and troubleshooting.

Impact:

- Zero manual deployment effort.
- End-to-end ingestion-to-dashboard pipeline built in under 10 minutes.
- Improved audit trail, version rollback, and team collaboration.

Best Practices:

Area	**Recommendation**
Versioning	Use Git SHA or tags in image tags (for example, etl:v1.2.3)
Security	Scan images with Trivy or Aqua
Data Pipeline	Separate dev/stage/prod pipelines with ArgoCD projects
Secrets	Use sealed secrets or external secret stores (Vault, AWS Secrets Manager)
Resilience	Use liveness/readiness probes, HPA, and retry logic in pipeline containers

***Table 5.8**: Best Practices of Streaming Data Pipeline in Production*

Conclusion

This chapter provided a practical deep dive into implementing CI/CD pipelines within Kubernetes environments using tools such as Jenkins, GitHub Actions, ArgoCD, and Flux. It explained the transition from traditional CI/CD to GitOps-driven, cloud-native automation and covered essential workflows for building, testing, and deploying containerized applications. The chapter showcased how to integrate CI/CD with container image builds, automate versioning and rollbacks, and enforce secure, scalable deployments across environments. Real-world YAML labs, pipeline blueprints, and case studies helped bridge theory with practice. Most importantly, it demonstrated how data engineers and DevOps teams can orchestrate complete data ingestion, transformation, and deployment pipelines using Kubernetes-native CI/CD strategies, ensuring agility, reliability, and observability at scale.

In the next chapter, we will focus on scaling strategies that ensure your applications and data pipelines can handle production-grade workloads. We will explore horizontal and vertical scaling, Kubernetes autoscalers, and performance monitoring techniques to drive intelligent scaling decisions. This chapter is essential for engineers and architects designing systems that must adapt to fluctuating demand, while maintaining high availability and performance.

CHAPTER 6A
Scaling Applications Horizontally and Vertically Part A

Introduction

In this chapter, we will explore the vital concepts and techniques behind scaling applications within Kubernetes. The ability to scale applications efficiently is key to handling increased demand and ensuring optimal performance.

We will cover the basics of both **horizontal scaling** and **vertical scaling**, starting with how to scale applications by adding more instances (horizontal scaling) and then by adjusting resources on individual instances (vertical scaling).

Structure

In this chapter, we will cover the following topics:

- Introduction to Kubernetes Scaling
- Horizontal Scaling with Horizontal Pod Autoscaler (HPA)
- Industry Case Study
- Vertical Scaling with Vertical Pod Autoscaler (VPA)

Scaling in Kubernetes

Modern applications are expected to handle millions of users, terabytes of streaming data, and operate 24/7 without downtime. Kubernetes was built to meet these demands, but the architecture must scale efficiently, both horizontally (adding more pods) and vertically (adding more resources to pods).

The Need for Scaling in Cloud: Native Systems

- Microservices communicate via APIs and often require elasticity.
- Real-time systems demand rapid adaptation to changing loads.
- Cost-efficiency mandates right-sizing both compute and storage.

- Scaling is essential:
  - To maintain performance under load.
  - To ensure high availability.
  - To optimize infrastructure cost.
  - To enable elastic growth in DevOps and data pipelines.

Scalability is not just a feature; it is a survival mechanism in production-grade systems.

Understanding the Types of Scaling in Kubernetes

Let us explore Horizontal and Vertical Scaling to understand scaling types:

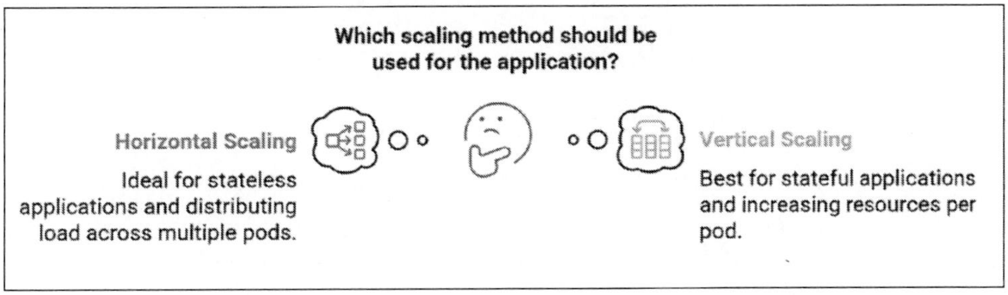

***Figure 6a.1:** Understanding the Types of Scaling in Kubernetes*

Horizontal Scaling versus Vertical Scaling

The following figure illustrates the concepts of Scaling method for Kubernetes deployment:

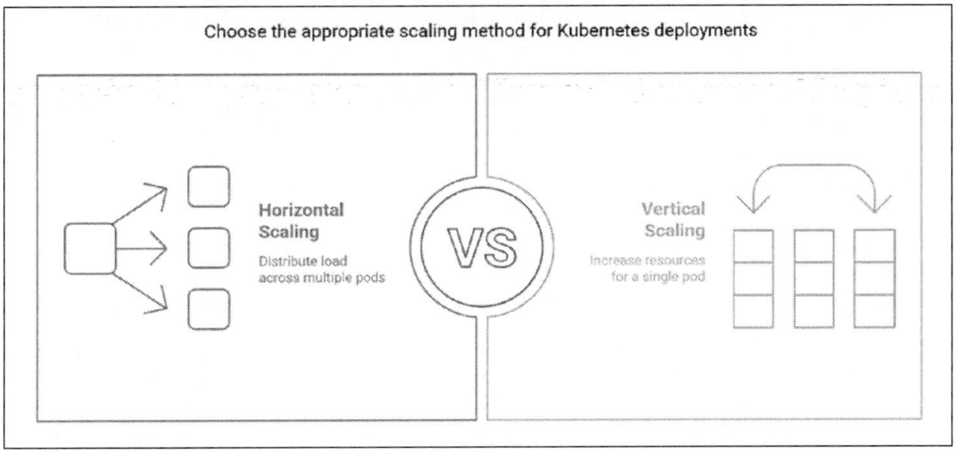

***Figure 6a.2:** Horizontal Scaling versus Vertical Scaling Concepts in Kubernetes*

- **Horizontal Scaling (Scale-out):** Add more replicas/pods to distribute the load.
- **Vertical Scaling (Scale-up):** Allocate more CPU/memory to a single pod.

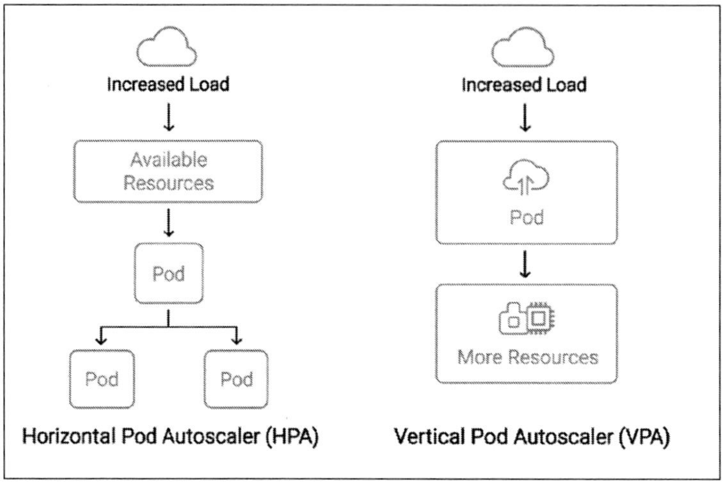

Figure 6a.3: *Horizontal versus Vertical Scaling Concepts*

Defining Horizontal Pod Autoscaler (HPA) and Vertical Pod Autoscaler (VPA)

The preceding figure illustrates the conceptual difference between Horizontal Pod Autoscaler (HPA) and Vertical Pod Autoscaler (VPA), which are two primary scaling strategies used in Kubernetes to handle increased application load.

On the **left side**, the figure represents the working of **Horizontal Pod Autoscaler (HPA)**. When the system detects an increase in load (such as higher CPU or memory utilization), the HPA responds by scaling **horizontally**—it adds more **pods** to distribute the load across multiple instances. Initially, a single pod is running with available resources. As demand grows, the HPA creates additional pod replicas, effectively balancing the incoming traffic or workload among them. This scaling happens without modifying the resources of individual pods but instead focuses on **increasing the quantity of pods** to meet performance requirements. This approach is highly effective for **stateless applications** where each pod can independently handle requests.

On the **right side**, the figure shows the functioning of the **Vertical Pod Autoscaler (VPA)**. Similar to HPA, it starts with a pod responding to an increased load. However, instead of creating new pods, the VPA adjusts the **resource allocation** (CPU, memory) of the existing pod to make it more powerful. This process is known as **vertical scaling** or scaling up. The pod remains a single entity, but with increased resource capacity to handle the additional workload. This is particularly useful for **stateful applications** or workloads that cannot easily be split across multiple pods but instead require more computational power within a single instance. In many cases, increasing resources with VPA may trigger a pod restart to apply the updated configuration.

In summary, the figure effectively compares two scaling mechanisms: HPA focuses on **scaling out** by adding more pods, while VPA focuses on **scaling up** by increasing the resources allocated to a pod. The choice between the two depends on the application's architecture and scaling requirements—HPA suits distributed, stateless workloads, while VPA is preferable for resource-intensive, stateful workloads.

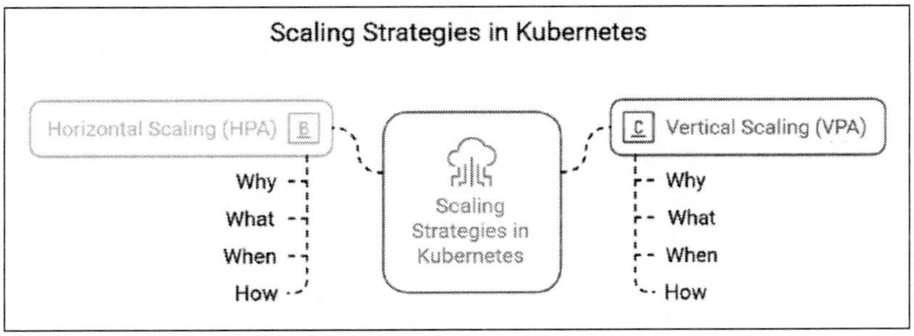

Figure 6a.4: *Scaling Strategies in Kubernetes*

Horizontal Scaling (HPA) allows automatic scaling of pod replicas based on resource usage.

Why: Because Kubernetes pods can only serve a limited number of requests based on CPU/memory/network limits. As traffic grows, a single pod is not enough.

What: Horizontal scaling adds more replicas of the same pod to distribute the load across nodes.

When: Ideal for stateless applications, REST APIs, frontend services, and ingestion layers.

How: Kubernetes uses **Horizontal Pod Autoscaler (HPA)** based on metrics such as CPU, memory, or custom Prometheus metrics to scale pod replicas.

YAML Example: HPA Using CPU

```yaml
apiVersion: autoscaling/v2
kind: HorizontalPodAutoscaler
metadata:
  name: api-hpa
spec:
  scaleTargetRef:
    apiVersion: apps/v1
    kind: Deployment
    name: api-deployment
  minReplicas: 2
  maxReplicas: 10
  metrics:
  - type: Resource
    resource:
      name: cpu
      target:
        type: Utilization
        averageUtilization: 60
```

Vertical Scaling (VPA) adjusts the CPU and memory of pods automatically.

Why: Sometimes workloads (for example, Spark, ML model training) need more resources per pod, not more pods.

What: Vertical scaling adjusts the CPU/memory limits of running pods to handle heavier computation inside each pod.

When: Best suited for **stateful applications**, **long-running batch jobs**, or **ML pipelines** that require consistent resource usage.

How: Use **Vertical Pod Autoscaler (VPA)** to monitor usage and automatically update pod resource requests/limits.

YAML Example for VPA

```
apiVersion: autoscaling.k8s.io/v1
kind: VerticalPodAutoscaler
metadata:
  name: ml-vpa
spec:
  targetRef:
    apiVersion: apps/v1
    kind: Deployment
    name: ml-job
  updatePolicy:
    updateMode: Auto
```

Real-Time versus Batch Workload Scaling

- **Real-time:** Requires consistent latency (for example, event-driven APIs, Kafka consumers).
- **Batch:** Needs heavy compute for short durations (for example, Spark ETL jobs).

Use Case Examples: When to Scale What

- **Horizontal (HPA):** REST APIs, frontend microservices, Kafka consumers.
- **Vertical (VPA):** Machine learning inference pods, data transformers.

Batch Workloads

- Run on schedule (for example, hourly/daily ETL).
- Require large but temporary compute (for example, Spark).
- Need vertical scaling + on-demand cluster autoscaling.

Real-Time Workloads

- Constant streaming (such as, Kafka consumers).
- Require **horizontal scaling** for message throughput.
- Benefit from **HPA** + **Cluster Autoscaler** combo.

Scaling in DevOps and Data Workflows

The following table illustrates examples of scaling in DevOps and data workflows:

Scaling Layer	Use Case	Scaling Strategy
CI/CD Pipelines	Jenkins Agents, GitHub Actions	Horizontal scaling of agents using HPA
Streaming Jobs	Kafka, Flink, Spark Streaming	Horizontal pod scaling + partition awareness
Batch ETL	Nightly Spark jobs	Vertical scaling + node pool provisioning
Data Ingestion	Airflow, Logstash, Debezium	Mixed: HPA + storage scaling

***Table 6a.1**: Scaling in DevOps and Data Workflows with Use Case and Scaling Strategy*

Scaling Decision Framework

Understanding Kubernetes Scaling Strategies

The following figure provides a clear visual representation of the two primary scaling approaches in Kubernetes: Horizontal Scaling and Vertical Scaling. It outlines the decision-making process that occurs when scaling needs are identified in a Kubernetes environment.

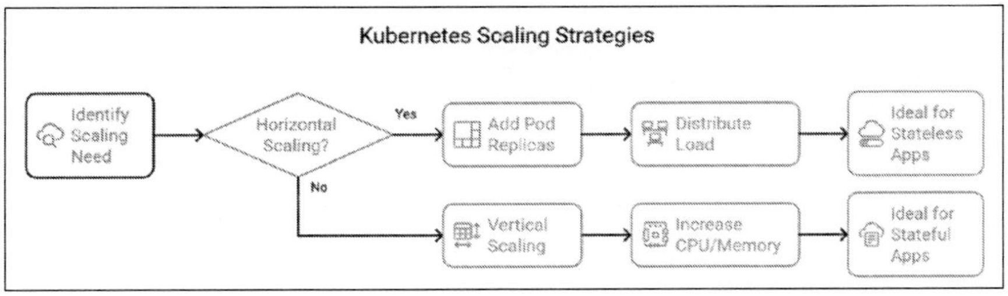

***Figure 6a.5**: Scaling Strategy Decision Flow – Identify Scaling Needs*

At the starting point, the system or operator first identifies a scaling need–this is triggered by factors such as increased traffic, higher resource utilization, or performance degradation. Once a scaling requirement is detected, a key decision must be made: **"Should the application be scaled horizontally or vertically?"** This choice depends on the application's design, architecture, and scalability characteristics.

If the answer is **"Yes"** to horizontal scaling, the system opts to add more pod replicas. This means creating additional instances of the same pod to share the workload across multiple pods. As a result, the load is effectively **distributed** among these pods, improving the application's ability to handle increased demand. This strategy is particularly **ideal for stateless applications**, where any pod can independently process requests without relying on shared or persistent internal state. Examples include web servers, REST APIs, and microservices, where requests can be handled by any replica.

On the other hand, if the answer is **"No"** to horizontal scaling, the system moves toward vertical scaling. Instead of adding more pods, vertical scaling involves increasing the resource capacity (CPU, memory) allocated to an existing pod, making it more powerful. This approach is beneficial when the application cannot be easily distributed across multiple pods, typically in **stateful applications** that maintain internal state or require a single instance to process transactions or hold data. Examples include databases or applications with session-based data that cannot be shared across multiple replicas without significant complexity.

In essence, the figure maps out a simple yet critical scaling decision tree:

- Identify the scaling need.
- **Decide between horizontal and vertical scaling.**
- For horizontal scaling: add pods → distribute load → ideal for stateless apps.
- For vertical scaling: increase resources → strengthen pod → ideal for stateful apps.

This decision flow helps Kubernetes administrators and architects choose the right scaling strategy based on application type and system requirements. By understanding this process, teams can ensure optimal resource utilization, application performance, and cost efficiency in their Kubernetes deployments.

Kubernetes Scaling Strategy Decision Flow: A Practical Framework

The following figure presents a **structured decision-making flowchart** for selecting the right scaling strategy in Kubernetes based on the nature of the application. It guides Kubernetes administrators and architects through a logical sequence of choices, helping them align scaling mechanisms with application characteristics for optimal performance and resource efficiency.

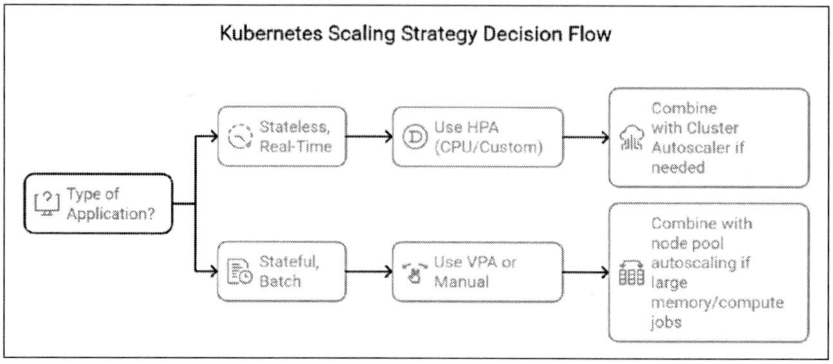

Figure 6a.6: *Kubernetes Scaling Decision Framework*

At the core of this decision flow lies the **"Type of Application"**—the first and most critical factor to evaluate when determining how to scale. Applications in Kubernetes broadly fall under two categories:

- Stateless, Real-Time Applications
- Stateful, Batch Applications

Stateless, Real-Time Applications

Stateless applications do not maintain any client session or internal state across requests. Examples include web servers, REST APIs, and microservices handling independent transactions. These applications are highly scalable horizontally because each instance (pod) can handle any incoming request without relying on a shared state.

For such applications, the recommended scaling approach is to use:

- **Horizontal Pod Autoscaler (HPA):** HPA automatically adjusts the number of pod replicas based on observed CPU utilization or other custom metrics (for example, memory, queue length, application-specific indicators). This allows the application to dynamically respond to fluctuating workloads.

If further scaling is needed beyond pods (that is, the cluster runs out of nodes to schedule new pods), the flow recommends combining HPA with:

- **Cluster Autoscaler:** Cluster Autoscaler automatically adds (or removes) nodes in the cluster to accommodate additional pods that cannot be scheduled due to resource constraints. This ensures that horizontal scaling at the pod level is not bottlenecked by the underlying infrastructure.

Flow Summary:

- Stateless → HPA (CPU/Custom Metrics) → +Cluster Autoscaler if more nodes required

Stateful, Batch Applications

Stateful applications maintain persistent data or session information, requiring pods to preserve state across transactions. Examples include databases, stateful workloads, or batch processing systems. These applications are less suited for horizontal scaling due to the complexity of distributing state.

For these workloads, the figure recommends:

- **Vertical Pod Autoscaler (VPA)** or **Manual Resource Adjustment:** VPA automatically recommends or applies changes to pod CPU and memory requests/limits based on observed usage patterns. Alternatively, administrators may manually fine-tune resources if autoscaling introduces risk or unpredictability.

However, stateful/batch workloads may still encounter limits where a single node's capacity is insufficient. To accommodate jobs needing very large memory or compute power, the flow advises combining vertical scaling with:

- **Node Pool Autoscaling:** This involves using node pools (groups of nodes with specific hardware profiles) and enabling autoscaling at the node pool level to add nodes with higher capacity. For example, a large-memory node pool might be scaled up to run data-intensive batch jobs that exceed standard node resources.

Flow Summary:

- Stateful → VPA or Manual Scaling → +Node Pool Autoscaling for large jobs

Why This Decision Flow Matters?

This decision flowchart provides an operationally practical framework by:

- Aligning scaling strategies to application statefulness and workload patterns.
- Highlighting combinatory scaling techniques (for example, combining HPA with Cluster Autoscaler or VPA with Node Pool Autoscaler).
- Promoting cost-effective scaling by using resources only as needed, instead of overprovisioning.
- Simplifying Kubernetes scaling complexity into an actionable step-by-step guide.

It underscores that there is no "one-size-fits-all" scaling solution in Kubernetes; rather, the right approach must account for both application architecture and infrastructure limitations.

- The flow helps engineers choose HPA or VPA based on the workload nature.
- For stateless workloads, prefer Horizontal Pod Autoscaling (HPA).
- For stateful or batch workloads, vertical scaling and proper node provisioning become critical.
- In both cases, Cluster Autoscaler ensures that the underlying infrastructure is elastic.

Industry Case Study: Scaling Strategy in a Large-Scale Retail Analytics Platform

In this case study, we examine how a retail analytics company successfully implemented a multi-faceted Kubernetes scaling strategy to support a highly diverse workload comprising over 5,000 microservices. The platform was designed to handle **real-time data ingestion**, **batch-oriented machine learning workflows**, and **orchestrated ETL pipelines using Airflow**. This combination of workload types presented unique scaling challenges across application layers.

Scenario Overview

The company operates a modern data analytics ecosystem with three major workload categories:

- **Real-Time Log Ingestion:** Responsible for collecting and processing high-velocity data streams from retail systems, requiring low latency and continuous availability.
- **Machine Learning (ML) Workloads:** Running scheduled retraining of predictive models on large datasets, characterized by compute and memory-intensive batch jobs.
- **Airflow ETL Pipelines:** Executing complex, multi-step data workflows using Directed Acyclic Graphs (DAGs) for scheduled data transformation and loading.

Each of these workloads has distinct scaling characteristics, necessitating **tailored scaling strategies** rather than a one-size-fits-all approach.

Solution Design

The engineering team implemented a **layered scaling approach** that aligned Kubernetes scaling primitives with the workload requirements of each application type:

- **Real-Time Ingestion Layer: Horizontal Pod Autoscaler (HPA)**
  - For the real-time log ingestion services, the team deployed a **Horizontal Pod Autoscaler (HPA)** configured with **CPU-based thresholds**. Since these services are stateless and require rapid adjustment to variable input rates, HPA enables automatic scaling of pods based on CPU utilization.
  - Why HPA?

    CPU usage serves as a direct indicator of workload stress in ingestion pipelines. As ingestion rates spike, CPU utilization increases, triggering HPA to provision more pods to handle the load without latency degradation.
  - **Outcome:** Ensured **elastic scaling** to match real-time traffic patterns, preventing data loss or ingestion lag.
- **Airflow DAG Runners: Vertical Pod Autoscaler (VPA)**
  - The Airflow scheduler and worker pods responsible for running DAGs were scaled using a **Vertical Pod Autoscaler (VPA)** with **memory-based adjustments.**
  - **Why VPA?**

    Airflow tasks are often memory-bound rather than CPU-intensive. DAG execution failures were frequently traced back to insufficient memory allocation rather than compute bottlenecks. By enabling VPA, the system automatically adjusted memory requests/limits based on historical and real-time usage metrics.
  - **Result:** Achieved higher task completion reliability without overprovisioning all pods upfront.
- **Machine Learning Model Retraining: Dedicated High-Memory Node Pool**
  - ML retraining workloads were scheduled onto a **dedicated node pool configured with high-memory instances**. Instead of relying solely on autoscalers to manage pod-level resources, the team statically allocated ML retraining jobs to nodes capable of supporting large in-memory datasets.
  - Why a dedicated node pool?

    ML training workloads often require **predictable, guaranteed access to large memory resources** that standard nodes could not provide. By isolating these jobs to a specialized node pool, contention with other workloads was avoided, and the risk of resource starvation was minimized.
  - **Scheduling Strategy:** Kubernetes **node affinity and taints/tolerations** ensured that ML pods were scheduled only onto these high-memory nodes.
- **Infrastructure Scaling: Cluster Autoscaler with Spot VMs (GKE)**
  - At the infrastructure level, the company leveraged Google Kubernetes Engine (GKE) with Cluster Autoscaler enabled to automatically scale the number of nodes in the cluster based on pending pod scheduling needs. Additionally, they utilized preemptible (spot) VMs to reduce infrastructure costs without sacrificing availability for fault-tolerant workloads.
  - **Why Spot VMs?**

    Non-critical or retriable workloads (such as batch ML training and background data loads) were excellent candidates for cost-optimized, short-lived compute resources.

- **Outcome:** Achieved significant cost savings while maintaining workload execution guarantees for stateless and non-latency-sensitive jobs.

Unified Monitoring and Observability

To ensure transparency and proactive scaling management, the company implemented **Prometheus** for metrics collection and **Grafana** for dashboard visualization. This allowed operators and developers to monitor:

- Scaling events (both pod and node level)
- Resource utilization trends
- Trigger thresholds for autoscalers
- Health of ingestion, DAG, and ML pipelines

By unifying monitoring across application and infrastructure layers, the team could continuously refine scaling thresholds and parameters based on empirical evidence.

Outcomes Achieved

The multi-layer scaling strategy resulted in measurable improvements across operational and financial metrics:

- **32% reduction in cloud infrastructure costs:** Achieved through optimized autoscaling policies and the use of cost-effective spot VMs for suitable workloads.
- **Improved SLA compliance to 99.99%:** Scaling bottlenecks and resource starvation were eliminated, leading to more predictable and reliable service availability.
- **Operational simplicity via centralized observability:** Monitoring dashboards provided a single pane of glass to track scaling behavior, and identify anomalies early.

Key Lessons and Takeaways:

- **Different workloads require different scaling strategies.** No single Kubernetes autoscaler addresses all workload types; combining HPA, VPA, cluster autoscaling, and node pool specialization yields optimal results.
- **Observability is integral to scaling success.** Without metrics-driven monitoring, scaling thresholds may be misaligned with real-world demands.
- **Cost efficiency and SLA improvements are not mutually exclusive.** With thoughtful scaling architecture, organizations can achieve both financial savings and higher service reliability.

This case study illustrates the **power of customized, workload-aware scaling strategies in Kubernetes environments.** By aligning scaling mechanisms with application patterns and leveraging the right tools at each layer, organizations can simultaneously achieve **resilience, cost efficiency, and operational simplicity**—even at the scale of thousands of microservices.

Horizontal Scaling with HPA

Kubernetes was designed with **horizontal scaling** as a primary mechanism to handle load variations. Applications that need to serve unpredictable or bursty traffic patterns benefit from the ability to add more replicas dynamically without human intervention.

In production systems, scaling decisions **cannot rely on static configuration**. The Horizontal Pod Autoscaler (HPA) enables applications to self-adjust based on observed metrics such as CPU, memory, or custom Prometheus metrics.

Scaling is not just adding pods—it is about **balancing performance, cost, and availability automatically**.

Working of Horizontal Pod Autoscaler

Let us break this down:

- **Why:**
  - To ensure **application responsiveness under load.**
  - To avoid **over-provisioning resources upfront.**
  - To **reduce manual intervention** in scaling decisions.
  - To enable **elastic scaling** based on real-time demand.
- **What:**
  - HPA is a **Kubernetes controller** that monitors specific metrics and adjusts the **replica count** of a Deployment, StatefulSet, or ReplicaSet accordingly.
  - Default metrics are **CPU utilization** and **memory utilization**, but it can also use **custom metrics** (for example, request queue length, Prometheus alerts).
- **When:**
  - Ideal for **stateless applications** that can handle requests independently across replicas (for example, web servers, APIs, ingestion pipelines).
  - Use when application performance is **directly tied to request load.**
  - Not suitable for **stateful apps without replication support.**
- **How**
  - HPA controller queries the metrics server at a defined interval (default: 15 seconds).
  - Compares actual metric (for example, CPU%) with target metric.
  - Calculates desired replicas: `DesiredReplicas = CurrentReplicas * (CurrentMetric / TargetMetric)`
  - Adjusts replica count if the threshold is crossed.
  - Writes the updated replica count to the Deployment or ReplicaSet spec.

Scaling Based on CPU, Memory, and Custom Metrics

Kubernetes offers powerful mechanisms to dynamically adjust application capacity based on real-time workload demands. This elasticity is achieved through autoscaling, where the system automatically increases or decreases the number of pods or resources allocated to a deployment. Scaling decisions can be driven by various metrics, with CPU and memory utilization being the most commonly used default metrics, while custom metrics allow for application-specific or business-driven scaling triggers.

Default Metrics:

- **CPU-Based Scaling:** CPU-based scaling is the **default and most widely adopted scaling metric in Kubernetes.** It relies on monitoring the CPU utilization across pods in a deployment or replica set and adjusting the number of pods accordingly to maintain a target utilization.

  How it works: Kubernetes uses the **Horizontal Pod Autoscaler (HPA)** to monitor average CPU utilization and compares it to a predefined target.

  For example:

  - **Target CPU utilization = 50%** (desired baseline usage)
  - **Observed CPU utilization = 80%** (current workload pressure)

Since the observed value exceeds the target, HPA triggers a **scale-up action**, increasing the number of pods to distribute the CPU load more evenly and bring utilization closer to the target.

Key characteristics of CPU-Based Scaling:

- Well-suited for **CPU-bound applications**, such as compute-intensive APIs, real-time processing pipelines, or data transformation services.
- Responds to workload spikes caused by increased computational needs.
- **Granularity**: scaling is reactive to **averaged metrics** across all pods, not per-pod.

- **Memory-Based Scaling:** Memory-based scaling works similar to CPU-based scaling but uses **memory utilization as the primary scaling signal.** This is particularly valuable for workloads that are constrained by memory availability rather than CPU performance.

  Why memory scaling?

  Certain applications (such as, caching systems, machine learning inference engines, in-memory databases) are highly **memory-dependent**. When these workloads approach their memory limits, failure risks increase (for example, Out-of-Memory (OOM) errors, eviction), requiring scaling actions to avoid service degradation.

  In this model:

  - **Target memory utilization = 70%**
  - **Observed memory utilization = 85%**

  The autoscaler will **scale up pods** to reduce memory pressure and maintain performance stability.

  Considerations:

  - Kubernetes' native HPA **does not support memory-based scaling by default** in some distributions.
  - A **metrics server** that exposes memory metrics must be properly configured for this scaling strategy to work.

- **Custom Metrics-Based Scaling:** In addition to CPU and memory, Kubernetes allows **scaling based on external or application-specific metrics** through the **Custom Metrics API.** This opens up a highly flexible way to scale applications using business logic, operational thresholds, or user-defined signals.

  What are custom metrics?

  Custom metrics can represent any measurable aspect of application health or demand, including but not limited to:

  - **HTTP request rate (requests per second)**: scale up web servers when traffic increases.
  - **Kafka queue length**: scale up consumers to process message backlogs faster.
  - **Database query throughput**: scale read replicas based on query volume.
  - **Business KPIs**: scale depending on domain-specific indicators (for example, number of active shopping carts, and orders placed per minute).

Implementation of Custom Metrics Scaling

To enable custom metrics scaling, Kubernetes requires an **adapter or bridge service** that connects an external monitoring system to the Kubernetes API. A common approach is to use the **Prometheus Adapter**, which exposes Prometheus-collected metrics to the Kubernetes autoscaling API.

How it works in practice:

- Metrics are collected and stored in Prometheus (or another monitoring backend).
- Prometheus Adapter translates specific metrics into a format that Kubernetes HPA can query.
- HPA consumes these metrics and compares them against a scaling threshold.
- Based on the comparison, Kubernetes scales the deployment up or down.

Comparing Scaling Strategies

The following table provides a comparison of scaling strategies with metrics and use cases:

Scaling Metric	Best For	Example Use Cases
CPU	CPU-bound workloads	Web servers, data processing pipelines
Memory	Memory-bound workloads	Caching layers, ML inference, and DB engines
Custom Metrics	Domain-specific scaling triggers	Web traffic scaling, message queues

Table 6a.2: *Comparing Scaling Strategies with Metrics and Use Cases*

Benefits of Metric-Driven Scaling:

- **Improved Resource Efficiency:** Scale only when metrics justify it, avoiding overprovisioning.
- **Higher Application Reliability:** Proactive scaling prevents resource exhaustion under load.
- **Alignment with Business KPIs:** Custom metrics enable scaling aligned with real-world demand, not just infrastructure health.

Important Considerations:

- CPU and memory metrics are **available out of the box**, but **custom metrics require extra setup** (metrics adapters, monitoring pipelines).
- Scaling decisions should consider **metric granularity, collection frequency, and delay** to avoid oscillations or lag in scaling responses.
- Overly aggressive scaling thresholds can lead to unnecessary scaling events and cost increases; tuning is critical.

Scaling in Kubernetes is **not limited to infrastructure metrics such as CPU and memory**—it can extend to **application-specific metrics via custom metrics integration**, allowing organizations to design highly responsive and business-aligned scaling strategies. Thus, by selecting the appropriate scaling metric for each workload, platforms can achieve a balance between **performance, reliability, and cost-efficiency.**

Hands-On YAML Lab: Deploying Horizontal Pod Autoscaler in Kubernetes

In this lab, we will walk through a **practical example of configuring and deploying a Horizontal Pod Autoscaler (HPA)** for a Node.js API running on Kubernetes. This will help readers understand the end-to-end process of setting up autoscaling based on CPU utilization.

Let us break it down step by step.

Scenario Overview

Imagine you have deployed a **Node.js API service named** my-api in a Kubernetes cluster. Initially, you want it to run **2 replicas** to ensure availability. However, you also want the system to **automatically**

scale up to 10 replicas, if CPU demand increases, ensuring that your API can handle traffic spikes without manual intervention.

You also aim to optimize resource consumption by **scaling back down to 2 replicas** during low traffic periods.

The goal is to maintain an **average CPU utilization of 60%** across all running pods.

Key objectives:

- Scale **up to 10 pods** when CPU usage is high.
- Scale **down to 2 pods** when CPU usage is low.
- Maintain CPU utilization around **60%**.

Step 1: Defining the Deployment YAML

We first define a Kubernetes **Deployment** resource to manage our Node.js API pods.

```yaml
yaml

apiVersion: apps/v1
kind: Deployment
metadata:
  name: my-api
spec:
  replicas: 2
  selector:
    matchLabels:
      app: my-api
  template:
    metadata:
      labels:
        app: my-api
    spec:
      containers:
      - name: my-api
        image: myregistry/my-api:latest
        resources:
          requests:
            cpu: "100m"
            memory: "128Mi"
          limits:
            cpu: "500m"
            memory: "512Mi"
        ports:
        - containerPort: 3000
```

Explanation of the key fields:

- **`replicas: 2`**: Starts with 2 pods.
- **`resources.requests`**: Reserves **100m (0.1 CPU)** and **128Mi memory** per pod as a baseline guarantee.
- **`resources.limits`**: Caps usage at **500m CPU** and **512Mi memory** per pod.
- **`image`**: Points to the container image hosted in **`myregistry`**.
- **`selector`** and **`labels`**: Used by Kubernetes to manage which pods belong to this deployment.

Why set resource requests and limits?

HPA uses **CPU utilization relative to requests.cpu** as the basis for scaling. Without defined resource requests, the HPA would not know what "100%" utilization represents.

Step 2: Defining the Horizontal Pod Autoscaler (HPA) YAML

Next, we create an HPA resource to manage autoscaling based on CPU utilization.

```
yaml

apiVersion: autoscaling/v2
kind: HorizontalPodAutoscaler
metadata:
  name: my-api-hpa
spec:
  scaleTargetRef:
    apiVersion: apps/v1
    kind: Deployment
    name: my-api
  minReplicas: 2
  maxReplicas: 10
  metrics:
  - type: Resource
    resource:
      name: cpu
      target:
        type: Utilization
        averageUtilization: 60
```

Explanation of key fields:

- **`scaleTargetRef`:** Points to the **my-api deployment** we want to scale.
- **`minReplicas`: 2:** Never scale below 2 pods.
- **`maxReplicas: 10`:** Never scale above 10 pods.
- **`metrics`:** Defines the scaling metric.
  - **`type: Resource`:** Scaling is based on a built-in resource metric.
  - **`resource.name: cpu`:** We are scaling based on CPU.
  - **`target.averageUtilization: 60`:** Target CPU utilization per pod is **60% of the requested CPU**.

What happens internally?

- Kubernetes measures the average CPU usage across all pods.
- If the **average exceeds 60%**, it increases the number of pods to reduce the load per pod.
- If the **average drops below 60%**, it reduces the number of pods to conserve resources.

Step 3: Applying the YAML Files

Finally, we deploy both resources to Kubernetes using kubectl:

```
bash

kubectl apply -f my-api-deployment.yaml
kubectl apply -f my-api-hpa.yaml
```

Explanation:

- The deployment starts running **2 replicas** of the Node.js API.
- The HPA controller **monitors pod CPU usage every 15 seconds** (default interval).
- Scaling decisions are made automatically by Kubernetes based on observed CPU metrics.
- If utilization exceeds 60%, it increases replicas (up to 10).
- If utilization drops below 60%, it scales down (not below 2 replicas).

How It Works in Practice?

Once deployed, the **Horizontal Pod Autoscaler continuously monitors CPU utilization** reported by the Kubernetes metrics server.

Example behavior:

The following table explains the Average CPU utilization with actions:

Average CPU Utilization	Action Taken	Number of Pods
55%	No scaling (near target)	2
75%	Scale up	3 or more
95%	Scale up aggressively	4-6+
40%	Scale down	back to 2

Table 6a.3: *CPU Usage Utilization with Actions*

Each time Kubernetes checks CPU utilization:

- If usage exceeds **60%**, more pods are added (but not exceeding 10).
- If usage drops below **60%**, pods are reduced (but never below 2).

This automated elasticity ensures:

- Consistent performance under load.
- Reduced resource waste during quiet periods.

Why This Approach Matters?

Autoscaling is critical for modern, cloud-native applications that experience **variable traffic patterns.** Rather than manually resizing deployments, Kubernetes can dynamically adjust the number of pods based on **real-time usage metrics.**

Key benefits:

- **Improved application availability** under spikes.
- **Optimized cost efficiency** (no overprovisioning).
- **Minimal operational overhead** (hands-off scaling).

Important Notes for Readers:

- **Metrics Server Required:** For HPA to function, a **Kubernetes metrics server** must be installed and configured to provide resource metrics such as CPU and memory.
- **Scaling Granularity:** Scaling actions may take a few minutes to stabilize, depending on:
  - Metric collection intervals
  - Pod startup time
  - Application readiness

- **Resource Requests Mandatory:** Always define **`resources.requests.cpu`** for containers. Without it, HPA cannot calculate a meaningful percentage for CPU utilization.

This hands-on example demonstrates how Kubernetes autoscaling can be implemented with just **two YAML files**, enabling your applications to **automatically scale between 2 and 10 pods based on CPU usage, targeting 60% utilization.**

It showcases how Kubernetes' simple yet powerful declarative scaling empowers developers and operators to build **resilient, responsive, and cost-effective cloud-native applications.**

HPA Trigger Lifecycle

The **Horizontal Pod Autoscaler (HPA)** in Kubernetes automatically scales the number of pods in a deployment, replica set, or stateful set based on observed metrics such as CPU utilization or custom metrics. The following figure illustrates the lifecycle or flow of how an HPA trigger works from the initial increase in load to the point where Kubernetes schedules new pods.

- User requests increase → application load increases.
- Pods experience higher CPU utilization → the metrics server observes metrics.
- HPA retrieves metrics → checks against target utilization.
- HPA calculates required replicas → updates the deployment.
- Kubernetes schedules additional pods to new nodes if needed (triggers the cluster autoscaler if nodes are exhausted).

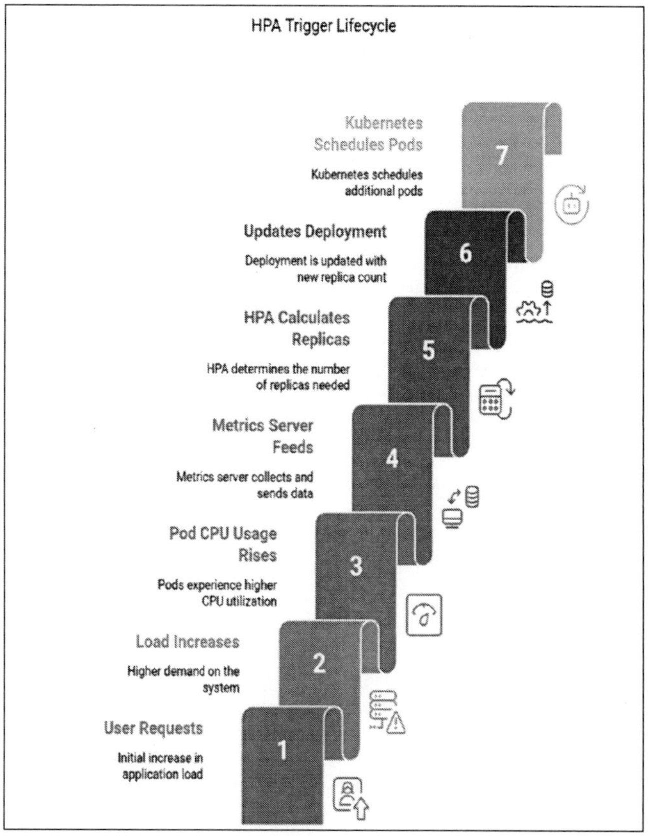

Figure 6a.7: *HPA Trigger Lifecycle*

The preceding figure shows that scaling is a **closed feedback loop**, dynamically adjusting without manual scaling commands.

Let us go step-by-step:

1. **User Requests (Initial increase in application load)**

   This stage represents the starting point:

   - Users or clients initiate more requests to the application, resulting in a spike in traffic.

     Example: A web application receiving more visits during peak hours or a marketing campaign driving more users.

Key idea: This increase in demand puts more load on the backend systems (API servers, databases, processing services, and so on).

2. **Load Increases (Higher demand on the system)**

   Due to increased user requests:

   - The system's workload rises–more HTTP requests, database queries, or computations.
   - The existing pods are now handling more transactions per second or connections.

Result: Pods are required to process more data and handle more concurrent connections, which leads to resource pressure.

3. **Pod CPU Usage Rises (Pods experience higher CPU utilization)**

   At this point:

   - The CPU utilization of the running pods increases because they are working harder to serve the increased load.
   - This metric (CPU usage) crosses the **threshold** or target defined in the HPA configuration (for example, 80% CPU utilization).

Note: *The HPA monitors pod metrics to decide when to scale. By default, it focuses on CPU, but can be configured for memory or custom metrics.*

4. **Metrics Server Feeds (Metrics server collects and sends data)**

   The **Kubernetes Metrics Server** comes into play:

   - It continuously collects resource usage data (such as CPU and memory) from the Kubelet running on each node.
   - These metrics are aggregated and sent to the Kubernetes control plane.
   - HPA queries this metrics API to get up-to-date usage stats.

Note: *Without the metrics server running and properly configured, HPA will not be able to retrieve these usage metrics.*

5. **HPA Calculates Replicas (HPA determines the number of replicas needed)**

   With the data from the Metrics Server:

   - HPA compares the current utilization against the target utilization (configured in the HPA spec).
   - Based on the difference, HPA calculates the desired number of replicas needed to bring resource usage back within the target.

Example: If the CPU target is 70%, but the current usage is 95%, HPA will increase the number of pods to balance the load.

Formula (simplified):

```
desiredReplicas = currentReplicas * (currentMetric / targetMetric)
```

6. **Updates Deployment (Deployment is updated with new replica count)**

   Once the desired replica count is calculated:

   - HPA **updates the deployment** (or replica set) with the new number of replicas.

     This is a declarative update, meaning Kubernetes will ensure the new desired state (increased pods) is achieved.

   - **Behind the scenes:** The deployment controller notices the updated replica count and takes action to adjust pod numbers.

7. **Kubernetes Schedules Pods (Kubernetes schedules additional pods)**

   Finally:

   - The Kubernetes Scheduler allocates the new pods onto nodes in the cluster that have sufficient resources (CPU, memory).
   - These pods are created and started to serve incoming requests, thereby distributing the load across more pods.

   Outcome:

   - System load is balanced.
   - User requests are handled efficiently, without overloading any single pod.

Horizontal Pod Autoscaler Trigger Lifecycle

In a Kubernetes environment, scaling an application automatically in response to load is critical for maintaining performance and reliability. The Horizontal Pod Autoscaler (HPA) facilitates this by monitoring specific metrics such as CPU or memory utilization and adjusting the number of pods accordingly.

The lifecycle begins when user demand increases, leading to higher application load and increased CPU usage in the existing pods. The Kubernetes Metrics Server plays a pivotal role by collecting real-time usage statistics from pods and feeding this data to the HPA controller. Based on these metrics, the HPA calculates the number of replicas required to maintain target utilization levels. Once calculated, the deployment is updated with the new replica count, prompting Kubernetes to schedule the additional pods onto available nodes.

This automated flow ensures that applications dynamically adapt to fluctuating workloads without manual intervention, maintaining service stability and performance even during unexpected traffic spikes.

Industry Case Study: Scaling an E-commerce Platform for Flash Sales

Background: Sudden Load Spikes in E-commerce Flash Sales

In online retail, **flash sales** are promotional events where products are offered at significant discounts for a limited time, usually resulting in a dramatic surge in user traffic. A leading e-commerce platform faced such a scenario, experiencing a **20x increase in traffic every Friday at 6 PM** when flash sales went live.

This surge placed immense strain on their backend APIs, particularly the **product listing API**, responsible for fetching and displaying product information to millions of customers in real-time.

Previous Challenge: Static Scaling Failed

Initially, the system was configured with a **fixed number of replicas (5 pods)** to serve API requests. Under normal load, this configuration was sufficient. However, during flash sales:

- Traffic increased 20-fold.
- API response time degraded drastically from **100 milliseconds to 4 seconds**.
- Users frequently encountered **502 Bad Gateway errors**, signaling backend overload.

The static infrastructure was incapable of handling such unpredictable and sudden spike in demand, leading to poor user experience and revenue loss during these critical sales events.

Solution Implemented: Dynamic Scaling with HPA and Cluster Autoscaler

To address these scaling bottlenecks, the engineering team introduced a **dynamic and automated scaling strategy** leveraging Kubernetes features.

Key components of the solution:

- **Horizontal Pod Autoscaler (HPA):** Configured to target **70% CPU utilization**. This allowed the system to automatically increase or decrease the number of API pods based on real-time CPU load.
- **Replica Settings:** Set **minimum replicas to 5** (ensuring baseline capacity) and **maximum replicas to 50** (providing headroom for flash sale traffic surges).
- **Custom Metrics Integration:** Integrated **Prometheus Adapter** to feed a custom metric into the HPA: → **"Requests in Queue"** – measuring how many requests were waiting to be served. This ensured that scaling decisions were not based solely on CPU usage but also accounted for pending user requests, leading to more responsive scaling.
- **Cluster Autoscaler:** Implemented alongside HPA to automatically provision additional nodes when the cluster lacked sufficient resources to schedule new pods. This ensured infrastructure elasticity beyond just pod-level scaling.

Outcome: Sustained Performance Under Extreme Load

This solution resulted in significant improvements during flash sales:

- Successfully handled **20x traffic spike** without service disruptions or 502 errors.
- Maintained **API response times below 200 milliseconds** – a vast improvement from earlier degraded performance.
- Achieved **40% reduction in cloud infrastructure costs** by dynamically scaling resources only when required, instead of overprovisioning 24/7.

Key Learnings from the Case Study

This real-world example offers valuable lessons for any platform anticipating sudden, unpredictable spikes in traffic:

- **Benchmark Resource Requirements:** Before configuring autoscaling, it is crucial to profile and understand your application's CPU, memory, and request handling characteristics. Misconfigured thresholds can lead to either under-provisioning or unnecessary scaling.
- **HPA Scales Pods, Not Nodes:** Horizontal Pod Autoscaler can only scale pods within the capacity of the existing cluster nodes. To enable true elasticity, it must be paired with a **Cluster Autoscaler** to automatically add nodes when needed.

- **Avoid Scaling Flapping:** Without proper configuration, autoscalers can oscillate between scaling up and down rapidly (known as "flapping"), causing instability. Introducing **cooldown periods** and **stabilization windows** helps prevent such behavior.
- **Use Business-Relevant Metrics:** While CPU and memory metrics are useful, they may not fully represent real-world load. Integrating **custom metrics** (such as queue depth, transactions per second, and more) provides more application-specific scaling triggers, aligning infrastructure scaling with business demands.

Takeaway

Scaling dynamic workloads in Kubernetes is not just a matter of turning on an autoscaler. It requires a **layered approach**, combining metric-driven decisions with infrastructure-aware scaling mechanisms. By leveraging both **pod-level autoscaling (HPA)** and **cluster-level scaling (Cluster Autoscaler)**, platforms can achieve **cost-effective, resilient, and performant scaling strategies** tailored to real-world usage patterns.

Vertical Scaling with VPA

Introduction: Why Vertical Pod Autoscaler Matters?

In Kubernetes, **resource requests and limits** are crucial for optimal scheduling and performance. However, static configurations often fall short in dynamic workloads, especially **data-intensive, memory-hungry, or CPU-bound applications**. This is where **Vertical Pod Autoscaler (VPA)** enters.

Unlike Horizontal Pod Autoscaler (HPA), which scales by adding/removing pods, **VPA adjusts the resource requests/limits of a pod vertically**, by increasing or decreasing **CPU and memory allocations per pod**.

In enterprise workloads such as **machine learning model training**, **data science pipelines**, or **high-memory ETL jobs**, scaling "out" (horizontal) may be ineffective because these applications are **not easily parallelized**. Instead, they need **more power per pod**.

How Vertical Pod Autoscaler (VPA) Works?

Let us explore this through:

Why:

- To prevent **Out-of-Memory (OOM) kills or CPU throttling** in workloads with unpredictable memory or CPU demands.
- To **optimize cluster resources** by avoiding over-provisioning static requests.
- To **improve application stability** for memory/CPU-intensive, non-parallelizable workloads.
- To enable **auto-tuning resource settings** without manual adjustments.

What:

- **VPA is a Kubernetes controller** that recommends or automatically adjusts the `resources.requests`, and `resources.limits` fields in a Pod Spec.
- VPA continuously **monitors actual resource consumption** and **recommends new values or applies them automatically** (depending on mode).
- Modes:
    - `"Off"` → generates recommendations but does not apply them.
    - `"Auto"` → applies recommendations (recreates pods with new settings).
    - `"Initial"` → applies recommendations only during pod creation.

Unlike HPA, **VPA triggers pod restarts** to apply new settings because resource fields are immutable on a running container.

When:

- Use VPA when:
  - The application **cannot scale horizontally** (for example, singleton workloads, stateful ML jobs).
  - The application requires **occasional but unpredictable resource spikes**.
  - Workload exhibits **resource misconfiguration**, causing waste or crashes.
- Not ideal for:
  - Stateless, horizontally scalable applications.
  - High-availability workloads where **pod restarts must be avoided**.

How:

- VPA monitors resource usage via the **metrics-server** or **Prometheus adapter**.
- It calculates **recommended CPU/memory** using historical and observed metrics.
- Based on mode:
  - Generates a recommendation (logs/status API).
  - Or triggers **`pod eviction`** → new pod created with updated **`requests/limits`**.
- Scheduler places a new pod based on the updated resource profile.

Understanding Vertical Pod Autoscaler in Kubernetes

In Kubernetes, applications often experience varying workloads, leading to unpredictable resource consumption over time. While Horizontal Pod Autoscaler (HPA) scales the number of pods based on metrics such as CPU or memory, sometimes what is needed is **adjusting the resource allocation per pod** instead of adding more pods.

This is where the **Vertical Pod Autoscaler (VPA)** comes in – it automatically adjusts CPU and memory **requests and limits** for containers in a pod, ensuring that each pod has sufficient resources for its workload without manual tuning.

Let us break this down using an example.

Scenario: Automatically Adjusting Resources for a Machine Learning Trainer

Imagine you are running a **machine learning training application** in Kubernetes. The application is deployed as a pod called ml-trainer. Initially, you configure static CPU and memory requests/limits. However, during different training runs, resource needs can fluctuate – sometimes using less, sometimes spiking higher.

Manually tuning these values after every job is inefficient and error-prone. By enabling a **Vertical Pod Autoscaler**, we allow Kubernetes to analyze actual resource usage and automatically recommend or apply adjustments.

Step-by-Step YAML Configuration

1. **Defining the Deployment**

   We start with a standard Deployment definition for **`ml-trainer`**:

   ```
   yaml

   apiVersion: apps/v1
   ```

```
kind: Deployment
metadata:
  name: ml-trainer
spec:
  replicas: 1
  selector:
    matchLabels:
      app: ml-trainer
  template:
    metadata:
      labels:
        app: ml-trainer
    spec:
      containers:
      - name: trainer
        image: myregistry/ml-trainer:latest
        resources:
          requests:
            cpu: "500m"
            memory: "1Gi"
          limits:
            cpu: "1"
            memory: "2Gi"
```

In this deployment:

- We launch a single replica of a container named trainer.
- We assign initial resource **requests** (minimum guaranteed resources) and **limits** (maximum allowed resources).

This ensures the pod will reserve at least 500 millicores of CPU and 1 GB of memory, but cannot exceed 1 CPU and 2 GB memory.

2. **Defining the Vertical Pod Autoscaler**

   Next, we configure a **Vertical Pod Autoscaler** for the deployment:

```
yaml

apiVersion: autoscaling.k8s.io/v1
kind: VerticalPodAutoscaler
metadata:
  name: ml-trainer-vpa
spec:
  targetRef:
    apiVersion: "apps/v1"
    kind: Deployment
    name: ml-trainer
  updatePolicy:
    updateMode: "Auto"
  resourcePolicy:
    containerPolicies:
    - containerName: trainer
      minAllowed:
        cpu: "300m"
        memory: "512Mi"
      maxAllowed:
        cpu: "4"
        memory: "8Gi"
```

Let us break this down:

- **`targetRef`:** This links the VPA to the **`ml-trainer`** deployment, specifying **which application** to manage.
- **`updatePolicy.updateMode: "Auto"`:** This tells Kubernetes to **automatically apply recommended resource adjustments** by evicting and restarting pods. Every time the VPA determines a better resource configuration, it replaces the current pod with a new one using updated settings.
- **`resourcePolicy`:** This defines resource guardrails - the VPA can only assign CPU and memory within the minimum and maximum values specified.

In this case:

- Minimum allowed: 300 millicores CPU, 512 MB memory.
- Maximum allowed: 4 CPU cores, 8 GB memory.

By setting these bounds, we prevent VPA from under-provisioning (which could cause crashes) or over-provisioning (which wastes resources).

How It Works in Practice?

When deployed:

- Kubernetes monitors the actual CPU and memory usage of the trainer container over time.
- The VPA controller analyzes these metrics and computes optimal **resource requests**.
- If the recommended resources differ significantly from the current values, the VPA evicts the pod.
- The pod restarts with the new recommended resource configuration.

Note: *Every time VPA applies an update, the pod is **restarted** - this may temporarily interrupt running workloads. Therefore, VPA is best suited for **batch jobs, long-running computations, or applications that tolerate restarts.***

Applying the YAML Files

To deploy both the application and its autoscaler, use:

```
bash

kubectl apply -f ml-trainer-deployment.yaml
kubectl apply -f ml-trainer-vpa.yaml
```

After deployment:

- Kubernetes will gradually collect metrics.
- VPA will periodically update resource recommendations.
- Pods will be restarted as needed to apply changes.

Key considerations when using Vertical Pod Autoscaler are listed as follows:

- **Pod Restarts are Required for Updates:** Unlike HPA, VPA changes require evicting and recreating pods. Plan for disruption or design around workloads that tolerate restarts.
- **Not Compatible with HPA (Scaling on CPU/Memory):** If using HPA based on CPU/memory metrics, VPA and HPA can conflict. Kubernetes recommends avoiding using both together for CPU/memory-based scaling.
- **Use Resource Boundaries to Prevent Extremes:** Always define **`minAllowed`** and **`maxAllowed`** values to avoid over-scaling or under-provisioning.

- **Ideal for Long-Running Workloads:** VPA is most effective for applications with relatively stable, predictable usage patterns over time, less suitable for highly dynamic, short-lived workloads.

Takeaway

The Vertical Pod Autoscaler automates the tedious process of tuning pod resource requests and limits by learning from actual usage over time. It allows Kubernetes to make **data-driven resource allocation decisions**, leading to improved efficiency, reduced waste, and less manual intervention.

In production environments, combining **careful resource policies, appropriate update modes, and workload understanding** is essential to leveraging VPA effectively, without unintended disruptions.

Use Cases in Machine Learning and Heavy ETL

Machine Learning Training Jobs

In model training, memory and CPU needs **grow over training epochs** or **based on the dataset size.**

Example:

- First few epochs: 2GiB memory sufficient.
- Later epochs: peaks at 6GiB memory.

Without VPA:

- You would over-provision at 6GiB → wasting 4GiB idle memory.
- Or under-provision → leading to **OOMKilled pods**.

With VPA:

- The system auto-tunes memory upwards as the job progresses.
- Prevents manual resizing mid-job.

Heavy ETL Workloads

Some ETL pipelines:

- Use dynamic SQL → memory load fluctuates per query plan.
- Pull **varying volumes of data** depending on day/time.

Without VPA:

- Static resources force choosing "worst-case" over-provision.
- Or unpredictable crashes when large data are ingested.

With VPA:

- Auto-adjusts memory as input volume increases.
- Reduces cost by scaling down during smaller jobs.

Pitfalls: Why VPA is Tricky in High-Availability Systems

Although powerful, VPA introduces challenges for **high-availability, low-downtime workloads.**

Main challenges:

- **Pod Eviction = Downtime:**
    - VPA applies updates by **terminating pods and recreating them.**
    - Each update incurs **disruption window** → unsuitable for zero-downtime apps.

- **Conflicts with HPA:**
  - Both HPA and VPA modify pod resources.
  - If configured simultaneously, → **resource conflict** → HPA sees "new" pod sizes every update.
- **No Fine-Grained Scheduling Control:**
  - Re-scheduled pods may land on different nodes → breaking **node affinity or topology spread constraints.**
- **Scaling Delay:**
  - Recommendations based on historical metrics.
  - Slow to react to **sudden spikes** → pod gets evicted, recreated, rescheduled → delay of seconds to minutes.

Therefore, **VPA is better suited for batch workloads**, **offline processing**, or **training jobs**, **rather than always-on web services or real-time APIs.**

VPA Update Lifecycle

The Vertical Pod Autoscaler (VPA) is a Kubernetes mechanism that dynamically adjusts the CPU and memory resource requests for running pods based on their actual usage. The goal is to ensure that pods have the optimal amount of resources: neither under-provisioned (which could lead to performance issues) nor over-provisioned (which wastes resources).

The following figure illustrates the lifecycle of how the VPA updates pod resources in a Kubernetes cluster. This process is continuous and cyclical, involving observation, analysis, recommendation, and application.

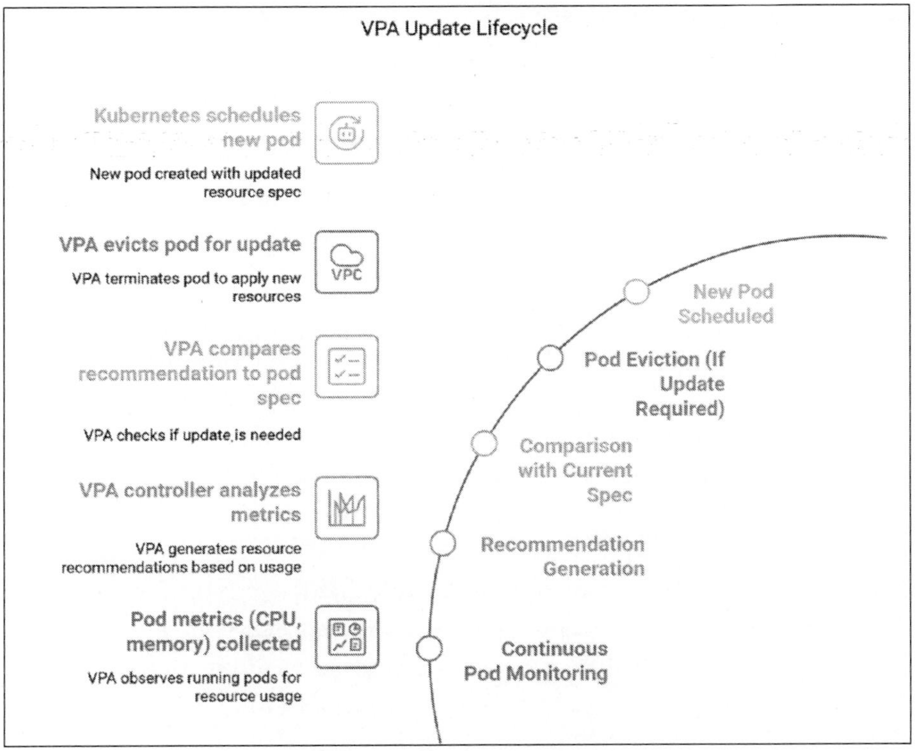

Figure 6a.8: *VPA Update Lifecycle*

The following is a step-by-step theoretical explanation of each stage in the lifecycle:

1. **Continuous Pod Monitoring**

   At the foundation of the VPA lifecycle is the continuous collection of **pod metrics**. The VPA continuously monitors the running pods to collect real-time data on **CPU and memory usage**. This data collection is crucial for understanding how each pod consumes resources over time under different workloads.

   - *Purpose*: To establish a baseline of actual resource consumption patterns.

2. **Recommendation Generation**

   Once sufficient usage data is collected, the **VPA controller analyzes these metrics**. This involves evaluating CPU and memory utilization trends, spikes, and sustained loads to generate a **recommended resource specification** for each pod.

   - *Purpose*: To calculate the optimal CPU and memory requests that balance performance and efficiency.

3. **Comparison with Current Spec**

   The next stage is for the VPA to **compare the recommended resource settings with the pod's current resource specification**. This step determines whether an adjustment is needed.

   If the current resources are already close to optimal, no action is taken. But if the difference between the current and recommended values exceeds a threshold (configured by policies), the VPA considers an update necessary.

   - *Purpose*: To prevent unnecessary updates and ensure updates only happen when beneficial.

4. **Pod Eviction (If Update Required)**

   When an update is deemed necessary, the VPA initiates a process to **evict the pod**. Eviction here refers to gracefully terminating the running pod so that Kubernetes can recreate it with the updated resource requests.

   It is important to note that the VPA does not directly modify a running pod; instead, it relies on Kubernetes to reschedule a new instance with the updated specification.

   - *Purpose*: To apply new resource settings by recreating pods with the recommended values.

5. **New Pod Scheduled**

   Following the eviction, Kubernetes **schedules a new pod** to replace the terminated one. This new pod is created using the **updated CPU and memory specifications** recommended by the VPA.

   Once the new pod is up and running, it re-enters the monitoring phase, continuing the cycle.

   - *Purpose*: To complete the update and ensure the pod operates with optimal resources moving forward.

VPA Lifecycle Summary

- Running pod is continuously **monitored by VPA** (via metrics-server).
- VPA analyzes historical + live usage → **generates a recommendation**.
- Compares the recommendation against current requests/limits.
- If adjustment is needed:

- **VPA evicts pod** (terminates).
- **New pod created automatically** → carries updated resource spec.
- Kubernetes schedules a pod (might be on the same or a new node).

This lifecycle highlights a **trade-off between optimization and availability**: every resource adjustment forces pod restart → introduces momentary unavailability.

Putting It All Together

This lifecycle creates a **closed feedback loop** where the Vertical Pod Autoscaler continuously:

- Monitors pod usage
- Analyzes data
- Generates recommendations
- Compares with current specs
- Evicts pods if needed
- Reschedules pods with improved resources

This automated cycle enables Kubernetes environments to **self-tune pod resource requests** without manual intervention, leading to better **resource efficiency**, **application stability**, and **cost optimization** in production workloads.

Note: *It is important to understand that* **VPA** ***does not scale the number of pod replicas*** *(which is the responsibility of the Horizontal Pod Autoscaler, HPA). Instead, it focuses purely on* ***adjusting the size of resources assigned to a single pod*** *instance over time.*

Also, the eviction process may impact pod availability if not configured with disruption budgets or tolerations - readers should consider workload criticality when enabling VPA in production systems.

Conclusion

In this chapter, we delved into the foundational concepts of scaling applications horizontally and vertically within a Kubernetes environment. We explored Horizontal Scaling using the Horizontal Pod Autoscaler (HPA) to scale services across multiple instances based on load. Additionally, we discussed Vertical Scaling with the Vertical Pod Autoscaler (VPA), which adjusts the CPU and memory resources of individual pods to meet varying demands.

The Industry Case Study helped demonstrate these scaling techniques in real-world scenarios, giving us practical insights into how organizations handle scaling challenges effectively.

As we conclude this chapter, you should now have a solid understanding of how Kubernetes enables efficient scaling to maintain application performance and availability.

In Part 2, we will continue with a deeper dive on Industry Case Study, Resource Requests, Limits, and Quality of Service (QoS), examining how these configurations help ensure optimal resource allocation and prevent bottlenecks. We will also explore Cluster Autoscaler and Node Pool Management to automate scaling at the infrastructure level, and discuss scaling real-world data pipelines to handle large-scale data processing efficiently.

CHAPTER 6B
Scaling Applications Horizontally and Vertically Part B

Introduction

In the second part, we will dive deeper into the practical aspects of scaling applications both horizontally and vertically. Scaling is crucial for improving performance, handling growing traffic, and maintaining high availability. This chapter explores advanced techniques for resource management, autoscaling, and managing large-scale data pipelines. Thus, by understanding these concepts, you can make your applications more resilient and adaptable to varying workloads.

Structure

In this chapter, we will cover the following topics:

- Industry Case Study
- Resource Requests, Limits and Quality of Service (QoS)
- Cluster Autoscaler and Node Pool Management
- Scaling Real-World Data Pipelines

Industry Case Study: Optimizing Resource Allocation in an AI Research Cluster

A prominent research organization operates a Kubernetes-based GPU cluster dedicated to running **nightly deep learning experiments**. The workloads involved multiple training jobs scheduled concurrently, each requiring significant GPU and memory resources. The experiments were time-sensitive, with results feeding into the next day's research cycles.

However, despite having powerful hardware and dedicated infrastructure, the team faced persistent resource allocation challenges affecting job completion rates and overall cluster efficiency.

Challenges Identified

The **organization observed two primary issues**:

- **Out-of-Memory (OOM) Failures:** Some training jobs failed unpredictably, terminated by the system with an **OOMKilled** status. This indicated that the pods consumed more memory than originally requested, leading the Kubernetes scheduler to kill them to protect node stability.

- **Over-Provisioning Waste:** In contrast, other jobs requested far more memory than they actually needed. These pods ended up **hoarding unused memory**, preventing Kubernetes from scheduling additional parallel jobs, even though physical resources were technically available.

Both situations resulted in **inefficient resource utilization** and **reduced experiment throughput**. Developers attempted to fix this manually by adjusting pod memory requests and limits daily, but this was labor-intensive, inconsistent, and unsustainable at scale.

Implemented Solution

To solve these problems, the team deployed the **Vertical Pod Autoscaler (VPA)** on their **training deployments**. The VPA was configured in **automatic update mode**, allowing it to dynamically adjust pod resource requests without manual intervention.

The key configuration choices included:

Minimum and Maximum Memory Bounds: The team set a memory floor and ceiling by configuring:

- `minAllowed.memory: 4Gi`
- `maxAllowed.memory: 24Gi`

This ensured that no pod would request below 4Gi or above 24Gi, providing guardrails while still allowing flexibility within an acceptable range.

`updateMode`: Auto: The VPA was set to automatically update resource requests and evict pods as needed to apply new recommendations. This was well-suited for **batch workloads** such as training jobs that could tolerate pod restarts.

Resource Policy to Exclude GPU Containers: Since GPU allocations are typically handled separately (for example, via device plugins or static assignments), the team configured a **resourcePolicy** to exclude the GPU containers from vertical scaling. This prevented VPA from attempting to adjust GPU-related requests, focusing only on CPU and memory.

Outcomes

After deploying the VPA with these settings, the organization observed significant improvements over the next 30 days:

- **Zero OOMKills:** No training jobs failed due to out-of-memory errors, indicating that pods were consistently allocated sufficient memory for their workloads.
- **~18% Memory Savings:** The cluster's overall memory usage decreased by approximately **18%**, thanks to the elimination of unnecessary static over-provisioning. This freed up memory to allow more jobs to run concurrently.
- **Eliminated Manual Tuning:** Developers no longer needed to manually tweak resource requests each day. This freed up engineering time and reduced operational burden, allowing the team to focus on model development instead of infrastructure troubleshooting.

Practical Insights and Lessons Learned

This case study demonstrates that the **Vertical Pod Autoscaler is highly effective for dynamic, short-lived, or batch workloads such as machine learning training, ETL pipelines, or simulation jobs.** These workloads benefit from automatic tuning because they:

- Can tolerate pod restarts.
- Run for defined durations rather than continuously.

- Often vary in resource needs depending on the dataset or model parameters.

However, the team noted that **VPA may not be suitable for always-on, highly available, or zero-downtime applications**, since eviction-based updates can temporarily disrupt service. For such applications, additional measures such as **Pod Disruption Budgets (PDBs)** or static provisioning might be more appropriate.

Conclusion: When to Choose Vertical Pod Autoscaler

Based on this implementation, the key takeaways for deciding when to use VPA are:

Ideal for workloads where **occasional pod eviction is acceptable**, such as:

- Machine learning model training
- ETL or data processing pipelines
- Simulation or rendering workloads
- Batch computing tasks

Avoid using for workloads that:

- Require **continuous uptime** without disruption.
- Cannot tolerate automatic restarts or evictions.
- Depend on static resource reservations for predictable latency.

When applied thoughtfully, the **Vertical Pod Autoscaler offers a powerful mechanism to automate and optimize resource allocation**, reducing both over-provisioning waste and under-provisioning risks. It enhances cluster efficiency while reducing manual intervention, but it must be configured with workload characteristics and availability needs in mind.

Resource Requests, Limits, and Quality of Service (QoS)

In Kubernetes, containers compete for **shared compute resources** on nodes: CPU and memory. Without boundaries, **one container can starve others** or overload the node, leading to failures or unpredictable performance.

To solve this, Kubernetes allows you to define **resource requests and limits**:

- **Request:** Minimum resources a container needs to run.
- **Limit:** Maximum resources a container is allowed to consume.

These definitions not only control resource fairness but also influence **pod scheduling** and **Quality of Service (QoS) classification**.

Misconfigured resource definitions can cause:

- Pods failing to schedule.
- Containers killed by the Out-of-Memory (OOM) killer.
- Unstable autoscaling behavior.

Let us break this down.

- **Why:**

  You define resource requests and limits to:

  - Prevent **resource starvation** and ensure fair sharing on the node.
  - Guarantee **critical workloads are scheduled** even during node contention.

  - Avoid **"noisy neighbor" problems** where low-priority apps impact high-priority services.
  - Enable **predictable autoscaling and scheduling decisions.**
- **What:**

  There are **two types of resource controls as follows:**

Term	Meaning
Request	Scheduler uses this to place pods; reserved minimum.
Limit	Runtime ceiling enforced by the kernel; container cannot exceed.

Table 6b.1: *Types of Resource Controls: Request and Limit*

Kubernetes uses these definitions to assign QoS Classes (Quality of Service):

QoS Class	Criteria
Guaranteed	requests == limits for **all containers** in the pod.
Burstable	requests < limits for **at least one container**.
BestEffort	**No requests/limits** specified.

Table 6b.2: *QoS Classes with the Criteria*

These QoS classes determine **OOM killer preference** under node pressure:

  - Guaranteed → killed last
  - Burstable → killed second
  - BestEffort → killed first
- **When:**

  You define requests and limits:

  - **Always** for production workloads.
  - **Optional (but recommended)** for staging/test environments.
  - Critical for:
    - **Stateful workloads** (databases, ML pipelines).
    - **Business-critical services** needing high uptime.
  - Avoid for:
    - Short-lived batch jobs (can tolerate OOM).
    - Development/testing workloads.
- **How:**

  Kubernetes scheduler:

  - Reads pod requests to find nodes with enough **allocatable resources.**
  - Places pod on a node meeting those requests.
  - Once running, the **kernel enforces limits** → if a container crosses a limit, it gets throttled (CPU) or killed (memory).

YAML Walkthrough: Defining Resources and Understanding QoS in Kubernetes

When deploying applications in Kubernetes, it is critical to define resource requests and limits for each container. These specifications allow Kubernetes to schedule workloads intelligently and manage resources efficiently under varying load conditions.

Let us walk through an example where we define a **Deployment** for a RESTful API service called **`data-api`**. This API has **moderate CPU requirements** but **variable memory usage** depending on request patterns or data volume.

Deployment YAML Definition

Here is the deployment manifest for this scenario:

```
yaml

apiVersion: apps/v1
kind: Deployment
metadata:
  name: data-api
spec:
  replicas: 2
  selector:
    matchLabels:
      app: data-api
  template:
    metadata:
      labels:
        app: data-api
    spec:
      containers:
      - name: api-container
        image: myregistry/data-api:v1
        resources:
          requests:
            cpu: "500m"
            memory: "512Mi"
          limits:
            cpu: "1"
            memory: "1Gi"
```

Key Points in the YAML

Let us unpack what this YAML configuration is doing:

Deployment with Two Replicas: We are running **two identical pods** to handle incoming API requests, providing basic scalability and redundancy.

Container Resource Requests: Each container inside the pod specifies the following **resource requests**:

- **`cpu: "500m"`** → This container requests **500 millicores** (half a CPU core) from the node scheduler.
- **`memory: "512Mi"`** → This container requests **512 megabytes of memory**.

A request acts as a reservation: Kubernetes guarantees that at least this much CPU and memory will be available when scheduling the pod onto a node. Hence, without sufficient free capacity, the pod will not be scheduled there.

Container Resource Limits: In addition to requests, we define **resource limits**:

- `cpu: "1"` → This container will be allowed to use up to **1 full CPU core** at maximum.
- `memory: "1Gi"` → This container's memory consumption is capped at **1 gigabyte**.

The **limit** acts as an enforcement boundary:

- If the container exceeds **1 CPU**, Kubernetes throttles CPU usage to bring it back within the limit.
- If the container tries to consume more than **1Gi of memory**, the system will **terminate the container with an Out-of-Memory (OOM) kill** to protect the node.

Scheduling Behavior

With these specifications:

- The Kubernetes scheduler will only assign pods to nodes that have **at least 500 millicores of CPU and 512Mi of memory available for reservation**.
- The node's kubelet will enforce the limits at runtime, ensuring the container never exceeds its resource cap.

This combination balances predictability and flexibility such as: the application can burst up to 1 CPU or 1Gi of memory temporarily if needed, while always reserving a baseline.

Kubernetes Quality of Service Classification

Kubernetes assigns every pod a **Quality of Service (QoS) class,** based on how its resource requests and limits are configured. QoS affects how pods are prioritized for eviction when nodes experience memory pressure or other constraints.

In this example:

Requests equal limits for both CPU and memory. This means:

Request (CPU)	Limit (CPU)	Request (Mem)	Limit (Mem)
500m	1	512Mi	1Gi

Table 6b.3: *Requests Equal Limits for Both CPU and Memory*

Since both resources have **equal requests and limits**, Kubernetes classifies this pod as:

QoS Class: Guaranteed

A pod in the **Guaranteed** class gets the **highest priority** to stay running under resource contention. If the node is under memory pressure and needs to evict pods, Guaranteed pods will be the **last to be terminated**.

In contrast:

- If requests < limits → QoS becomes **Burstable** (lower priority)
- If no requests/limits are specified → QoS is **BestEffort** (lowest priority)

Thus, Guaranteed QoS is ideal for critical workloads where uptime and resource protection are essential.

Why This Matters?

By explicitly defining both requests and limits equally:

- Developers ensure **predictable application performance**, as each pod gets at least 500m CPU and 512Mi memory with permission to scale up to 1 CPU/1Gi.
- Operators achieve **resource fairness**, as no pod can monopolize resources beyond its allocated maximum.
- The workload gains **resilience under node pressure**, being protected from premature eviction thanks to the Guaranteed QoS class.
- The cluster improves **scheduling precision**, since pods declare exactly how much they need (and no more).

Broader Insights

This example illustrates an important principle:

Resource definitions in Kubernetes are not just optional configuration - they directly influence scheduling decisions, runtime behavior, and application survivability.

A well-defined resource configuration:

- Prevents resource starvation of critical apps.
- Improves multi-tenant workload fairness.
- Enables Kubernetes to make smarter decisions under stress.

For production systems, especially APIs, databases, and user-facing workloads, adopting a **Guaranteed QoS** profile is often recommended to ensure reliability, especially when cluster nodes have variable loads.

Summary

In this YAML walkthrough, we configured a deployment for a REST API with explicit requests and limits, resulting in:

Predictable scheduling → placed only on nodes with sufficient reserved capacity.

Runtime enforcement → capped at 1 CPU, 1Gi memory.

Highest QoS → Kubernetes prioritizes this pod's survival under memory pressure.

By setting `requests == limits`, this pod achieves **Guaranteed** quality of service, offering a strong balance of resource protection, stability, and fairness in a shared Kubernetes environment.

Resource Requests, Limits, and QoS Flow

The following is a conceptual diagram:

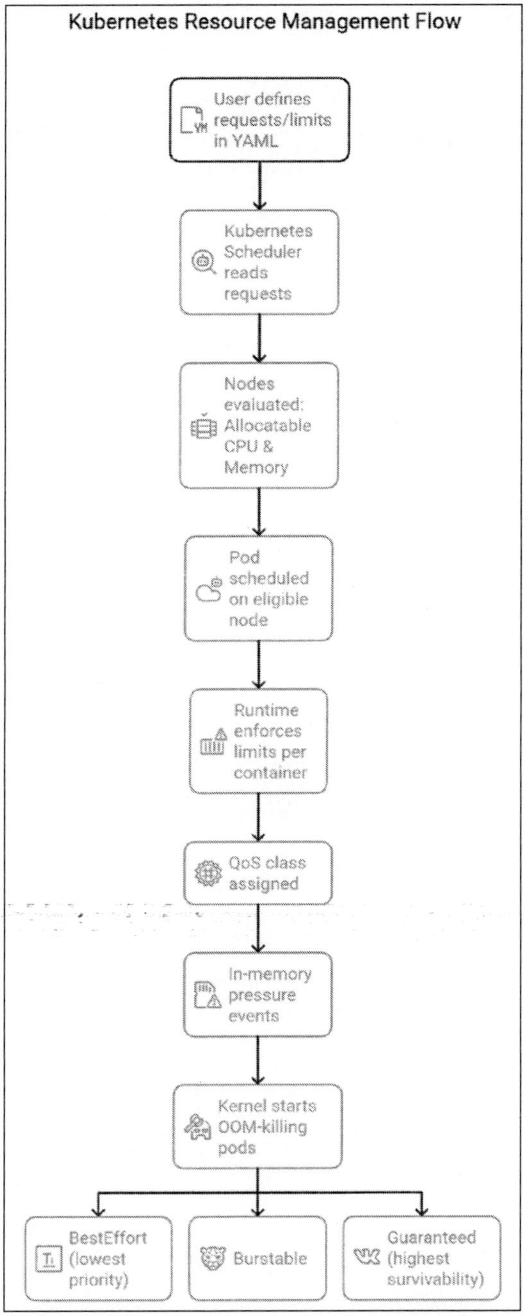

Figure 6b.1: *Resource Requests, Limits, and QoS Flow*

Understanding Kubernetes Resource Management Flow

Kubernetes provides a sophisticated mechanism to manage CPU and memory resources for containers running inside pods. This resource management flow ensures optimal scheduling, fair allocation, and graceful degradation under resource constraints. The diagram represents this flow step-by-step:

1. **User Defines Requests and Limits in YAML**

   The resource management process begins when the user specifies **resource requests and limits** inside a Kubernetes manifest file (usually in YAML format).

   a. **Requests** indicate the minimum resources a container needs to run.

   b. **Limits** define the maximum resources a container is allowed to consume.

   Example:

   ```
   yaml

   resources:
     requests:
       memory: "256Mi"
       cpu: "500m"
     limits:
       memory: "512Mi"
       cpu: "1"
   ```

   This acts as a contract between the user and Kubernetes for resource allocation.

2. **Kubernetes Scheduler Reads Requests**

   The **Kubernetes Scheduler** reads the declared resource requests when scheduling a pod. It uses these values to decide **which node has enough allocatable resources** to accommodate the pod.

   At this point:

   a. No actual allocation has happened yet.

   b. It is only a selection process based on theoretical capacity.

3. **Nodes Evaluated for Allocatable CPU and Memory**

   Each node in the cluster reports its **allocatable resources** (total capacity minus reserved system resources). The scheduler evaluates each node to find one that can fulfill the pod's requested CPU and memory.

   If no node satisfies the request → pod remains **Pending**.

   This step prevents overcommitment and ensures fair distribution across nodes.

4. **Pod Scheduled on Eligible Node**

   Once an eligible node is found, the **pod is scheduled** onto that node. Kubernetes updates its internal state to reflect this assignment, and the kubelet on the node takes over to create the pod and its containers.

   Pod now moves from **Pending → Running (creating phase)**.

5. **Runtime Enforces Limits Per Container**

   At runtime, the container engine (for example, containerd, CRI-O, Docker) enforces the **limits** specified earlier:

   a. Containers cannot exceed the set CPU limit (throttling will occur).

   b. Containers consuming more memory than the limit → **OOMKilled** by the kernel.

This enforcement is critical for multi-tenant environments to avoid "noisy neighbor" issues.

6. **QoS Class Assigned**

   Kubernetes assigns the pod a **Quality of Service (QoS) Class** based on how the user specified requests and limits:

   a. **Guaranteed**: If every container in the pod has **equal requests and limits** for both CPU and memory.

   b. **Burstable**: If requests < limits for at least one container.

   c. **BestEffort**: If no requests or limits are specified.

   QoS impacts **eviction priority** under resource pressure (as follows).

7. **In-memory Pressure Events**

   As pods run, the node may encounter **memory pressure** (free memory dropping below a threshold). The kubelet monitors such events and reports to the OS kernel.

   When memory pressure becomes critical, action is needed to prevent a system crash.

8. **Kernel Starts OOM-Killing Pods**

   The **Linux kernel's Out-Of-Memory (OOM) killer** selects processes (containers) to terminate to free up memory.

   This is where **QoS class influences survivability**:

   a. **BestEffort pods** → first to be killed

   b. **Burstable pods** → next

   c. **Guaranteed pods** → last to be killed (highest survivability)

   The kernel prioritizes killing lower QoS classes to keep the most critical workloads alive.

9. **Resulting Pod Priority and Survivability**

   The preceding figure shows the final state:

   a. **BestEffort** → Lowest priority, killed first

   b. **Burstable** → Medium priority, killed after BestEffort

   c. **Guaranteed** → Highest priority, survives longest under memory pressure

This hierarchical QoS system enables **predictable application behavior** even when nodes are oversubscribed or under pressure.

Kubernetes manages container resources through a declarative process where users specify requests and limits in YAML. The scheduler ensures that pods land on nodes capable of fulfilling these requests. Runtime enforces limits to isolate workloads, while Kubernetes assigns QoS classes that dictate pod priority under memory pressure. The kernel uses these QoS classes to determine which pods to kill during critical memory shortages, allowing higher-priority workloads to survive.

This flow ensures:

- Fairness and predictability
- Resource isolation
- Resilience during oversubscription

Why This Matters?

Understanding this resource management flow is **critical for developers and platform engineers** to:

- Prevent resource starvation.
- Ensure critical applications have the highest survivability.
- Design efficient, multi-tenant Kubernetes clusters.
- Troubleshoot pod evictions and OOM kills effectively.

By following this flow, Kubernetes achieves **balanced resource utilization while maintaining workload priorities under stress.**

Case Study: Improving ETL Stability with Resource Profiles

Background:

A data engineering team ran an ETL container that occasionally **crashed due to memory spikes.** Initially:

- **No requests/limits defined** → pod fell under **BestEffort class.**
- During high memory usage from other pods → **ETL pod frequently killed** by the OOM killer.

Issue:

- Job failures.
- Data pipeline interruptions.
- Wasteful reruns.

Solution:

- Defined `requests` and `limits` in YAML:

```
yaml

resources:
  requests:
    cpu: "1000m"
    memory: "2Gi"
  limits:
    cpu: "2"
    memory: "4Gi"
```

- Pod moved from **BestEffort → Burstable QoS** (since requests < limits).
- Node reserved `≥2Gi memory for ETL pod` → prevented preemption.
- Reduced crash frequency by **80%** (remaining 20% due to real node exhaustion).

Optional improvement: Moved to **Guaranteed QoS** by setting `requests == limits` for even higher survivability.

How Resource Profiles Affect Autoscaling and Scheduling?

Defining requests and limits impacts:

- **Scheduler behavior:**
  - Scheduler ignores nodes that cannot satisfy requests.

    - Prevents pods from being scheduled where resources are unavailable.
- **Cluster utilization:**
    - High requests block scheduling even if the node has idle capacity (but below the request).
    - Over-provisioned requests → underutilized nodes.
- **Autoscaling:**
    - HPA calculates scaling based on requests → inaccurate requests lead to **under-scaling or over-scaling.**
    - Example: Setting low requests → HPA thinks pod using high % of requests → triggers unnecessary scale-up.
- **Pod survivability:**
    - QoS class governs which pods survive under memory pressure.
    - Guaranteed class → least likely to be killed.

Practical Recommendations:

- Always define **requests and limits** for production workloads.
- Use **Guaranteed QoS** for stateful, critical apps.
- Use **Burstable QoS** for moderately important but elastic apps.
- Avoid **BestEffort** unless for disposable workloads.
- Regularly **review resource metrics (Prometheus, metrics-server)** to fine-tune requests/limits.

Hands-On Lab: Tuning Resource Profiles

1. Deploy the **`data-api`** deployment above.
2. Run **`kubectl describe pod <pod-name>`** → verify QoS Class.
3. Simulate load using stress tool inside the container → observe **`kubectl top pod`**.
4. Increase memory usage → intentionally cross memory **`limit`** → verify **`kubectl describe pod`** → check **`State: OOMKilled`**.

Validation Checklist:

- Pod correctly scheduled.
- Pod QoS class shows **Guaranteed** (or Burstable, if modified).
  Kernel kills the pod if memory > limit.
- Pod restarted per deployment spec → **no manual intervention.**

Closing Thoughts:

Correctly configuring resource requests, limits, and QoS is **not optional** for production-grade Kubernetes deployments. They form the foundation of **predictable scheduling, reliable autoscaling, and workload stability under node pressure.**

Skipping or misconfiguring these parameters risks:

- Poor autoscaling performance.
- Unreliable deployments.
- Increased operational toil during outages.

Every workload should have an intentional **resource profile aligned to business criticality and failure tolerance.**

Cluster Autoscaler and Node Pool Management

In Kubernetes, pods are scheduled onto nodes with available resources. But what happens when **no node has enough capacity to schedule a pod?** Kubernetes, by default, **will not automatically provision a new node**.

This is where the **Cluster Autoscaler** comes in. It dynamically **adds nodes to a cluster** when pods cannot be scheduled due to insufficient resources and **removes underutilized nodes** when no longer needed, reducing cost.

Cluster Autoscaler is supported across major managed Kubernetes providers:

- **Amazon EKS**
- **Google Kubernetes Engine (GKE)**
- **Azure Kubernetes Service (AKS)**

It integrates deeply with **node pools (node groups)** to scale them up/down in response to workload needs.

Let us explore this using the structured way:

- **Why:**

  You use Cluster Autoscaler to:

  - Match compute capacity to workload demand dynamically.
  - Eliminate manual node provisioning/scaling.
  - Optimize infrastructure cost by removing idle nodes.
  - Ensure pods are not left pending due to lack of nodes.

  In today's cloud-native environments, this is critical to balance **agility, reliability, and cost-efficiency.**

- **What:**

  Key components and concepts are as follows:

Concept	Description
Cluster Autoscaler	Controller that scales node groups up/down.
Node Pool/Group	Logical set of nodes with the same VM type/config.
Taints/Tolerations	Control what pods can run on which nodes.
Spot/Preemptible nodes	Cheaper but interruptible instances.

Table 6b.4: *Key Components and Concepts of Cluster*

  Cluster Autoscaler works by:

  - Monitoring pending pods.
  - Determining if any node group can scale up to accommodate pods.
  - Interacting with the cloud provider API to add/remove nodes.

- **When:**

  Use Cluster Autoscaler when:

  - Running workloads with **variable traffic patterns** (for example, retail apps, event-driven systems).

  - Managing **multi-tenant clusters** where workload sizes fluctuate.
  - Trying to **optimize cost with minimal manual ops overhead.**
  - Supporting **CI/CD pipelines that need burst compute capacity.**

  Do not use autoscaler **alone** for horizontal pod scaling; it is designed to **complement the Horizontal Pod Autoscaler (HPA).**

- **How:**

  How it works step-by-step:

  1. Scheduler places pods → if no node can host → pod stays **Pending**.
  2. **Cluster Autoscaler detects an unschedulable pod**.
  3. Checks which node pool can be scaled to accommodate the pod's requests.
  4. If an eligible node group is found → sends a **scale-up request to the cloud provider API**.
  5. Cloud spins up a node → node joins cluster → scheduler reschedules pod.
  6. Later, if a node becomes **underutilized and empty**, the autoscaler removes the node.

Note: *It only removes nodes if:*

- Pods can be moved elsewhere.
- No DaemonSets or pod disruption budgets block eviction.

Supported Providers (EKS, AKS, and GKE)

Each major provider implements autoscaling with native integrations.

Provider	Integration
EKS	Autoscaler deploys as a pod; scales EC2 Auto Scaling Groups (ASG).
GKE	Cluster Autoscaler is **built-in, enabled per node pool**.
AKS	Autoscaler managed at node pool level via Azure APIs.

Table 6b.5: *Public Cloud Providers and Integration*

Regardless of the provider, **Cluster Autoscaler logic stays the same**, but implementation details and APIs differ.

For cloud-native apps, using the provider-native autoscaler ensures:

- Integration with managed node pools.
- Native support for **spot/preemptible nodes**.
- Security and IAM aligned with cloud provider standards.

Integrating Cluster Autoscaler and Horizontal Pod Autoscaler: A Practical YAML Walkthrough

In Kubernetes, scaling can happen at two levels:

- **Pod-Level Scaling (Horizontal Pod Autoscaler, HPA):** Automatically increases or decreases the number of pod replicas based on resource utilization (such as, CPU, memory).
- **Node-Level Scaling (Cluster Autoscaler):** Automatically adds or removes nodes from the cluster based on resource demands.

To build a resilient and cost-efficient system, we often use both **HPA** and **Cluster Autoscaler** together. Let us break down how they work together through a real-world YAML configuration.

The YAML Configuration

```yaml
yaml

apiVersion: apps/v1
kind: Deployment
metadata:
  name: web-api
spec:
  replicas: 2
  selector:
    matchLabels:
      app: web-api
  template:
    metadata:
      labels:
        app: web-api
    spec:
      containers:
      - name: api-container
        image: myregistry/web-api:v1
        resources:
          requests:
            cpu: "500m"
            memory: "512Mi"
          limits:
            cpu: "1"
            memory: "1Gi"
---
apiVersion: autoscaling/v2
kind: HorizontalPodAutoscaler
metadata:
  name: web-api-hpa
spec:
  scaleTargetRef:
    apiVersion: apps/v1
    kind: Deployment
    name: web-api
  minReplicas: 2
  maxReplicas: 10
  metrics:
  - type: Resource
    resource:
      name: cpu
      target:
        type: Utilization
        averageUtilization: 60
```

What is Happening Here?

- **Deployment Defined with Resource Requests and Limits**

  We define a **Deployment** named **`web-api`** with:

  - Two initial replicas.
  - Each container requests **500 millicores of CPU** and **512Mi of memory.**

  - Each container is capped (limited) at **1 CPU** and **1Gi memory.**

  This sets both the minimum resource guarantee (requests) and maximum allowed consumption (limits) for each pod.

- **Horizontal Pod Autoscaler (HPA) Targets Deployment**

  An **HPA resource** named **`web-api-hpa`** is attached to this deployment. It is configured to:

  - Keep **at least 2 replicas** running.
  - Scale up to **10 replicas maximum.**
  - Scale based on **CPU utilization target of 60%.**

  Meaning:

  - If average CPU utilization across all pods exceeds 60%, Kubernetes will add more pods (up to 10).
  - If utilization falls below 60%, it may reduce replicas, but never below 2.

How Scaling Works?

Scenario 1: Scaling Pods (Horizontal Scaling)

Let us say traffic increases → CPU load rises → average CPU utilization hits 75%.

- The HPA detects that utilization exceeds the 60% threshold.
- The HPA requests to increase replicas from 2 → 3 → 4... and so on, trying to bring utilization down toward 60%.

Scenario 2: Scaling Nodes (Cluster Autoscaler)

Each pod requests **500m CPU + 512Mi memory**.

When the deployment scales toward **10 replicas**, the current nodes may lack sufficient resources (since each pod needs at least those requested resources).

At this point:

Kubernetes will try to schedule pods onto existing nodes.

If nodes **do not have enough allocatable CPU/memory** → new pods enter the **Pending** state because no node has enough resources.

Here is where the **Cluster Autoscaler** comes in.

- Cluster Autoscaler monitors pending pods.
- If pods cannot be scheduled due to a lack of node capacity → Cluster Autoscaler automatically **provisions new nodes** (adds nodes to the node pool) until enough capacity is available to host the new pods.

The Coordination: HPA + Cluster Autoscaler

- HPA focuses on adding/removing pods based on workload.
- Cluster Autoscaler focuses on adding/removing nodes to ensure pods can be scheduled.

Together:

- HPA increases pod replicas to handle more load.
- Cluster Autoscaler ensures that the underlying infrastructure grows to provide space for new pods.

- Without a Cluster Autoscaler, HPA could increase pod count, **but some pods would remain Pending forever** if there is no node with free capacity.

Why Is This Integration Important?

- Prevents **unschedulable pods** during scaling spikes.
- Avoids **manual node management** in dynamic environments.
- Achieves **both application elasticity and infrastructure elasticity**.
- Saves cost by **removing unused nodes automatically** when the load drops.

In plain words, imagine a restaurant:

- Pods are waiters.
- **Nodes are tables.**
- When more customers arrive → you hire more waiters (HPA).
- But if you do not add more tables (Cluster Autoscaler), those new waiters will have nowhere to serve.

By combining HPA and Cluster Autoscaler, you scale both the **number of waiters (pods)** and the **number of tables (nodes)** in sync to meet demand.

Key Takeaways:

- HPA scales the **application layer (pods)**.
- Cluster Autoscaler scales the **infrastructure layer (nodes)**.
- Both autoscalers work independently but **complement each other** to achieve seamless elasticity.
- Kubernetes will not create new nodes for pod scaling **unless a Cluster Autoscaler is configured and enabled.**
- Resource **requests must be properly defined** for Cluster Autoscaler to understand scheduling needs.

Requests and Limits

If you skip defining requests:

- Kubernetes will not reserve resources during scheduling → leading to oversubscription.
- Cluster Autoscaler cannot detect pending pods needing more resources → no scaling action → pods stay Pending forever.

By explicitly setting **requests**, you ensure that:

- Pods are scheduled onto nodes with sufficient resources.
- Cluster Autoscaler knows how much extra capacity is needed to fit pending pods.

This example illustrates a **real-world integration of HPA and Cluster Autoscaler**: Without node scaling, pod scaling alone will hit a wall. Without pod scaling, node scaling serves no workload growth.

In Kubernetes, achieving true elastic scalability requires **both dimensions to work together—automatically, dynamically, and efficiently.**

Detailed Explanation of the Autoscaling Flow in Kubernetes

Autoscaling is a fundamental capability in Kubernetes that ensures an application can automatically handle fluctuations in demand by dynamically adjusting the number of pods and nodes. It involves both **Horizontal Pod Autoscaler (HPA)**, which scales the number of pods, and **Cluster Autoscaler (CA)**, which adds or removes nodes from the cluster depending on scheduling needs.

The following two figures represent this process in different visual styles: the first as a staircase journey, and the second as a flowchart:

Conceptual Architecture:

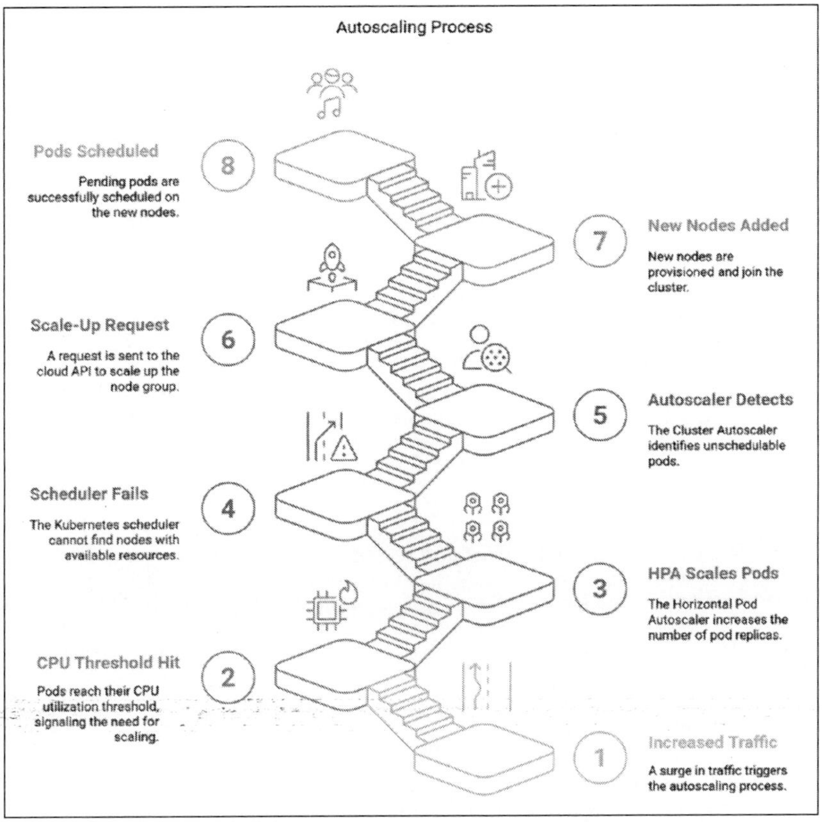

Figure 6b.2: *Autoscaling Flow in Kubernetes*

Autoscaling Process (Staircase Visual)

The preceding figure outlines **8 steps** in the autoscaling journey, with a colorful staircase metaphor indicating progression:

1. **Increased Traffic**
    a. A surge in user traffic or requests triggers higher demand on the application.
    b. This is the starting point of the autoscaling process, signaling that the system needs more resources to maintain performance.
2. **CPU Threshold Hit**
    a. Pods start reaching their **CPU utilization threshold** (or memory/other metrics if configured).
    b. This threshold breach acts as a signal for Kubernetes that existing pod capacity may be insufficient.

3. **HPA Scales Pods**
    a. The **Horizontal Pod Autoscaler** (HPA) responds by increasing the **number of pod replicas** to handle the increased load.
    b. It uses metrics such as CPU, memory, or custom metrics (via the Metrics Server) to determine scaling needs.
4. **Scheduler Fails**
    a. Kubernetes tries to **schedule the new pods** on existing nodes.
    b. If no node has enough resources (CPU, memory), the scheduler fails to place these pods, leaving them in a **Pending** state.
5. **Autoscaler Detects**
    a. The **Cluster Autoscaler** monitors unschedulable pods (pods stuck in Pending because no node can accommodate them).
    b. It identifies that more node capacity is required.
6. **Scale-Up Request**
    a. The Cluster Autoscaler issues a **scale-up request** to the cloud provider's API to add more nodes to the cluster.
    b. This may involve provisioning new virtual machines in the cloud environment.
7. **New Nodes Added**
    a. New nodes are **provisioned and added** to the cluster.
    b. They register with the Kubernetes control plane and are ready to host workloads.
8. **Pods Scheduled**
    a. Previously unschedulable pods are now **successfully scheduled** on the new nodes.
    b. The system returns to a balanced state, capable of handling the increased demand.

Key Takeaway: This process illustrates the interplay between **pod scaling (HPA)** and **node scaling (CA)**, showing how Kubernetes ensures both workload and infrastructure scale in response to demand.

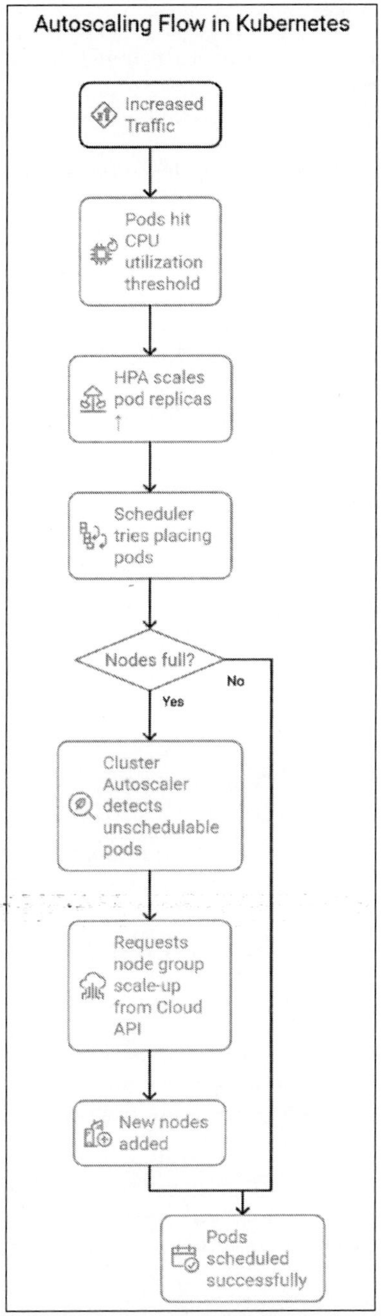

Figure 6b.3: *Autoscaling Flow in Kubernetes*

Autoscaling Flow in Kubernetes (Flowchart Visual)

This figure presents the same process in a **flowchart style**, emphasizing decision points and logical flow.

Start: Increased Traffic

- Increased application usage triggers the autoscaling logic.

Pods hit the CPU utilization threshold

- Pods begin breaching the configured **CPU threshold** (for example, 80% utilization), notifying HPA that more pods are needed.

HPA scales pod replicas

- HPA increases the **desired replica count** of the deployment to meet performance needs.

Scheduler tries to place pods:

- The Kubernetes **scheduler** attempts to assign the new pods to available nodes.

Decision Point: Nodes Full?

- If a node with sufficient resources is available → pods get scheduled immediately → **Pods scheduled successfully**.
- If no node has enough resources → the system moves to scale infrastructure.

Cluster Autoscaler detects unschedulable pods

- CA recognizes pods are **unschedulable** due to insufficient capacity.

Requests a node group scale-up from the Cloud API

- CA sends an API request to the cloud provider (for example, AWS, GCP, Azure) to **increase the node count** in the node group or auto-scaling group.

New nodes added

- Cloud provisions additional nodes, which then join the cluster.

Pods scheduled successfully

- Scheduler retries placing the unschedulable pods; this time, they succeed because new resources are available.

Key Takeaway: This flowchart emphasizes the **decision point** (whether nodes are full or not) and how Kubernetes escalates from pod scaling to infrastructure scaling.

Case Study: Leveraging Spot Nodes for Cost-Optimized Kubernetes Autoscaling

A leading fintech company operated a nightly **batch fraud detection pipeline** that processed large volumes of transactional data. This pipeline required significant computational power—**about 80 CPUs—from 10:00 PM to 4:00 AM**. However, outside these hours, the workload dropped to nearly zero.

Initially, the company provisioned its Kubernetes cluster with **10 static nodes**, designed to handle peak demand at all times. While this guaranteed resource availability, it resulted in **significant overprovisioning and underutilization** for approximately **18 hours daily**, leading to unnecessary infrastructure expenses.

Challenge: How to **reduce infrastructure costs** without compromising the workload's **Service Level Agreements (SLAs)**?

Solution: Introducing Spot Nodes and Dynamic Autoscaling

To address the inefficiency, the engineering team implemented a **cost-optimized autoscaling strategy** combining on-demand and spot (or preemptible) nodes with Kubernetes-native features:

Migrating to a Mixed Node Pool

Instead of relying solely on on-demand instances, the cluster was reconfigured to use a **hybrid node pool**:

- **On-demand nodes**: For critical, always-available services that could not tolerate disruption.
- **Spot nodes**: For interruptible, cost-sensitive workloads such as the nightly fraud detection jobs.

Spot nodes (also known as preemptible nodes in some clouds) are **significantly cheaper–often 60–80% less expensive than on-demand instances**–but come with the risk of being terminated by the cloud provider with little notice.

Configuring Cluster Autoscaler with "Least-Waste" Expansion Strategy

The **Kubernetes Cluster Autoscaler** was enabled and configured with the `expander=least-waste` **strategy**. This strategy selects node groups for scaling that result in **the least unused capacity per node**, improving resource efficiency.

With autoscaler enabled:

- The cluster could **scale up** spot nodes automatically during peak demand.
- The cluster could **scale down** idle nodes when demand subsided.

Using Taints and Tolerations to Control Workload Placement

To ensure only **interruptible workloads** ran on spot nodes, the spot node pool was configured with a **taint**:

```
yaml

spec:
  taints:
  - key: "spot"
    value: "true"
    effect: "NoSchedule"
```

This taint instructed Kubernetes **not to schedule any pods on these nodes unless the pod explicitly tolerated the taint**.

Workloads that were **designed to tolerate interruption** (such as batch fraud detection jobs) were configured with a **matching toleration**:

```
yaml

tolerations:
- key: "spot"
  operator: "Equal"
  value: "true"
  effect: "NoSchedule"
```

As a result:

- Critical services remained protected on **on-demand nodes**.
- Cost-sensitive, interruptible jobs were scheduled on **spot nodes**, taking advantage of the lower cost.

Pods **without the toleration** would **never be scheduled on spot nodes**, ensuring the separation of workload types.

Results Achieved

By implementing this strategy, the company achieved:

- **~65% reduction in infrastructure cost:** Since spot nodes were approximately **70% cheaper**, shifting most of the workload to them drove major savings.
- **Preserved SLAs:** Critical services remained unaffected, while batch workloads completed successfully even with occasional preemptions.

Dynamic scaling:

- Cluster autoscaled from **5 nodes (baseline)** → up to **30 nodes at night** to meet peak demand.
- Automatically scaled back down to **3 nodes during the day**, minimizing idle resources.

Broader Concept: Managing Node Pools with Taints and Tolerations

This case study demonstrates a broader Kubernetes principle: **using taints and tolerations to control workload placement** across specialized node pools.

Such strategies are applicable beyond spot instances:

- **GPU node pools** (for machine learning workloads) can be tainted with a key like **"nvidia.com/gpu"**.
- **High-memory nodes** can be tainted to reserve them for in-memory databases.

Example for GPU nodes:

```
yaml

spec:
  taints:
  - key: "nvidia.com/gpu"
    value: "true"
    effect: "NoSchedule"
```

Pods needing GPUs must declare a **matching toleration**:

```
yaml

tolerations:
- key: "nvidia.com/gpu"
  operator: "Equal"
  value: "true"
  effect: "NoSchedule"
```

Without a toleration, the pod **will not be scheduled** on a tainted node.

This mechanism allows operators to:

- Control the placement of specialized workloads.
- Prevent general-purpose workloads from occupying expensive nodes.

Key Takeaways: Interplay of Autoscaling and Node Pool Strategies

The synergy of **Cluster Autoscaler** for elastic scaling, **Node pool specialization with taints/tolerations, and Horizontal Pod Autoscaler (if workload-driven scaling is needed)** enables organizations to:

- Optimize cloud infrastructure costs.
- Maintain high availability and resiliency.
- Ensure workloads are correctly placed according to resource, cost, and reliability requirements.

This approach is a hallmark of **mature, cloud-native Kubernetes operations**, providing the balance between **cost efficiency and reliability at scale**.

Note: *By combining* ***spot instances, taints/tolerations, and autoscaling****, Kubernetes offers a powerful platform to optimize workloads both for cost and performance. This case study demonstrates how thoughtful configuration, rather than just scaling blindly, can unlock* ***significant savings*** *while maintaining* ***service quality and reliability****.*

Scaling Real-World Data Pipelines

Introduction: The Challenge of Scaling Data Pipelines

In modern distributed systems, **data pipelines are the backbone of real-time insights and operational intelligence.** But scaling these pipelines is non-trivial when:

- Data volume grows exponentially.
- Latency requirements tighten.
- Source/target systems change dynamically.

Traditionally, scaling big data platforms such as **Apache Spark, Apache Kafka, or Apache Flink** involved managing large clusters outside Kubernetes. But today, organizations seek:

- Cloud-native deployment of big data engines.
- Elastic scaling within Kubernetes.
- Seamless integration with DevOps and SRE tooling.

Scaling a data pipeline is more than adding CPU – it is about designing for **resilience, elasticity, and observability** at every stage: **ingestion, processing, storage, and serving.**

We will break this down in detail.

- **Why:**

  Scaling real-world data pipelines is needed because:

  - **Workload patterns fluctuate.** Example: A stock exchange platform sees 10x traffic during market open/close.
  - **Data volumes increase over time.** Static capacity leads to failures or backlogs.
  - **Business requirements evolve.** Adding new data sources → ingest more.
  - **Cost control.** Over-provisioning wastes money; under-provisioning causes SLA breaches.

  Scaling ensures:

  - Predictable throughput under load.
  - Low-latency processing.
  - Cost-optimized infrastructure.
  - Meeting regulatory/operational SLAs.

- **What:**

  Scaling data pipelines involves:

Component	Scaling Concern
Apache Spark	Scaling drivers and executors for batch/stream workloads.

Apache Kafka	Scaling brokers, partitions, and consumer groups.
Apache Flink	Scaling job managers and task managers.
Ingestion (Debezium, Kafka Connect)	Scaling connectors and tasks dynamically.

Table 6b.6: *Scaling Data Pipelines and Scaling Concerns*

Scaling must balance:

- Compute (CPU, memory)
- Storage (disk, throughput)
- Network I/O (bandwidth, latency)

- **When:**

  When to scale:

  - Traffic surge windows (example, Black Friday, IPO trading day).
  - Persistent lag in Kafka consumer groups.
  - Spark executors hitting memory/CPU bottlenecks.
  - Flink checkpoint delays increase over the SLA.
  - Kafka Connect task failures/restarts due to throughput bottleneck.

  Scaling is reactive (in response to alerts) **or proactive (based on historical usage trends).**

- **How:**

  Scaling inside Kubernetes → achieved via:

  - **Custom Resource Definitions (CRDs)** for Spark, Flink, Kafka (for example, Spark Operator, Strimzi).
  - **Horizontal scaling of Kubernetes pods** running brokers, connectors, or processing tasks.
  - **Auto-scalers:**
    - Horizontal Pod Autoscaler (HPA)
    - Vertical Pod Autoscaler (VPA)
    - Cluster Autoscaler (adds/removes nodes)

  Scaling strategy:

  - Spark → adjust executor count + dynamic allocation
  - Kafka → increase partitions + broker pods
  - Flink → scale task manager replicas
  - Kafka Connect → scale connector tasks per throughput

Scaling Spark, Kafka, and Flink Natively on Kubernetes

Each system has specific scaling characteristics.

- **Scaling Apache Spark:**

  In Kubernetes:

  - Spark driver runs as a pod.
  - Executors launched dynamically as pods → tied to **`spark.dynamicAllocation.enabled=true`**.

Example YAML for SparkJob:

```yaml
apiVersion: sparkoperator.k8s.io/v1beta2
kind: SparkApplication
metadata:
  name: spark-batch-job
spec:
  type: Scala
  mode: cluster
  image: gcr.io/spark-image:3.4.0
  mainClass: com.example.DataProcessor
  sparkVersion: "3.4.0"
  driver:
    cores: 1
    memory: "2g"
    serviceAccount: spark-sa
  executor:
    cores: 2
    instances: 5
    memory: "4g"
  dynamicAllocation:
    enabled: true
    initialExecutors: 2
    minExecutors: 2
    maxExecutors: 10
```

`dynamicAllocation` scales executors between 2 and 10 based on workload.

Explanation:

- Driver orchestrates the job lifecycle.
- Executors are added/removed automatically by Spark's shuffle-aware scheduler.

Scaling **reacts to stage queue size → no manual node tuning.**

- **Scaling Apache Kafka:**

  In Kubernetes, Kafka is deployed via operators (example, **Strimzi**).

  Kafka scaling happens at:

  - **Broker count** → add broker pods.
  - **Partition count** → re-partition topics.

  Scaling Brokers Example (Strimzi Kafka CRD):

```yaml
apiVersion: kafka.strimzi.io/v1beta2
kind: Kafka
metadata:
  name: kafka-cluster
spec:
  kafka:
    version: 3.5.0
    replicas: 5
    listeners:
      - name: plain
        port: 9092
```

```
        type: internal
    resources:
      requests:
        cpu: "1"
        memory: "4Gi"
      limits:
        cpu: "2"
        memory: "8Gi"
    storage:
      type: persistent-claim
      size: 100Gi
```

Scaling from **`replicas: 3 → replicas: 5`** adds brokers.

Important: Scaling brokers does not automatically rebalance partitions → must trigger **`kafka-reassign-partitions`** tool externally.

Scaling consumers → **add pod replicas in consumer deployment** → **increases parallelism.**

- **Scaling Apache Flink:**

  Kubernetes-native Flink deployment scales **TaskManagers** horizontally:

  Example YAML:

```yaml
apiVersion: flink.apache.org/v1beta1
kind: FlinkDeployment
metadata:
  name: flink-stream-job
spec:
  image: flink:1.17
  flinkVersion: v1_17
  taskManager:
    resource:
      cpu: 2
      memory: "4Gi"
    replicas: 4
  job:
    jarFile: local:///opt/flink/job.jar
    parallelism: 8
```

  Increasing replicas → increases available task slots → more parallelism.

  Scaling triggers:

  - Lag in Flink processing (example, checkpoint time increases).
  - Input Kafka partition count increases.
  - Stateful operators overwhelmed.

Designing Scalable Ingestion Pipelines: Debezium, Kafka Connect

Ingestion scaling differs → focuses on **connector tasks**.

Kafka Connect deploys **worker pods** running connectors. Each connector → internally parallelized via **tasks**.

Scaling ingestion = increase:

- **Connector tasks count** → parallelism
- **Worker pods count** → throughput/load

Example KafkaConnect CRD (Strimzi):

yaml

```
apiVersion: kafka.strimzi.io/v1beta2
kind: KafkaConnect
metadata:
  name: connect-cluster
spec:
  replicas: 3
  bootstrapServers: kafka-cluster-kafka-bootstrap:9092
  config:
    group.id: connect-cluster
    offset.storage.topic: connect-offsets
    config.storage.topic: connect-configs
    status.storage.topic: connect-status
  resources:
    requests:
      cpu: "1"
      memory: "2Gi"
```

Scaling from `replicas: 1 → replicas: 3` allows more connector workers.

The connector config also specifies `tasks.max` → controls parallel task count inside the connector.

Scaling bottleneck → observe **connector lag metrics** (example, Debezium lag).

Case Study: Streaming Financial Data at Scale

Context:

A stock exchange platform ingests **market trades, quotes, and orders (~20K messages/sec)**.

Architecture:

- Market feeds → Debezium → Kafka topics
- Stream processors → Flink jobs → derived streams
- Downstream apps → consume via REST/gRPC

Challenges:

- Data bursts during market open/close.
- Must scale ingestion and processing dynamically.
- SLA: **end-to-end latency <1 sec.**

Scaling decisions:

- Kafka brokers scaled from 3 → 6 during market open.
- Flink task managers scaled from 4 → 8 replicas dynamically at peak load. - Debezium connectors configured with `tasks.max: 4` → each connector handles 4 partitions.

  Observability → Prometheus + Grafana dashboards monitored:

  - Kafka consumer lag

- Flink checkpoint time
- Debezium task latency
- JVM heap/memory utilization

Automated scaling driven via **custom Kubernetes metrics → KEDA.**

Result → **zero lag, sustained <800ms latency under 20K msg/sec load.**

Observability Tools to Fine-Tune Scaling

Scaling decisions must be **data-driven.** The following table shows the key observability stack:

Tool	Purpose
Prometheus	Metrics collection (CPU, JVM, lag)
Grafana	Visualization and dashboards
JMX Exporter	JVM internals (GC, heap)
Kafka Exporter	Kafka topic lag, partition state

Table 6b.7: *Key Observability Stack – Tools and Purpose*

Metrics drive scaling triggers:

- Kafka lag spikes → scale consumers
- Flink checkpoint delay → scale task managers
- Spark stage runtime → increase executors
- Debezium connector lag → scale connector tasks

Architecture Diagram

Scaling Data Pipeline Flow:

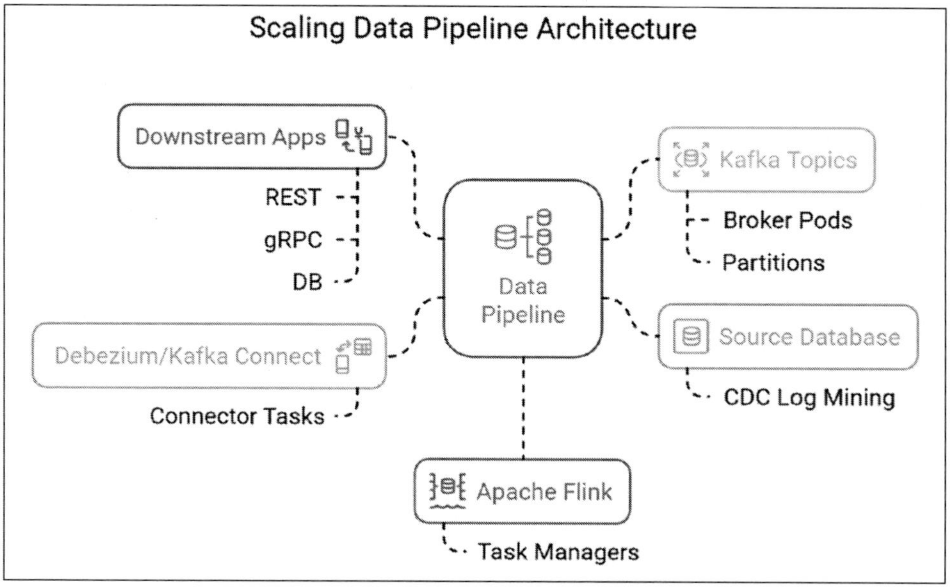

Figure 6b.4: *Scaling Data Pipeline Architecture*

The following figure demonstrates the Scaling Data Pipeline Flow:

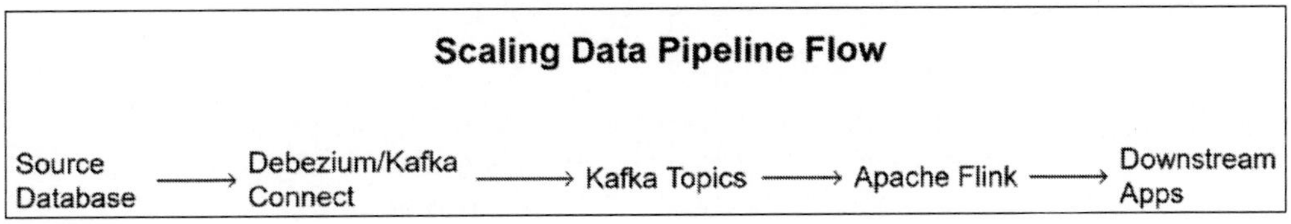

Figure 6b.5: *Scaling Data Pipeline Flow*

Scaling Data Pipeline Architecture: Explanation

This architecture represents a **scalable, event-driven data pipeline** built to handle high-velocity data flows with real-time processing and integration across systems. It demonstrates how various components work together in a streaming data pipeline, with each layer designed for independent scalability.

The pipeline follows this flow:

- **Source Database (CDC Log Mining):** The journey begins with a transactional source database (example, PostgreSQL, MySQL) configured for **Change Data Capture (CDC)**. This mechanism continuously monitors and captures insert, update, and delete operations from the database's transaction log without impacting transactional performance. These changes are transformed into event streams ready for downstream processing.
- **Debezium/Kafka Connect:** The captured CDC events are consumed by **Debezium**, an open-source distributed platform for change data capture, integrated with **Kafka Connect**. Debezium connectors read from the source database's transaction logs and publish change events into **Kafka topics**.
    - **Scaling point:** Debezium allows horizontal scaling by increasing **connector tasks**, enabling more parallel ingestion streams.
- **Kafka Topics:** Kafka acts as the **central event backbone**, storing incoming events in **topics** partitioned across **broker pods**. Partitioning enables parallelism, while replication ensures fault tolerance and durability. Kafka decouples producers (Debezium) from consumers (Flink and other consumers), providing a buffer and replayability.
    - **Scaling point:** Kafka scales horizontally by adding **broker pods** and increasing **topic partitions.**
- **Apache Flink (Stream Processing):** Kafka topics feed into **Apache Flink**, a distributed stream processing engine. Flink jobs perform real-time data transformations, enrichments, aggregations, or filtering as required by downstream business logic. Flink's **Task Managers** execute parallel processing tasks across a cluster.
    - **Scaling point:** Flink scales via **task managers** and **parallel processing slots.**
- **Downstream Applications:** Once processed, the data is delivered to **downstream applications**. These could be REST APIs, gRPC services, or directly to downstream databases and data warehouses. Applications consume the enriched and curated data for reporting, analytics, ML models, or operational use cases.
    - **Scaling point:** Downstream services can scale horizontally through **API replicas**, **load balancers**, or **database shards/replicas,** depending on consumer needs.

Key Design Principle: Independent Scalability

Each component in this architecture is designed to **scale independently**:

- **Debezium:** Scale the number of connector tasks for more ingestion throughput.

Kafka: Scale broker pods and partitions to increase ingestion and consumption parallelism.

Flink: Scale task managers and slots to boost processing throughput.

Consumers: Scale API servers, gRPC endpoints, or database replicas to serve more requests.

This scalability is managed inside a **Kubernetes-based deployment**, where containerized components can auto-scale based on observability metrics (example, CPU usage, lag in Kafka, Flink backpressure). Kubernetes controllers dynamically adjust replicas, ensuring high availability, throughput, and low latency under varying load conditions.

The **Scaling Data Pipeline Architecture** is a highly resilient and scalable design pattern for modern data platforms. By decoupling ingestion, processing, and consumption stages, organizations gain flexibility to independently scale each layer based on business needs and system demands, while maintaining data consistency, freshness, and availability.

Conclusion

Scaling real-world data pipelines is far from a one-time task - it is an ongoing process that requires continuous attention and adjustment. The process involves observing key metrics to identify performance bottlenecks, analyzing where improvements are needed, and then adjusting resources whether manually or through automated systems to address these issues. After adjustments are made, it is crucial to verify their impact to ensure that the changes have the desired effect. Kubernetes provides powerful platform primitives, such as **Custom Resource Definitions (CRDs), Horizontal Pod Autoscaler (HPA), Vertical Pod Autoscaler (VPA)**, and autoscalers, which enable the scaling of large data pipelines without the need for external orchestrators. When these tools are combined with robust observability, they empower cloud engineers, data engineers, and architects to build scalable, resilient, and cost-efficient data pipelines that can dynamically adapt to changing business requirements. The next chapter will delve into the intricacies of Role-Based Access Control (RBAC).

CHAPTER 7

Securing Kubernetes Workloads and DevSecOps

Introduction

Role-Based Access Control (RBAC) in Kubernetes is a fundamental security mechanism that governs access to cluster resources. By assigning permissions to roles and binding them to users or service accounts, RBAC ensures that entities have only the necessary access to perform their tasks, adhering to the principle of least privilege. This chapter delves into the intricacies of RBAC, providing a comprehensive understanding tailored for Cloud Engineers, DevOps professionals, Data Engineers, Data Architects, and Software Architects.

Structure

In this chapter, we will cover the following topics:

- Kubernetes Role-Based Access Control (RBAC)
- Securing Sensitive Data with Kubernetes Secrets
- Implementing Network Policies and Pod Security Policies
- Integrating DevSecOps into CI/CD Pipelines
- Vulnerability Scanning and Compliance Checks for Secure Data Pipelines

Essential Role of RBAC in Kubernetes

In a Kubernetes environment, multiple users and services interact with the cluster, each requiring specific permissions. Without a robust access control mechanism, there is a risk of unauthorized access, accidental misconfigurations, or malicious activities. RBAC addresses these concerns by:

- **Enforcing Least Privilege**: Ensuring users and services have only the permissions they need.
- **Enhancing Security Posture**: Reducing the attack surface by limiting access.
- **Facilitating Compliance**: Meeting regulatory requirements by controlling and auditing access.
- **Supporting Multi-Tenancy**: Isolating access in shared clusters to prevent cross-tenant interference.

Core Components of Kubernetes RBAC

RBAC in Kubernetes revolves around four primary components:

- **Role:** A Role defines a set of permissions within a specific namespace. It specifies allowed actions (verbs) on resources. **Example:**

  ```yaml
  yaml

  apiVersion: rbac.authorization.k8s.io/v1
  kind: Role
  metadata:
    namespace: development
    name: pod-reader
  rules:
  - apiGroups: [""]
    resources: ["pods"]
    verbs: ["get", "list"]
  ```

- **ClusterRole:** ClusterRoles are similar to Roles but are cluster-scoped. They can define permissions across all namespaces or for cluster-wide resources. **Example:**

  ```yaml
  yaml

  apiVersion: rbac.authorization.k8s.io/v1
  kind: ClusterRole
  metadata:
    name: cluster-admin
  rules:
  - apiGroups: ["*"]
   resources: ["*"]
    verbs: ["*"]
  ```

- **RoleBinding:** A RoleBinding grants the permissions defined in a Role to a user or service account within a specific namespace. **Example:**

  ```yaml
  yaml

  apiVersion: rbac.authorization.k8s.io/v1
  kind: RoleBinding
  metadata:
    name: read-pods
    namespace: development
  subjects:
  - kind: User
    name: alice
    apiGroup: rbac.authorization.k8s.io
  roleRef:
    kind: Role
    name: pod-reader
    apiGroup: rbac.authorization.k8s.io
  ```

- **ClusterRoleBinding:** A ClusterRoleBinding grants the permissions defined in a ClusterRole to a user or service account across the entire cluster. **Example:**

  ```yaml
  yaml

  apiVersion: rbac.authorization.k8s.io/v1
  kind: ClusterRoleBinding
  metadata:
    name: admin-binding
  ```

```
subjects:
- kind: User
  name: admin
  apiGroup: rbac.authorization.k8s.io
roleRef:
  kind: ClusterRole
  name: cluster-admin
  apiGroup: rbac.authorization.k8s.io
```

Roles versus ClusterRoles:

- **Roles:** Use when you want to grant permissions within a specific namespace. Ideal for applications or users that operate in a confined environment.
- **ClusterRoles:** Use when you need to grant permissions across the entire cluster or for cluster-scoped resources such as nodes or persistent volumes.

Implementing RBAC in Kubernetes

Step-by-Step Guide:

1. **Identify the Subjects:** Determine the users, groups, or service accounts that need access.
2. **Define Roles or ClusterRoles:** Specify the permissions required.
3. **Create RoleBindings or ClusterRoleBindings:** Associate the roles with the subjects.
4. **Apply the Configurations:** Use kubectl apply `-f` to deploy the YAML files.
5. **Verify Access:** Test the permissions to ensure that they work as intended.

Hands-On YAML Lab: Namespace-Restricted Access

Scenario: Grant a developer read-only access to pods in the "development" namespace.

Role Definition:

```
yaml

apiVersion: rbac.authorization.k8s.io/v1
kind: Role
metadata:
  namespace: development
  name: pod-reader
rules:
- apiGroups: [""]
  resources: ["pods"]
  verbs: ["get", "list"]
```

RoleBinding:

```
yaml

apiVersion: rbac.authorization.k8s.io/v1
kind: RoleBinding
metadata:
  name: read-pods
  namespace: development
subjects:
- kind: User
  name: dev-user
```

```
    apiGroup: rbac.authorization.k8s.io
roleRef:
    kind: Role
    name: pod-reader
    apiGroup: rbac.authorization.k8s.io
```

Apply the Configurations:

```
bash

kubectl apply -f role.yaml
kubectl apply -f rolebinding.yaml
```

Use Cases: Multi-Team Environments and Least-Privilege Enforcement

Multi-Team Environments

In organizations where multiple teams share a Kubernetes cluster, RBAC ensures that each team has access only to their respective namespaces. For instance, the "frontend" team can be granted permissions in the "frontend" namespace, while the "backend" team operates in the "backend" namespace.

Least-Privilege Enforcement

RBAC enables administrators to grant the minimal necessary permissions to users and services. For example, a CI/CD pipeline service account can be given permissions only to deploy applications, without access to modify cluster-wide settings.

Kubernetes Role-Based Access Control

Imagine a Kubernetes cluster with multiple namespaces: "development," "staging," and "production." Each namespace has its own set of Roles and RoleBindings. Users and service accounts are bound to roles within their respective namespaces. ClusterRoles and ClusterRoleBindings exist at the cluster level, granting permissions across all namespaces when necessary.

- **Namespace Isolation:** Roles and RoleBindings ensure that users operate within their designated namespaces, preventing unauthorized access to other environments.
- **Cluster-Wide Permissions:** ClusterRoles and ClusterRoleBindings are used sparingly, typically for administrators who require access across the entire cluster.
- **Service Accounts:** Applications running within the cluster use service accounts bound to specific roles, ensuring that they have only the permissions necessary for their operation.

  The following figure illustrates the core components and relationships involved in managing access permissions within a Kubernetes cluster. RBAC in Kubernetes is a mechanism for defining **who can perform what actions on which resources**, enforcing the principle of least privilege and improving security and governance in multi-tenant or enterprise environments.

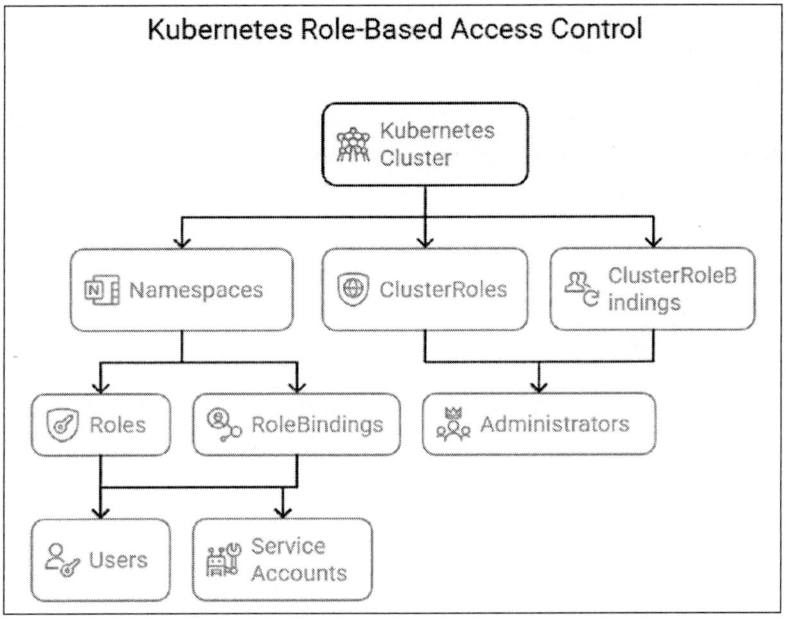

Figure 7.1: *Kubernetes Role-Based Access Control*

Let us break down each element in the preceding figure:

- **Kubernetes Cluster**
  - This represents the entire Kubernetes environment, hosting all deployed workloads, services, configurations, and administrative objects. RBAC policies are applied at either the **cluster level** or **namespace level** to control access.
- **Namespaces**
  - Kubernetes supports the logical separation of resources into **namespaces**. Each namespace acts as an isolated environment, allowing different teams or applications to share the same cluster without interfering with one another.
  - Within each namespace, **Roles** and **RoleBindings** are defined to restrict access at a fine-grained level.
- **Roles**
  - A **Role** defines a set of **permissions** (verbs such as get, list, create, delete) that apply to resources **within a namespace** (example, pods, deployments, services).
  - Example: A Role might allow a user to read pods but not delete them in the "development" namespace.
- **RoleBindings**
  - A **RoleBinding** associates a **Role** with a specific **user** or **service account** inside a namespace. It "binds" users to the permissions defined in a Role.
  - This ensures that only authorized users or service accounts can perform actions in that namespace.
- **Users and Service Accounts**
  - **Users** represent human operators or developers who interact with the Kubernetes API (example, via kubectl).

- **Service Accounts** represent **machine identities**–commonly used by applications running inside the cluster to authenticate with the API server securely.

- **ClusterRoles**
  - While Roles are namespace-scoped, **ClusterRoles** define permissions **across the entire cluster** (including non-namespace resources such as nodes and persistent volumes).
  - ClusterRoles are essential for cluster-wide administrative tasks.
- **ClusterRoleBindings**
  - Similar to RoleBindings, but at the **cluster level**. A **ClusterRoleBinding** binds a **ClusterRole** to a user or service account globally, granting permissions across all namespaces or cluster-level resources.
- **Administrators**
  - Administrators are typically assigned **ClusterRoles** via **ClusterRoleBindings**, giving them broad or full access across the Kubernetes cluster.
  - They are responsible for managing RBAC policies, roles, and access boundaries.

How RBAC Works Together?

When a user or service account makes an API request, Kubernetes checks: Does this user have a **Role** or **ClusterRole** granting the requested action? Is there a **RoleBinding** or **ClusterRoleBinding** that associates this role to the user or service account?

If both are true, access is granted. Otherwise, the action is denied.

Why RBAC Matters?

RBAC enables:

- **Separation of Duties:** Dev teams can manage their namespace without impacting others.
- **Compliance:** Restrict sensitive operations (such as node manipulation) to specific admins.
- **Auditability:** Trace which user or service account performed critical actions.

By structuring access control around **roles and bindings**, organizations gain fine-grained governance over their Kubernetes environments, reduce the risk of accidental misconfigurations, and ensure that production workloads remain secure.

Key Takeaways:

- **RBAC policies are layered:** Role → RoleBinding → User/ServiceAccount.
- **Namespace versus Cluster scope:** **`Roles/RoleBindings`** apply **within namespaces** and **`ClusterRoles/ClusterRoleBindings`** apply **cluster-wide**.
- **RBAC is declarative:** You define roles and bindings using YAML files that can be version-controlled alongside application code.

Best Practices:

- **Principle of Least Privilege:** Always grant the minimal permissions necessary.
- **Use Namespaces**: Leverage namespaces to isolate resources and access.
- **Regular Audits**: Periodically review roles and bindings to ensure that they align with current requirements.
- **Avoid Wildcards:** Be cautious with wildcard permissions (*), as they can grant broader access than intended.
- **Document Roles**: Maintain clear documentation of roles and their purposes for transparency and ease of management.

Implementing RBAC in Kubernetes is essential for securing cluster resources and ensuring that users and services operate within their intended boundaries. By understanding and applying the concepts of Roles, RoleBindings, ClusterRoles, and ClusterRoleBindings, organizations can enforce fine-grained access control, enhance security, and maintain compliance in multi-tenant environments.

Securing Sensitive Data with Kubernetes Secrets

In modern distributed systems, applications frequently need to access sensitive data–such as database passwords, API keys, TLS certificates, SSH credentials, and encryption keys. If improperly handled, these secrets become the weakest link in the security chain.

- **Why does this problem exist:** Traditionally, developers hardcoded credentials into application configs or environment variables checked into version control systems. This practice exposes secrets to unauthorized users, leading to data breaches, compliance violations, and attacks.
- **Why is Kubernetes impacted:** Kubernetes deployments often use declarative YAML manifests stored in Git or CI/CD pipelines. If secrets are not isolated, they risk exposure in plain text through logs, manifests, or Git histories.

Key Risks:

- Hardcoded passwords in manifests.
- Unauthorized access to etcd (the cluster data store).
- Insecure transmission of secrets to containers.
- Accidental disclosure through CLI tools.

Kubernetes Secrets

Kubernetes **Secrets** are specialized Kubernetes objects designed to securely store small pieces of sensitive data. Unlike ConfigMaps, secrets are encoded and optionally encrypted at rest in etcd.

Core Features:

- Stored as **base64-encoded values** (not encrypted by default, encoding is for transport).
- **Mounted as environment variables or volumes** inside pods.
- **Access controlled** via RBAC (can restrict who/what reads secrets).
- Supports **encryption at rest** with Kubernetes Encryption Configuration.
- Used by pods transparently, without exposing in logs or process lists.

Types of Secrets:

- **Opaque:** General key-value pairs
- **docker-registry:** For Docker credentials
- **tls:** For certificate pairs

When Should You Use Kubernetes Secrets:

- When applications need runtime credentials (DB password, token).
- When automating sensitive workflows inside CI/CD pipelines.
- When credentials must rotate or expire periodically.
- When multi-tenant clusters require isolated secret access per namespace.

In production, use secrets **any time credentials are referenced by containers, scripts, or services running inside Kubernetes**.

Important: Secrets should never be stored in plaintext YAML repos. Always use sealed secrets, GitOps workflows with encryption, or external secret managers for long-term storage.

Implementing Secrets Securely in Kubernetes

Step-by-Step Workflow:

1. **Creating a Kubernetes Secret**

   Example: Store **`DB_PASSWORD=supersecure123`** as a secret.

   a. Encode Secret Value:

   ```
   bash

   echo -n "supersecure123" | base64
   # Output: c3VwZXJzZWN1cmUxMjM=
   ```

   b. Define Secret YAML:

   ```
   yaml

   apiVersion: v1
   kind: Secret
   metadata:
     name: db-credentials
   type: Opaque
   data:
     DB_PASSWORD: c3VwZXJzZWN1cmUxMjM=
   ```

   c. Apply Secret:

   ```
   bash

   kubectl apply -f db-secret.yaml
   ```

2. **Accessing Secrets in a Pod (Env Vars)**

   ```
   yaml

   apiVersion: v1
   kind: Pod
   metadata:
     name: db-app
   spec:
     containers:
     - name: app
       image: alpine
       env:
       - name: DB_PASSWORD
         valueFrom:
           secretKeyRef:
             name: db-credentials
             key: DB_PASSWORD
   ```

   Inside the container:

   ```
   bash

   echo $DB_PASSWORD
   # Prints: supersecure123
   ```

3. **Accessing Secrets as Mounted Volumes**

```yaml
yaml

apiVersion: v1
kind: Pod
metadata:
  name: db-app
spec:
  containers:
  - name: app
    image: alpine
    volumeMounts:
    - name: secret-vol
      mountPath: "/etc/secret"
      readOnly: true
  volumes:
  - name: secret-vol
    secret:
      secretName: db-credentials
```

The file `/etc/secret/DB_PASSWORD` will contain the value.

Industry Best Practices for Secret Management:

- **Encrypt Secrets at Rest:** Use Kubernetes encryption providers (KMS, AWS KMS, Azure Key Vault) so that etcd stores encrypted secrets.
- **Avoid Inline Base64 Secrets in Git:** Avoid checking base64 strings in Git. Use sealed secrets, SOPS, or tools such as Helm Secrets to encrypt data before committing.
- **Leverage External Secret Managers:** For higher compliance, use integration with Vault, AWS Secrets Manager, Azure Key Vault, or Google Secret Manager.
- **Use Least-Privilege RBAC:** Limit access to secrets through namespace RBAC. Only apps or users who require secrets should be able to retrieve them.
- **Rotate Secrets Periodically:** Design apps to re-read secrets from mounted paths or environment variables to allow secret updates without restarts.
- **Audit Secret Access:** Enable audit logging in Kubernetes to monitor which subjects access secrets.

Integration with External Secret Managers

Organizations often extend Kubernetes Secrets with **external secret managers** for enterprise-grade security.

Vault Example:

- Vault stores secret values outside Kubernetes.
- Use a vault-agent injector to inject secrets as environment variables or volumes.
- Supports secret leasing, automatic rotation.

Kubernetes Secret Management with Vault

The following figure illustrates the integration of **HashiCorp Vault** as a secure, centralized solution for managing secrets in Kubernetes. Vault plays a critical role in securely storing, distributing, and accessing sensitive data such as API keys, database credentials, and encryption keys in a cloud-native environment.

Architecture Flow:

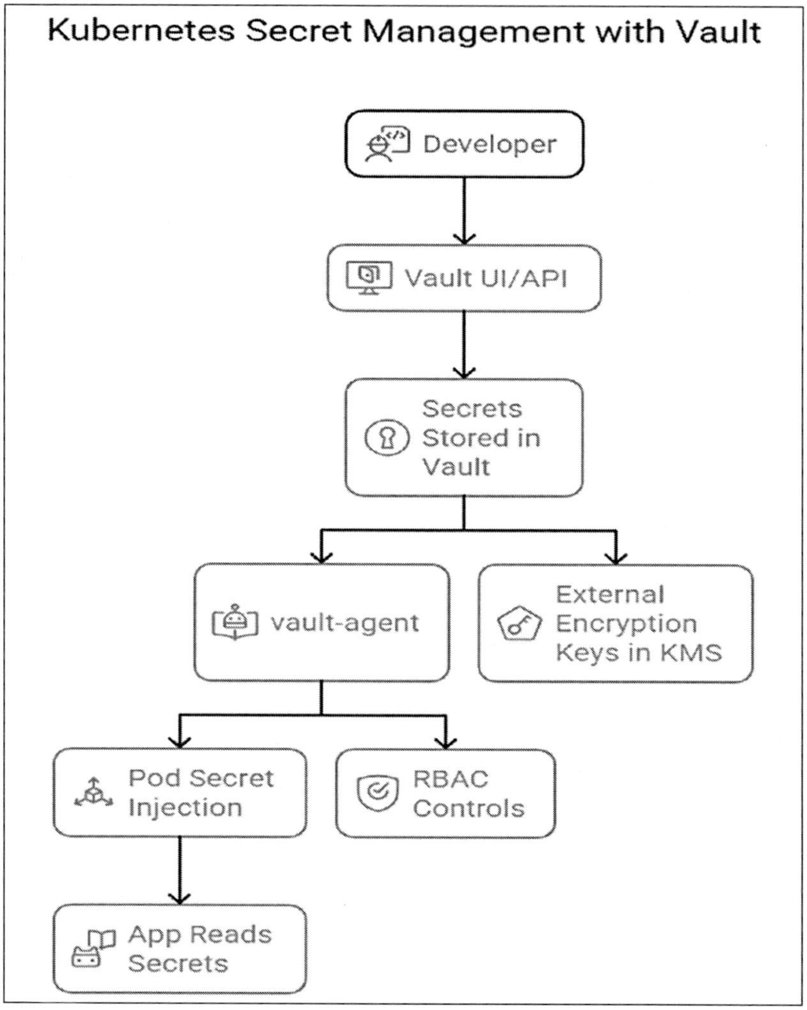

Figure 7.2: *Kubernetes Secret Management with Vault*

Let us walk through the preceding figure step by step:

Developer Interaction

At the top of the flow, a **developer** interacts with Vault through either its **UI (Web interface)** or its **API (programmatic access)**.

- This allows the developer to write, read, and manage secrets inside Vault.
- The UI/API acts as the entry point for secret lifecycle management (creation, update, deletion).

Secrets Stored in Vault

Once a secret is submitted by the developer, it is securely **stored inside Vault**.

- Vault encrypts the secrets at rest using strong cryptographic algorithms.
- Secrets can be organized into key-value pairs, or structured data (for example, JSON), depending on application needs.

Integration Paths: Vault-Agent and External KMS

From this point, the workflow splits into **two main integration paths**:

- **Vault-Agent Path**
  - A **vault-agent** runs inside the Kubernetes cluster.
  - It acts as an intermediary, authenticating with Vault and retrieving secrets securely without requiring the application to directly handle Vault tokens.
  - The vault-agent can inject secrets directly into pods via **sidecar containers** or **init containers**.
- **External Encryption Keys (KMS)**
  - Vault itself can be configured to use an external **Key Management System (KMS)** (such as AWS KMS, Google Cloud KMS, or Azure Key Vault) for managing its own encryption keys.
  - This adds another layer of protection. If the Vault storage backend is compromised, secrets remain protected by the external KMS.
- **Pod Secret Injection and RBAC Controls**

  Pod Secret Injection
  - Using the vault-agent, secrets are **injected directly into running Kubernetes pods** either as environment variables or mounted files.
  - This eliminates the need to store secrets in Kubernetes native Secrets objects (which may be less secure without extra protections).
- **RBAC Controls**
  - Vault applies **Role-Based Access Control (RBAC)** policies to enforce **who or what has access to specific secrets**.
  - These RBAC rules ensure least-privilege access, controlling which applications or teams can access certain keys or credentials.
- **App Reads Secrets**

  Finally, inside the pod, the **application reads the injected secrets** securely:
  - Secrets may be accessed from files mounted into the container filesystem.
  - Or the application can read from pre-populated environment variables injected by the vault-agent.
  - The application never needs to directly query Vault or manage Vault tokens–improving security and simplifying integration.

Importance of Vault Integration Kubernetes

Figure 7.2 encapsulates the **best practices for secret management in Kubernetes**, avoiding common pitfalls such as:

- Storing unencrypted secrets in version control.
- Using static Kubernetes Secrets without encryption at rest.
- Hardcoding credentials into application images.

Vault enables:

- Dynamic secret generation (for example, temporary database passwords).
- Centralized audit logging for secret access.

- Seamless rotation and revocation of credentials without restarting applications.

Key Takeaways:

- Vault acts as the central source of truth for secrets, not Kubernetes Secrets objects.
- vault-agent bridges Vault and Kubernetes workloads securely, automating token handling and secret delivery.
- External KMS integration provides an additional security boundary for encrypting Vault data at rest.
- RBAC policies in Vault control fine-grained access to secrets for both human and machine users.

Final Thought: By integrating Vault into a Kubernetes cluster following this architecture, organizations can achieve a secure, scalable, auditable secret management workflow suitable for compliance-driven or highly regulated environments.

Real-World Case Study

Context:

A fintech company runs multi-tenant SaaS on Kubernetes. Security audits flagged hardcoded database (DB) passwords inside deployment YAML files.

Problem (Why): The company initially encoded passwords in base64 inside manifests stored in Git, exposing secrets to DevOps team members.

Modern Solution (What): The company integrated Vault with Kubernetes using vault-agent injector sidecars.

When: Secrets required live rotation every 24 hours to comply with PCI-DSS.

How:

- Vault centrally stores secrets.
- vault-agent injects secrets into pods on startup.
- Containers read secrets from `/vault/secrets/`.
- No secrets persisted in environment variables or YAML files.

Result:

- Zero secrets stored in etcd or Git.
- Dynamic secrets rotated daily without app restarts.
- Compliance passed with no findings.

Common Pitfalls and Mitigations:

- **`Base64 ≠ Encryption`:** Base64 is encoding, NOT encryption. Always enable encryption at rest in Kubernetes.
- **Plaintext Secrets in CI/CD Logs:** Mask secret values in pipelines to prevent leaks.
- **Excessive RBAC Permissions:** Avoid giving ClusterRole with `get secrets` to service accounts unless required.

Secret Management in Kubernetes with Vault

In modern cloud-native applications, managing secrets such as database passwords, API tokens, and encryption keys securely is critical. Kubernetes provides a native way to store secrets, but enterprises often use tools such as **HashiCorp Vault** for centralized and robust secret management. The following figure illustrates how Vault integrates with Kubernetes to manage secrets securely:

The concept of the following figure:

- External Vault server
- Kubernetes API server
- vault-agent sidecar
- Application container

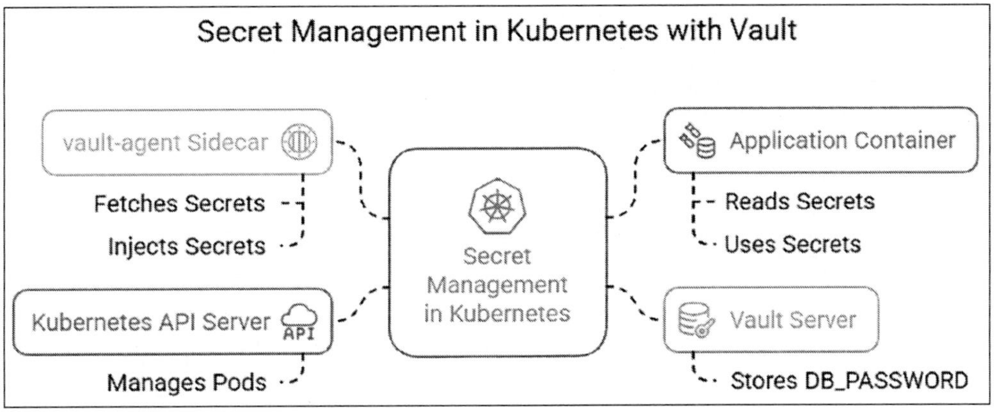

***Figure 7.3:** Secret Management in Kubernetes with Vault*

The preceding figure shows the secret flow:

- Vault stores **`DB_PASSWORD`**
- vault-agent fetches and injects secret
- The application reads from **`/vault/secrets/DB_PASSWORD`**

Architecture Overview

Figure 7.3 shows an overview of how **Vault integrates with Kubernetes** to manage secrets dynamically.

Key Components:

- **Vault Server:** This is the core secret store where sensitive information such as **`DB_PASSWORD`** is stored securely. It handles encryption, access control, and audit logging.
- **vault-agent Sidecar:** A lightweight agent that runs alongside the application container (as a sidecar pod). Its job is to **fetch secrets** from the Vault Server and **inject them into the application's environment** (often as files or environment variables). It keeps secrets updated without restarting the app.
- **Kubernetes API Server:** Acts as the control plane in Kubernetes, managing pods and their lifecycle. It ensures the pod is running with the right configuration and permissions.
- **Application Container:** This is your main application workload that needs access to secrets. Once the **`vault-agent`** sidecar injects the secret (for example, a database password), the app reads it from a predefined location, such as a file path or environment variable.

Flow Summary:

1. The **Vault Server** stores the secret.
2. The **vault-agent** securely fetches the secret and injects it inside the application's pod.

3. The **application container** reads the secret and uses it in its runtime (for example, connecting to a database).
4. The **Kubernetes API Server** manages pod deployment and orchestrates the sidecar and app container lifecycle.

This design avoids storing secrets directly in Kubernetes Secret objects (which are base64 encoded but not encrypted by default) and instead uses Vault's encryption and access control capabilities.

Stepwise Flow:

Figure 7.4 presents a **step-by-step flow** of how secrets are injected into an application pod in Kubernetes using Vault.

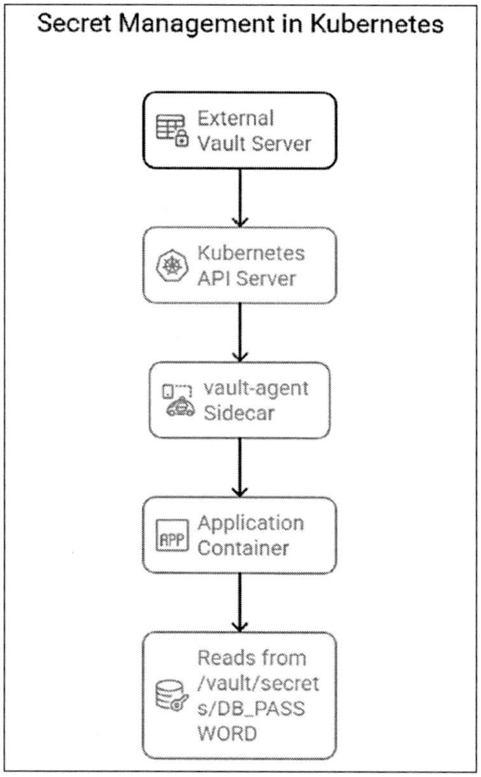

***Figure* 7.4:** *Secret Management in Kubernetes*

Step-by-Step Explanation:

1. **External Vault Server:** An external Vault server stores the secrets centrally. This server is independent of Kubernetes but exposes APIs to interact with the cluster.
2. **Kubernetes API Server:** When a pod is created, the Kubernetes API server manages its scheduling and lifecycle, coordinating its components.
3. **vault-agent Sidecar:** As part of the pod, a vault-agent sidecar container runs alongside the application. When the pod starts, the vault-agent authenticates to Vault (usually via Kubernetes Service Account) and fetches the secret (for example, `DB_PASSWORD`).
4. **Application Container:** The main app container starts and relies on the vault-agent sidecar to fetch and write the secret into a shared volume or environment variable.

5. **Reads from `/vault/secrets/DB_PASSWORD`:** The application reads the secret from a mounted path (such as **`/vault/secrets/DB_PASSWORD`**). This secret is now available in memory inside the pod without ever being persisted in the pod's YAML manifest or Kubernetes secrets API.

Why This Approach Matters:

- **Enhanced Security:** Secrets are never stored directly in Kubernetes objects; instead, they are dynamically injected at runtime.
- **Least Privilege:** Vault uses fine-grained RBAC policies to control which pods/roles can access specific secrets.
- **Automatic Secret Rotation:** Vault can rotate credentials or tokens without restarting the app, and vault-agent ensures that the app always has the latest secret.
- **Audit and Compliance:** All secret accesses are logged centrally by Vault for auditing purposes.

Use Case Example

Imagine a web app that needs a database password. Instead of hardcoding the password or passing it via Kubernetes Secret, the app's pod runs with a vault-agent sidecar that fetches the password from Vault every time the pod starts. The app simply reads from **`/vault/secrets/DB_PASSWORD`**, keeping the password out of code, YAML files, and Git repositories.

Figure 7.2 showcase a secure and automated workflow for handling secrets in Kubernetes using Vault. By combining **vault-agent sidecars, Kubernetes orchestration, and external Vault storage**, organizations can achieve a highly secure, auditable, and scalable secret management solution for cloud-native applications.

By leveraging Kubernetes Secrets **with encryption, RBAC, and optionally external secret managers**, engineers can securely manage sensitive data in a cloud-native environment. Combining these practices ensures:

- Stronger compliance,
- Reduced insider threats,
- Secure runtime secret delivery, and
- Support for automated secret rotation.

Final Words: For production, never treat Kubernetes Secrets as a full security solution alone. Pair with encryption at rest, RBAC, audit logging, and optionally, external secret managers for a defense-in-depth approach.

Implementing Network Policies and Pod Security Policies

In Kubernetes, **Pods can freely communicate across the cluster by default.** While this open communication simplifies deployment, it **increases the attack surface and violates security best practices** in multi-tenant, sensitive, or regulated workloads.

Without network isolation:

- A compromised Pod can laterally move to access other Pods or services.
- Malicious actors inside one namespace could scan and attack Pods across namespaces.
- Compliance frameworks (PCI DSS, HIPAA, ISO 27001) require **segmentation between workloads handling sensitive versus non-sensitive data.**

Therefore, network isolation is critical to enforce least-privilege communication, limit blast radius, and comply with security standards.

Network Policies and Pod Security Policies

Network Policies: A NetworkPolicy is a Kubernetes object that controls which Pods can communicate with each other or external endpoints.

Key properties:

- Works at **Layer 3 and 4 (IP + port level).**
- Requires a **CNI plugin that supports NetworkPolicies** (for example, **Calico, Cilium, and Weave Net).**
- Default behavior: **deny nothing until a policy is defined.**

Example actions:

- Allow traffic **only from the same namespace.**
- Deny all **external inbound traffic.**
- Allow **DNS and logging egress** but deny internet access.

Pod Security Policies (PSPs): ***(deprecated)***

Originally, PSPs were Kubernetes' built-in mechanism for controlling security contexts at the Pod level, such as:

- Prevent privileged containers,
- Restrict hostPath volume usage, and
- Limit Linux capabilities.

However:

- PSPs were deprecated in **Kubernetes 1.21** and removed in **1.25.**
- Replacement solutions: **OPA Gatekeeper, Kyverno, Pod Security Admission (PSA).**

When should you use NetworkPolicies and Pod Security:

- Anytime you run **multi-tenant clusters (shared Dev, QA, Prod environments).**
- To **segregate workloads** (frontend → backend → DB tiers).
- To comply with **PCI DSS requirement 1.2.1** (restrict traffic to that which is necessary).
- When hosting **stateful workloads (such as, Kafka, Redis)** that should not expose internal ports globally.
- Before deploying third-party apps from unknown sources.

Implementing Network Policies in Practice

Example 1: "Deny All by Default" Network Policy

```
yaml

apiVersion: networking.k8s.io/v1
kind: NetworkPolicy
metadata:
  name: deny-all
  namespace: sensitive-ns
spec:
  podSelector: {}
  policyTypes:
  - Ingress
  - Egress
```

Explanation:

- Applies to **all Pods** in namespace sensitive-ns.
- **Blocks all inbound and outbound traffic** unless another policy explicitly allows.

Use this as a **baseline policy**, layering selective allow-policies on top.

Example 2: Allow Only Namespace Internal Traffic

```
yaml

apiVersion: networking.k8s.io/v1
kind: NetworkPolicy
metadata:
  name: allow-ns-internal
  namespace: sensitive-ns
spec:
  podSelector: {}
  ingress:
  - from:
    - podSelector: {}
  egress:
  - to:
    - podSelector: {}
```

Explanation:

- Pods in sensitive-ns can only talk **to other Pods inside the same namespace.**
- No external or cross-namespace communication permitted.

Real-world: This setup enforces **namespace-level segmentation for PCI DSS zones.**

PCI DSS Network Segmentation in Kubernetes

The following figure illustrates how to design a Kubernetes cluster architecture that aligns with **Payment Card Industry Data Security Standard (PCI DSS)** compliance by implementing network segmentation:

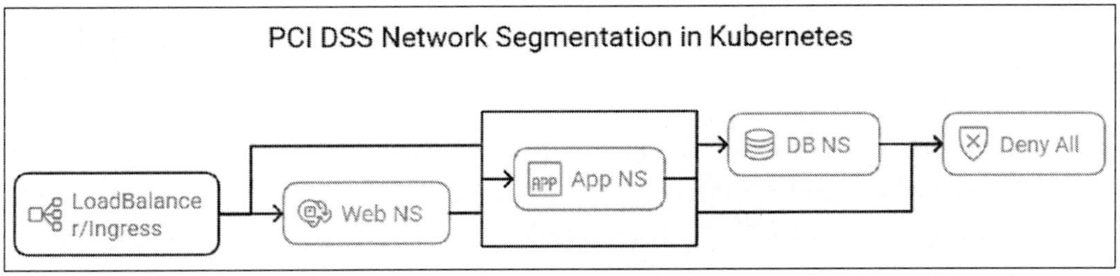

Figure 7.5: *PCI DSS Network Segmentation in Kubernetes*

This approach ensures sensitive systems including databases are isolated from less-trusted zones such as web-facing applications, reducing attack surfaces and limiting lateral movement.

Breakdown of the Architecture:

- **LoadBalancer / Ingress:**

  At the entry point of the Kubernetes cluster, a **LoadBalancer** or **Ingress Controller** handles incoming HTTP/HTTPS traffic from external users or systems. This component acts as the

gateway, routing requests to internal namespaces while enforcing initial security measures such as TLS termination, IP whitelisting, and Web Application Firewalls (WAF).

Purpose: Controls and secures external traffic access into the Kubernetes environment.

- **Web NS (Namespace):**

  Once traffic passes through the ingress layer, it enters the **Web Namespace (Web NS)**–a Kubernetes namespace dedicated to hosting **frontend or public-facing applications** (for example, a web server or API gateway). This namespace is isolated to handle internet-facing workloads and has limited permissions to internal services.

  Purpose: Acts as the **first security boundary** between external users and internal applications.

  Security policies: Can enforce **network policies** to only allow outbound connections to authorized backend services.

- **App NS (Namespace):**

  Requests forwarded from the web tier are sent to the **App Namespace (App NS)**, which houses the **application logic layer** (for example, business APIs, backend services). This namespace is **segregated from the web namespace** to reduce direct exposure to public traffic.

  Purpose: Contains the backend services that process sensitive data or logic, protected from direct internet access.

  Security policies: Only accepts traffic from the Web NS; no direct external access.

- **DB NS (Namespace):**

  The **Database Namespace (DB NS)** holds the **databases and data storage services**, which contain sensitive payment data or cardholder information. Under PCI DSS, databases must be protected in their own isolated zone to prevent unauthorized access.

  Purpose: Keeps **Cardholder Data Environment (CDE)** separate from application and web layers.

  Security policies: Strict network controls to only allow inbound connections from App NS.

- **Deny All (Default Deny Policy):**

  At the far end of the architecture, the preceding figure shows a **Deny All** policy, representing a **default-deny network policy** applied cluster-wide or namespace-level. This policy blocks **all traffic by default** except explicitly permitted connections defined earlier (for example, from App NS to DB NS).

  Purpose: Acts as a **fail-safe mechanism** to block unauthorized or unintended connections, enforcing **zero-trust networking**.

How This Architecture Enforces PCI DSS Compliance:

The PCI DSS standard requires:

- Segmentation between trusted and untrusted networks.
- Restricting access to cardholder data strictly on a need-to-know basis.
- Limiting inbound and outbound traffic to essential connections.

This architecture fulfills those requirements by:

- Using **namespaces** as **logical security zones** (Web, App, DB).
- Applying **network policies** (such as Kubernetes NetworkPolicy or Calico policies) to control which namespaces can communicate.

- Employing a **default-deny stance** to block all other traffic, reducing accidental exposures.

Each namespace operates like an isolated security zone similar to network VLANs in traditional data centers. Policies define **explicit allowed connections between namespaces** while denying everything else by default.

Benefits of This Design:

- Reduces the risk of **lateral movement** inside the cluster if an app is compromised.
- Simplifies **auditing and compliance reporting** for PCI DSS.
- Supports a **defense-in-depth** security posture.
- Flexible scaling: You can scale services independently inside each namespace without breaching segmentation.

Real-World Example

Consider an online store processing credit card payments. The web server (frontend) lives in Web NS, the order processing API in App NS, and the payment database in DB NS. With segmentation:

- Only the web server can talk to the API server.
- Only the API server can query the database.
- The database never receives traffic from the internet or frontend directly.

This controlled flow ensures **no unauthorized direct access** to sensitive data.

Conclusion: *Figure* 7.5 exemplifies how Kubernetes can be architected to meet PCI DSS network segmentation requirements by using namespaces and network policies as the core building blocks. It demonstrates the principle of **least privilege networking**, and provides a scalable, modern equivalent of traditional firewall segmentation for containerized environments.

Industry Case Study: Securing a Financial Services Platform with Kubernetes Network Policies

In this real-world example, a financial services company deployed a fraud detection platform built on Kubernetes using multiple microservices. Security and compliance were critical requirements due to the sensitive nature of financial transactions and the need to adhere to regulatory standards such as PCI DSS.

To protect its infrastructure, the company implemented a robust **network segmentation strategy using Kubernetes Network Policies.** This approach enabled fine-grained control over how pods and services could communicate within the cluster.

Solution Design and Implementation

The company applied the following key configurations:

- **Deny-All Baseline Policy:** They enforced a *default deny-all network policy* at the namespace level for each workload environment. This meant that no pod was allowed to send or receive traffic unless explicitly permitted by an allow rule. This baseline policy significantly reduced the attack surface by blocking unauthorized communications.
- **Controlled Internal Communications:** For the fraud detection service, they created an allow policy only for gRPC traffic from the App Namespace (App NS) to the Scoring Namespace (Scoring NS). This ensured that only authorized application pods responsible for fraud analysis could invoke scoring services. No other namespaces or workloads could access the scoring engine, protecting it from lateral movement within the cluster.

- **Restricted Egress Traffic:** The platform also restricted outbound network connections. By default, pods could not access the internet. An exception was configured to allow outbound traffic only through a controlled proxy. This design prevented pods from accidentally or maliciously leaking data directly to the internet while still allowing approved outbound communications through monitoring and security appliances.

Outcomes Achieved

The implementation of these policies delivered several measurable security and compliance benefits, such as:

- **Prevented Lateral Movement:** During penetration testing, security teams attempted lateral traversal within the cluster. The network segmentation successfully blocked these attempts, confining each service to its designated communication scope.
- **Passed PCI DSS Compliance Controls:** The platform achieved compliance with PCI DSS control 1.2.1 (restrict inbound traffic to necessary components) and control 1.3.4 (restrict outbound traffic to necessary destinations) thanks to the enforced deny-by-default approach and explicit allow policies.
- **Avoided Production Outage from Misconfigured Container:** A third-party logging container was later discovered to be misconfigured, attempting to send logs directly to an external endpoint. Because of the enforced egress restrictions, this misconfiguration did not result in data exposure or production instability. The policy effectively contained unintended traffic until the issue was resolved.

Key Takeaways

This case study demonstrates that **network segmentation using Kubernetes Network Policies** is a powerful strategy to enforce the principle of least privilege, contain security breaches, and satisfy compliance requirements in regulated industries.

By combining a deny-all baseline with selective allow rules and controlled egress policies, the organization achieved a **resilient, compliant, and secure microservices architecture** without sacrificing operational agility.

This example underscores the importance of integrating security controls directly into Kubernetes workloads rather than relying solely on perimeter defenses or external firewalls.

Integrating DevSecOps into CI/CD Pipelines

In traditional software delivery, **security checks were performed at the end of the development cycle** – causing last-minute delays, costly fixes, and production risks.

In modern cloud-native architectures:

- Rapid deployments happen daily (or hourly).
- Microservices independently evolve and deploy in parallel.
- Containerized workloads increase surface area (vulnerabilities in base images, dependencies, Kubernetes manifests).

Security **cannot be bolted on later; it must be integrated from Day 1.**

This shift is called **DevSecOps: embedding security into DevOps workflows.**

Without DevSecOps:

- Vulnerable container images shipped to production.
- Misconfigured Kubernetes manifests expose privileged workloads.

- Compliance violations (PCI, HIPAA) discovered **after release.**

For cloud engineers, DevSecOps is no longer optional–it is a critical success factor for secure, scalable, and compliant systems.

DevSecOps in Kubernetes CI/CD Pipelines

DevSecOps in Kubernetes integrates security scanning, policy enforcement, and compliance validation as automated stages inside CI/CD pipelines.

Key goals:

- Scan every container image for known CVEs before deploying.
- Validate Kubernetes manifests (YAML linting, security policies).
- Enforce admission control to block non-compliant deployments.
- Shift-left security so that vulnerabilities are caught early.

Common tools for Kubernetes DevSecOps:

Tool	**Function**
Trivy	Vulnerability scanner for container images and IaC files
Snyk	Dependency scanning, license checks
Polaris	Kubernetes YAML policy validation
Kube-bench	CIS Kubernetes benchmark checks
OPA Gatekeeper	Admission controller for policy enforcement

Table 7.1: *Common Tools Used for Kubernetes DevSecOps*

When should DevSecOps practices be implemented:

- At every build stage: Scan container images before they are pushed to the registry.
- At every pull request: Validate Kubernetes manifests before merging to the main branch.
- At every deploy step: Enforce policies at the Kubernetes admission controller before workloads are admitted to the cluster.
- Before compliance audits: Run automated CIS, NIST, and PCI compliance checks.

In a CI/CD pipeline, DevSecOps gates happen automatically–no manual intervention needed.

Implementing DevSecOps

Example Workflow: DevSecOps in GitHub Actions Pipeline

Let us look at a typical Kubernetes CI/CD pipeline integrating DevSecOps:

```
yaml

name: DevSecOps Pipeline

on:
  push:
    branches: [ main ]

jobs:
  security-scan:
    runs-on: ubuntu-latest
```

```
      steps:
        - name: Checkout Code
          uses: actions/checkout@v3

        - name: Scan Kubernetes YAML with Polaris
          uses: FairwindsOps/polaris-action@master
          with:
            config: ".polaris.yaml"

        - name: Scan Container Image with Trivy
          run: |
            docker build -t myapp:${{ github.sha }} .
            trivy image myapp:${{ github.sha }}

        - name: Build & Push Image
          run: |
            docker login -u ${{ secrets.DOCKER_USER }} -p ${{ secrets.DOCKER_
PASS }}
            docker push myregistry/myapp:${{ github.sha }}

        - name: Deploy to Kubernetes
          run: kubectl apply -f deploy/

        - name: Run kube-bench
          run: kube-bench --version 1.27
```

Explanation:

- Polaris validates Kubernetes manifests statically (for example, missing resource limits, privileged containers).
- Trivy scans container image for known vulnerabilities.
- Build and push step uploads image only if scans pass.
- Deploys YAMLs only after security scans are green.
- Runs kube-bench post-deploy to validate live cluster configuration against CIS benchmark.

DevSecOps Pipeline Stages

The following figure shows a **multi-stage DevSecOps pipeline**. **Polaris** checks YAML manifests for Kubernetes security compliance. **Trivy** checks container images for known vulnerabilities. **kube-bench** validates the running Kubernetes cluster against CIS standards. Arrows indicate a **"gate" mechanism** → deployment proceeds **only if all stages pass. This ensures that insecure images, configurations, or clusters never make it to production**.

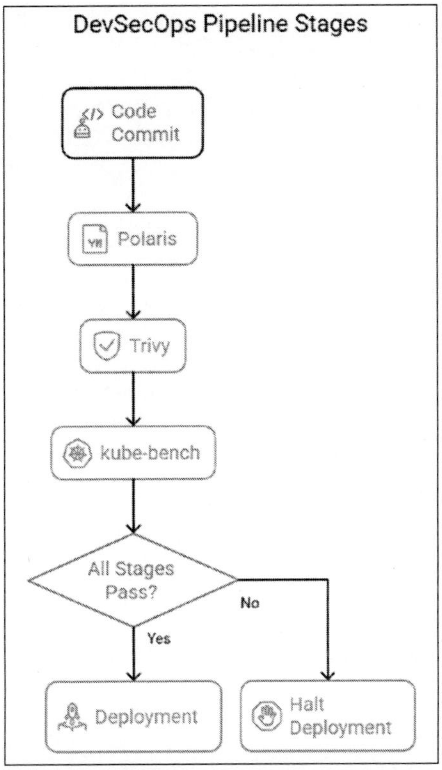

Figure 7.6: *DevSecOps Pipeline Stages*

A Secure Deployment Workflow

In modern cloud-native application delivery, **DevSecOps** integrates security checks directly into the continuous integration and continuous deployment (CI/CD) pipeline. The preceding figure illustrates a typical DevSecOps pipeline for Kubernetes deployments, emphasizing the inclusion of automated security tools at critical stages before production deployment.

Let us break down each stage in the process:

1. **Code Commit**

   The pipeline begins when a developer pushes code to a version control repository (for example, GitHub, GitLab). This commit could include application code, Kubernetes manifests, Helm charts, or infrastructure-as-code (IaC) definitions.

   Trigger: The code commit automatically triggers the CI/CD pipeline to start running the defined validation and security checks.

2. **Polaris: YAML Policy Validation**

   At this stage, **Polaris** - a Kubernetes configuration auditing tool - analyzes the YAML files associated with the deployment. Polaris scans for common misconfigurations such as:

   - Missing resource limits
   - Containers running as root
   - Lack of readiness or liveness probes
   - Insecure privileges or capabilities

Goal: Ensure Kubernetes manifests follow best practices before being applied to the cluster.

3. **Trivy: Vulnerability Scanning**

   After configuration validation, the pipeline invokes **Trivy**, a popular vulnerability scanner for container images. Trivy inspects the container images defined in the manifests for:

   - Known vulnerabilities in OS packages (CVEs)
   - Application library vulnerabilities (npm, pip, Maven, and so on)
   - Policy violations or deprecated dependencies

   Goal: Detect security risks in the application's dependencies **before deployment.**

4. **Kube-bench: Cluster Security Benchmark**

   Next, the pipeline runs **kube-bench**, a tool that checks the cluster environment against the CIS Kubernetes Benchmark - a widely accepted set of security best practices. This stage verifies:

   - Proper API server configuration
   - RBAC permissions are scoped appropriately
   - Secure kubelet and etcd settings
   - Minimal privilege access

   Goal: Validate the underlying Kubernetes cluster's security posture to ensure a compliant environment.

5. **Decision Gate: "All Stages Pass?"**

   Once the scans are complete, the pipeline evaluates whether all checks have passed. This decision acts as a **policy gate** in the DevSecOps workflow:

   - **Yes:** If all validation and scanning stages pass, the pipeline proceeds to deploy the workload to the cluster.
   - **No:** If any stage reports a critical issue or failure, the pipeline halts deployment automatically.

   This gate ensures that only validated, secure, and compliant workloads are promoted into production or staging environments.

6. **Deployment or Halt Deployment**

   The pipeline takes the final action based on the security gate:

   - **Deployment:** Kubernetes resources are applied using tools such as kubectl, Helm, or GitOps controllers, safely launching the application in the cluster.
   - **Halt Deployment:** No resources are deployed, and the pipeline logs the issues for developer remediation.

Benefit: This proactive approach shifts security left, preventing vulnerabilities or misconfigurations from reaching runtime.

Why This Matters: This DevSecOps pipeline illustrates **"security as code"**–embedding security validations directly into CI/CD pipelines. The automation ensures that:

- Security does not slow down deployment velocity.
- Human error is reduced by codifying security checks.
- Compliance mandates (example, SOC2, ISO27001) are satisfied through repeatable controls.

- Developers receive **immediate feedback** on issues in their code or infrastructure definitions.

By running **Polaris, Trivy, and kube-bench** before deployment, organizations strengthen both **application security** and **infrastructure hardening** in a Kubernetes environment.

Conclusion: *Figure* 7.6 represents a **modern security-first deployment model** for Kubernetes-based applications. Integrating configuration validation, image scanning, and cluster compliance checks into the delivery pipeline ensures secure, reliable, and compliant software releases.

This approach aligns with **DevOps culture**, while embedding security without friction, offering a scalable way to secure cloud-native systems.

Real-World Case Study: DevSecOps for Data Pipeline Deployment

A fintech company was deploying **Kafka, Spark, and Airflow** on Kubernetes to process **real-time financial transactions**.

Challenge: Their data engineers had frequent YAML changes, custom container builds, and non-standard base images.

Security risks observed:

- Insecure container images with high CVEs.
- YAML manifests missing resource limits or security contexts.
- Unintentional exposure of internal services (no NetworkPolicy).

DevSecOps solution implemented:

- Polaris + Trivy scans in the **GitLab pipeline.**
- Gatekeeper enforced **PodSecurityPolicies replacement at admission.**
- CI pipeline **failed builds automatically if CVEs above Medium found.**
- Post-deploy audit with kube-bench.

Outcome:

- Reduced CVE count by 85% across the container fleet.
- Prevented misconfigured workloads from reaching production.
- Passed SOC2 compliance without a manual security review.

Key Recommendations:

- **Never skip static manifest validation** (example, Polaris, kube-linter).
- Always integrate **image scanning before push** (Trivy/Snyk).
- Use **OPA Gatekeeper/Kyverno** for runtime policy enforcement.
- Embed **security gates early (PR checks, pre-deploy).**
- Monitor cluster compliance **continuously, not just once.**

Vulnerability Scanning and Compliance Checks for Secure Data Pipelines

In modern cloud-native systems, **each container image bundles hundreds of dependencies (OS packages, libraries, runtimes)**. Every added dependency increases the **attack surface**.

Without vulnerability scanning:

- A critical CVE in a base image layer can expose the entire app.
- An outdated dependency in a YAML manifest can violate compliance (PCI, HIPAA, GDPR).
- Data pipelines processing sensitive records risk **data breaches** due to unpatched vulnerabilities.

Every container image, YAML manifest, and deployed workload must be scanned for security and compliance—continuously, not just once.

For Kubernetes-based data pipelines:

- Insecure Kafka/Spark/ZooKeeper images can compromise real-time workloads.
- Misconfigured manifests can unintentionally expose sensitive ports.
- Inadequate RBAC or missing pod security settings lead to privilege escalation.

In regulated industries (finance, healthcare), failing compliance checks → hefty fines + reputational damage. Therefore, integrating vulnerability scanning and compliance gates into CI/CD is mandatory—not optional.

Vulnerability Scanning and Compliance in Kubernetes

Vulnerability scanning: Automatically detect known CVEs in container images, YAML manifests, and infrastructure code.

Compliance checks: Validate Kubernetes cluster + workloads adhere to standards (CIS benchmarks, PCI DSS, NIST, HIPAA).

Scanning is not just "one-time before deploy"—it must happen:

- At build time (before image push)
- At deploy time (validate YAML manifests)
- At runtime (audit deployed workloads)

The following table lists typical scanning coverage:

Resource	Check Type
Docker image	CVEs in OS packages, libraries
Helm charts	YAML misconfigurations
Live cluster	CIS Benchmark compliance
Kubernetes API	Admission policy violations

Table 7.2: *Scanning Coverage*

The following table lists common scanning tools:

Tool	Function
Trivy	Image scanning + IaC scanning
Aqua Microscanner	Container security
Anchore	Image policy enforcement
kube-bench	CIS Kubernetes benchmark validation
OPA Gatekeeper	Admission controller for policies

Table 7.3: *Common Scanning Tools*

These tools automate security assurance as part of DevSecOps pipelines.

When should scanning and compliance be performed:

- **During container build:** Scan base image + app layers before pushing to registry.
- **At CI pipeline step:** Scan YAML/Helm manifests for misconfigurations (missing resource limits, privilege escalation).
- **Pre-deploy:** Admission controllers reject manifests failing policies (OPA Gatekeeper, Kyverno).
- **Post-deploy audits:** Run kube-bench or kubesec to validate running cluster compliance.

Pipeline must enforce "fail if vulnerabilities or policy violations exceed the threshold."

Implementing Scanning and Compliance in Kubernetes Pipelines

Sample Workflow: GitHub Actions DevSecOps Pipeline

```
yaml

name: CI Pipeline with Vulnerability Scanning

on:
  push:
    branches: [ main ]

jobs:
  scan-and-deploy:
    runs-on: ubuntu-latest

    steps:
      - name: Checkout Code
        uses: actions/checkout@v3

      - name: Scan Docker Image with Trivy
        run: |
          docker build -t myapp:${{ github.sha }} .
          trivy image --exit-code 1 --severity HIGH,CRITICAL myapp:${{ github.
sha }}

      - name: Scan Kubernetes YAML with Polaris
        uses: FairwindsOps/polaris-action@master
        with:
          config: ".polaris.yaml"

      - name: Push Image (if scan passed)
        run: |
          docker push myregistry/myapp:${{ github.sha }}

      - name: Deploy to Kubernetes
        run: kubectl apply -f deploy/
```

Explanation of workflow:

- Trivy scans container image → fails to build if HIGH/CRITICAL vulnerabilities found.
- Polaris validates YAML for Kubernetes best practices.
- Only after both scans pass → image is pushed + deployed.

YAML Lab: OPA Gatekeeper Policy Example (Deny privileged containers)

```
yaml

apiVersion: constraints.gatekeeper.sh/v1beta1
kind: K8sPSPPrivilegedContainer
metadata:
  name: prevent-privileged-containers
spec:
  match:
    kinds:
      - apiGroups: [""]
        kinds: ["Pod"]
```

Explanation:

- This policy blocks any pod using securityContext.privileged: true.
- Enforced by OPA Gatekeeper at admission → prevents privileged containers from reaching cluster.

Vulnerability Scanning and Compliance Flow in CI/CD

The following figure represents Vulnerability Scanning and Compliance Flow in CI/CD:

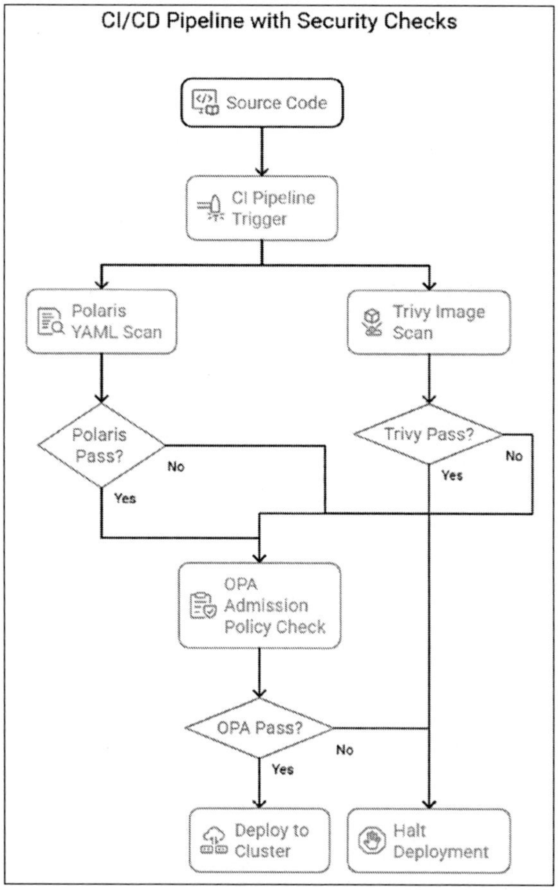

***Figure 7.7**: Vulnerability Scanning and Compliance Flow in CI/CD*

CI/CD Pipeline with Security Checks: Integrating Security into Deployment Workflows:

- Shows flow where:
  - Code triggers pipeline
  - Polaris validates YAML
  - Trivy scans image
  - OPA Gatekeeper enforces admission policies
- Arrows show conditional "pass gates" → deployment is only allowed if all scans pass.

The preceding figure illustrates a modern **Continuous Integration and Continuous Deployment (CI/CD) pipeline that embeds security controls at every stage of the software delivery process.** This approach represents a shift from traditional post-deployment security audits to a **"shift-left" security model**, where security checks are automated and integrated early into the development lifecycle.

At the top of the pipeline, the process begins when a developer pushes changes to the source code repository. This **code commit** triggers the CI pipeline, automatically initiating a sequence of validation and scanning steps designed to ensure the deployment meets both functional and security requirements.

The pipeline splits into two parallel validation tracks. On the left, the pipeline runs **Polaris YAML Scan**, a configuration auditing tool for Kubernetes manifests. Polaris checks the deployment YAML files for misconfigurations or insecure defaults, such as missing resource limits, containers running as privileged, or lack of pod security policies. Once the Polaris scan completes, the pipeline evaluates whether the scan **passed or failed**. If Polaris detects critical issues, the pipeline moves to further evaluation under **Open Policy Agent (OPA) Admission Policy Check**; otherwise, it proceeds directly to the next gate.

In parallel, on the right branch of the pipeline, the process runs a **Trivy Image Scan**, scanning container images for known vulnerabilities (CVEs) in the base OS packages and application dependencies. If Trivy identifies vulnerabilities exceeding acceptable severity thresholds, the deployment is halted immediately. If the scan passes, the workflow continues to the same OPA Admission Policy Check step as the Polaris branch.

The **OPA Admission Policy Check** represents a critical final security gate in the pipeline. Open Policy Agent (OPA) evaluates whether the deployment complies with custom organizational policies, which may include namespace restrictions, required labels, resource quotas, or compliance mandates such as CIS benchmarks or PCI-DSS controls. If OPA approves the deployment, the pipeline proceeds to **Deploy to Cluster**, automatically applying the Kubernetes manifests to the cluster. If OPA denies the deployment, the pipeline is **halted to prevent insecure or non-compliant workloads from reaching production.**

By combining multiple security controls–**configuration scanning (Polaris), vulnerability scanning (Trivy), and policy enforcement (OPA)**–this CI/CD pipeline ensures defense-in-depth throughout the deployment process. Each tool targets a specific security layer: configuration, container image, and runtime admission. Together, they prevent security issues such as misconfigurations, known vulnerabilities, or policy violations from reaching the production cluster.

This pipeline model provides multiple benefits. It improves compliance with security standards, reduces the likelihood of introducing vulnerabilities into production, and gives developers **early feedback** on security issues, enabling faster remediation. Importantly, by automating these checks as part of CI/CD, security validation becomes **continuous, scalable, and consistent**, rather than relying on manual post-deployment reviews.

In summary, *Figure* 7.7 demonstrates how DevSecOps principles can be operationalized in Kubernetes deployments by integrating automated security gates into CI/CD workflows. It enables organizations to deliver secure applications rapidly, while maintaining governance, risk, and compliance requirements in dynamic cloud-native environments.

Real-World Case Study: Compliance and Vulnerability Scanning for Financial Data Pipelines

A banking analytics company running **Kafka, Spark, and Airflow pipelines** on Kubernetes faced a PCI-DSS compliance audit.

Problems:

- Base container images inherited **critical vulnerabilities from the Alpine/Ubuntu base.**
- YAML manifests missed resource limits → **violated CIS benchmark.**
- No admission control → **developers accidentally deployed privileged containers.**

DevSecOps implementation:

- Integrated **Trivy in Jenkins pipeline** (fail if HIGH/CRITICAL CVEs found).
- Added **OPA Gatekeeper policies** for PodSecurity.
- Scanned manifests with **Polaris + kube-score.**
- Ran **kube-bench** nightly to audit live clusters.

Outcome:

- Reduced container CVEs by 90% within 3 months.
- Passed PCI-DSS audit **without manual evidence collection.**
- Prevented privilege escalation vulnerabilities **from entering the cluster.**

Key Recommendations:

- Never skip image scanning at build time (Trivy, Anchore).
- Validate YAML manifests pre-deploy (Polaris, kube-linter).
- Enforce runtime policy compliance (OPA Gatekeeper, Kyverno).
- Run CIS benchmark validation continuously (kube-bench).
- The pipeline must fail builds if CVEs/policy violations breach thresholds.

Conclusion

This chapter provided a practical roadmap for securing Kubernetes workloads, covering RBAC, Secrets management, network and pod security policies, DevSecOps integration, and vulnerability scanning—all essential for building secure, compliant, and resilient cloud-native systems. As we continue our journey, the next chapter will dive into Kubernetes networking strategies, exploring how services communicate securely and efficiently, and how Service Mesh solutions such as Istio enable observability, traffic control, and zero-trust architectures in modern distributed applications.

Chapter 8
Networking Strategies and Service Mesh with Istio

Introduction

In modern cloud-native applications, efficient and secure communication between services is critical. Kubernetes provides a powerful but sometimes complex networking model that requires a clear understanding to design scalable, reliable, and secure systems. As applications grow in complexity, service-to-service communication demands more than what basic Kubernetes networking can offer—enter service meshes such as Istio, which bring advanced traffic management, security, and observability to microservices.

In this chapter, we will begin with the foundational concepts of Kubernetes networking and progressively move towards more sophisticated strategies. We will learn how to manage external traffic using Ingress controllers, secure communications with TLS termination, and explore Istio's architecture to understand how it enhances networking in Kubernetes. We will also cover traffic control techniques such as routing and circuit breaking, and examine how Istio provides observability through tracing and monitoring to deliver deep insight into service behavior.

By the end of this chapter, we will be equipped to design and manage robust networking layers in your Kubernetes environments using Istio.

Structure

In this chapter, we will cover the following topics:

- Kubernetes Networking Fundamentals
- Ingress Controllers and TLS Termination
- Introduction to Service Mesh and Istio Architecture
- Traffic Routing, Load Balancing, Circuit Breaking
- Observability with Istio (Tracing and Monitoring)

Kubernetes Networking Fundamentals

Kubernetes networking provides the essential foundation for communication between pods, services, and external clients within a cluster. Unlike traditional networking, Kubernetes enforces a flat, routable network where every pod receives its own unique IP address, enabling direct pod-to-pod communication without the need for Network Address Translation (NAT). Networking in Kubernetes is governed by key concepts such as ClusterIP, Services, DNS resolution, Ingress controllers, and Network Policies, ensuring reliable, scalable, and secure traffic flow inside and outside the cluster. Understanding these core principles is critical for designing resilient, high-performance cloud-native applications.

Kubernetes Networking: An Introduction

In traditional infrastructure, networking was largely static. Each server had a fixed IP address, firewall rules were manually configured, and service discovery often relied on hardcoded endpoints. But Kubernetes breaks that model—**containers are ephemeral, pods come and go, IP addresses are dynamic, and workloads scale elastically.**

This fundamental shift introduces unique challenges, such as:

- How do we ensure pods can communicate even as they get recreated on different nodes?
- How do external clients reach internal services when pod IPs are temporary?
- How do we load-balance traffic without manual intervention?

Kubernetes solves these challenges by building an **internal, software-defined network abstraction layer.** Engineers must understand this layer to architect resilient, scalable, and secure systems.

In Kubernetes, networking is not optional—it is the backbone of distributed, microservices communication.

Understanding the Kubernetes Networking Model

Kubernetes makes three fundamental promises about networking:

- Every Pod gets its own unique IP address.
- Every Pod can communicate directly with every other Pod, **without NAT or port mapping.**
- Containers inside a Pod share a network namespace and local ports.

Unlike Docker bridge networks, Kubernetes implements **flat networking across the cluster** (using CNI plugins such as Calico, Flannel, and Weave).

What does this mean in practice? Whether a Pod runs on Node A or Node B, it can reach another Pod **using its cluster IP directly**, without needing proxy hops or NAT translations.

Kubernetes Services: The Missing Abstraction

While direct Pod-to-Pod networking works, it is unreliable at scale:

- Pods are destroyed and recreated dynamically → IPs change.
- Scaling up/down alters which Pods exist.
- Load balancing needs to distribute traffic across replicas.

If clients connect to Pods directly by IP, they would constantly fail as Pods churn.

Solution: Kubernetes Service abstraction

A **Service** provides:

- A stable, virtual IP address (called ClusterIP).
- DNS entry inside the cluster (`my-service.default.svc.cluster.local`).
- Built-in load balancing across matching Pods.

"Services decouple consumers from the dynamic nature of Pod IPs by acting as a fixed front door."

Types of Kubernetes Services

Kubernetes offers different types of Services depending on where and how traffic needs, to flow.

ClusterIP (default)

- Only accessible from inside the cluster.

- Used for internal microservices-to-microservices communication.
- For example, the frontend pod talks to the backend pod via `http://backend-service:8080`.

Use case: APIs used by other Pods but not exposed to the internet (for example, database service, internal API gateway).

NodePort

- Opens a fixed port (30000-32767) on **every node in the cluster**.
- External clients send traffic to any node IP at that port → routed internally to the Service.
- Simple, but lacks cloud-native load balancing.

Use case: Quick external access in dev/testing or bare-metal clusters **without a cloud load balancer.**

Note: Not recommended for production large-scale traffic due to lack of health-check/load-balancing features.

LoadBalancer

- Provisions a **cloud provider's load balancer** (AWS ELB, Azure LB, GCP LB).
- Exposes Service via public IP and DNS managed by cloud.
- Traffic passes from Load Balancer → NodePort → Service → Pod.

Use case: Production-ready external services, highly available ingress endpoints.

When to Use Which Service Type

Scenario	Recommended Type
Internal-only microservices	ClusterIP
Quick, manual external access	NodePort
Production external endpoint (cloud env)	LoadBalancer

Table 8.1: *When to Use Which Service Type*

Example: A data pipeline exposes an internal API for ingestion (ClusterIP), but also exposes a public analytics API endpoint (LoadBalancer).

How Kubernetes Routes Traffic Internally (Flow Explanation)?

Let us break down what happens when **Pod A calls `http://my-service`**:

- **DNS Resolution:**
  - Pod A queries Kubernetes DNS for `my-service`.
  - DNS responds with **ClusterIP virtual IP** (for example, 10.96.100.5).
- **Traffic Redirection:**
  - Pod A sends traffic to 10.96.100.5 (ClusterIP).
  - Node intercepts traffic → kube-proxy rewrites → forwards to backend Pod IP selected by Service selector.
- **Backend Response:**
  - Pod X (backend) receives requests, processes, and replies → response flows back to Pod A.

Key Insight: kube-proxy (iptables or IPVS mode) manages packet forwarding on every node without user intervention.

Kubernetes Internal Traffic Flow

The following figure explains internal traffic resolution and load balancing:

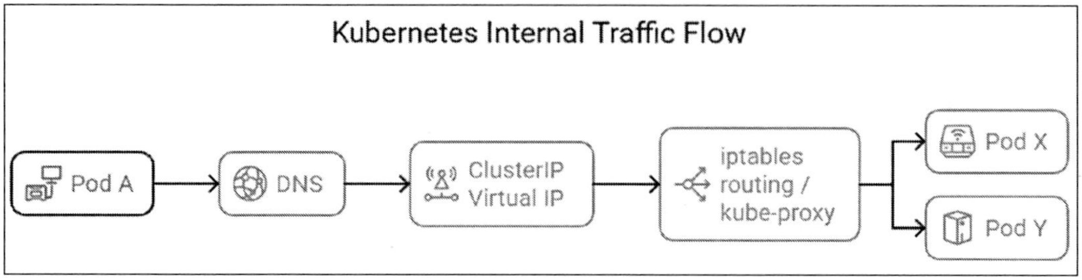

Figure 8.1: *Kubernetes Internal Traffic Flow*

- Use arrows to show the request path from Pod A → DNS → ClusterIP → backend Pods.
- Annotate "kube-proxy forwards" at routing hop.
- Label each Pod and Service clearly.

The figure illustrates the internal network communication flow in a Kubernetes cluster, specifically how one pod communicates with another service-backed pod. This process involves several key components that abstract service discovery and routing within the cluster.

- **Pod A (Client Pod):** The communication begins from a source pod–Pod A–which initiates a request to reach a Kubernetes service (for example, a backend API or database service).
- **DNS Resolution:** Rather than using direct pod IPs (which are ephemeral), Pod A typically makes requests to a **service name** (such as **`my-service.default.svc.cluster.local`**). Kubernetes CoreDNS resolves this name to a **ClusterIP**, a stable virtual IP representing the service.
- **ClusterIP (Virtual IP):** The DNS resolution returns a **ClusterIP**, which is a virtual IP address managed by Kubernetes. This IP does not belong to any one pod but instead abstracts access to a group of pods behind the service.
- **iptables/kube-proxy Routing:** Once the request reaches the ClusterIP, **kube-proxy** (running on each node) or **iptables** (or IPVS) rules take over. These components handle routing decisions and load balance the traffic across the pods selected by the service.
- **Destination Pods (Pod X/Pod Y):** Finally, the request is forwarded to one of the available pods (for example, Pod X or Pod Y) that match the service's selector labels. The selection is done using round-robin or other routing algorithms to ensure an even distribution of traffic.

Key Insight:

This internal traffic flow abstracts away the complexity of discovering and communicating with dynamically assigned pod IPs. By using DNS, ClusterIP, and kube-proxy, Kubernetes ensures **reliable, scalable, and transparent service-to-service communication** within the cluster.

Example: Deploying a Sample Service

Suppose, you have an **ETL processing API running on port 8080 inside Pods.** You want:

- Internal access only → ClusterIP.
- Optional external access → NodePort for testing.

YAML Example: ClusterIP

```
yaml

apiVersion: v1
kind: Service
metadata:
  name: etl-api
spec:
```

```
  selector:
    app: etl
  ports:
    - protocol: TCP
      port: 80
      targetPort: 8080
  type: ClusterIP
```

Now, other pods can call **`http://etl-api:80`** internally.

YAML Example: NodePort

```
yaml

apiVersion: v1
kind: Service
metadata:
  name: etl-api
spec:
  selector:
    app: etl
  ports:
    - protocol: TCP
      port: 80
      targetPort: 8080
      nodePort: 30080
  type: NodePort
```

Now reachable externally at **`http://<NodeIP>:30080`**.

Real-World Insight:

A retail analytics company deployed an ETL pipeline in Kubernetes:

- ETL API exposed via ClusterIP internally → only frontend Pods consume.
- Admin dashboard exposed via LoadBalancer → accessible to BI analysts over HTTPS.
- NodePort used in staging → external testers validated APIs.

Outcome: Decoupled internal/external traffic, optimized security, and used the right service types per endpoint.

Key Takeaways:

- Kubernetes Services abstract the complexity of ephemeral Pod IPs.
- ClusterIP keeps traffic internal and secure by default.
- NodePort enables external dev/test access but does not scale well.
- LoadBalancer integrates with cloud infra for production-grade exposure.
- Understanding Service types is critical for designing scalable, secure architectures.

Ingress Controllers and TLS Termination

In traditional web systems, reverse proxies (such as Nginx or Apache) handle incoming HTTP(S) traffic, routing it to backend servers. In Kubernetes, things work differently: Pods are ephemeral, IP addresses are dynamic, and service endpoints change as workloads scale or restart.

Without a centralized traffic gateway, exposing multiple applications would require managing separate NodePorts or LoadBalancers per service—leading to inefficiency, higher costs, and operational complexity.

Ingress solves this problem by providing a unified entry point for HTTP and HTTPS traffic into the Kubernetes cluster.

Ingress allows external traffic to enter the cluster **based on hostname, URL paths, or rules**, routing it to the correct internal service–**just like a reverse proxy for multiple services running inside Kubernetes.**

Why do we Need Ingress?

Without Ingress:

- Every external app would need its own LoadBalancer or NodePort.
- TLS certificates must be manually applied to each exposed endpoint.
- DNS entries must point to multiple external IPs.

For a microservices system with dozens of APIs, this approach **does not scale.**

Ingress simplifies:

- Centralized traffic management.
- Single external IP/DNS for multiple services.
- Centralized TLS termination (handling HTTPS certificates at entry point).
- URL/path-based routing → multiple services behind the same domain.

For data engineers/architects deploying APIs, dashboards and ETL endpoints, ingress eliminates duplicated infra and simplifies routing.

Ingress and Ingress Controller

Ingress is a Kubernetes API object:

- Defines routing rules → how external HTTP(S) traffic maps to internal services.
- Does not process traffic directly → acts as a configuration.

An **Ingress Controller** is:

- The actual software handling traffic (NGINX, Traefik, HAProxy, Istio ingress gateway).
- Reads Ingress objects → configures underlying proxy dynamically.

Think of:

Ingress → high-level routing policy (like a config file).

Ingress Controller → reverse proxy that applies those rules.

Without an Ingress Controller installed, Ingress resources will not function–they are "just definitions."

When Should we use Ingress?

Ingress is essential when:

- You need to expose **multiple HTTP/S apps under the same DNS** (for example, `api.mycompany.com`, `dashboard.mycompany.com`).
- You want **TLS termination centrally** → manage certs once, not per service.
- You need **path-based routing** → `/api → backend-api-service`, `/ui → frontend-service`.
- You want **external traffic control, rate limiting, auth, and WAF** via proxy plugins.

Ingress is not needed for:

- Exposing single app → LoadBalancer is simpler.
- Exposing non-HTTP traffic (TCP, UDP) → use `Service.Type=LoadBalancer`.

How Does Ingress Work?

High-level flow:

1. External DNS (for example, **`myapp.com`**) → points to LoadBalancer IP of Ingress Controller.
2. The client sends an HTTPS request to `myapp.com`.
3. LoadBalancer forwards → Ingress Controller pod.
4. Ingress Controller inspects hostname/path.
5. Matches route → forwards to target Kubernetes Service → Pod.

Ingress Controller terminates SSL/TLS **at edge** → backend traffic is HTTP (optional re-encrypt if needed).

Ingress Controller Traffic Routing

Visuals should include:

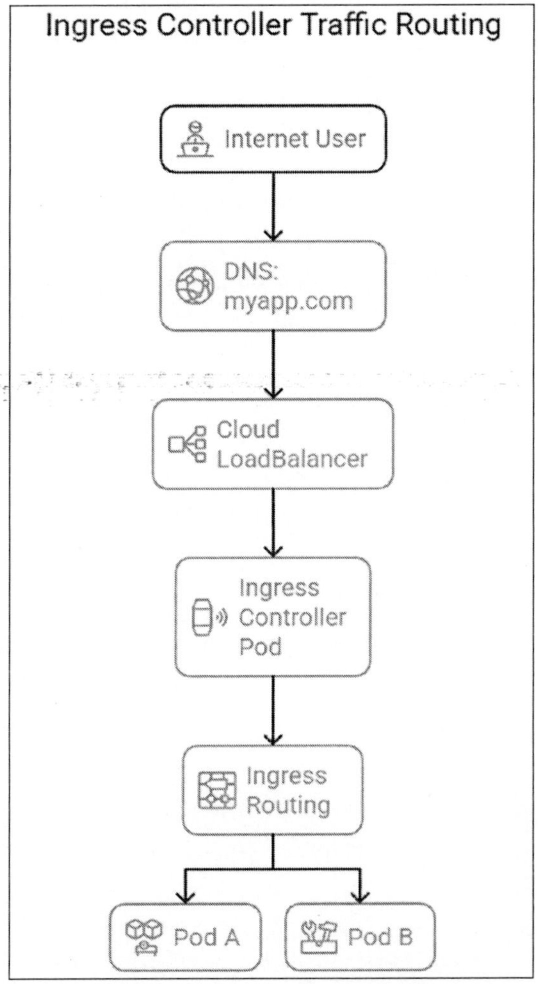

Figure 8.2: *Ingress Controller Traffic Routing*

In Kubernetes, external traffic access to services running inside the cluster is efficiently managed by an **Ingress Controller**. The preceding figure illustrates the step-by-step routing flow that takes place when a user from the internet accesses an application deployed within a Kubernetes cluster.

- **Internet User Initiates Request:** The journey begins when an external user sends a request–for example, opening `https://myapp.com` in a web browser. This request needs to reach the appropriate backend service hosted inside the Kubernetes cluster.
- **DNS Resolution:** The DNS system translates the domain name `myapp.com` into an IP address, which typically belongs to a **Cloud LoadBalancer** service that fronts the cluster. This DNS record is often managed by cloud DNS providers such as Route53 (AWS), Cloud DNS (GCP), or Azure DNS.
- **Cloud LoadBalancer:** The DNS-resolved request is received by a **cloud-provisioned LoadBalancer**, which serves as the public entry point to the Kubernetes cluster. It forwards the request to the Ingress Controller.
- **Ingress Controller Pod:** Inside the cluster, a specialized pod known as the **Ingress Controller** listens for HTTP/HTTPS traffic on specific ports (often 80 and 443). Common implementations include NGINX Ingress, HAProxy Ingress, and Traefik. The controller references Kubernetes **Ingress resources** to determine how requests should be routed.
- **Ingress Routing:** The controller examines the request's hostname and path. Based on defined routing rules in the Ingress resource (**`myapp.com/api → Pod A`**, **`myapp.com/web → Pod B`**, and so on), the controller decides which backend pod should receive the request.
- **Pod A or Pod B (Backend Pods):** The traffic is ultimately directed to the appropriate application pod (for example, Pod A or Pod B) that handles the user's request. These backend pods are part of services registered with the Ingress controller, and the traffic is load-balanced as needed.

Key Takeaway:

This architecture ensures a clean separation between external traffic handling and internal application logic. By leveraging Ingress Controllers and cloud LoadBalancers, Kubernetes provides a **secure, scalable, and manageable** entry point for multi-service web applications–all governed by declarative routing rules.

Figure 8.2 highlights the key components involved in routing external traffic into a Kubernetes cluster. DNS resolution maps the application domain name to the cloud LoadBalancer IP address, which acts as the public entry point. Traffic flow arrows illustrate the path taken by incoming requests from the internet through the LoadBalancer to the Ingress Controller.

The Ingress Controller performs TLS termination for HTTPS traffic and applies routing rules defined in the Ingress resource. Based on the request hostname and path (for example, **`/api`** routed to **`svc-api`**), the controller forwards traffic to the appropriate backend service. This emphasizes the Ingress Controller's role as both the central traffic router and the TLS endpoint for applications running inside the cluster.

Example: Exposing Multiple Services via Ingress

Suppose:

- **`api.mycompany.com`** → routes to backend API service.
- **`dashboard.mycompany.com`** → routes to frontend UI service.

Ingress YAML Example (Basic):

```
yaml

apiVersion: networking.k8s.io/v1
kind: Ingress
```

```
metadata:
  name: my-ingress
  annotations:
    nginx.ingress.kubernetes.io/rewrite-target: /
spec:
  tls:
  - hosts:
    - api.mycompany.com
    - dashboard.mycompany.com
    secretName: mycompany-tls-secret
  rules:
  - host: api.mycompany.com
    http:
      paths:
      - path: /
        pathType: Prefix
        backend:
          service:
            name: backend-api
            port:
              number: 80
  - host: dashboard.mycompany.com
    http:
      paths:
      - path: /
        pathType: Prefix
        backend:
          service:
            name: frontend-ui
            port:
              number: 80
```

This YAML:

- Routes two hostnames → different services.
- Enables TLS via **mycompany-tls-secret**.
- Uses NGINX-specific rewrite annotation.

Deploying NGINX Ingress Controller

Example install (using Helm):

```
bash

helm repo add ingress-nginx https://kubernetes.github.io/ingress-nginx
helm install my-ingress-nginx ingress-nginx/ingress-nginx
```

This deploys:

- Ingress Controller Pod(s).
- LoadBalancer Service → exposes Ingress Controller.
- Configures proxy rules dynamically via CRDs.

Real-World Example

A **financial SaaS platform** needed:

- **Single public IP/DNS** for 12 microservices.

- **TLS offloading at ingress**, avoid embedding certs in apps.
- **Custom paths and subdomains** per client API.

Solution:

- Deployed NGINX Ingress Controller + cert-manager for automatic TLS.
- Configured multi-host Ingress rules for per-client isolation.
- Scaled ingress with horizontal pod autoscaler under peak load.

Result: Achieved centralized TLS management, API gateway pattern, and simplified DNS.

Key Takeaways:

- Ingress centralizes routing, TLS, and traffic management in Kubernetes.
- Ingress Controllers implement the routing logic → required for Ingress objects to work.
- NGINX Ingress → default popular choice; alternatives: Traefik, Istio Gateway.
- Supports advanced plugins: WAF, authentication, rate limiting.

Introduction to Service Mesh and Istio Architecture

In large-scale Kubernetes deployments, handling communication between microservices reliably and securely becomes a critical architectural concern. As applications expand from a few services to dozens or even hundreds of interconnected workloads, managing traffic routing, securing communication, enforcing policies, and gathering observability data pose serious challenges. Traditional Kubernetes networking, while powerful for service discovery and basic load balancing, lacks built-in mechanisms for traffic control, security enforcement, retries, circuit breakers, or distributed tracing at the service level.

Why is a service mesh necessary in modern Kubernetes environments?

At its core, a service mesh addresses the operational challenges that arise once an organization moves from monolithic or small microservice deployments to **distributed, cloud-native architectures with complex traffic patterns.** Without a service mesh, engineers must embed logic for retrying failed calls, handling timeouts, enforcing mutual TLS encryption, collecting telemetry, and applying routing rules inside each microservice's codebase or Kubernetes manifests. This approach leads to **code duplication, inconsistent implementations, and increased operational risk.**

A service mesh such as **Istio** abstracts these networking responsibilities from the application code and shifts them into the platform layer. Istio injects lightweight proxy sidecars (Envoy) next to every Pod in the cluster, intercepting all inbound and outbound traffic transparently. These proxies form the **data plane** of the service mesh, while Istio's **control plane** centrally manages policies, routing rules, security configurations, and observability settings. The data plane enforces; the control plane configures.

What is Istio and what problems does it solve?

Istio provides a programmable infrastructure layer enabling:

- **Secure communication** between services via mutual TLS encryption without requiring application code changes.
- **Traffic management policies** such as traffic splitting, mirroring, or weighted routing for progressive delivery (canary deployments, A/B testing).
- **Centralized observability** through automatic collection of metrics, distributed tracing, and logging.

- **Resiliency patterns** such as retries, timeouts, and circuit breakers applied uniformly to all services.
- **Policy enforcement** for rate limiting, access control, and quota management.

Without Istio, teams face the burden of configuring these capabilities per application or using disparate tools, leading to fragmentation and scalability bottlenecks.

When should a team implement Istio?

For small projects or low-complexity systems, basic Kubernetes networking may suffice. However, as soon as **service-to-service communication grows in scale, crosses trust boundaries, needs encryption, or requires policy enforcement across teams, Istio becomes critical.** Organizations pursuing **zero-trust security architectures, regulated compliance needs, or requiring sophisticated traffic control during software releases** will benefit significantly from adopting Istio earlier in their Kubernetes adoption journey.

Teams should also consider Istio when:

- Microservices span multiple namespaces, clusters, or cloud providers.
- The organization mandates encryption for all internal traffic (compliance with PCI DSS, HIPAA, SOC2).
- Operations require progressive delivery techniques such as canary or blue-green deployments at the platform level.
- Teams struggle with inconsistent telemetry, monitoring blind spots, or lack of distributed tracing.

How does Istio architecture achieve these goals?

Istio's architecture is divided into the **control plane** and the **data plane.** The control plane configures and manages the behavior of the data plane proxies. The key components of Istio's control plane include:

- **Pilot**: Distributes service discovery, traffic management, and routing rules to the Envoy proxies.
- **Citadel (deprecated in newer versions)**: Responsible for issuing and rotating TLS certificates to enable secure service-to-service communication.
- **Galley (deprecated in newer versions)**: Responsible for configuration validation and distribution.
- **Istiod**: Unified control plane component in newer Istio versions, combining Pilot, Citadel, and Galley into a single binary.

The **data plane** consists of **Envoy sidecar proxies** automatically injected next to each application Pod in the mesh. These proxies handle **traffic interception, TLS encryption, telemetry gathering, and enforcing control-plane policies.**

Istio Architecture: Traffic Management and Security in Kubernetes

The following figure illustrates the architectural flow of how **Istio**, a popular open-source service mesh, is deployed and functions within a Kubernetes cluster to enhance microservices communication, security, and observability:

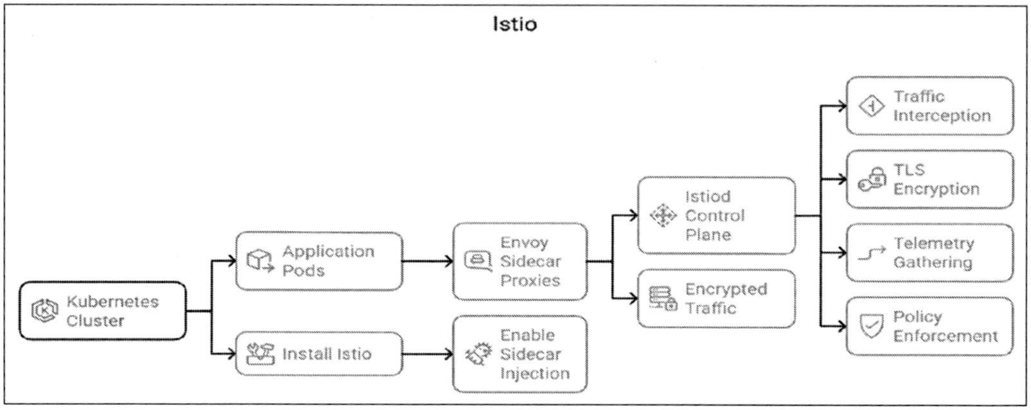

Figure 8.3: *How does Istio Architecture Achieve These Goals*

The flow begins with a **Kubernetes Cluster**, where application workloads run inside **application pods**. To integrate Istio's service mesh capabilities, the cluster is configured with Istio via a separate installation process, depicted as **Install Istio**. Once Istio is installed, **sidecar injection** is enabled–either automatically or manually–which deploys **Envoy sidecar proxies** alongside each application pod. These proxies intercept all inbound and outbound traffic for their associated pods.

The **Envoy sidecars** are central to Istio's functionality. They work under the orchestration of the **Istiod Control Plane**, which manages configurations, propagates policies, and maintains service discovery. The sidecars relay service-to-service communication through **encrypted traffic**, leveraging **mTLS (Mutual TLS)**, ensuring secure communication between services even over untrusted networks.

This setup allows Istio to deliver powerful features:

- **Traffic Interception**: Every packet between services is routed through the Envoy proxy, enabling precise control over routing, retries, timeouts, and traffic splitting.
- **TLS Encryption**: Built-in mutual TLS secures communication, enforcing authentication and data privacy across services.
- **Telemetry Gathering**: The Envoy proxies capture rich metrics and traces (for example, Prometheus, Jaeger), feeding them to observability platforms for real-time monitoring.
- **Policy Enforcement**: Administrators can define fine-grained access policies such as rate limits, quotas, and RBAC rules that are enforced at the proxy level.

Through these components, Istio provides a **non-intrusive, scalable, and consistent mechanism** to manage service communication and security in microservices-based applications. This makes it particularly valuable for regulated industries, zero-trust environments, and teams seeking to decouple infrastructure concerns from application logic.

To install Istio in a cluster, platform engineers typically use **`istioctl`**. A minimal installation uses:

```
bash
istioctl install --set profile=demo
```

This command deploys Istio's core components with default configurations suitable for experimentation or dev environments. Production installations require tighter control over profiles, mTLS settings, ingress/egress gateways, and resource limits.

Once Istio is installed, enabling automatic sidecar injection for an application namespace is performed using:

```
bash
kubectl label namespace my-app istio-injection=enabled
```

Any new Pods created in **`my-app`** will automatically receive an Envoy sidecar, onboarding them into the mesh.

A real-world **example** of Istio adoption comes from a financial institution operating over 70 microservices across two Kubernetes clusters spanning AWS and GCP. Their engineering team faced challenges deploying secure multi-cloud services while maintaining compliance with financial regulations mandating encryption of all data in transit.

By implementing Istio with mutual TLS enabled cluster-wide, they achieved:

- Complete encryption of internal service communication without modifying application code.
- Centralized observability using Prometheus + Grafana integrated via Istio telemetry adapters.
- Gradual rollout of a new risk-scoring service using traffic splitting (90/10 → 50/50 → 100% routing).
- Dynamic failure handling with retries and circuit breaking applied platform-wide via Istio virtual services and destination rules.

The outcome was a **40% reduction in release rollback incidents**, and a **single policy source of truth for security and traffic management.**

In conclusion, Istio enables organizations to **decouple critical networking, security, and observability concerns from application teams, empowering platform engineers to provide these features as infrastructure-level capabilities.** It elevates Kubernetes networking from basic routing to a programmable, policy-driven service communication layer essential for secure, reliable, and scalable microservices operations.

This foundational understanding sets the stage for exploring **advanced Istio traffic routing, load balancing, and circuit-breaking mechanisms** in the next part of the chapter.

Traffic Routing, Load Balancing, and Circuit Breaking in Istio

In the world of distributed systems, resilient service communication is not just about connecting two endpoints. It is about doing so **intelligently, securely, and predictably under dynamic load conditions**. Kubernetes offers basic service discovery and routing, but for production-grade traffic shaping, Istio service mesh unlocks an entirely new class of capabilities. Among them, **traffic routing, load balancing, and circuit breaking** are foundational to delivering high availability and stability in microservices systems.

Why is advanced traffic control needed in Kubernetes microservices?

Traditional routing models based on simple DNS or Kubernetes Service abstraction fail to handle real-world challenges such as **gradual deployment**, **A/B testing**, **request-level failure containment**, or **graceful service failover**. When a team deploys a new version of a critical service (for example, payment gateway or inventory processor), sending 100% of the production traffic to it immediately introduces risk. If something goes wrong, customers are affected, and rollback becomes disruptive.

Additionally, services often depend on other downstream services. If a downstream service fails or slows down, it can **cascade into system-wide outages**. In large systems, engineering teams need fine-grained control over how requests flow between services – including **rate limiting, retry logic, and circuit breaking** – without embedding these concerns into every application.

Key Features of Istio for Routing, Balancing, and Fault Tolerance

Istio's traffic management is built around two Custom Resources:

- `VirtualService`: Defines how requests are routed to different versions of a service.
- `DestinationRule`: Defines policies for subsets of services, including load balancing, TLS, and circuit breakers.

With these two constructs, platform teams can define how traffic is split across service versions, how failover works, what retries should be attempted, and under what conditions a service should be temporarily bypassed.

A **VirtualService** allows teams to configure rules such as "send 90% of traffic to v1 and 10% to v2," enabling progressive delivery patterns such as **blue-green** or **canary** rollouts. It also supports **header-based routing**, which can direct traffic from specific users, geographies, or test groups to different service versions.

A **DestinationRule** lets teams apply **load balancing policies** (for example, round-robin, least connections), configure **connection pools**, or **trigger circuit breaking** if services are slow or unresponsive.

Together, these tools form the backbone of intelligent, fault-tolerant traffic management in Kubernetes.

Implementing Traffic Routing and Circuit Breaking

Teams should adopt these strategies **early in the service lifecycle**, especially when deploying user-facing applications, payment systems, or data ingestion services. They are also vital during **high-risk deployments**, such as major version upgrades, schema changes, or experimental features.

In data-heavy environments, especially those running real-time pipelines (Kafka consumers, stream processors), circuit breakers prevent a single bad node from overloading downstream systems.

If the system runs on shared infrastructure (multi-tenancy), routing traffic gradually across updates avoids resource contention and throttling problems.

Configuring Routing and Circuit Breaking in Istio

Let us walk through a scenario where a platform team wants to perform a **canary rollout** of a new service version and protect the system from overload using circuit breaking.

Step 1: Define a DestinationRule

```
yaml

apiVersion: networking.istio.io/v1beta1
kind: DestinationRule
metadata:
  name: reviews-destination
spec:
  host: reviews
  subsets:
  - name: v1
    labels:
      version: v1
  - name: v2
    labels:
```

```
        version: v2
  trafficPolicy:
    connectionPool:
      tcp:
        maxConnections: 100
      http:
        http1MaxPendingRequests: 100
        maxRequestsPerConnection: 10
    outlierDetection:
      consecutiveErrors: 5
      interval: 10s
      baseEjectionTime: 30s
      maxEjectionPercent: 50
```

This rule defines two subsets: **v1** and **v2**. It enables circuit breaking by applying thresholds. For example, if five consecutive errors are observed, the service instance is **ejected** from the load-balancing pool for 30 seconds.

Step 2: Define a VirtualService

```
yaml

apiVersion: networking.istio.io/v1beta1
kind: VirtualService
metadata:
  name: reviews-route
spec:
  hosts:
  - reviews
  http:
  - route:
    - destination:
        host: reviews
        subset: v1
      weight: 90
    - destination:
        host: reviews
        subset: v2
      weight: 10
```

This routes 90% of the traffic to **`reviews-v1`**, and only 10% to **`reviews-v2`**, enabling a canary rollout without changing the application code or reconfiguring the deployment pipeline.

Canary Rollout and Traffic Flow

The following figure illustrates the Canary Rollout and Traffic Flow:

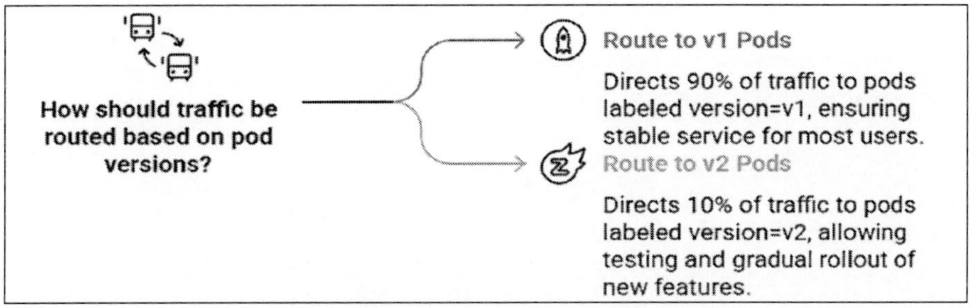

Figure 8.4: *Canary Rollout and Traffic Flow*

- A user request arrives at the Istio ingress gateway.
- The gateway applies routing rules from the VirtualService.
- 90% of traffic is routed to pods labeled `version=v1`, while 10% goes to pods labeled `version=v2`.
- The DestinationRule enforces circuit-breaking policies on each pod instance.

Each time a request is made, the Envoy sidecar evaluates whether a particular pod is healthy or should be skipped, ensuring **resilience and stability during rollout.**

The following figure illustrates a controlled **Canary deployment strategy** implemented using **Istio**, enabling progressive delivery and safe rollouts of application updates within a Kubernetes environment:

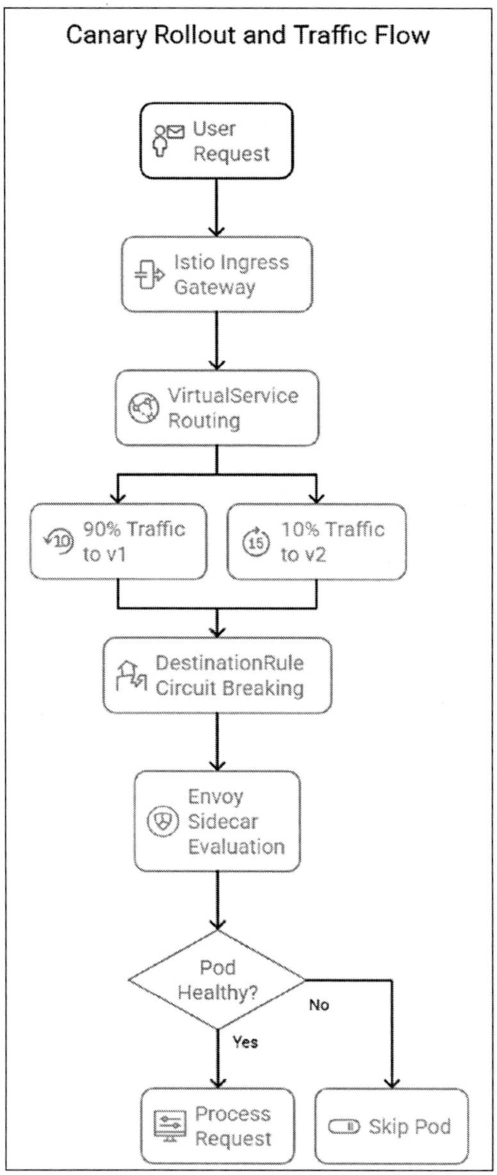

Figure 8.5: *Canary Rollout and Traffic Flow*

This approach helps reduce deployment risk by gradually shifting traffic from an old version to a new version of an application, while monitoring performance and stability.

The flow begins with a **User Request**, which first passes through the **Istio Ingress Gateway**. This gateway acts as the entry point for external traffic into the Kubernetes cluster. Once inside the mesh, the request is routed using a **VirtualService** configuration. This Istio resource defines how traffic is split between different versions of a service. In this example, 90% of the traffic is routed to **version v1** (stable release) and 10% to **version v2** (new canary release). This gradual traffic allocation allows real-world testing of v2 under real conditions without fully exposing it to all users.

After routing, traffic flows through **DestinationRules** that apply **circuit-breaking policies**, such as connection limits and timeouts. This protects the system from cascading failures in the event that the new version misbehaves or becomes overwhelmed.

Next, each request is processed through an **Envoy Sidecar Proxy**, which is deployed alongside every application pod in the mesh. Envoy performs intelligent traffic management, applying retries, load balancing, and health checks.

Before the request reaches a pod, the **Envoy sidecar** checks if the **pod is healthy**. This check ensures traffic is only directed to functioning application instances. If the pod fails the health evaluation, the proxy **skips the pod** and reroutes the request to a healthy one. If the pod passes, the **request is processed** normally.

This canary strategy allows engineers to safely introduce new code to production, monitor real-time metrics, and **roll back instantly** if issues are detected. It ensures **resilience**, **progressive traffic shifting**, and **service reliability**, making it a crucial practice in **cloud-native DevOps workflows.**

Real-World Case Study: Protecting a Machine Learning API with Circuit Breakers

At a major retail analytics company, a real-time ML scoring API deployed on Kubernetes was experiencing sporadic failures due to a downstream feature extraction service under high load. Without traffic management, all requests would eventually pile up and time out, causing cascading failures across the pipeline.

The platform team implemented an Istio-based solution:

- Added a `DestinationRule` with outlier detection to remove slow service instances temporarily.
- Configured retry policies with capped timeouts to avoid hammering the downstream service.
- Gradually rolled out new model versions using **canary deployments** and **`VirtualService` routing**.

The result was a **40% reduction in 5xx errors**, **zero downtime during ML model upgrades**, and enhanced developer confidence to deploy frequently.

Final Thoughts

Advanced traffic management, load balancing, and circuit breaking are **essential to the stability and agility of modern Kubernetes environments**. Using Istio's programmable routing layer, teams can deploy with confidence, reduce failure impact, and enforce intelligent traffic flows tailored to system health and business logic. Rather than pushing these patterns into code, Istio elevates them to platform-level constructs that operate across the entire mesh – consistent, scalable, and secure.

This understanding of routing and failover lays the foundation for the final part of this chapter: **how to visualize, observe, and debug service communication using tracing and observability tools within Istio.**

Observability with Distributed Tracing and Monitoring

In a distributed, cloud-native environment powered by Kubernetes and microservices, the **ability to observe system behavior is as critical as the ability to deploy services**. When dozens of services are interconnected, a single slowdown in one component can ripple across the entire system. Traditional logs are no longer sufficient. Engineers must rely on **end-to-end observability**—including metrics, traces, and logging—to understand service behavior, latency patterns, and request failures.

Why is observability essential in Kubernetes + Istio environments?

Unlike monolithic architectures, where internal function calls are simple to follow, **microservices-based systems introduce complexity through network boundaries, retries, and asynchronous messaging**. A single client request can span multiple services. If there is latency or a failure, how do you find out which service is responsible?

Without proper observability:

- Debugging a slowdown can take hours if not days.
- DevOps teams cannot trace bottlenecks or failure patterns.
- Resource utilization goes unchecked, leading to overspending or under-provisioning.

Istio service mesh natively enables distributed tracing and metrics collection using sidecar proxies (Envoy) without requiring any modification in application code. This gives engineers fine-grained insights across the entire service communication path.

What observability tools does Istio integrate with?

Istio supports out-of-the-box integration with the following industry-standard observability tools:

- **Prometheus**: For collecting metrics (latency, request count, error rates).
- **Grafana**: For building custom dashboards to visualize Prometheus metrics.
- **Jaeger**: For distributed tracing (visual call graphs, trace spans).
- **Kiali**: For mesh topology visualization and health inspection.

These tools allow engineers to **ask questions such as**:

- Which service is experiencing the highest request latency?
- What is the success rate of my canary rollout?
- How is traffic distributed among service versions?
- Which pod or node is experiencing resource exhaustion?

When should observability be implemented?

Observability should not be an afterthought or added during troubleshooting. In modern CI/CD workflows:

- **Tracing and metrics should be enabled during staging** to validate rollout health.
- Production environments must include automated dashboards and alerts.
- During **chaos testing or load testing**, observability helps understand how services behave under stress.

Data-driven decisions (for example, autoscaling thresholds, and circuit breaker tuning) are only possible when telemetry is available and accessible.

How to enable tracing and monitoring with Istio?

Istio injects an **Envoy sidecar proxy** into each pod. This proxy automatically:

- Captures metrics such as request count, duration, and status codes.
- Creates trace spans and sends them to the Jaeger backend.
- Passes tracing headers (**`x-request-id`**, **`x-b3-traceid`**) to downstream services.

The observability stack can be deployed using Istio's built-in **demo profile**, or manually via Helm or IstioOperator for production-grade setups.

YAML Lab: Enabling Telemetry in Istio

For quick setup in a non-production cluster, use:

```
bash

istioctl install --set profile=demo -y
```

This installs:

- Prometheus
- Grafana
- Jaeger
- Kiali

You can access them via port-forwarding:

```
bash

kubectl -n istio-system port-forward svc/jaeger 16686:16686
kubectl -n istio-system port-forward svc/grafana 3000:3000
kubectl -n istio-system port-forward svc/prometheus 9090:9090
```

For application instrumentation, **no code changes** are needed. The Envoy sidecar already captures and sends spans to Jaeger.

Example: Debugging Slow Requests via Jaeger

Imagine a retail application where users experience intermittent slowdowns during checkout. With tracing enabled:

- Engineers open Jaeger and filter traces for the **`checkout-service`**.
- Traces show a spike in latency when **`inventory-service`** is called.
- A deeper trace view reveals that **`inventory-service`** had retries and timeouts.

The engineering team inspects Prometheus metrics and finds that a node running **`inventory-service`** is under CPU pressure. Autoscaler policies are updated, and latency normalizes.

Without tracing, identifying this root cause across microservices would take hours.

Distributed Tracing Lifecycle in Istio

Distributed tracing is a fundamental observability practice in microservices environments. In Kubernetes, Istio provides seamless tracing capabilities across services by leveraging sidecar proxies (Envoy) and integration with tools such as **Jaeger**, **Prometheus**, and **ELK/Fluentd**. The following figure visualizes how a client request is traced across multiple services in the service mesh and how telemetry data is collected along the way:

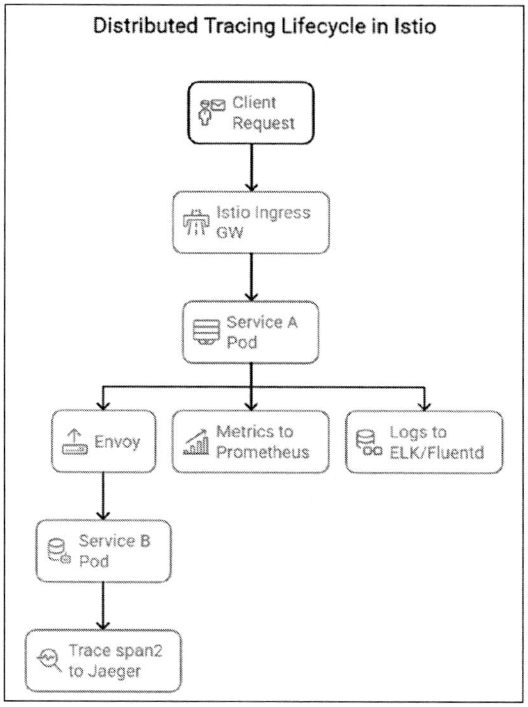

Figure 8.6: *Distributed Tracing Lifecycle in Istio*

Explanation:

- Every inbound/outbound request goes through the Envoy sidecar.
- The proxy captures trace headers and generates spans.
- Metrics are pushed to Prometheus (for example, request duration).
- Spans are batched and sent to Jaeger.
- Grafana dashboards can correlate CPU usage with request latency.

Here is a breakdown of the lifecycle stages:

1. **Client Request**

   The lifecycle begins when a client (user or system) makes an HTTP/gRPC request to a service hosted within the Kubernetes cluster. This request is intended for a specific application service exposed to the internet.

2. **Istio Ingress Gateway**

   The external request first reaches the **Istio Ingress Gateway**, which acts as the edge proxy for incoming traffic. This gateway terminates the connection and routes it internally based on the virtual service and gateway rules configured in Istio. Crucially, the request receives a **trace context header**, which is used to track the request throughout the entire service mesh.

3. **Service A Pod**

   The request is then forwarded to **Service A**, the first internal microservice. Because Service A runs within the Istio mesh, it has an **Envoy sidecar** proxy injected, which intercepts inbound and outbound traffic. At this stage:

   a. **Trace Span 1** is initiated.

b. The sidecar automatically logs and forwards telemetry data (latency, status codes, and so on).

4. **Telemetry Routing from Service A**

   Service A produces various types of telemetry data:

   a. **Metrics to Prometheus**: Resource usage, request rates, and latencies are pushed to Prometheus, a time-series database used for monitoring.

   b. **Logs to ELK/Fluentd**: Application and infrastructure logs are shipped to an ELK stack (Elasticsearch, Logstash, Kibana) or Fluentd for log aggregation and search.

   c. These parallel flows ensure full-stack observability, capturing different dimensions of service behavior.

5. **Envoy Proxy and Service B Pod**

   As Service A makes a downstream call to **Service B**, the request again passes through the **Envoy sidecar proxy**. Here, the trace context is propagated, and **Trace Span 2** is created for the communication between Service A and Service B. The Envoy proxy on both ends tracks this call, measures the latency, and applies routing or retry policies if needed.

   Service B then handles the request. It may also make further downstream calls, generating additional trace spans to build a complete picture of the request lifecycle.

6. **Tracing Data Sent to Jaeger**

   Finally, **tracing spans**—including metadata such as service name, latency, success/failure, and timestamps—are forwarded to **Jaeger**, a distributed tracing platform. Jaeger stitches together the spans to provide an end-to-end view of the request's journey across services. Developers and operators can use this information to:

   a. Debug performance bottlenecks,

   b. Identify failing services, and

   c. Trace root causes of errors.

This tracing lifecycle ensures that each request moving through an Istio-managed Kubernetes cluster is tracked, measured, and visualized across all services. The combination of **sidecar injection**, **telemetry collection**, and **trace visualization** provides a robust observability foundation—critical for debugging microservices and achieving production-grade reliability.

Real-World Case Study: Distributed Tracing in Financial Transactions

A financial institution deployed over 60 microservices, including transaction processors, fraud engines, and customer APIs. During peak hours, intermittent transaction delays occurred.

By deploying Istio with tracing enabled:

- Traces showed that the `risk-evaluation-service` had inconsistent response times.
- Prometheus data revealed garbage collection spikes in the JVM-based service.
- Engineers optimized heap settings and introduced VPA policies.

Result:

- P95 latency dropped by 47%.
- Deployment velocity increased since trace-based validation became part of CI/CD.

Final Thoughts

Observability is not just about dashboards–it is about engineering feedback loops. With Istio's native telemetry stack, DevOps and data teams can measure everything from **service reliability** to **request-level behavior**. In Kubernetes, where services scale dynamically and fail gracefully, **tracing is the only way to truly understand behavior in production.**

As service architectures grow in complexity, **Istio becomes the operational lens** through which teams monitor, trace, and secure modern applications.

Conclusion

In this chapter, we explored the foundational and advanced components of Kubernetes networking–from exposing services using ClusterIP, NodePort, and LoadBalancer to building secure, intelligent traffic control using Ingress controllers. We also introduced Istio, the powerful service mesh that transforms basic connectivity into secure, observable, and policy-driven service communication. With hands-on labs, diagrams, and production-grade configurations, you have gained the tools to confidently architect and troubleshoot real-world network flows in distributed environments. The next chapter takes you into the art and science of Kubernetes troubleshooting. You will learn how to debug broken pods, failed deployments, misconfigured services, and control plane issues using built-in tools such as kubectl, events, logs, and probes. We will also explore real-world failure patterns and walk through resolution strategies to help you master Kubernetes reliability.

CHAPTER 9
Debugging Kubernetes

Introduction

Kubernetes offers powerful abstractions for deploying and managing containerized applications, but diagnosing issues in a distributed, dynamic environment can be challenging. Thus, whether it is a pod failing to start, a node going offline, or an obscure networking glitch, effective debugging is essential for maintaining system reliability and uptime. This chapter focuses on practical techniques and tools you can use to identify and resolve common issues in Kubernetes environments. From basic troubleshooting with 'kubectl' to more advanced root cause analysis for production incidents, this chapter will equip you with a systematic approach to tackling Kubernetes problems confidently and efficiently.

Structure

In this chapter, we will cover the following topics:

- Debugging Pods, Nodes, and Clusters
- **`CrashLoopBackOff`** and **`ImagePullBackOff`**
- kubectl Logs, Events and Exec-Based Debugging
- Network Debugging and Port Forwarding
- Root Cause Analysis (RCA) for Production Incidents

Debugging Pods, Nodes, and Clusters in Kubernetes

As cloud-native applications grow in complexity and scale, Kubernetes has emerged as the standard platform to orchestrate and manage containerized workloads. However, with this power comes added operational intricacy. Unlike traditional monolithic systems where debugging often happens within a single host or application instance, Kubernetes distributes workloads across multiple pods, nodes, and clusters. These workloads are ephemeral, dynamically scheduled, and interdependent - making failures harder to isolate.

- Ephemeral workloads (pods that restart or disappear)
- Dynamic scheduling decisions
- Complex service dependencies
- Asynchronous failures (logs/events stored separately)

Debugging in Kubernetes is not optional - it is essential. A small misconfigured YAML file, an incorrect environment variable, or a failed image pull can lead to pod crashes, infinite restarts, **`CrashLoopBackOff`** or node-level pod evictions or resource starvation, often affecting downstream services in production.

Core Debugging Dimensions in Kubernetes

Kubernetes debugging spans three major components:

- **Pod Lifecycle and Health Monitoring**

  Kubernetes tracks pod status through distinct lifecycle **phases**, helping administrators' pinpoint issues related to startup, execution, or termination:

  - **Pending:** Pod is accepted by the control plane but has not yet been scheduled onto a node.
  - **Running:** At least one container is executing without errors.
  - **Succeeded/Failed:** Containers have terminated with/without error.
  - **Unknown:** The system cannot determine the pod status due to node or network failure.

Understanding each of these phases helps isolate problems related to scheduling, image pull issues, liveness/readiness probe failures, or unfulfilled resource constraints.

- **Node-Level Failures**

  Nodes can become unavailable or unsuitable for scheduling due to:

  - **Disk Pressure:** Insufficient storage space on the node.
  - **Memory Pressure:** Lack of allocatable RAM to serve new workloads.
  - **Network Partitioning:** Loss of connectivity, affecting pod communication or control plane signals.

Such conditions often trigger Kubernetes to **taint** or **cordon** the affected node, preventing new pods from being scheduled.

- **Cluster Events**

  Kubernetes continuously emits structured **event logs** to describe what is occurring within the system. These logs provide valuable context for:

  - Image pull failures
  - Taint violations
  - Insufficient CPU/memory
  - Crash loops
  - Liveness/readiness probe failures

These are accessible via `kubectl get events` and should be your first stop in tracing deployment issues.

When Do These Issues Arise?

Problems often surface during high-pressure phases of software delivery or scaling. Common production scenarios include:

- Application rollouts failing due to bad YAML configurations.
- Pods stuck in Pending due to lack of resources or taints.
- Intermittent node failures leading to cascading scheduling failures.
- DaemonSets failing to deploy due to incorrect selectors.
- Cross-zone deployments where availability zones run out of capacity.
- During CI/CD deployments with invalid manifests.
- At peak traffic hours, leading to resource exhaustion.

- While performing infrastructure upgrades or security patching.
- When cluster autoscalers lag behind demand spikes.
- In cross-zone deployments, where some availability zones may hit capacity limits.

Each of these conditions can lead to cascading failures if not debugged promptly.

These issues become **critical** during:

- Release cycles
- Peak traffic spikes
- Node autoscaler adjustments
- Security patches or infrastructure upgrades

How Do We Debug These Issues?

Let us walk through common practices, supported by **tools**, **commands**, and **real examples**.

Action	Command Example
View Pod Status	`kubectl get pods`
Detailed Pod View	`kubectl describe pod <pod-name>`
View Cluster Events	`kubectl get events --sort-by=.metadata.creationTimestamp`
Inspect Node Health	`kubectl describe node <node-name>`
View Resource Utilization	`kubectl top pods, kubectl top nodes`
Delete Faulty Pod	`kubectl delete pod <pod-name>`
View Scheduler Logs (advanced)	`kubectl logs kube-scheduler -n kube-system`

Table 9.1: *Tooling and CLI Reference*

Hands-on Lab: Debugging Pod Scheduling Failures

Scenario:

You deploy a Spark job in Kubernetes, but the pod remains in the **Pending** state indefinitely.

Step-by-Step Debugging:

1. **Check Pod Status**

```
kubectl get pod spark-job-pod
```

2. **Describe Pod to View Event Reasons**

```
kubectl describe pod spark-job-pod
```

Example Output:

```
Events:
  Type     Reason            Age   From               Message
  ----     ------            ----  ----               -------
  Warning  FailedScheduling  2m    default-scheduler  0/5 nodes are
available: 5 Insufficient memory.
```

3. **Verify Node Resources**

```
kubectl top nodes
```

Shows all nodes are over-utilized - the scheduler cannot place the pod.

If nodes are over-utilized, the scheduler cannot assign the pod.

4. **Resolution:**
    a. Scale up node pool size using your cloud provider.
    b. Optimize the Spark job's resource requests.
    c. Manually assign **`requests.memory`** to a lower value in the pod spec.
    d. Reduce **`resources.requests`** in your Spark deployment.
    e. Adjust pod memory to fit current cluster capacity.

Node Unavailability: Taints and Cordons

Kubernetes uses **taints** to mark nodes as unsuitable for general scheduling. For example: Nodes can be **tainted** to repel pods:

```
kubectl taint nodes node-1 key=value:NoSchedule
```

If a node is **cordoned**, no new pods will be scheduled for it (nodes can also be **cordoned** to temporarily prevent new scheduling):

```
kubectl cordon node-1
```

Use Case: A pod will not schedule, and you see this in `kubectl describe`:

```
node(s) had taints that the pod didn't tolerate
```

Add appropriate tolerations in the YAML to override this behavior.

YAML Lab: Simulate Pod Scheduling Failure

```
yaml

apiVersion: v1
kind: Pod
metadata:
  name: memory-hog
spec:
  containers:
  - name: hog
    image: busybox
    command: ["sh", "-c", "sleep 3600"]
    resources:
      requests:
        memory: "32Gi"
```

This YAML will fail to schedule on a standard cluster with 4–8 GiB RAM nodes.

Use **`kubectl describe pod memory-hog`** to view events and confirm failure.

Real-World Case Study: Unhealthy Spark Driver Pod

Scenario: A data engineering pipeline deployed a Spark application that consistently failed.

Why: The pod was crashing due to a missing environment variable required for authentication.

What: The application spec had **`envFrom`** referring to a missing ConfigMap.

When: During a scheduled CI/CD rollout triggered by GitOps.

How: Used **`kubectl describe pod`** and **`kubectl logs`** to identify:

```
Exception: ENV_VAR not found
```

- Added the correct ConfigMap and redeployed the application.

Kubernetes Scheduling and Failure Tracing

The following figure demonstrates Kubernetes Scheduling and Failure Tracing:

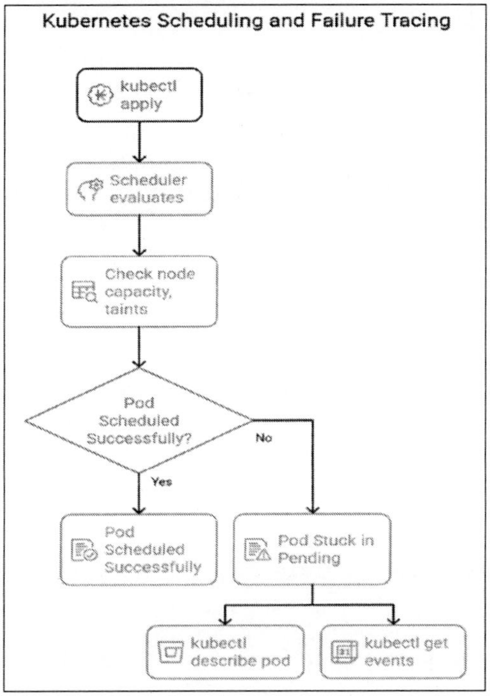

Figure 9.1: *Kubernetes Scheduling and Failure Tracing*

Explanation:

1. The developer applies a manifest using **`kubectl apply`**.
2. The Kubernetes scheduler evaluates the pod's requirements (CPU, memory, tolerations).
3. The scheduler checks node conditions and taints.
4. If all conditions are met, the pod is scheduled.
5. If not, the pod remains in a Pending state.
6. Use **`kubectl describe pod`** and **`kubectl get events`** to investigate the reason (for example, no resources, taint mismatch).

Key Takeaways:

- Debugging in Kubernetes is not just about logs; it is about **correlating events, pod states, and cluster conditions**.
- Most scheduling issues relate to **resource requests**, **taints**, or **node health**.
- Mastering basic tools such as **`kubectl describe`**, **`kubectl top`**, and **`kubectl logs`** builds your confidence to troubleshoot production workloads.
- Kubernetes debugging blends **observation**, **event tracing**, and **resource analysis**.
- The **`kubectl CLI`** is your first line of defense - use it often and fluently.

- Scheduling failures usually stem from insufficient resources, taints, or malformed YAML specs.
- Always inspect **event logs**, **node conditions**, and **container exit codes**.
- Consider using observability tools such as **Lens**, **Grafana**, or **Prometheus** for more visual context.
- Simulating failures (such as, over-provisioning pods) is a great way to train your team on production-ready diagnostics.

`CrashLoopBackOff` and `ImagePullBackOff`

In Kubernetes production environments, two of the most common and disruptive errors are **`CrashLoopBackOff`** and **`ImagePullBackOff`**. These failures not only cause application downtime but can also introduce cascading issues across distributed systems if left unaddressed. In this section, we will deep-dive into understanding, reproducing, diagnosing, and resolving these issues, with hands-on YAML labs and root cause simulations.

Why These Errors Occur?

`CrashLoopBackOff`:

This error occurs when a container repeatedly crashes after starting successfully. Kubernetes automatically tries to restart it but backs off exponentially after continuous failures. The root causes may include:

- Misconfigured environment variables or missing secrets.
- Runtime exceptions in the application startup logic.
- Misconfigured **`livenessProbe`** or **`readinessProbe`** causing premature restarts.

`ImagePullBackOff`:

This error happens when Kubernetes fails to fetch the container image from a registry. Common reasons are:

- Incorrect image name, tag, or registry URL.
- Lack of credentials for private registry access.
- Network or DNS issues preventing communication with the image source.

Understanding the Core Concepts

`CrashLoopBackOff` Lifecycle:

- Container starts successfully → exits (**`code != 0`**) → restarts → fails repeatedly → enters backoff.

`ImagePullBackOff` Lifecycle:

- Kubernetes tries to pull an image → fails → retries → enters backoff.

Key Tools for Diagnosis:

- `kubectl describe pod <pod-name>`
- `kubectl get events --sort-by=.metadata.creationTimestamp`
- `kubectl logs <pod-name> -c <container-name>`
- Azure-specific: Azure Monitor, Container Insights, Log Analytics workspace

When to Apply the Fixes?

You should investigate these errors:

- Immediately during development or CI/CD pipeline builds to prevent broken releases.

- When production workloads fail to start, especially on deployment.
- During new image rollout, environment changes, or after secret/config updates.

How to Investigate and Fix?

YAML Lab: Reproducing and Resolving `CrashLoopBackOff`

```yaml
yaml

apiVersion: v1
kind: Pod
metadata:
  name: crashloop-demo
spec:
  containers:
  - name: faulty-app
    image: busybox
    command: ["sh", "-c", "exit 1"]
    livenessProbe:
      exec:
        command: ["sh", "-c", "exit 1"]
      initialDelaySeconds: 5
      periodSeconds: 5
```

Fix: Update command to avoid exit failure.

```yaml
yaml

command: ["sh", "-c", "sleep 3600"]
```

Also, correct faulty probes.

YAML Lab: Simulating and Fixing `ImagePullBackOff`

```yaml
yaml

apiVersion: v1
kind: Pod
metadata:
  name: imagepull-demo
spec:
  containers:
  - name: faulty-container
    image: myregistry.azurecr.io/nonexistent-image:latest
```

Fix:

1. Check Azure ACR registry name and image tags.
2. Validate image availability using **`az acr repository show-tags`**.
3. Ensure Azure Kubernetes Service (AKS) is connected to ACR:

```
az aks update -n <aks-cluster-name> -g <resource-group> --attach-acr <acr-name>
```

Real-World Use Case: Environment Variable/Secret Misconfigurations

Scenario:

A Data Engineering pipeline failed during CI/CD deployment with **`CrashLoopBackOff`**.

Root Cause: A missing secret (**DB_PASSWORD**) required at startup. The container tried connecting to the DB and failed.

Fix:

1. **Validate secret:**

   yaml

   ```
   kubectl get secret db-secrets -o yaml
   ```

2. **Patch deployment with correct reference:**

   yaml

   ```
   env:
   - name: DB_PASSWORD
     valueFrom:
       secretKeyRef:
         name: db-secrets
         key: db-password
   ```

Pod Lifecycle and Error Transition Flow

The following figure captures how a pod transitions from scheduling → container start → readiness OR crash. The backoff logic protects the node from constant restart attempts.

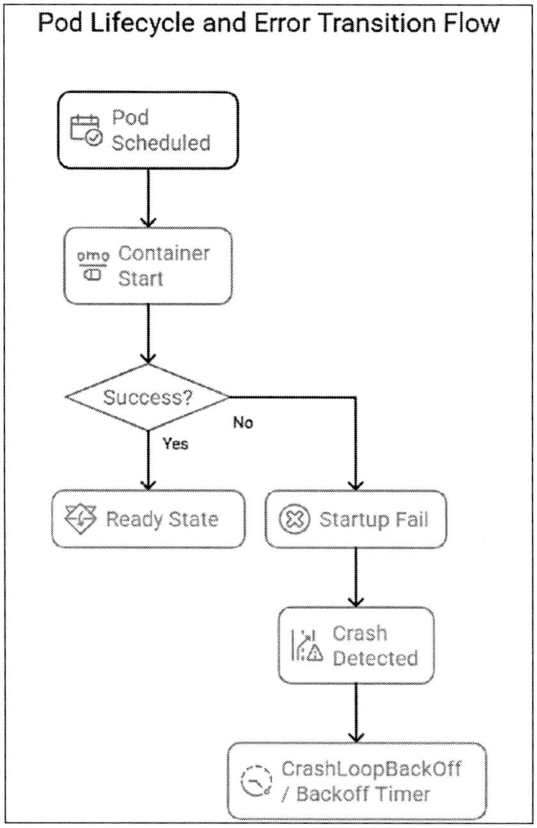

Figure 9.2: *Pod Lifecycle and Error Transition*

In Kubernetes, understanding the pod lifecycle is essential for debugging and operational reliability. The preceding figure illustrates the transition of a pod from creation through execution, highlighting both **successful readiness paths** and **error-handling states** such as **`CrashLoopBackOff`**.

Let us walk through each stage in detail:

1. **Pod Scheduled**

   This is the initial point in the lifecycle. Once the Kubernetes scheduler has selected a suitable node (based on CPU, memory, affinity, taints, and so on), the pod enters the **"Scheduled"** state. At this point:

   - The pod has not yet begun running.
   - The scheduler has determined a node that satisfies the resource and scheduling constraints.
   - If no suitable node is found, the pod remains in **Pending**, and events like **`FailedScheduling`** are triggered.

Transition Condition: The kubelet on the selected node begins initializing the pod containers.

2. **Container Start**

   Next, the kubelet starts pulling the container image and attempts to launch the container(s) defined in the pod specification. This is where most startup-related issues emerge.

   Possible reasons for failure at this step include:

   - Image not found (**`ErrImagePull`**)
   - Image pull secrets not configured (**`ImagePullBackOff`**)
   - Misconfigured command/entrypoint
   - Invalid environment variables

Transition Condition: The container entrypoint executes, and Kubernetes monitors for success/failure.

3. **Success Check**

   This is a critical decision point in the flow. After the container starts, Kubernetes checks if it launches successfully and passes its startup conditions.

   - **Success:** The container initializes, optionally runs any startup probes, and begins responding to readiness probes.
   - **Failure:** The container exits with a non-zero code, or fails a startup probe (if configured).

This is evaluated based on:

   - Exit codes
   - Health probes (for example, **`startupProbe`**, **`livenessProbe`**, **`readinessProbe`**)
   - Container logs

Success Path: Pod Enters Ready State

If the container starts successfully and passes readiness checks, the pod enters the **Ready** state. At this point:

- Kubernetes service endpoints include the pod.
- Load balancers or ingress controllers may route traffic to the pod.
- This state is stable until either the pod is terminated or crashes.

Failure Path: Startup Failure

If the container fails to start, the pod enters a **Startup Fail** state. Common reasons include:

- Missing configuration (for example, required environment variable)
- Crash during entrypoint script
- Permission denied errors
- Dependencies not available (for example, missing volume mount, service unready)

Kubernetes captures the failure in the event stream, and depending on **`restartPolicy`**, may attempt to relaunch the container.

Crash Detected

When a container terminates unexpectedly (non-zero exit code), Kubernetes records the failure and attempts a restart (if **`restartPolicy is Always`** or **`OnFailure`**). The pod does **not** enter Ready and the process restarts.

If this failure recurs quickly, Kubernetes interprets it as a **crash loop**.

`CrashLoopBackOff` / `Backoff` Timer

This is a special state where Kubernetes backs off before attempting the next restart. This is implemented to:

- Avoid overwhelming the system with rapid restarts.
- Give operators time to investigate before further resource consumption.

Backoff intervals typically follow an **exponential retry** pattern – for example, 10s, 20s, 40s – up to a maximum threshold.

Pods in this state show up with:

```
kubectl get pods
NAME          READY   STATUS             RESTARTS
app-crasher   0/1     CrashLoopBackOff   5
```

To investigate further, the operator would typically run:

```
kubectl describe pod app-crasher
kubectl logs app-crasher
```

Operational Implications

Understanding this lifecycle is crucial for:

- Building effective liveness/readiness probes.
- Handling misconfigurations gracefully.
- Designing fault-tolerant applications.
- Monitoring restart counts and pod status for SRE alerting.

The Pod Lifecycle and Error Transition Flow is not just an academic concept; it is a practical framework that every DevOps engineer must internalize. Whether it is a failed startup probe, a missing image, or a crash-looping pod, this model helps dissect where things go wrong and how to fix them quickly.

By embedding this lifecycle in observability tools (for example, Prometheus alerts, Grafana dashboards), teams can proactively detect and resolve issues – reducing Mean Time to Recovery (MTTR) and improving system reliability.

Symptom	Diagnostic Tool	Command
Pod not scheduled	Describe pod	kubectl describe pod <name>
CrashLoopBackOff	Check logs	kubectl logs <name>
Probes failing	Inspect pod spec	kubectl get pod <name> -o yaml
Environment variable missing	Confirm ConfigMaps/ Secrets	kubectl describe pod + kubectl get cm / secret

Table 9.2: *Common Troubleshooting Checklist*

Diagnosing pod failures such as **CrashLoopBackOff** and **ImagePullBackOff** is a critical skill for any Kubernetes practitioner. These failures usually stem from configuration errors, missing dependencies, or registry mismanagement. With hands-on experience in reading logs, reviewing pod events, and understanding readiness probes, you can drastically improve recovery time, and maintain availability in production environments.

kubectl Logs, Events and Exec-Based Debugging

In a production Kubernetes environment, being able to quickly investigate and resolve issues in Pods and services is crucial to ensure application reliability and uptime. This part focuses on real-world debugging using native Kubernetes tooling–specifically kubectl logs, kubectl describe, kubectl get events, and kubectl exec–for interacting with containers, identifying anomalies, and resolving them effectively. All practices here align with industry use cases in both managed services such as Azure Kubernetes Service (AKS) and self-managed clusters.

Command-line debugging is critical in Kubernetes for the following reasons:

- **Dynamic Infrastructure:** Kubernetes environments constantly scale and mutate. Debugging via logs and CLI allows engineers to understand problems without disrupting services.
- **Lack of GUI Visibility:** In many enterprise setups (especially in CI/CD pipelines), CLI tools are the only immediate way to observe and react to issues.
- **Minimal Downtime:** When pods crash, timing is critical. Using tools such as **kubectl logs** or **exec** enables near real-time debugging and faster Mean Time to Resolution (MTTR).
- **Cloud-Native Complexity:** In AKS or other cloud providers, workloads are often abstracted–direct host access is restricted. CLI-based debugging is the most viable strategy.

What are the core CLI tools for Kubernetes debugging?

kubectl logs

- **Purpose:** Fetches logs from running or previously terminated containers.
- **Usage:** For inspecting error messages, stack traces, or container-specific logging output.

```
kubectl logs <pod-name>
kubectl logs <pod-name> -c <container-name>   # For multi-container pods
kubectl logs --previous <pod-name>            # View logs from a crashed pod
```

kubectl describe

- **Purpose:** Provides detailed information about a resource (Pod, Node, Deployment).
- **Includes:** Events, state transitions, probe status, volume mounts, and container specs.

```
kubectl describe pod <pod-name>
```

kubectl get events

- **Purpose:** Retrieves cluster events in reverse chronological order.

- **Use case:** Excellent for identifying resource scheduling issues, restarts, and probe failures.

  ```
  kubectl get events --sort-by='.lastTimestamp'
  ```

kubectl exec

- **Purpose:** Executes a command inside a running container. Helpful for live debugging of files, environments, or dependencies.

  ```
  kubectl exec -it <pod-name> -- /bin/bash
  ```

Debug Pods (Ephemeral Containers)

Purpose: Introduced in Kubernetes v1.23+, ephemeral containers allow attaching a debug container to a running Pod without restarting it.

```
kubectl debug -it <pod-name> --image=busybox --target=<container-name>
```

Scenario	Tool
Pod is crashing repeatedly (CrashLoopBackOff)	`kubectl logs -previous`
Application timing out or failing to start	`kubectl describe, kubectl get events`
Need to inspect environment, installed libraries	`kubectl exec`
Node taints or scheduling delays	`kubectl describe node`
Real-time troubleshooting in distributed apps	`kubectl exec + kubectl logs`

Table 9.3: *When Should These Commands be Used*

In Azure Kubernetes Service (AKS), these tools are often the first line of defense before consulting Log Analytics or Azure Monitor.

Hands-on Debugging in Action

Scenario: API Server Request Timeout in AKS

Issue:

Users are reporting timeout errors while accessing a REST API deployed in AKS.

Step-by-Step Debug:

1. **Check Pod Status**

   ```
   kubectl get pods -n prod-api
   ```

2. **Describe the Pod**

   ```
   kubectl describe pod rest-api-78f5 -n prod-api
   ```

   Outcome: Shows readiness probe failing after 10s. Events show "Readiness probe failed" for three consecutive tries.

3. **Inspect Logs**

   ```
   kubectl logs rest-api-78f5 -n prod-api
   ```

   Outcome: Reveals the container fails to connect to its PostgreSQL database due to DNS resolution issues.

4. **Inspect Node's DNS Config**

   ```
   kubectl get pods -n kube-system -l k8s-app=kube-dns
   kubectl logs -n kube-system <dns-pod-name>
   ```

   Outcome: DNS pod shows high latency. CPU is throttled.

5. **Exec into Pod for More Clarity**

```
kubectl exec -it rest-api-78f5 -n prod-api -- /bin/bash
nslookup postgres-db
```

Outcome: Delayed or failed resolution confirms DNS stress.

Resolution:

- Updated resource limits for CoreDNS.
- Used Azure DNS zones for external DB and configured appropriate caching.

Command-Line Debugging Lifecycle in Kubernetes

This flow represents how engineers progress through layered debugging:

- From high-level object status → to event logs → to container internals.
- Supports incident triage, proactive analysis, and deep troubleshooting.

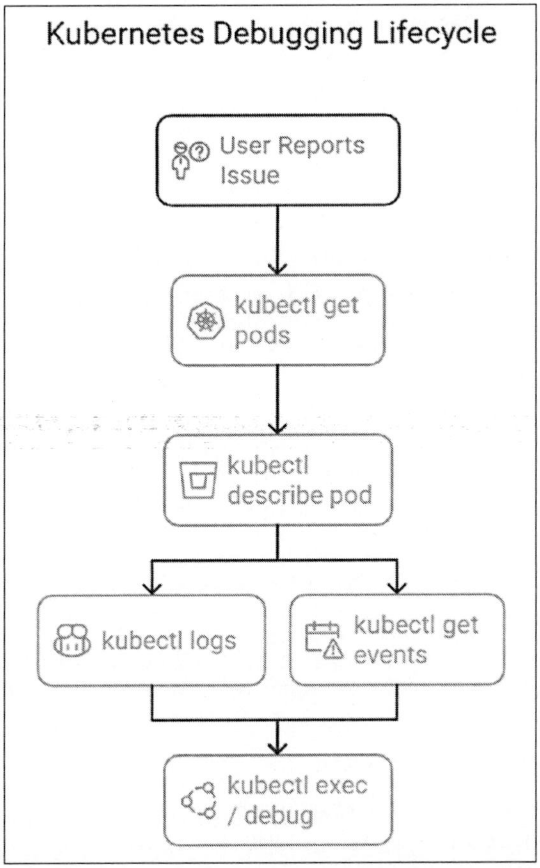

Figure 9.3: *Command-Line Debugging Lifecycle in Kubernetes*

The preceding figure outlines a structured process that engineers follow when investigating pod-level issues in Kubernetes. This lifecycle is built on a logical series of CLI-based interactions using **`kubectl`**, the primary command-line interface for Kubernetes. Whether you are responding to an incident or performing root cause analysis, following this lifecycle reduces the time to resolution and increases debugging accuracy.

Let us walk through each stage:

1. **User Reports Issue**

   The lifecycle begins with a problem being surfaced – either through monitoring systems (like Prometheus/Grafana), log aggregation alerts, or direct user feedback.

   Common symptoms reported include:

   - A web service becoming unresponsive.
   - CronJob outputs not reaching a downstream system.
   - An application deployment failing after a CI/CD rollout.

   This is the cue for operators or SREs to start their investigation with **`kubectl`**.

2. **`kubectl get pods` – Identify Pod State**

   The first diagnostic step is to list the pods in the relevant namespace to check their current status:

   ```
   kubectl get pods -n <namespace>
   ```

   This command provides a snapshot view of:

   - Pod health (**`Running`**, **`Pending`**, **`CrashLoopBackOff`**, and so on)
   - Container readiness (**`0/1`**, **`1/1`**)
   - Restart counts

   Why it matters: This instantly helps filter whether the pod is running, failing, or stuck in scheduling. It sets the investigation context.

3. **`kubectl describe pod` – Inspect Pod Events and Conditions**

   Next, the pod's detailed metadata and event history are queried using:

   ```
   kubectl describe pod <pod-name> -n <namespace>
   ```

   This command returns critical insights such as:

   - Node assignment and tolerations
   - Volume mounts, environment variables
   - Lifecycle probe configurations
   - The last few Kubernetes event messages (such as, **`FailedScheduling`**, **`BackOff`**, **`PullImageError`**)

   Why it matters: This often reveals the *why* behind the pod's condition – for instance, it may show that the pod failed to mount a volume, or is restarting due to a misconfigured health check.

4a. **`kubectl logs` – View Container Output**

   If the pod is in **`Running`** or **`CrashLoopBackOff`**, the next logical step is to inspect container logs:

   ```
   kubectl logs <pod-name> -n <namespace>
   ```

   In multi-container pods:

   ```
   kubectl logs <pod-name> -c <container-name>
   ```

   Logs are critical for:

   - Detecting stack traces or runtime errors.
   - Identifying missing environment variables.

- o Catching dependency failures (for example, DB connection refused).

Why it matters: Logs provide application-level errors, which are usually not exposed in Kubernetes events.

4b. **`kubectl get events` – Analyze Cluster Events Chronologically**

This command fetches all events in the namespace, ordered by time:

```
kubectl get events -n <namespace> --sort-by=.metadata.creationTimestamp
```

Events help identify:

- o When a pod was scheduled.
- o If it failed due to node resource constraints.
- o If there was a preemption or eviction.

Why it matters: It helps trace *what happened and when*. This is essential in environments with multiple autoscalers or competing workloads.

5. **`kubectl exec` or `kubectl debug` – Interact with the Container**

When the logs and events are not enough, you move into the container shell:

```
kubectl exec -it <pod-name> -n <namespace> -- /bin/sh
```

For deeper diagnosis of a broken container image or a pod that failed to start, use ephemeral debugging:

```
kubectl debug pod/<pod-name> -n <namespace> --image=busybox
```

This allows actions such as:

- Inspecting mounted filesystems
- Testing network reachability (such as, DNS, curl, ping)
- Manually executing binaries

Why it matters: This is the "break-glass" phase where engineers perform hands-on inspection inside a live or replica environment.

From Incident to Resolution

Figure 9.3 visually conveys the operational reality of debugging in Kubernetes environments. It emphasizes a practical, tool-driven flow that DevOps teams rely on during real-world incidents. When captured in dashboards or runbooks, this lifecycle ensures consistent incident response and shortens recovery time during outages.

By standardizing this CLI-based debugging process, teams can:

- Train junior engineers effectively.
- Reduce on-call burnout through faster root cause analysis.
- Integrate observability tools with command-line flows for better context switching.

Summary

This section equips engineers with hands-on strategies for diagnosing common Kubernetes issues using native tooling. In production-grade AKS environments, these CLI tools offer real-time visibility into workload health, reducing the time to detect and resolve errors. Understanding how to correlate events, logs, and container states is essential for high availability in cloud-native pipelines.

Network Debugging and Port Forwarding

Why do network debugging challenges arise in Kubernetes?

Kubernetes introduces an abstraction over traditional networking using internal DNS, service discovery, pod-to-pod communication, and layered overlay networks such as CNI plugins (for example, Azure CNI, Calico). In complex data-driven or microservices-based environments, network failures are inevitable due to:

- Misconfigured Services or missing endpoints.
- Internal DNS resolution failures between pods.
- Broken NetworkPolicies or Azure NSG rules.
- Ingress traffic not routing correctly or backend pods failing readiness.
- Inaccessible internal APIs causing ETL pipelines or microservices to fail silently.

When microservices rely on real-time connectivity (for example, a Spark job calling a metadata catalog or an ingestion pipeline pinging Kafka over internal DNS), diagnosing such issues is critical for maintaining SLAs.

What are key tools and scenarios?

Kubernetes provides the following tools and techniques to debug network issues:

Tool	Purpose
`kubectl exec`	Launch the interactive shell inside the container to test connectivity.
`kubectl port-forward`	Expose a pod or service port on localhost for access.
`kubectl get svc/endpoints`	Check if service endpoints are correctly mapped to pods.
`netshoot` (diagnostic pod)	Advanced networking tools (curl, dig, nslookup, traceroute).
`dnsutils`	Lightweight pod image to test DNS issues from within the cluster.

***Table 9.4**: Debugging Tools and Scenarios*

In Azure Kubernetes Service (AKS), network debugging often includes checking:

- Azure Network Security Group (NSG) rules blocking pod CIDRs.
- Azure CNI IP exhaustion issues or VNet misconfigurations.
- DNS timeouts due to CoreDNS misbehavior (visible in logs).

Network debugging becomes critical when:

- **Services Not Accessible:** Microservice A cannot reach Service B via its ClusterIP.
- **DNS Failures:** `curl` to service name fails; pods cannot resolve internal hostnames.
- **Connection Timeouts:** Load balancers route traffic but backend pods don't respond.
- **Pod Logs Show Errors:** Errors such as `connection refused`, `no route to host`, `504 gateway timeout.`

Especially in large-scale ETL workloads and streaming data pipelines (for example, Kafka Connect, Debezium), internal service communication is fundamental. One broken hop in the pipeline can delay the entire workflow or crash dependent services.

How do we diagnose network problems in Kubernetes?

Step 1: Start with kubectl get and describe

```
        kubectl get svc -n data-pipeline
kubectl describe svc kafka-broker -n data-pipeline
kubectl get endpoints kafka-broker -n data-pipeline
```

Check if the service has any associated endpoints (i.e., backing pods).

Step 2: Deploy a Diagnostic Pod (Netshoot)

Use **`netshoot`** to run tools such as **`curl`**, **`dig`**, **`nslookup`**, and `traceroute` from inside the cluster.

```
kubectl run -it netshoot --rm --image=nicolaka/netshoot - bash
```

Inside netshoot container:

```
dig kafka-broker.data-pipeline.svc.cluster.local
curl http://kafka-broker:9092
```

Step 3: Use Port Forwarding for External Access

```
kubectl port-forward svc/kafka-broker 9092:9092 -n data-pipeline
```

This allows developers to run local tools (example, Kafka clients) against cluster services.

Step 4: Check DNS Resolution Failures

```
kubectl logs -n kube-system -l k8s-app=kube-dns
kubectl get pods -n kube-system -l k8s-app=kube-dns -o wide
```

In Azure, CoreDNS failures are common if Azure DNS endpoints are not reachable due to NSG rules.

YAML Lab: Using BusyBox and Netshoot for Network Testing

```
yaml

apiVersion: v1
kind: Pod
metadata:
  name: net-debugger
  namespace: debug
spec:
  containers:
  - name: net-toolbox
    image: nicolaka/netshoot
    command: ["sleep", "3600"]
    securityContext:
      capabilities:
        add: ["NET_ADMIN"]
```

After deploying:

```
bash

kubectl exec -it net-debugger -n debug -- bash
curl kafka-service:9092
dig kafka-service.data-pipeline.svc.cluster.local
```

Case Study: Debugging an Unreachable Kafka Cluster in Azure AKS

Scenario:

A real-time financial processing pipeline on AKS was failing. Kafka producer logs showed `broker not reachable`.

Diagnosis Steps:

- Checked Kafka service and endpoints: all looked healthy.
- Used **netshoot** from a different namespace; DNS resolution to Kafka service failed.
- Found a `NetworkPolicy` applied at the namespace level blocking inter-namespace communication.
- Modified policy to allow traffic from producer namespace.

Fix Applied:

```
yaml

apiVersion: networking.k8s.io/v1
kind: NetworkPolicy
metadata:
  name: allow-producer-to-kafka
  namespace: kafka
spec:
  podSelector:
    matchLabels:
      app: kafka
  ingress:
  - from:
    - namespaceSelector:
        matchLabels:
          name: kafka-producers
```

Kubernetes Networking and Port Forwarding

Explanation:

- The developer uses `kubectl port-forward` to forward the local port to the cluster pod port.
- Netshoot or BusyBox pod can test connectivity from within the cluster.
- Kubernetes DNS (`svc.cluster.local`) is resolved by CoreDNS.
- Azure CNI routes traffic through VNet, impacted by NSGs.

The following figure illustrates the internal and external networking flow that enables developers to debug or interact with Kubernetes-based applications running in a cluster—specifically via `kubectl port-forward`. It covers not only how local traffic is tunneled to Kubernetes pods or services, but also how that traffic navigates within the Azure Container Networking Interface (CNI) environment and is influenced by Network Security Groups (NSGs).

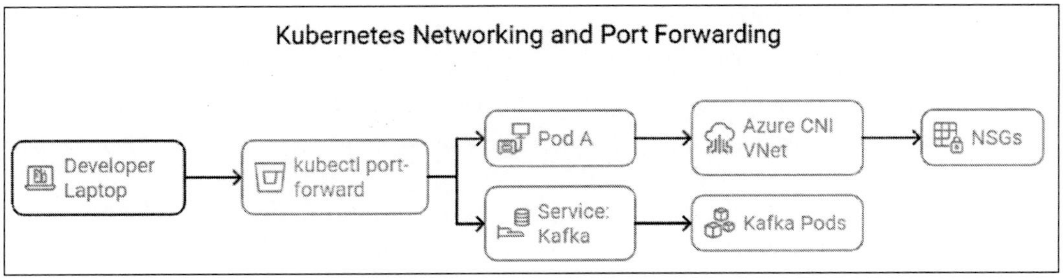

***Figure 9.4**: Kubernetes Networking and Port Forwarding*

Let us walk through each component and the flow involved:

1. **The Developer Laptop Initiates Port Forwarding**

   At the edge of this flow sits the developer's laptop. From here, the user executes a command such as:

   `kubectl port-forward svc/kafka 9092:9092`

   or:

   `kubectl port-forward pod/pod-a 8080:80`

   This command establishes a local TCP tunnel that forwards traffic from a port on the local machine (e.g., **`localhost:9092`**) directly to the target pod or service in the Kubernetes cluster.

   Use Case: This is especially helpful for local testing, debugging Kafka brokers, REST APIs, or internal web interfaces without exposing them publicly via Ingress or LoadBalancer.

2. **`kubectl port-forward` Bridges Local and Cluster Network**

   `kubectl port-forward` works by leveraging the Kubernetes API server. Once invoked, it:

   - Establishes a connection to the Kubernetes API server over HTTPS.
   - Proxies local traffic via that connection to the internal Pod/Service.
   - Uses SPDY (or HTTP/2) to multiplex the port-forward session.

   Note: This process bypasses the usual service discovery mechanisms (such as DNS resolution inside the cluster), making it ideal for troubleshooting isolated workloads.

3. **Pod-Level or Service-Level Forwarding**

   Depending on the object selected, the traffic flow diverges slightly:

- **To a Pod (example, Pod A):**
  - Traffic is directly forwarded to the IP and port of the container inside the pod.
  - This is ideal when testing a single-instance application or debugging at the container level.
- **To a Service (example, Kafka):**
  - The request is forwarded to the ClusterIP of the service.
  - Kube-proxy (via iptables or IPVS) routes the traffic to one of the backend pods (example, Kafka Pods) using round-robin or other load-balancing algorithms.

  Best Practice: Use service-level forwarding to validate how load balancing is behaving across replicas.

4. **Azure CNI Integration**

   In the case of an Azure Kubernetes Service (AKS) deployment using **Azure CNI:**

   - Each pod gets an IP address from the virtual network (VNet).
   - These IPs are routable within the VNet and can communicate with other Azure services or networked systems.

   Implication: Any traffic flowing to pods—either from other pods or from developer laptops via port-forward—is effectively routed over Azure's virtual network fabric.

5. **Network Security Groups (NSGs)**

   NSGs define the **allow/deny rules** that govern traffic flowing into and out of subnets and network interfaces in Azure. Even though **`kubectl port-forward`** uses a local-to-API server proxy, certain traffic scenarios (such as backend Kafka pod access or inter-pod communication) are still impacted by NSG configurations.

   Examples:

   - An NSG rule that denies inbound TCP on port 9092 may prevent intra-pod Kafka communication.
   - Misconfigured NSGs may block pod-to-pod DNS or health check probes.

6. **Optional: Netshoot or BusyBox for In-Cluster Testing**

   Figure 9.4 implicitly supports the use of diagnostic containers such as:

   ```
   kubectl run -it netshoot --rm --image=nicolaka/netshoot -- bash
   ```

These tools help developers test:

- DNS resolution via `dig` or `nslookup`
- Network reachability via **`curl`** or **`telnet`**
- Kafka port availability using **`nc`** (netcat)

This is crucial for confirming service discovery (**`svc-name.namespace.svc.cluster.local`**) via **CoreDNS** and for diagnosing NSG or network policy issues.

Practical Use and Debugging Benefits

This networking model is foundational for:

- Debugging service-to-service communication (especially for brokers such as Kafka).
- Running integration tests locally against real cluster workloads.
- Diagnosing service discovery, NSG blocking, or DNS resolution failures.

By understanding this flow, Kubernetes engineers can confidently:

- Test internal applications without LoadBalancers or Ingress.
- Validate cluster DNS and routing logic.
- Use Azure-specific tools (example, Network Watcher) to correlate NSG rules with traffic behaviors.

Summary:

- Kubernetes networking issues often stem from broken DNS, service misconfiguration, or network policies.
- Tools such as **`kubectl`**, **`netshoot`**, and **`port-forward`** provide visibility and interactivity.

- YAML-based labs and diagnostic pods help replicate, isolate, and resolve complex issues quickly.
- On Azure, additional layers such as NSGs and Azure DNS introduce platform-specific debugging layers.

Root Cause Analysis for Production Incidents

The Problem with Diagnosing Production Incidents

In cloud-native environments such as Kubernetes, production issues are not just about *what failed*, but *why*, *where*, and *how*. A simple `CrashLoopBackOff` or service timeout can spiral into downtime, missed SLAs, or revenue loss. Without a structured RCA process, organizations face:

- **Reactive firefighting** with no systemic resolution.
- **Blame games** instead of accountability.
- **Lack of traceability** in distributed microservices.
- **Regulatory gaps**, especially in industries such as finance or healthcare.

Example:

A large Azure-based ETL pipeline failed during peak business hours due to an unhandled exception in a container. Because no audit trail or metric correlation was in place, the issue took hours to isolate – costing critical business hours and trust.

RCA Process and Its Core Components

Root Cause Analysis (RCA) is a structured investigation to identify the underlying cause of a production failure, followed by preventive remediations.

RCA Workflow Stages:

1. **Incident Detection:** Triggered by alerts (Prometheus, Azure Monitor).
2. **Timeline Reconstruction:** What happened *when*, *where*, and in *what sequence*?
3. **Correlation of Logs and Events:** Aligning logs, pod failures, node taints, and events.
4. **Isolating the Culprit:** Component, config, or code causing the chain reaction.
5. **Fix + Prevent:** Patch, rollback, or redeploy; followed by observability improvement.

RCA Artifacts:

- **Incident Report Template:** Includes impact, timeline, and affected systems.
- **Post-Mortem Doc:** Non-blaming doc used to institutionalize learnings.
- **Azure Workbooks + Log Analytics:** Dashboards to visualize cluster-level breakdown.

Applying RCA in Real-World Scenarios

Perform RCA in the following critical conditions:

- **Persistent Pod Failures** even after restarts or redeployments.
- **Latency Spikes** with no obvious application changes.
- **Node Failures** affecting HA workloads or StatefulSets.
- **Data Pipeline Failures** (example, Kafka broker deadlock or Spark executor timeout)

Production Context in Azure

When dealing with Spark on Azure Kubernetes Service (AKS), for instance:

- Spark driver logs might be in Azure Blob storage.
- Cluster diagnostics might appear in **Azure Monitor Logs**.
- Pod crash info can be collected from `kubectl logs` and correlated with **Kusto queries** in **Log Analytics Workspace**.

Performing RCA with Tools, Templates, and Hands-On Lab

RCA Flow Diagram:

```
Alert → Timeline → Logs → Events → Correlation → Root Cause → Fix → Prevention
```

RCA YAML Lab:

Simulate failure in the Spark app:

YAML: Faulty Spark Executor Pod

```yaml
yaml

apiVersion: v1
kind: Pod
metadata:
  name: spark-executor-failure
spec:
  containers:
  - name: executor
    image: apache/spark:3.3.0
    command: ["sh", "-c"]
    args: ["exit 1"]  # Simulate crash
```

Diagnostic CLI:

```bash
bash

kubectl describe pod spark-executor-failure
kubectl logs spark-executor-failure
kubectl get events --sort-by='.metadata.creationTimestamp'
```

Observation: You will note repeated crash loops with **`Exit Code 1`**, no liveness probe, and memory over-usage.

Real-World Case Study: High Latency in Spark ETL on AKS

Scenario:

A financial service company runs Spark jobs on Azure Kubernetes Service. During one critical run, latency in the fraud detection pipeline increased from 400ms to over 5 seconds.

RCA Walkthrough:

- **Timeline Reconstruction:** Alerts from Azure Monitor revealed that the latency began after a new image was pushed.
- **Log Correlation:** Spark driver logs showed multiple retries on Kafka consumer connections.
- **Pod-Level Debugging:** Spark executors had CPU throttling due to incorrect `requests/limits`.

- **Root Cause:** Misconfigured resource limits in Spark driver and Kafka pod affecting inter-service communication.

YAML Fix: Updated Resources

```yaml
yaml

resources:
  requests:
    cpu: "2"
    memory: "4Gi"
  limits:
    cpu: "3"
    memory: "6Gi"
```

Prevention:

- Added Prometheus-based resource alerts.
- Introduced retry policies using Istio for downstream services.
- Enforced container linting with Polaris before deployment.

Area	Best Practice
Observation	Enable Azure Monitor + Prometheus for layered visibility
Metrics	Correlate CPU/Memory with logs and HPA behaviors
Logging	Use centralized EFK/ELK or Azure Log Analytics
Preventive RCA	Automate linting and validation (example, OPA Gatekeeper + Polaris)
RCA Templates	Maintain RCA Playbook for fast, repeatable incident resolution

***Table 9.5**: Best Practices and Recommendations*

Final Thoughts

Root Cause Analysis in Kubernetes environments is both an art and a science. The complexity of containerized workloads, especially in distributed systems such as Spark, Kafka, and Flink, demands structured RCA workflows. Integrating observability tools, resource tracking, and detailed post-mortems ensures operational excellence.

By mastering RCA practices tailored to Azure Kubernetes environments, modern engineering teams can reduce MTTR, prevent repeat outages, and build trust in mission-critical data pipelines.

Root Cause Analysis Template for Kubernetes Incidents

- **Incident Summary**
  - Incident Title:
  - Date and Time:
  - Reported By:
  - Severity Level:
  - Impact Summary:
- **Affected Components**
  - Cluster Name/Environment (Dev/Stage/Prod):
  - Namespace(s):
  - Affected Services/Pods:

  - Nodes involved:
- **Timeline Reconstruction**
  - Detection Time:
  - Incident Start:
  - Key Events and Timestamps:
  - Incident End:
  - Alert Source (example, Prometheus, Azure Monitor):
- **Root Cause Analysis**
  - Logs and Metrics Reviewed:
  - Tools Used (kubectl logs, describe, Azure Monitor, Grafana):
  - Findings:
  - Root Cause Identified:
- **Remediation**
  - Temporary Fix Applied:
  - Permanent Fix Implemented:
  - Configuration/Code Changes Made:
- **Preventive Measures**
  - Monitoring Improvements:
  - Resource Limit Adjustments:
  - CI/CD Enhancements:
  - Policy/Governance Update:
- **Lessons Learned**
  - What worked well:
  - What could have been improved:
  - Documentation Updates Required:
- **Approvals and Follow-Up**
  - RCA Owner:
  - Approved By:
  - Next RCA Review Date:
  - Jira Ticket or Tracker ID:

Conclusion

In this chapter, we thoroughly explored the nuances of debugging Kubernetes applications and clusters, covering everything from resource-level issues and event logs to advanced troubleshooting with kubectl, ephemeral containers, and cloud-native tools. By mastering these techniques, engineers and architects can confidently identify and resolve challenges that arise in modern containerized environments.

In the next chapter, we will build upon this foundation by diving into Monitoring, Logging, and Observability. We will cover essential strategies for collecting, analyzing, and visualizing telemetry data, using tools such as Prometheus, Grafana, Fluentd, and Azure Monitor to gain holistic insights into cluster health, performance, and security.

CHAPTER 10
Monitoring, Logging, and Observability

Introduction

As applications scale in Kubernetes, ensuring visibility into system behavior becomes critical for performance, reliability, and troubleshooting. Monitoring, logging, and observability provide the foundation for understanding what is happening inside your clusters and services. This chapter explores the tools and practices needed to collect metrics, aggregate logs, trace requests, and set up real-time alerts. Whether you are managing a small setup or a large-scale Kubernetes deployment, mastering observability empowers you to detect anomalies early, debug issues faster, and optimize system health with confidence.

Structure

In this chapter, we will cover the following topics:

- Prometheus and Grafana Monitoring Stack for Kubernetes
- Centralized Logging with Fluentd and Elasticsearch
- Custom Alerts and Threshold-Based Dashboards
- Metrics, Logs, Traces: The 3 Pillars of Observability
- Real-Time Monitoring for Large Clusters

Prometheus and Grafana Monitoring Stack for Kubernetes

Modern Kubernetes workloads—especially data-heavy pipelines, real-time analytics engines, and distributed microservices—require deep visibility to ensure reliability and performance. Traditional logging and basic CPU/memory stats are no longer enough. Engineers need fine-grained metrics, historical visualizations, and intelligent alerting.

Without observability:

- Performance bottlenecks go unnoticed until SLAs are breached.
- Root cause analysis becomes guesswork.
- Teams lack visibility into resource wastage and scaling needs.
- Real-time workloads (for example, streaming Kafka/Spark jobs) suffer from hidden anomalies.

Core Concept

Prometheus is the de facto standard for collecting time-series metrics from Kubernetes components, pods, and nodes. It scrapes metrics using the HTTP pull model via *exporters* such as **`node-exporter`**, **`kube-state-metrics`**, and application-specific endpoints (for example, **`/metrics`**).

Grafana is the visualization layer for Prometheus, turning raw metrics into actionable dashboards and custom alerts.

Together, they enable:

- Real-time health checks on pods, nodes, and cluster infrastructure.
- Custom dashboards for ETL jobs, Spark workloads, Kafka throughput, and so on.
- Alerting for latency spikes, pod failures, memory leaks, and CPU saturation.

Use Cases

Use Prometheus and Grafana when:

- You are running production clusters with uptime requirements.
- You are managing high-throughput workloads such as data ingestion, ML model serving, or stream processing.
- You want proactive alerts instead of reactive incident response.
- You need compliance-grade logging and metric retention for audit trails.

For example, in Azure Kubernetes Service (AKS), native integration with Prometheus and Grafana enhances visibility while leveraging Azure Monitor and Azure Log Analytics for hybrid insights.

Implementation

1. **Install Prometheus and Grafana via Helm (Azure AKS Friendly)**

Use Helm 3 and install both components into a **`monitoring`** namespace:

```
bash

helm repo add prometheus-community https://prometheus-community.github.io/
helm-charts
helm repo update

kubectl create namespace monitoring

helm install prometheus prometheus-community/kube-prometheus-stack \
  --namespace monitoring \
  --set grafana.service.type=LoadBalancer \
  --set prometheus.service.type=LoadBalancer
```

This deploys: Prometheus, Alert Manager, Grafana, node-exporter, kube-state-metrics—all pre-wired.

2. **Enable Node-Level Metrics**

Ensure the **`node-exporter`** is installed (comes with the preceding Helm chart):

- Exposes CPU, disk, and memory usage for each AKS node
- Default scrape endpoint: **`http://<node-ip>:9100/metrics`**

3. **Enable Cluster Metrics with `kube-state-metrics`**

Tracks Kubernetes objects:

- Deployments
- DaemonSets
- CronJobs
- Pod conditions (example, CrashLoopBackOff)
- PVC statuses

4. **Configure Grafana Dashboards**

Grafana UI (default login: **`admin/prom-operator`**):

- Navigate to "**`Import Dashboard`**".
- Use ID **`6417`** for Kubernetes cluster monitoring.
- Use ID **`1860`** for the node exporter dashboard.
- Create alerts for: high pod restarts, high CPU, and disk saturation.

5. **Sample YAML Lab: Service Monitor for a Custom App**

```
yaml

apiVersion: monitoring.coreos.com/v1
kind: ServiceMonitor
metadata:
  name: myapp-servicemonitor
  labels:
    release: prometheus
spec:
  selector:
    matchLabels:
      app: myapp
  endpoints:
    - port: http
      interval: 15s
  namespaceSelector:
    matchNames:
      - default
```

Prometheus and Grafana Pipeline: Observability Architecture in Kubernetes

The following figure provides a high-level architectural view of how observability is established in a Kubernetes environment using **Prometheus** for metrics collection and **Grafana** for visualization. It showcases how multiple data sources - including nodes, Kubernetes API, and application endpoints - are instrumented, scraped, stored, and finally visualized through dashboards and alerts.

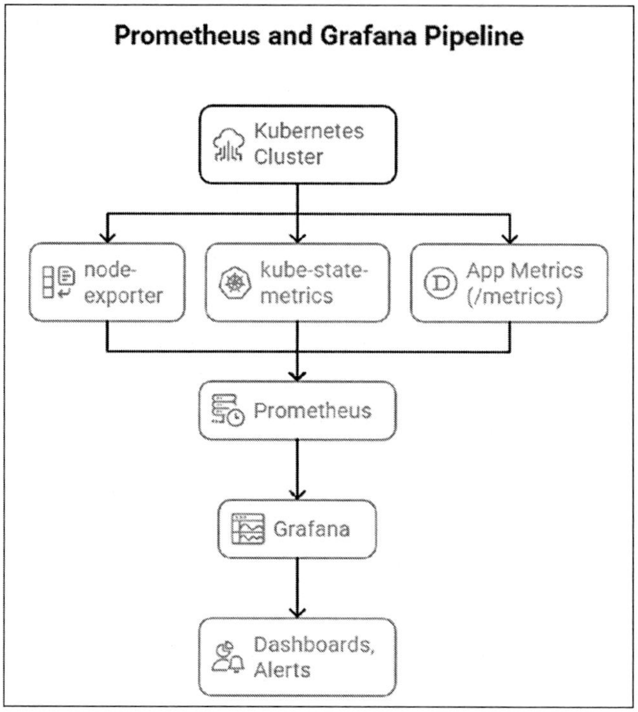

Figure 10.1: *Prometheus and Grafana Pipeline*

This architecture relies on a few core components and operational steps:

- **Exporters** collect data from nodes and workloads.
- **Prometheus** scrapes data at regular intervals and stores time-series metrics.
- **Grafana** visualizes metrics and triggers alerts.
- Works in AKS or on-prem with identical configuration.

Here is a step-by-step explanation of each step:

1. **Kubernetes Cluster (AKS, GKE, EKS, On-Prem)**

At the top of the stack is the Kubernetes cluster, which serves as the source of operational and application metrics. This includes:

a. Nodes (compute infrastructure)

b. Kubernetes control plane objects (pods, deployments, daemonsets, and so on)

c. Custom workloads and services running inside the cluster

Regardless of the deployment environment (cloud-managed services such as AKS/GKE or on-prem), the core pipeline remains the same.

2. **Exporters: Data Producers**

These components are responsible for exposing metrics in Prometheus-compatible formats (`/metrics` endpoint).

a. **node-exporter**

i. Collects system-level metrics (CPU, memory, disk, network) from each Kubernetes node.

ii. Runs as a DaemonSet so every node has one instance of the exporter.

iii. Provides host-level telemetry such as:

- Filesystem saturation
- CPU load
- Memory pressure

b. **kube-state-metrics**

i. Monitors the **state** of Kubernetes objects (Deployments, Pods, ReplicaSets).

ii. Reads from the Kubernetes API server and exports metrics, such as:

- Deployment desired versus available replicas
- Pod phase distribution (Pending, Running, Failed)
- Resource limits/requests per namespace

c. **App Metrics (`/metrics`)**

i. Custom metrics exposed by application containers (for example, Node.js, Go, Python apps).

ii. Libraries such as **`prom-client`** or **`prometheus_client`** instrument the code to expose business logic metrics, such as:

- HTTP request duration
- Error rates
- Queue length
- Custom counters and gauges

These endpoints are scraped by Prometheus using service discovery or direct configuration.

3. **Prometheus: Metrics Collection and Storage**

Prometheus acts as the central metrics engine in this pipeline. Its key functions include:

a. Scraping exposed metrics from exporters and application endpoints.

b. Storing metrics as **time series**, indexed by metric name, labels, and timestamps.

c. Applying rules for:

i. Alert generation

ii. Recording complex queries into new series for faster dashboarding

Prometheus provides a built-in query language called **PromQL** to extract meaningful patterns from the collected metrics.

4. **Grafana: Visualization and Alerting**

Grafana is the visual front end of the observability stack. It connects to Prometheus as a data source and enables users to:

a. Build dynamic and customizable dashboards.

b. Monitor live metrics with auto-refresh intervals.

c. Set up alert rules to notify on-call engineers when conditions are met (for example, CPU > 80%)

Grafana Alerts can integrate with:

i. Slack

ii. Microsoft Teams

iii. PagerDuty

iv. Email

Bonus: Grafana allows templating and variable support, so users can dynamically switch between namespaces, pods, services, or clusters from a single dashboard.

5. **Dashboards and Alerts: Final Outcome**

The end result of this pipeline is:

a. Real-time dashboards showing infrastructure health, pod status, and application metrics.

b. Proactive alerting to ensure uptime and reliability.

This enables SREs, DevOps, and developers to:

i. Troubleshoot live issues faster

ii. Detect performance regressions

iii. Monitor SLA/SLO compliance

iv. Validate auto-scaling behavior

Key Takeaways:

Component	Role in Pipeline
node-exporter	Collects system metrics from cluster nodes
kube-state-metrics	Exposes Kubernetes object states as metrics
Application metrics	Business and service-specific metric endpoints
Prometheus	Scrapes, stores, and queries time-series data
Grafana	Visualizes metrics and sets up alert thresholds
Dashboards/Alerts	Final monitoring layer for observability

Table 10.1: *Key Takeaways*

Applicability to Azure AKS and Other Clouds

This architecture is **cloud-agnostic**. Whether deployed on AKS (Azure), GKE (Google Cloud), or EKS (AWS), the structure remains consistent. In Azure AKS, node-exporter and kube-state-metrics can be deployed via Helm charts or using Azure Monitor integrations, while Prometheus and Grafana can be managed via:

- Helm (community-managed)
- Prometheus Operator
- Azure Managed Grafana (for enterprise use cases)

Real-World Case Study: Monitoring Spark ETL Workloads on Azure Kubernetes Service

Scenario:

A data engineering team operates a large-scale **Spark-on-Kubernetes** environment to process scheduled Extract, Transform, Load (ETL) workloads on **Azure Kubernetes Service (AKS)**. These Spark jobs are resource-intensive, running daily with variable memory and CPU demands depending on data volume.

The team encountered **intermittent job failures**, especially under peak data ingestion cycles. These failures were unpredictable and difficult to isolate using logs alone, as they often occurred mid-way through execution and did not consistently reproduce.

Challenge:

Spark executor pods were **crashing with `OOMKilled` (Out-of-Memory)** errors during high-load periods. However, the symptoms were inconsistent across nodes. Some nodes completed their tasks, while others failed unexpectedly.

Initial debugging with **`kubectl describe pod`** showed memory limit violations, but the team needed a **system-wide view** to pinpoint:

- Which nodes were under pressure?
- When were resource limits exceeded?
- How frequently was the problem occurring?

Observability Pipeline Design

To build visibility across both infrastructure and Spark workloads, the team implemented a **Prometheus-Grafana observability pipeline** with the following components:

- **Node-Level Metrics**
    - **node-exporter** was deployed as a DaemonSet across all AKS nodes.
    - It collected kernel-level telemetry including:
        - Memory usage
        - CPU load
        - Disk IO
        - Swap usage (if enabled)

    This data was ingested by Prometheus and visualized in Grafana.
- **Cluster State Monitoring**
    - **kube-state-metrics** was used to export metadata about:
        - Spark executor pod status
        - Replica counts
        - Container restarts
        - Resource requests and limits

    This provided the context needed to correlate pod failures with node conditions.
- **Application-Level Instrumentation**
    - Spark was configured to expose **Prometheus-compatible metrics** on `/metrics`.

- Custom metrics such as:
  - Executor memory usage
  - JVM heap statistics
  - Task execution duration were scraped by Prometheus.

This enabled per-job and per-pod performance insight.

Grafana Dashboarding

Using Grafana, the team created custom dashboards with panels to track:

- Memory saturation per node
- **Spark executor pod memory usage** over time
- **Number of `OOMKilled` events** grouped by node and namespace
- Real-time alerts for:
  - Node memory usage > 85%
  - Executor container restarts
  - Spark job duration spikes

This visual and alerting layer replaced the manual log inspection cycle.

Alert-driven scaling with HPA and Cluster Autoscaler

To proactively mitigate memory exhaustion:

- The team defined **Prometheus alert rules** that triggered when memory usage crossed 85% on any node.
- These alerts are fed into a **Horizontal Pod Autoscaler (HPA)** configuration for Spark executor workloads.
- When executor pods scaled up and overwhelmed node capacity, the **Cluster Autoscaler** automatically added new nodes to the AKS node pool.

This closed the loop from **`metrics → alerting → automated scaling`**, and ensuring continuity of batch processing.

Outcome: The observability improvements had direct operational benefits:

Metric	Before Monitoring	After Implementation
Job Failure Rate	2–3 per day	Near-zero
Average Memory Usage	~80%	~65% (after scaling)
Mean Time to Resolution (MTTR)	3+ hours	<30 minutes
Spark Job SLA Adherence	~85%	>99%

Table 10.2: *Observability Improvements had Direct Operational Benefits*

Additionally, the team avoided **manual node resizing** and benefited from **cost-efficient autoscaling**, aligning resource usage with actual demand.

Key Learnings:

- **Node-level monitoring** is crucial for memory-bound workloads such as Spark.
- **Application metrics** enhance visibility beyond Kubernetes constructs.
- **Dashboards alone are not enough** – alerting and autoscaling ensure actionability.
- Integrated monitoring pipelines enable **self-healing infrastructure** under variable load.

By integrating Prometheus and Grafana in your AKS-based Kubernetes clusters, you gain end-to-end observability. Metrics drive scaling, alerting, and incident prevention. Custom dashboards allow deep insights into job health, pod status, and node saturation—transforming reactive firefighting into proactive engineering.

Centralized Logging with Fluentd and Elasticsearch

In Kubernetes, each Pod is ephemeral and logs are stored in container-specific runtimes on the node. Once a Pod is evicted, crashes or the node is drained, these logs are lost unless forwarded elsewhere. In real-world distributed systems—especially with ETL jobs, API microservices, and Spark/Kafka workloads—this becomes a serious **observability gap**.

Centralized logging is critical for operational success and security due to the following key reasons:

- **Multi-node context**: You cannot SSH into every node to check `/var/log/containers/`.
- **Pod volatility**: Logs disappear when pods restart or crash (for example, `CrashLoopBackOff`).
- **Compliance**: Enterprises (especially in BFSI, and healthcare) must retain logs for audits.
- **Debugging latency**: Logs help correlate events across services and nodes for RCA.
- **Data traceability**: Especially vital in data pipelines for trace-level lineage and tracking.

What is EFK: Fluentd + Elasticsearch + Kibana?

The most popular open-source logging stack is **EFK**:

- **Fluentd:** A log collector/forwarder that runs as a **DaemonSet** on every node. Parses, filters, and routes logs from containers.
- **Elasticsearch:** A search and analytics engine that stores structured log data and supports complex queries.
- **Kibana:** A UI frontend to visualize logs, build dashboards, and set alerts.

Why Fluentd:

- Native Kubernetes integration
- High performance, low footprint
- Supports multiple output backends (S3, BigQuery, Splunk, and so on)
- Parses both structured (`json`) and unstructured logs

Fluent Bit is a lightweight alternative to Fluentd for edge use cases, but Fluentd remains the most configurable for ETL-scale logs.

When to Centralize Logs in Kubernetes?

You should adopt centralized logging:

- When running multi-service or multi-tenant applications.
- In **production environments** where log retention is essential.
- When using **CI/CD**, tracing failures across multiple deployment stages.
- In **compliance-driven industries**: financial services, healthcare, government.
- When integrating with Azure-native services (example, Azure Monitor, Log Analytics).

Azure Kubernetes Service (AKS) integrates well with custom Fluentd + EFK stacks while also supporting native options such as Azure Monitor Logs for hybrid environments.

Deploying EFK on Kubernetes with Fluentd DaemonSet

Step-by-Step Implementation (AKS-compatible):

1. **Deploy Elasticsearch using Helm**

   ```bash
   helm repo add elastic https://helm.elastic.co
   helm repo update

   helm install elasticsearch elastic/elasticsearch \
     --namespace logging --create-namespace \
     --set replicas=1 \
     --set minimumMasterNodes=1
   ```

   You can scale up replicas for production or HA using StatefulSets.

2. **Deploy Kibana (UI frontend)**

   ```bash
   helm install kibana elastic/kibana \
     --namespace logging \
     --set service.type=LoadBalancer
   ```

   Once deployed, access Kibana using the external IP. The default port is `5601`.

3. **Deploy Fluentd as a DaemonSet**

   This Fluentd configuration tail logs from all pods and forwards them to Elasticsearch.

   ```yaml
   apiVersion: apps/v1
   kind: DaemonSet
   metadata:
     name: fluentd
     namespace: logging
   spec:
     selector:
       matchLabels:
         app: fluentd
     template:
       metadata:
         labels:
           app: fluentd
       spec:
         containers:
         - name: fluentd
           image: fluent/fluentd-kubernetes-daemonset:v1.14-debian-elasticsearch7
           env:
           - name: FLUENT_ELASTICSEARCH_HOST
             value: "elasticsearch.logging.svc.cluster.local"
           - name: FLUENT_ELASTICSEARCH_PORT
             value: "9200"
           volumeMounts:
           - name: varlog
             mountPath: /var/log
           - name: dockercontainers
             mountPath: /var/lib/docker/containers
   ```

```
        readOnly: true
      volumes:
      - name: varlog
        hostPath:
          path: /var/log
      - name: dockercontainers
        hostPath:
          path: /var/lib/docker/containers
```

This Fluentd setup tails container logs from **/var/log/containers/**, parses them, and forwards them to Elasticsearch.

YAML Lab: Parsing Structured JSON Logs from Applications

Assume your microservice writes structured logs such as:

```
json

{"timestamp":"2024-05-12T14:00:01Z", "level":"ERROR", "component":"api", "mes-
sage":"Failed to reach Kafka broker"}
```

Update Fluentd config to parse as JSON:

```
xml

<filter kubernetes.**>
  @type parser
  format json
  key_name log
  reserve_data true
</filter>
```

This ensures log attributes (for example, **level**, **component**, **message**) are extracted and indexed into Elasticsearch fields.

Fluentd to Elasticsearch Log Pipeline

The following figure illustrates the **Fluentd to Elasticsearch log pipeline**, detailing the functions and types involved in the log flow:

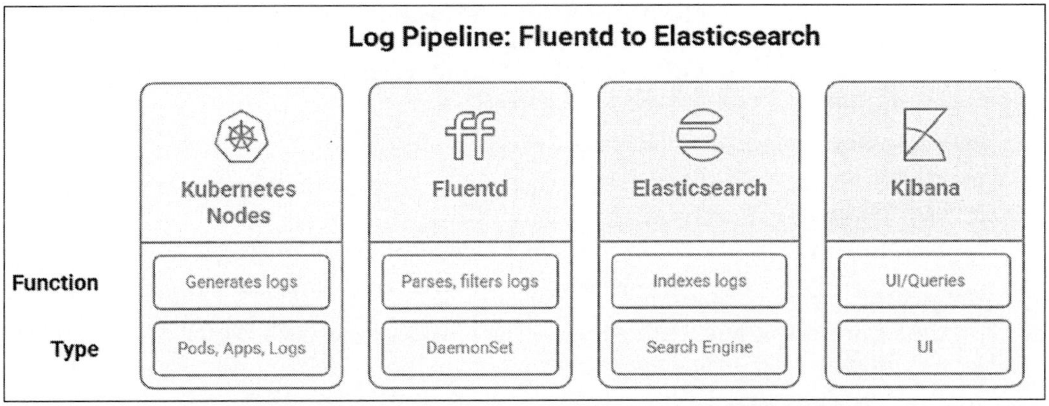

Figure 10.2: *Fluentd to Elasticsearch Log Pipeline with Functions and Types*

Log Pipeline: Fluentd to Elasticsearch

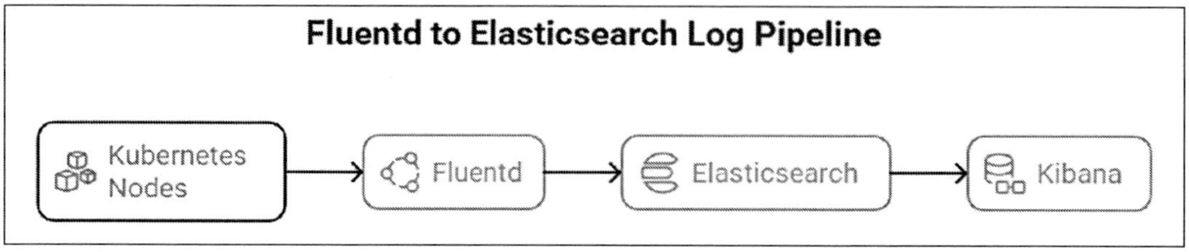

Figure 10.3: *Fluentd to Elasticsearch Log Pipeline*

- The steps of the Fluentd/Elasticsearch/Kibana (EFK) logging pipeline are listed as follows: **Fluentd** runs on every node as a DaemonSet and reads logs from the node's log directories.
- It filters and parses log lines (structured or plain text), then sends them to **Elasticsearch** via HTTP API.
- **Elasticsearch** indexes logs based on defined templates or auto-mappings.
- **Kibana** enables querying by label, namespace, pod name, timestamp, or message pattern.

In a Kubernetes environment, observability is incomplete without centralized logging. Kubernetes applications, system components, and container runtimes all generate logs that are critical for debugging, compliance, and performance monitoring. However, these logs are distributed across nodes and ephemeral containers, making aggregation a necessity. One of the most popular and production-grade logging pipelines involves using **Fluentd** to collect and ship logs to **Elasticsearch**, which then serves as a backend for visualization in **Kibana**.

Step 1: Kubernetes Nodes: Log Generation

At the source of this pipeline are the **Kubernetes nodes**, which run various components such as kubelet, container runtimes (example, containerd, Docker), and user-deployed pods. Each pod running on a node typically writes stdout and stderr logs to the node's file system, usually under the path `/var/log/containers/`. These logs may be in plain text or structured formats like JSON. The role of the node layer is **log generation**, and it is agnostic to where or how logs are consumed downstream.

Step 2: Fluentd – Log Aggregation and Processing

To collect logs from all nodes in a Kubernetes cluster, **Fluentd** is deployed as a **DaemonSet**. This ensures that one Fluentd pod runs on every node, allowing it to directly access local log files. Fluentd is a powerful data collector and router that supports filtering, parsing, buffering, and forwarding logs. In this pipeline, Fluentd performs several critical tasks:

- **Reads log files** from the local file system on each node.
- **Parses logs** into structured formats if needed (for example, parsing JSON or separating fields in plain-text logs).
- **Applies filters or tags** based on log content, labels, namespaces, or application types.
- **Sends logs** to Elasticsearch over HTTP, often using the `elasticsearch` output plugin.

This step is the **log processing and routing layer**, and it provides tremendous flexibility for enriching, dropping, or transforming logs before persistence.

Step 3: Elasticsearch – Indexing and Storage

Once Fluentd forwards logs to **Elasticsearch**, they are **indexed and stored**. Elasticsearch is a distributed search and analytics engine optimized for fast full-text search. It allows logs to be queried using powerful DSLs and APIs. In this context, logs are treated as structured documents, and Elasticsearch:

- Automatically or manually **indexes fields** such as **`pod_name`**, **`namespace`**, **`container_id`**, **`message`**, **`timestamp`**, and custom application metadata.
- Applies **retention policies**, sharding, and replication as part of log lifecycle management.
- Serves as the query backend for dashboards, alerting, or forensic investigations.

This is the **persistent and searchable data store layer** of the logging pipeline.

Step 4: Kibana – Visualization and Querying

Finally, logs stored in Elasticsearch are surfaced through **Kibana**, a browser-based visualization interface. Kibana connects directly to Elasticsearch and offers:

- **Real-time querying** using filters, wildcards, or JSON syntax.
- **Dashboards and visualizations** built on log data such as error rates per pod, latency distributions, or frequency of exception patterns.
- **Drill-down exploration** using fields such as namespace, pod name, or container label.

This completes the **user interaction and dashboard layer**, turning raw log data into actionable insights for DevOps, SRE, and engineering teams.

Benefits of Fluentd → Elasticsearch Logging Pipeline:

- **Node-Level Coverage:** Every log on every node is captured.
- **Scalable and Flexible:** Fluentd and Elasticsearch are both designed for large-scale environments.
- **Structured Search:** Logs become queryable by meaningful labels, not just plain text.
- **Real-Time Visibility:** Kibana enables near real-time detection of incidents or anomalies.

The Fluentd to Elasticsearch logging pipeline is a foundational component of modern Kubernetes observability stacks. Fluentd provides log aggregation and processing at the node level, Elasticsearch ensures scalable indexing and searchability, and Kibana delivers interactive exploration. This architecture helps teams **correlate logs across services, accelerate debugging, and meet compliance needs**—all from a unified platform.

Real-World Use Case: Debugging Kafka Data Loss in Azure AKS

Context: A Data Engineering team at a fintech firm ran Kafka producers in AKS for ingesting fraud alerts.

Problem: Alerts were dropped intermittently during peak hours. Application logs were inconsistent.

Solution:

- Fluentd collected logs from all producer pods.
- Logs were parsed into structured fields (**`topic`**, **`partition`**, **`error_code`**).
- Kibana dashboards highlighted that logs with **`timeout_exception`** clustered around a node running high CPU.
- Azure Monitor showed the node's vCPU usage >90%.

Action:

- The node pool was tuned with bigger VM SKUs.
- Kafka producer retry logic was adjusted.

- Fluentd retained logs for 14 days to validate post-deployment stability.

The Fluentd + Elasticsearch + Kibana (EFK) stack brings **real-time, centralized observability** to Kubernetes clusters, bridging the gap between containerized applications and long-term log analytics. This is vital for teams operating on Azure AKS who need:

- Fine-grained visibility into logs,
- Compliance-level log retention, and
- Seamless alerting and querying across namespaces and services.

It transforms logs from an afterthought to a **strategic observability asset**, especially in data-driven, real-time architectures.

Custom Alerts and Threshold-Based Dashboards

Need for Custom Alerts in Kubernetes

Monitoring metrics without actionable alerts is like having CCTV with no operator. In modern cloud-native environments-especially Kubernetes clusters running data-intensive pipelines -**automated, real-time alerting** is not a luxury but a critical necessity.

Why Alerting Matters:

- **Data Pipeline Reliability:** Catch ETL job failures, ingestion lag, or data loss proactively.
- **Operational Health:** Detect node memory leaks, container crashes, or latency spikes.
- **SRE and On-Call Efficiency:** Alert fatigue is reduced when alerts are well-tuned with thresholds.
- **Security and Compliance:** Alert on unusual patterns such as container restarts or unexpected traffic spikes.
- **Cost Optimization:** Alert on over-provisioned resources or underutilized nodes.

Alerts act as the **early warning system** - they reduce Mean Time to Detect (MTTD) and support faster Mean Time to Resolve (MTTR).

Tools: Prometheus Alertmanager + Grafana Alerting

Kubernetes alerting is typically handled through two key mechanisms:

- **Prometheus Alertmanager:**
    - Handles **routing**, **silencing**, **inhibition**, and **deduplication** of alerts generated by Prometheus.
    - Alerts are defined using PromQL expressions in **Prometheus rule files**.
    - Supports integrations with Slack, PagerDuty, email, MS Teams, and more.
- **Grafana Alerting:**
    - Native alerting engine integrated with dashboards.
    - Supports **multi-dimensional conditions** and **threshold-based triggers**.
    - Grafana alerts can evaluate Prometheus data sources, display visual thresholds, and push notifications.

  These two components can be **used together or independently**, depending on the organization's DevOps maturity.

Trigger-Based Thresholds versus Anomaly Detection

You should design alert rules based on **Kubernetes usage patterns** and the **nature of workloads**. Alerts should trigger:

- **Predictably** (threshold breach, CPU > 90% for 5 min).
- **Intelligently** (spikes versus long-term trend deviation).
- **With minimal noise** (avoid false positives).

Alerting Categories:

Type	Use Case
Static Thresholds	High memory, CPU, disk I/O
Rate of Change	Error rate increase, crash loops
Burn Rate Alerts	SLO/SLA violation risk (latency, errors)
Anomaly Detection	Resource usage drift, ingestion lag

Table 10.3: *Types of Alerting Categories*

In Azure Kubernetes Service (AKS), Prometheus can be integrated with Azure Monitor Logs and Alert Rules via Azure Managed Grafana for hybrid setups.

Creating Prometheus Alert Rules and Grafana Panels

Sample YAML: Prometheus Alert Rule (High Memory)

Create a rule file:

```
yaml

groups:
- name: pod-alerts
  rules:
  - alert: HighPodMemoryUsage
    expr: (container_memory_usage_bytes{container!="",pod!=""} / container_
spec_memory_limit_bytes{container!="",pod!=""}) > 0.85
    for: 5m
    labels:
      severity: warning
      team: data-platform
    annotations:
      summary: "High memory usage in pod {{ $labels.pod }}"
      description: "Memory usage > 85% for pod {{ $labels.pod }} in namespace
{{ $labels.namespace }}"
```

Apply this using your Prometheus Helm chart's **`prometheus.rules`** config or ConfigMap.

This alert ensures that **memory leakage or misconfigured limits** in pods running Spark, Kafka Connect, or ETL jobs are flagged before OOM kills.

Grafana Alert Panel: Memory Usage Threshold

In Grafana:

- Create a dashboard panel (for example, **`Pod Memory %`**).
- Add PromQL query:

```
(container_memory_usage_bytes / container_spec_memory_limit_bytes) * 100
```

- Set threshold: Red = 85%, Orange = 70%.
- Enable **Grafana Alert Rule**:
    - Condition: When the value is above 85% for 5 minutes.
    - Notification: Slack, email, Azure Monitor Webhook.

Custom Alerting in Kubernetes

In Kubernetes observability, real-time alerting is just as critical as logging and metrics collection. A robust alerting pipeline ensures that administrators and engineers are promptly notified of anomalies, resource exhaustion, failed pods, or performance degradation. The most common alerting stack in Kubernetes revolves around **Prometheus**, **AlertManager**, and **Grafana**, forming an integrated flow from metrics collection to actionable notification.

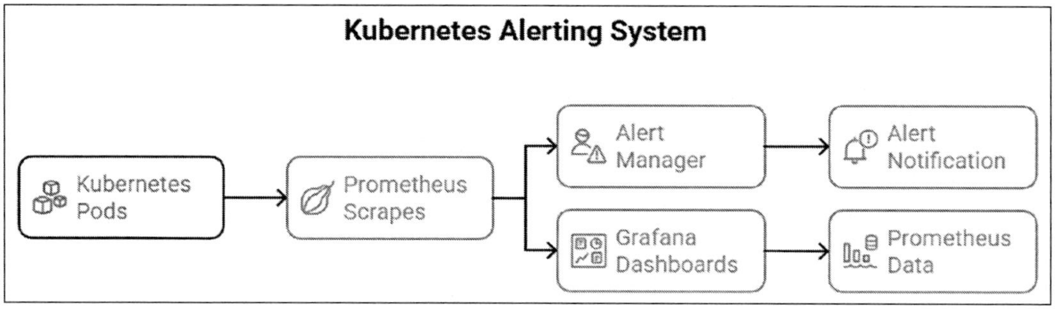

Figure 10.4: *Kubernetes Alerting System*

Here is a step-by-step explanation of the preceding figure:

Step I: Metrics Generation from Kubernetes Pods

The flow begins with **Kubernetes Pods** emitting metrics – either through application instrumentation (example, exposing **`/metrics`** endpoints in Prometheus format) or via system-level exporters such as **node-exporter**, **kube-state-metrics**, and **cAdvisor**. These metrics provide data on CPU usage, memory pressure, pod status, disk I/O, request latencies, and many other indicators.

Step II: Prometheus Scraping Metrics

Prometheus, configured with appropriate **`scrape_configs`**, **scrapes metrics from the exporters and pods** at regular intervals. It stores this time-series data internally in a high-performance Time-Series Database (TSDB). Prometheus also references **alerting rule files**, which define thresholds and conditions under which alerts should be triggered. For example, a rule might be: "Trigger an alert if node memory usage exceeds 90% for 5 minutes."

Step III: AlertManager Notification Routing

When an alert rule is breached, Prometheus **forwards the alert to AlertManager**, a dedicated component responsible for alert **deduplication, grouping, silencing, and routing**. AlertManager evaluates routing configurations to determine the correct notification channels – such as Slack, email, PagerDuty, Microsoft Teams, or Webhooks. This ensures that alerts are actionable and reach the right teams.

Step IV: Grafana Visualization and Alert Surfacing

While Prometheus handles alert logic, **Grafana offers a powerful visualization interface**. It connects to Prometheus as a data source and allows users to build **dashboards with real-time charts and thresholds**. Grafana can also define its own alert rules on visual panels – offering visual cues (for example, red bars for failures) and sending alerts independently of AlertManager if configured.

Step V: Data Flow to Prometheus and Visualization Tools

All components work in harmony: Prometheus maintains **centralized metric storage**, Grafana queries and **renders those metrics**, and AlertManager ensures that alerts **result in timely human notification**. This architecture makes it possible to not only detect failures but also correlate them visually through dashboards or respond automatically via notification systems.

Why This Architecture Matters:

- **Proactive Operations**: Prevent outages by alerting on early warning signs (such as, rising memory usage).
- **Flexible Routing**: AlertManager supports complex routing logic and integrations.
- **Decoupled Visualization**: Grafana operates independently but is tightly coupled via Prometheus metrics.
- **Scalable**: Prometheus supports federation and horizontal scaling for large clusters.
- **Open and Extensible**: Fully open-source, and integrates with Kubernetes natively.

This alerting system is indispensable in production Kubernetes environments, helping organizations **detect, visualize, and respond** to issues before they escalate into major incidents.

YAML Lab: Complete Alerting Stack

Install kube-prometheus-stack with Prometheus, Alertmanager, and Grafana:

```
bash

helm repo add prometheus-community https://prometheus-community.github.io/
helm-charts
helm install monitoring prometheus-community/kube-prometheus-stack \
  --namespace monitoring --create-namespace
```

Apply the `HighPodMemoryUsage` rule and verify in the **`Prometheus → Alerts`** tab.

Real-World Case Study: Alerting Kafka Lag in Azure AKS

Scenario:

A financial institution deployed a **Kafka Connect** pipeline in AKS to ingest high-frequency transactions into a fraud detection system.

Challenge:

- During peak hours, ingestion lag grew silently.
- Spark streaming jobs processed stale data, affecting detection latency.

Solution:

- Defined alert rule on Kafka consumer group lag: **`kafka_consumer_group_lag > 10000`**
- Set alert severity: **`critical`**, routed to PagerDuty.
- Also visualized lag across partitions in Grafana.

Outcome:

- Proactively detected lag buildup.

- Added horizontal pod autoscaling based on lag metrics.
- Ensured **zero customer-facing fraud detection latency** violations.

Custom alerting in Kubernetes is **mission-critical**–especially in data-driven architectures–because it allows teams to act before outages happen. Whether it is pod restarts, Kafka lag, or ETL memory bottlenecks, alert rules powered by **Prometheus + Grafana** offer:

- Predictability
- Scalability
- Automation

The key is not just collecting metrics but **interpreting them meaningfully** and **triggering timely actions**.

In the next section, we will dive into **how to interpret distributed traces, logs, and metrics together** for holistic observability.

Metrics, Logs, Traces: The Three Pillars of Observability

Why Observability Needs Metrics, Logs, and Traces?

In distributed, microservice-based Kubernetes environments, a single failed transaction might span multiple pods, services, and nodes–making root cause analysis non-trivial. Traditional monitoring tools show symptoms (such as, CPU usage), but **observability reveals the story behind the symptoms**.

Challenges without full observability:

- **Blind Spots**: High CPU usage does not explain *why* a service is slow.
- **No Context**: Logs without correlation do not show the end-to-end journey.
- **Slower RCA**: Teams waste time navigating across metrics, logs, and traces manually.

Without **metrics (what happened)**, **logs (what was recorded)**, and **traces (how and where it happened)**, SREs and platform teams operate in the dark.

The Observability Pillars and Tools

The following table describes the three pillars of Observability: metrics, logs, and traces, along with relevant examples:

Pillar	Description	Example Tooling
Metrics	Time-series numerical data on system behavior	Prometheus, Azure Monitor
Logs	Structured/unstructured messages and events	Fluentd, Log Analytics
Traces	End-to-end latency mapping across services	Jaeger, OpenTelemetry

Table 10.4: *Observability Pillars and Tools*

Key Tools:

- **Prometheus:** Scrapes and stores metrics from pods, containers, and nodes.
- **Fluentd:** Aggregates and routes logs to backends such as Elasticsearch or Azure Monitor.
- **Jaeger + OpenTelemetry:** Enables distributed tracing by capturing span data across service calls.

Azure AKS can integrate these tools with Azure Monitor Logs (for metrics/logs) and Application Insights (for tracing), or deploy open-source stacks such as Prometheus, Fluentd, and Jaeger.

Leveraging Full Observability

You should implement a 3-pillar observability approach in the following scenarios:

- **Production-Critical Applications:** Need real-time visibility for SLAs and uptime guarantees.
- **Multi-Service Pipelines:** Tracing is essential when a single user request passes through 5+ microservices.
- **Incident Investigation:** Correlation across logs, metrics, and traces speeds up root cause analysis.
- **Capacity Planning:** Resource trends from metrics + logs help optimize autoscaling and resource limits.

Implementing Metrics, Logs, and Traces in Kubernetes

Step 1: Deploy Prometheus (Metrics)

Use Helm in Azure AKS:

```
bash

helm install prometheus prometheus-community/kube-prometheus-stack \
  --namespace monitoring --create-namespace
```

- Prometheus scrapes from `kube-state-metrics`, `node-exporter`, and custom application endpoints.
- Use PromQL for building Grafana dashboards.

Step 2: Configure Fluentd for Logs

Use a DaemonSet to capture logs from all nodes:

Sample Fluentd DaemonSet YAML:

```
yaml

apiVersion: apps/v1
kind: DaemonSet
metadata:
  name: fluentd
  namespace: logging
spec:
  selector:
    matchLabels:
      app: fluentd
  template:
    metadata:
      labels:
        app: fluentd
    spec:
      containers:
      - name: fluentd
        image: fluent/fluentd-kubernetes-daemonset
        env:
        - name: FLUENT_ELASTICSEARCH_HOST
          value: "elasticsearch.logging.svc"
        - name: FLUENT_ELASTICSEARCH_PORT
          value: "9200"
```

This sends pod logs to Elasticsearch or Azure Log Analytics via Fluent Bit/Fluentd adapters.

Step 3: Setup Jaeger for Distributed Tracing

Use `istioctl` or Helm to install Jaeger in your cluster:

```
bash

istioctl install --set profile=demo
kubectl apply -f addons/jaeger.yaml
```

- Istio injects sidecar proxies (**Envoy**) into pods that generate tracing data.
- Traces are forwarded to the Jaeger backend via **OpenTelemetry**.

Example Trace Use Case: Tracing a Failing API Call:

- A Spark job initiates a REST call to a fraud-detection microservice.
- Trace data shows 800ms of latency at the **auth-service** level.
- Logs reveal slow database queries inside that service.
- Prometheus confirms that memory usage spiked during that window.

This illustrates **why traces are essential**: they pinpoint where to look and **logs/metrics confirm the cause**.

YAML Lab: Enable Tracing and Metric Exposure

Application Instrumentation Example (Python with OpenTelemetry):

```
python

from opentelemetry import trace
from opentelemetry.instrumentation.flask import FlaskInstrumentor

app = Flask(__name__)
FlaskInstrumentor().instrument_app(app)

@app.route("/checkout")
def checkout():
    with tracer.start_as_current_span("checkout-process"):
        time.sleep(0.3)
        return "Checkout complete"
```

- Use **otel-collector** to export traces to Jaeger.
- Use **Prometheus Python Client** to expose **/metrics** endpoint.

Kubernetes Observability Stack

Modern Kubernetes environments demand more than just uptime monitoring. Distributed systems need **holistic observability**–spanning **metrics, logs, and traces**–to troubleshoot failures, optimize performance, and ensure compliance. This observability stack integrates key open-source tools such as **Prometheus**, **Grafana**, **Fluentd**, **Elasticsearch**, **Jaeger**, and **OpenTelemetry** to create a unified view across system behavior.

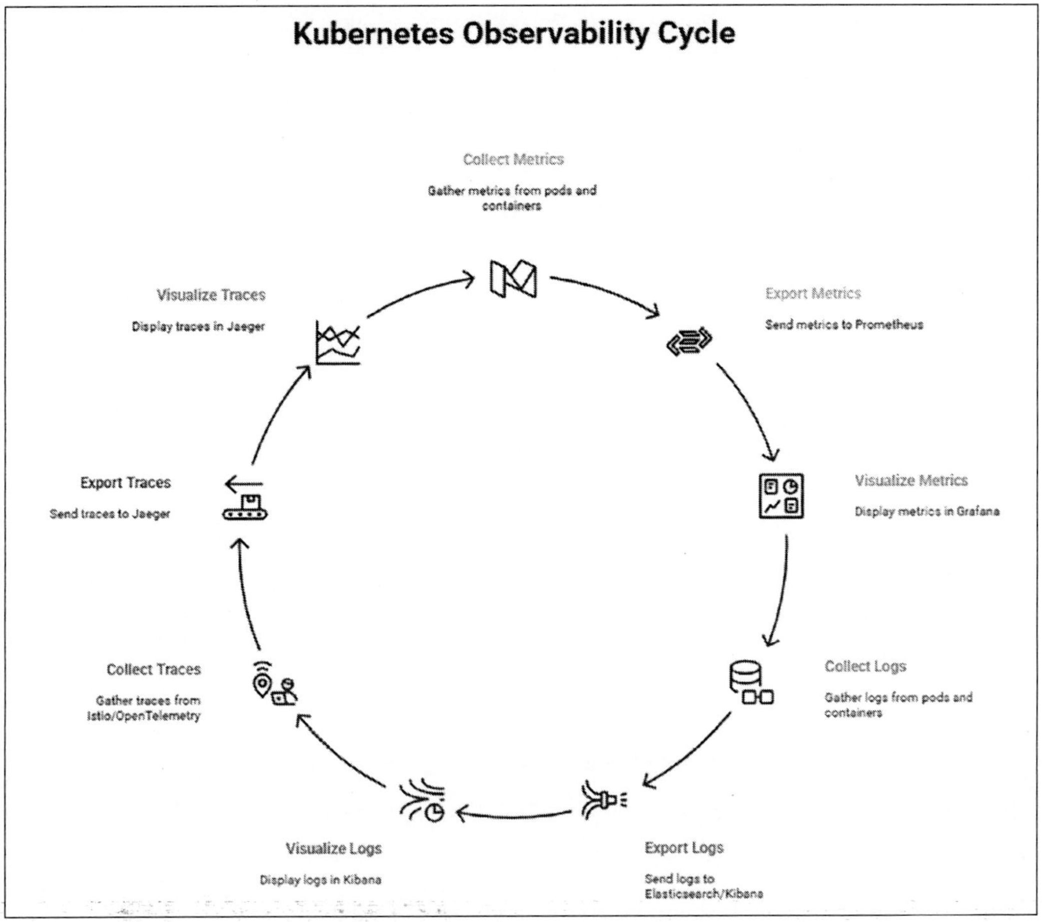

Figure 10.5: *Kubernetes Observability Stack*

How the Observability Stack Works in Practice

The following points explain how telemetry data flows from Kubernetes workloads through the observability stack, enabling end-to-end monitoring, troubleshooting, and performance analysis.

- **Pods** emit telemetry data: metrics (**`cAdvisor`**), logs (**`stdout/stderr`**), and traces (via instrumented code or sidecar).
- **Prometheus** scrapes metrics, while **Fluentd** ships logs to a centralized backend.
- **Istio or OpenTelemetry** instruments network-level traces.
- **Grafana**, **Kibana**, and **Jaeger UI** are the UIs for analysis and troubleshooting.

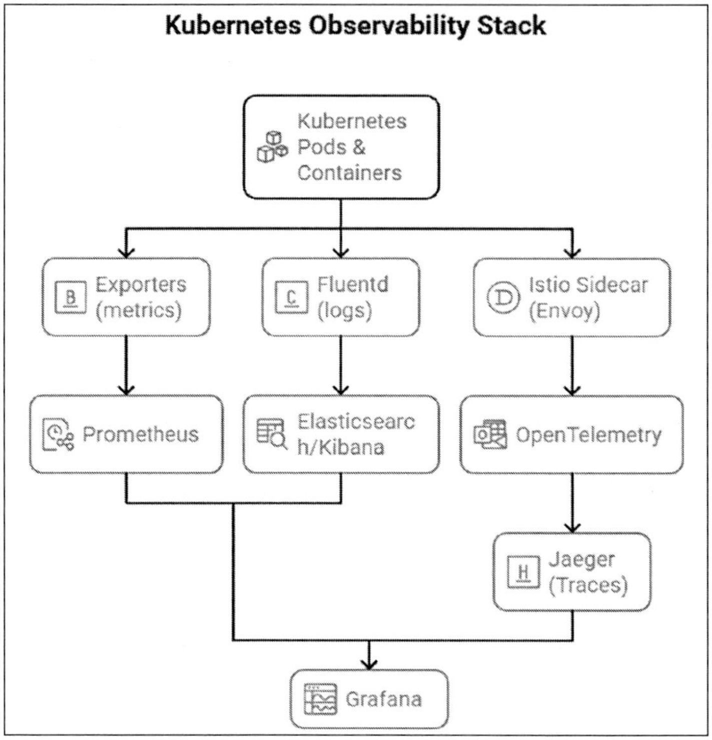

Figure 10.6: *Kubernetes Observability Stack*

Kubernetes Observability Stack End-to-End Visibility for Cloud-Native Workloads

This section explains how telemetry data flows through the Kubernetes observability stack, starting from application workloads and moving through metrics, logs, and tracing systems to provide complete end-to-end visibility across cloud-native environments.

Step I: Source of Truth – Kubernetes Pods and Containers

All telemetry data originates from **Kubernetes Pods and Containers**. Each pod produces:

- **Metrics:** CPU, memory, disk, and network utilization via components such as **`cAdvisor`**, **`node-exporter`**, or custom app endpoints (**`/metrics`**).
- **Logs:** Application output written to **`stdout/stderr`**.
- **Traces:** Distributed call chains across microservices, collected through sidecars or instrumentation libraries.

This raw data becomes the foundation for observability.

Step II: Metrics Collection via Exporters and Prometheus

Kubernetes integrates with **Prometheus exporters** to gather metrics:

- **node-exporter** captures host-level resource metrics.
- **kube-state-metrics** exposes Kubernetes object states (for example, pod status, deployment counts).
- Application-level exporters (such as for Redis and MySQL) reveal runtime health.

Prometheus then **scrapes these metrics on a schedule**, stores them in a Time-Series Database (TSDB), and makes them queryable using PromQL.

Step III: Log Aggregation Using Fluentd and Elasticsearch

While Prometheus handles numbers, **Fluentd** focuses on logs. Deployed as a **DaemonSet**, Fluentd runs on every node and:

- Watches **`/var/log/containers/`** for **stdout** logs.
- Parses and enriches logs with Kubernetes metadata (labels, namespaces).
- Filters unnecessary noise.
- Forwards structured logs to **Elasticsearch.**

Elasticsearch indexes and stores the logs for full-text querying. For visualization and log exploration, **Kibana** provides a powerful frontend UI.

Step IV: Distributed Tracing via Istio and OpenTelemetry

To capture inter-service latency and trace propagation:

- **Istio's Envoy proxy** acts as a sidecar injected into each pod, automatically capturing and forwarding spans.
- Alternatively, developers can use **OpenTelemetry SDKs** to instrument application code manually.
- Trace data is sent to a collector or directly into **Jaeger**, which builds and displays the call graph.

This helps pinpoint latency bottlenecks, dependency issues, and context-aware failures.

Step V: Unified Visualization with Grafana

While logs, metrics, and traces are collected separately, **Grafana acts as the unifying observability dashboard**:

- Connects to **Prometheus** for time-series metrics.
- Integrates with **Elasticsearch** for log queries (via plugin).
- Pulls traces from **Jaeger** for request path visualization.

Grafana supports advanced dashboards, alerting thresholds, and correlation features that give engineers a comprehensive troubleshooting tool.

Why This Observability Stack Matters:

- **Scalability:** Designed for multi-node clusters and microservices.
- **Modularity:** Each tool can be deployed independently or replaced.
- **Open Source:** No vendor lock-in, extensible via plugins.
- **Proactive Debugging:** Enables deep root cause analysis, not just monitoring.
- **Compliance Ready:** Helps meet auditing, tracing, and retention requirements.

Summary of Data Flow:

Data Type	Collector	Storage/Processing	Visualization Tool
Metrics	Exporters	Prometheus	Grafana
Logs	Fluentd	Elasticsearch	Kibana, Grafana (via plugin)
Traces	Envoy/OTel SDK	Jaeger (via OpenTelemetry)	Grafana (tracing view)

Table 10.5: *Data Types and Visualization Tools*

By combining these tools, platform engineers can establish an observability plane that supports real-time performance monitoring, historical trend analysis, and fast incident response. This stack is especially useful in **Azure Kubernetes Service (AKS)**, **EKS**, or **GKE**, where managed services simplify the deployment of these components.

Real-World Case Study: Debugging Streaming Latency in Azure AKS

Problem:

A financial services team reported that real-time analytics dashboards built on Kafka + Flink in AKS showed stale data during peak loads.

Investigation:

- **Grafana + Prometheus** showed CPU throttling in Kafka pods.
- **Fluentd + Log Analytics** logs confirmed high GC pause events in Kafka brokers.
- **Jaeger traces** pinpointed that the delay was at the **`Flink → Kafka`** consumer stage.

Remediation:

- Added CPU/memory limits and upgraded Kafka pod size.
- Introduced circuit breaking on Flink for backpressure.
- Added Prometheus alert: **`flink_consumer_lag > 5000`**.

Outcome:

- Reduced processing lag from 30s to <5s.
- Enabled proactive autoscaling based on metrics + traces.

Final Thoughts

Metrics, logs, and traces **should not be treated in isolation**. True observability comes when these pillars converge to provide a real-time, correlated view of system health.

- **Prometheus** gives quantitative system metrics.
- **Fluentd/Log Analytics** explains contextual logs.
- **Jaeger/OpenTelemetry** shows **where**, **how long**, and **why** things happened.

By combining these tools within your Azure Kubernetes or hybrid environment, teams gain **true visibility**, faster recovery, and better capacity planning.

Real-Time Monitoring for Large Clusters

Why Traditional Monitoring Breaks at Scale?

As Kubernetes clusters grow beyond hundreds of pods and services, traditional monitoring solutions such as local metrics stores, dashboards with high query frequency, or single-node Prometheus setups **begin to struggle** with:

- **High Cardinality:** Exploding label combinations in metrics (**`pod`**, **`job`**, **`instance`**, and so on).
- **Resource Constraints:** Prometheus uses in-memory storage; large-scale clusters exceed RAM limits.
- **Query Latency:** Grafana dashboards slow down as Prometheus TSDB grows.
- **Data Retention Issues**: Default Prometheus keeps data for 15 days or less without a long-term store.
- **Multi-Cluster Blind Spots:** In enterprise environments, dozens of clusters must be observed together.

As organizations move toward multi-tenant, multi-cluster, and cloud-native data processing workloads (Kafka, Spark, Flink, and more), they require horizontally scalable, multi-source monitoring pipelines.

Core Concepts of Scalable Monitoring Architecture

To overcome scale issues, organizations adopt the following architectural optimizations:

- **Remote Write to Long-Term Storage**

  Offload Prometheus metrics to scalable backends such as:

  - **Azure Monitor Managed Prometheus**
  - **Thanos**
  - **Cortex**
  - **VictoriaMetrics**

These tools store data in blob stores (Azure Blob, S3) while preserving queryability.

- **Prometheus Federation**

  Split monitoring into hierarchical layers:

  - **Leaf Prometheus** on each cluster scrapes node-local metrics.
  - **Central Prometheus** scrapes from the federated endpoints.

This allows **aggregate dashboards** without overloading any single server.

- **Loki + Grafana for Scalable Log Monitoring**

  Promtail pushes logs to Loki, which stores them efficiently using **index-less architecture** and compresses log streams by labels. Ideal for 10K+ container environments.

Applying Scalable Observability Techniques:

Scenario	Recommended Solution
>500 pods per cluster	Remote Write or Thanos
Multi-cluster observability	Federation or Cortex
Long-term metrics history (>30 days)	Azure Blob Storage with Thanos/Cortex
Data workloads with Kafka, Flink, Spark	Metric relabeling + custom alerts
Real-time SRE dashboards for C-level visibility	Grafana + Loki + Azure Monitor integration

***Table 10.6**: Scenario-Based Scalable Observability Techniques*

Implementing Real-Time Scalable Monitoring in Azure AKS

Step 1: Deploy Thanos with Prometheus

Thanos uses **sidecar containers** to stream data to object storage.

```
bash

# Sample Helm values.yaml (snippet)
thanos:
  objectStorageConfig:
    type: AZURE
```

```
      config:
        storage_account: <azure-storage-account>
        container: thanos-metrics
        storage_account_key: <key>
```

- Thanos Queries aggregates from all clusters.
- Store Gateway reads historical data.
- Azure Blob is used as the central metrics archive.

Step 2: Set Up Loki for Logs at Scale

```
bash

helm upgrade --install loki grafana/loki-stack \
  --namespace logging \
  --set loki.persistence.enabled=true \
  --set promtail.enabled=true
```

- **Promtail** scrapes logs from **`/var/log/containers`**.
- Loki stores logs with **efficient compaction and index sharding**.

Step 3: Enable Cross-Cluster Federation

On the Prometheus federation node:

```
yaml

- job_name: 'federate_cluster_aks-prod'
  scrape_interval: 30s
  honor_labels: true
  metrics_path: '/federate'
  params:
    'match[]':
      - '{__name__=~".+"}'
  static_configs:
    - targets:
      - 'prometheus.aks-prod.svc:9090'
```

This collects pre-aggregated time series from **`aks-prod`**.

Step 4: Build Multi-Cluster Dashboards in Grafana

Use templated variables such as:

```
label_values(cluster)
```

To allow dynamic selection between:

- **`aks-prod`**
- **`aks-staging`**
- **`aks-batch-processing`**

You can then create single dashboards visualizing **throughput across all environments**.

Case Study: Monitoring Real-Time Financial Pipelines in Azure AKS

Context: A fintech firm runs 200+ microservices and high-volume Kafka + Spark streaming pipelines on 5 Azure AKS clusters globally. They faced:

- Missed SLAs due to **monitoring blind spots**.

- Inconsistent dashboards across clusters.
- Alert fatigue from poorly defined thresholds.

Solution:

- **Prometheus + Thanos** deployed on each cluster.
- **Grafana Loki** replaced the expensive ELK logging pipeline.
- **Central Grafana instance** used dashboards templated by **`cluster`**, **`namespace`**, and **`app`**.
- **Custom Alert Rules**:
    - o Kafka consumer lag > 10s
    - o Spark executor memory > 80%
    - o Ingestion throughput deviation > 30%

Outcome:

- Reduced average incident detection time by 65%.
- Enabled a unified view across all streaming workloads.
- Saved $12K/month in storage and logging costs.

YAML Lab: Multi-Tenant Grafana Monitoring in Azure AKS

Create namespaces and RoleBindings to isolate tenants:

```yaml
yaml

apiVersion: rbac.authorization.k8s.io/v1
kind: RoleBinding
metadata:
  name: devops-monitoring
  namespace: devops
subjects:
- kind: User
  name: devops-team@example.com
roleRef:
  kind: ClusterRole
  name: view
  apiGroup: rbac.authorization.k8s.io
```

Enable **data source isolation** in Grafana per team.

Takeaways:

- At scale, **observability needs to be horizontally scalable**, decoupled from single clusters.
- Azure-native services (Azure Monitor, Container Insights) can be extended with open-source tooling such as **Prometheus + Thanos** and **Loki** for advanced use cases.
- Real-time monitoring should not just capture the current state but also enable **historic analysis, trend-based alerting, and cost-efficient logging**.

By adopting this architecture, organizations unlock **proactive insights** into mission-critical data pipelines, prevent failures, and empower cross-functional engineering teams with observability-driven reliability.

Conclusion

In this chapter, we built a solid foundation for Kubernetes observability using Prometheus, Grafana, Fluentd, and Elasticsearch. We explored how to implement real-time monitoring, centralized logging, and full-stack tracing for large-scale clusters. Through YAML labs and architectural best practices, we learned how to track performance, detect anomalies, and ensure system reliability across distributed data pipelines.

In the next chapter, we will shift focus to infrastructure automation. It dives into Helm for packaging Kubernetes applications, Terraform for infrastructure-as-code provisioning across cloud environments, and Ansible for configuration automation. These tools form the backbone of repeatable, scalable, and version-controlled Kubernetes operations.

CHAPTER 11
Automation with Helm, Terraform, and Ansible

Introduction

In the world of modern cloud-native applications, automation is essential for efficient, scalable, and error-free deployments. Helm, Terraform, and Ansible are powerful tools that streamline the management of Kubernetes resources, infrastructure provisioning, and configuration automation, offering a unified approach to infrastructure-as-code and application deployment.

This chapter will cover essential DevOps practices and tools, focusing on Helm Charts for Kubernetes packaging and deployment, Terraform for cloud infrastructure provisioning, and Ansible for Kubernetes configuration management. Finally, we will explore techniques for automating multi-cluster environments and integrating Infrastructure as Code (IaC) with CI/CD pipelines.

Structure

In this chapter, we will cover the following topics:

- Helm Charts for Kubernetes Packaging and Deployment
- Terraform for Cloud Infrastructure Provisioning
- Ansible for Kubernetes Configuration Management
- Automating Multi-Cluster Environments
- Integrating IaC with CI/CD Pipelines

Helm Charts for Kubernetes Packaging and Deployment

The complexity of managing Kubernetes deployments grows exponentially as applications evolve and environments expand. Relying on raw YAML manifests for each environment - whether for development, QA, or production - often leads to configuration drift, human error, and inconsistent configurations. Engineers frequently resort to copy-pasting YAML across environments, introducing hardcoded values and making it difficult to maintain and scale applications confidently. This manual process creates significant bottlenecks, especially in CI/CD pipelines, where quick, reliable deployments are critical. Helm alleviates this challenge by packaging Kubernetes applications into reusable, configurable charts, simplifying deployment and scaling while ensuring consistency across environments.

Why Does This Problem Exist?

Deploying applications on Kubernetes using raw YAML can quickly become unmanageable. As environments grow and apps evolve with new services, dependencies, environments (dev, QA, prod), and parameter overrides, engineers often copy/paste YAML across environments – which introduces configuration drift, hardcoded values, and human error.

Manually managing these manifests across CI/CD, staging, and prod becomes a bottleneck. You cannot scale changes safely or confidently.

What is Helm? What Does It Solve?

Helm is a **package manager** for Kubernetes. Just like **`apt`** or **`yum`** in Linux, Helm helps install, upgrade, and roll back Kubernetes applications using **pre-templated YAML files** (called Helm Charts).

Core Helm Concepts:

- **`Chart`:** A collection of YAML templates + configuration (**`values.yaml`**).
- **`Release`:** A running instance of a chart.
- **`values.yaml`:** Central config file to inject variables (example, port and image tag).
- **`templates/`:** Folder that holds Kubernetes manifest templates using Go templating syntax.

Helm simplifies the lifecycle of complex Kubernetes apps – parameterized, reusable, and upgradable.

When Should Helm Be Used: Helm is an indispensable tool when managing complex Kubernetes deployments, particularly for scenarios where consistency across environments is crucial. It excels in deploying the same application across dev, QA, and production environments, while also offering seamless customization through configurable parameters such as ports, replicas, and container images. Helm is ideal for GitOps pipelines, ensuring smooth and automated application releases, as well as for managing deployments in multi-tenant clusters, maintaining isolation and flexibility. While it can handle one-off YAML deployments, its true power lies in managing repeatable, scalable applications with ease and efficiency.

Use Case	Use Helm?
Deploying the same app across dev, QA, and prod	Yes
Customizing apps with different configs (ports, replicas, images)	Yes
Small, one-off YAML deployment	Maybe
Deploying apps as part of a GitOps pipeline	Yes
Releasing to multi-tenant clusters	Yes

Table 11.1: *Helm Use Cases*

How to Use Helm for Automation (Azure Example Included)

Step 1: Install Helm

```
Bash
curl https://raw.githubusercontent.com/helm/helm/master/scripts/get-helm-3 |
bash
```

Step 2: Add a Helm Repository

```
bash

helm repo add bitnami https://charts.bitnami.com/bitnami
helm repo update
```

Step 3: Install an App via Helm

```
bash

helm install my-mysql bitnami/mysql --set auth.rootPassword=adminpass
```

This creates a MySQL deployment with parameterized values.

YAML Lab: Create Your Own Helm Chart (Azure AKS Example)

```
bash

helm create azureapp
```

This generates a folder **`azureapp/`** with:

```
Chart.yaml
values.yaml
templates/
```

Modify `values.yaml`:

```
yaml

replicaCount: 3
image:
  repository: nginx
  tag: stable
  pullPolicy: IfNotPresent
```

Customize `templates/deployment.yaml`:

```
yaml

apiVersion: apps/v1
kind: Deployment
metadata:
  name: {{ .Release.Name }}-app
spec:
  replicas: {{ .Values.replicaCount }}
  template:
    spec:
      containers:
        - name: app
          image: "{{ .Values.image.repository }}:{{ .Values.image.tag }}"
```

Deploy on Azure AKS:

```
bash

helm install azureapp ./azureapp
```

Helm Lifecycle in Kubernetes: Declarative Deployment at Scale

The following figures represent the Helm Lifecycle in Kubernetes:

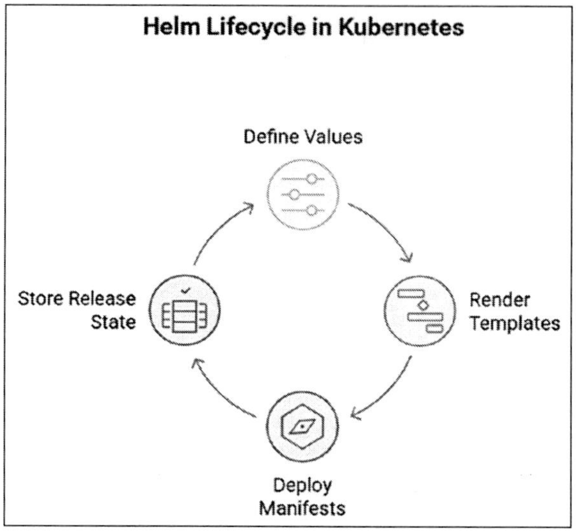

Figure 11.1: *Helm Lifecycle in Kubernetes - Cyclic*

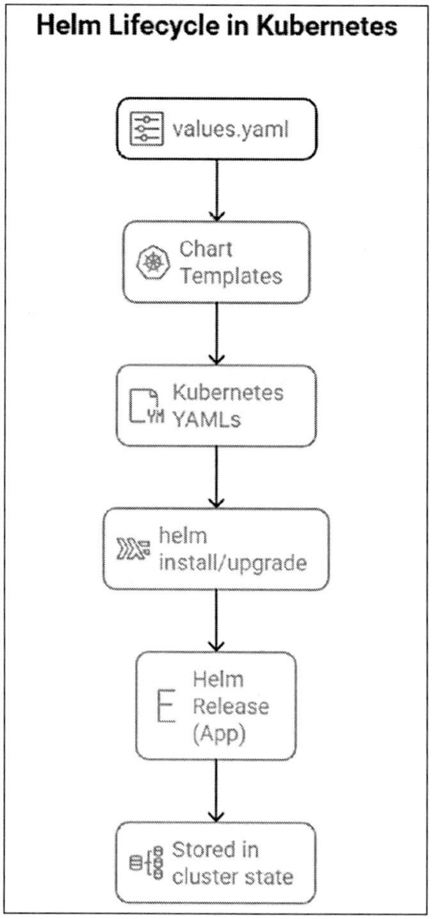

Figure 11.2: *Helm Lifecycle in Kubernetes*

Helm is often referred to as the **package manager for Kubernetes**, and rightly so - it brings standardization, versioning, and reusability to the process of deploying complex applications across Kubernetes clusters. The preceding figure outlines the full **Helm lifecycle**, showing how a Helm chart is rendered, applied, and tracked inside a Kubernetes environment.

Let us explore this lifecycle step by step:

1. `values.yaml` – Declarative Configuration Input

   The Helm lifecycle begins with a **`values.yaml` file**, which contains all user-defined configuration values. This file:

   - Acts as a single source of truth for input variables (for example, replica counts, image versions, and resource limits).
   - Allows users to **override default settings** provided in the chart.
   - Supports environment-specific customization (for example, **`values-dev.yaml`** and **`values-prod.yaml`**).

   Helm treats this file similarly to a config file for an application–it does not contain code, but it drives how the code (Kubernetes YAMLs) is generated.

2. **Chart Templates – `Parameterized` Blueprints**

   Next, Helm uses a directory called `templates/`, which holds **Kubernetes YAML templates** with Go-style templating syntax (**`{{ .Values.<key> }}`**). These templates define:

   - Deployments
   - Services
   - ConfigMaps
   - Ingress Resources
   - Custom Resource Definitions (CRDs)

   Templates enable reusability. For instance, one chart can deploy PostgreSQL in dev, staging, or prod, just by switching out the `values.yaml`.

3. **Rendering `Kubernetes` YAMLs**

   Using the **`helm template`** engine, Helm **combines the `values.yaml` file with the chart templates** to render complete Kubernetes manifests. These manifests are:

   - Fully valid Kubernetes YAML definitions (that is, what you would normally pass to **`kubectl apply`**).
   - Dynamically generated at runtime, ensuring tailored configuration per deployment.

   This decouples config from logic and reduces hardcoding in infrastructure code.

4. **`helm install` or `helm upgrade` – Execution and `Deployment`**

   Once manifests are rendered, Helm uses either:

   - **`helm install`** for first-time deployments.
   - **`helm upgrade`** to update existing deployments while preserving state.

   These commands:

   - Apply the generated manifests to the Kubernetes API server.
   - Create all the defined resources (pods, services, and more).
   - Track the release metadata and version in a ConfigMap or Secret.

This step is equivalent to **kubectl apply**—but with versioning, rollback, and state tracking.

5. **Helm Release – Versioned Deployment Unit**

   Every time you install or upgrade a chart, Helm creates a **Helm release**. A release is:

   - A logical unit containing all deployed resources + configuration + version metadata.
   - Stored inside the Kubernetes cluster (by default in the **kube-system** namespace).
   - Assigned a unique name and version number.

   This release abstraction enables:

   - Rollbacks (**helm rollback**)
   - Auditing of changes
   - Consistent upgrades

6. **Stored in Cluster State – Persistent History**

   Helm maintains the **release history** and state in the cluster:

   - Tracks what was installed, with which version, and which values were used.
   - Uses either ConfigMaps or Secrets to store release data.
   - Enables drift detection and diff comparisons (**helm diff** plugin).

   This internal storage allows Helm to perform operations such as:

   - Listing all releases (**helm list**)
   - Checking historical configurations (**helm history**)
   - Restoring previous states (**helm rollback**)

Why This Lifecycle Matters?

Helm's lifecycle brings **repeatability, predictability, and control** to Kubernetes deployments. It is particularly important in:

- CI/CD pipelines for versioned deployment artifacts.
- Multi-tenant environments for managing shared services.
- Platform engineering use cases where infrastructure is templated.

The following table summarizes the lifecycle stages:

Lifecycle Stage	Description
`values.yaml`	Defines variables and environment-specific configurations.
Templates	Parameterized YAML definitions for Kubernetes objects.
Rendered YAMLs	Final manifests that Kubernetes can understand.
Install/Upgrade	Applies manifests to the cluster with Helm commands.
Helm Release	Tracks deployed app with metadata and version.
Cluster State	Persistent storage of release history and configuration.

Table 11.2: *Summary Lifecycle Stages*

By following this structured Helm lifecycle, teams can deploy microservices, databases, and infrastructure components with confidence and reproducibility—critical capabilities in production-grade Kubernetes environments.

Use Case: When to Use Helm in Azure CI/CD?

Scenario: A data platform team wants to deploy a Kafka stack across AKS dev, QA, and prod clusters with different CPU limits and secrets.

- Helm lets them define CPU limits, image tags, and secrets via **`values.yaml`**.
- Reuse the same chart and override per environment (**`helm upgrade -f values-prod.yaml`**).
- Integrated with GitHub Actions to deploy automatically via CI/CD.

Key Takeaways:

- Helm abstracts away repetitive YAML and supports version-controlled, consistent releases.
- Ideal for large data workloads, repeatable environments, and CI/CD workflows.
- In Azure, Helm is used widely to automate app deployment into AKS environments and integrate with Azure DevOps/GitHub pipelines.

Terraform for Cloud Infrastructure Provisioning

Why Does This Problem Exist?

Manual provisioning of cloud infrastructure using portals or CLI tools leads to **inconsistency, configuration drift**, and **human error**, especially when teams need to replicate environments (dev, QA, prod) or manage dozens of clusters across regions. As infrastructure grows, reproducibility, auditing, and scalability become increasingly difficult.

Traditional scripts (for example, Azure CLI or ARM templates) are either too verbose or platform-specific, making multi-cloud provisioning brittle and hard to reuse.

What is Terraform and Why It is a Game-Changer?

Terraform is a widely adopted, open-source Infrastructure-as-Code (IaC) tool developed by HashiCorp. It allows engineers to define cloud infrastructure in a declarative format using HashiCorp Configuration Language (HCL). Unlike ARM, Bicep, or CloudFormation, terraform works across all major cloud platforms including Azure, AWS, and GCP, with consistent syntax.

With Terraform, you define the desired infrastructure state, and it handles the create/update/delete lifecycle, making it ideal for provisioning Kubernetes clusters (such as AKS), RBAC, virtual networks, storage, and monitoring integrations.

Key Features:

- **Declarative model** (you define the desired state)
- Multi-cloud support
- **Modules for reuse**
- **State tracking** and change planning
- **Versioning** for repeatable deployments

When Should Terraform Be Used: Terraform is the go-to solution for provisioning and managing complex, multi-resource infrastructures, especially when working with Azure AKS clusters, Kubernetes, VNets, and storage accounts. It excels in scenarios requiring multi-region cluster management across clouds, providing consistency and scalability across environments. Terraform is also ideal for team-based, version-controlled infrastructure pipelines, ensuring collaborative, reproducible deployments. However, for single resource provisioning, it may be overkill, as simpler tools could be more efficient for such tasks. In essence, Terraform is best suited for large-scale, collaborative infrastructure management, where consistency, version control, and cross-cloud coordination are paramount.

Scenario	**Use Terraform?**
Provisioning Azure AKS clusters	Yes
Creating Kubernetes + VNet + Storage accounts together	Yes
Managing multi-region clusters across clouds	Yes
Single resource provisioning	Not ideal
Team-based, version-controlled infra pipelines	Absolutely

Table 11.3: *Terraform Use Cases*

How to Use Terraform to Provision Azure Kubernetes Infrastructure?

Step-by-Step Breakdown

Step 1: Install Terraform (example: for Mac)

```
bash

brew install terraform
# or
choco install terraform
```

Step 2: Configure Azure CLI and Terraform

Login to Azure:

```
bash

az login
```

Export credentials if needed:

```
bash

az account set --subscription "<your-subscription-id>"
```

HCL Lab – Provision AKS Cluster + Node Pool

`main.tf` (core AKS provisioning)

```
hcl

provider "azurerm" {
  features {}
}

resource "azurerm_resource_group" "rg" {
  name     = "aks-iac-rg"
  location = "East US"
}

resource "azurerm_kubernetes_cluster" "aks" {
  name                = "aks-demo-cluster"
  location            = azurerm_resource_group.rg.location
  resource_group_name = azurerm_resource_group.rg.name
  dns_prefix          = "aksdemo"

  default_node_pool {
    name       = "default"
    node_count = 3
    vm_size    = "Standard_DS2_v2"
```

```
  }

  identity {
    type = "SystemAssigned"
  }

  network_profile {
    network_plugin = "azure"
    load_balancer_sku = "standard"
  }
}
outputs.tf
hcl

output "kube_config" {
  value = azurerm_kubernetes_cluster.aks.kube_config_raw
  sensitive = true
}
```

Step 3: Initialize and Apply Terraform

```
bash

terraform init
terraform plan
terraform apply
```

After provisioning, Terraform stores the state file (**`terraform.tfstate`**) locally or in a remote backend such as Azure Storage, which tracks infrastructure drift and enables future updates.

Real-World Azure Case Study: Terraform for Data Pipelines

Scenario: A Cloud Data Architect needs to provision an **AKS cluster, Azure Monitor logs, and Private DNS Zone**, and enable **AAD RBAC integration** for a scalable real-time analytics platform.

Terraform enables them to:

- Reuse AKS provisioning modules across regions.
- Add custom node pools for Spark, Kafka workloads.
- Integrate **`azurerm_monitor_diagnostic_setting`** to forward logs to Log Analytics.
- Manage secrets via Azure Key Vault modules.

This avoids the need for ARM templates, PowerShell, and separate pipelines.

Terraform Infrastructure Provisioning Lifecycle

The following figure represents the Terraform Infrastructure Provisioning Lifecycle:

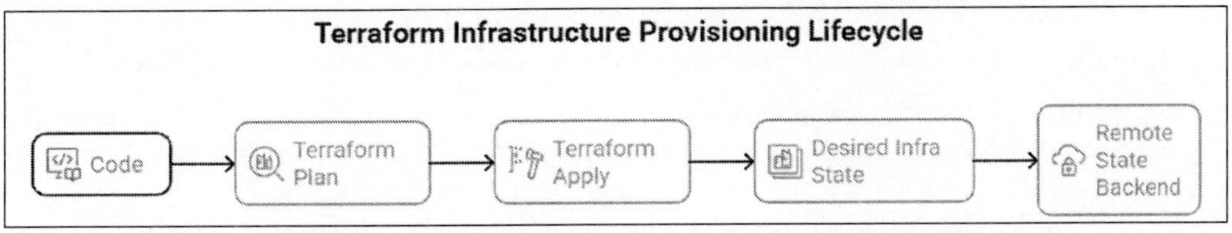

Figure 11.3: *Terraform Infrastructure Provisioning Lifecycle*

Explanation:

- Code (`*.tf`) defines infrastructure
- Terraform `plan` shows diff
- `apply` makes the changes
- State is saved for drift detection and updates

```
                     +--------------------+
                     |  main.tf / modules |
                     +--------------------+
                               |
               +---------------+---------------+
               |                               |
      +---------------+              +---------------------+
      |  azurerm_rg   |              |  azurerm_k8s_cluster|
      +---------------+              +---------------------+
               |                               |
    Terraform Plan → Terraform Apply → Desired Infra State
                               |
                +-----------------------------+
                |  Remote State Backend (Azure)|
                +-----------------------------+
```

Figure 11.4: *Terraform Infrastructure Provisioning Lifecycle*

Explanation:

Terraform is a declarative Infrastructure as Code (IaC) tool that allows you to define, version, and manage infrastructure through code. *Figure* 11.4 captures the complete lifecycle of provisioning infrastructure using Terraform on **Azure**, with emphasis on **remote state management, modularization, and resource orchestration.**

Let us walk through each stage of this lifecycle step-by-step:

1. `main.tf / modules` – Infrastructure Configuration Layer

   At the top of the lifecycle sits the **Terraform configuration files**:

   - **`main.tf`**: This is the primary configuration file where resources are defined.
   - **`modules/`**: Optional reusable building blocks that encapsulate logic for infrastructure components such as networks, storage accounts, or Kubernetes clusters.

   These files describe the *desired state* of your infrastructure using the **HashiCorp Configuration Language (HCL)**. This includes definitions for:

   - Resource groups (**`azurerm_resource_group`**)
   - Azure Kubernetes clusters (**`azurerm_kubernetes_cluster`**)
   - Virtual networks, subnets, and more

   Modules help promote **code reusability**, **abstraction**, and **clean separation of concerns**.

2. **Resource Definitions: `azurerm_rg` and `azurerm_k8s_cluster`**

   Once the configuration is authored, Terraform processes specific **resource blocks**:

   - **`azurerm_resource_group` (`azurerm_rg`):** Creates a logical container in Azure to group related resources. It is the foundational layer required before provisioning dependent resources.
   - **`azurerm_kubernetes_cluster` (`azurerm_k8s_cluster`):** Provisions a fully managed Azure Kubernetes Service (AKS) cluster within the specified resource group.

Each of these resources will:

- Reference input variables from **`variables.tf.`**
- Produce outputs for use in other modules or pipelines.
- Be tracked as part of the overall execution plan.

3. **Terraform Plan → Apply → Desired Infrastructure State**

   This is the heart of Terraforms provisioning engine.

   - **Terraform Plan**
     - Compares your configuration with the current state in Azure.
     - Produces a detailed execution plan showing what will be created, updated, or destroyed.
     - Does **not** make any actual changes—it is a dry run used for review and approval.
   - **Terraform Apply**
     - Executes the changes proposed in the `plan`.
     - Provisions resources in Azure using authenticated API calls.
     - Provides confirmation and resource IDs for traceability.
   - **Desired Infrastructure State**
     - After apply, the infrastructure in Azure matches the declared configuration.
     - Terraform ensures **idempotency**—running **`apply`** again with no changes results in no actions.

4. **Remote State Backend (Azure Storage)**

   Terraform uses a **state file (`terraform.tfstate`)** to track the deployed infrastructure.

   Why use a remote state:

   - Prevents conflicts in team environments.
   - Enables collaboration with **state locking.**
   - Secures infrastructure definitions in cloud-native backends.

Common Azure Backend:

```
hcl

terraform {
  backend "azurerm" {
    resource_group_name  = "tfstate-rg"
    storage_account_name = "mystatestorage"
    container_name       = "tfstate"
    key                  = "prod.terraform.tfstate"
  }
}
```

The remote state:

- Acts as the single source of truth.
- Enables **drift detection** and comparison.
- It is protected by RBAC, encryption, and versioning in Azure Blob Storage.

Lifecycle Recap: Step-by-Step Flow:

Step	Description
1	The developer defines infrastructure using `main.tf` and optional reusable modules.
2	Azure resources such as **`azurerm_resource_group`** and **`azurerm_kubernetes_cluster`** are declared.
3	**`terraform plan`** previews the intended changes.
4	**`terraform apply`** provisions the resources in Azure.
5	Resulting infrastructure reaches the **desired state** as declared in the code.
6	State is written to **Azure backend storage** to enable future updates, rollbacks, or comparisons.

Table 11.4: *Lifecycle Recap of Flow*

Why Does This Lifecycle Matters?

Using Terraform to manage infrastructure offers numerous benefits:

- **Repeatability:** Recreate the same environment across multiple regions or teams.
- **Auditability:** Every change is captured in version control and backed by state history.
- **Collaboration:** Teams can work on infrastructure confidently using remote backends and locking.
- **Automation:** Easily integrate with CI/CD pipelines to enable GitOps-style workflows.

This lifecycle is particularly powerful when provisioning **Azure Kubernetes clusters**, **networking stacks**, or **hybrid cloud infrastructure**.

Best Practices for Terraform on Azure

Adopting best practices for Terraform on Azure ensures robust, secure, and scalable infrastructure management. Utilizing a remote backend, such as Azure Blob Storage, for state files mitigates team collisions and supports version control while separating modules for AKS, VNet, and KeyVault enhances reusability and modularity. Locking Terraform versions via the **`.terraform.lock.hcl`** file guarantees consistency across environments, preventing unexpected changes. Additionally, integrating KeyVault to secure sensitive secrets prevents the exposure of credentials within **`.tf`** files, bolstering security and compliance. These practices collectively streamline collaboration, security, and maintainability in Azure-based infrastructure deployments.

Practice	Why It Matters
Use remote backend (Azure Blob) for state	Avoid team collisions, support version control
Separate modules for AKS, VNet, KeyVault	Better reusability
Lock Terraform versions via **`.terraform.lock.hcl`**	Ensure consistency
Secure secrets with KeyVault integration	Avoid putting secrets in `*.tf` files

Table 11.5: *Best Practice Use Cases for Terraform on Azure Cloud*

Final Thoughts

Terraform is a foundational tool in modern cloud-native Kubernetes automation. It allows cloud engineers and architects to:

- Manage large-scale AKS clusters reproducibly.
- Integrate IAM, logging, and secrets into provisioning.
- Automate multi-region and multi-cloud setups.

For Azure-specific use cases, Terraform supports advanced constructs such as:

- Azure AD integration
- Managed identities
- Virtual Node Pools with ACI
- Azure Policy-as-Code

Ansible for Kubernetes Configuration Management

Why Use Ansible After Terraform?

While **Terraform is ideal for infrastructure provisioning**, it is **declarative and limited** when it comes to **complex configuration tasks**, such as:

- Installing agents or software (for example, Prometheus and Fluentd).
- Modifying cluster configurations after deployment.
- Applying OS-level updates, patching, and reboots.
- Interacting with APIs to perform conditional tasks.

This is where **Ansible shines** – it enables **idempotent, task-oriented automation** for systems management and Kubernetes post-provisioning tasks. Ansible is **agentless** and uses **SSH or Kubernetes API** to perform operations.

In real-world Azure scenarios, DevOps and Platform teams use Terraform for AKS provisioning and Ansible to configure applications, deploy DaemonSets, enforce RBAC policies, or install monitoring agents across clusters.

What is Ansible and Its Role in Kubernetes Automation?

Ansible is an **open-source automation engine** that uses **YAML-based playbooks** to automate cloud, system, and Kubernetes configuration tasks. It is **imperative but idempotent**, meaning it runs instructions step-by-step but does not repeat successful steps.

Core Concepts:

Component	Description
Inventory	Hosts to be managed (example, AKS worker nodes or API endpoints).
Playbook	A YAML file containing automation tasks.
Role	A reusable directory structure with tasks, handlers, defaults.
Module	Building blocks (example, `k8s`, `shell`, and `copy`) used inside tasks.

Table 11.6: *Components and Description*

When to Use Ansible in a Kubernetes Environment?

Ansible is particularly valuable in Kubernetes environments for post-deployment operations and security automation, excelling in scenarios such as installing observability tools such as Fluentd, node-exporter, and security agents. It is also indispensable for managing dynamic configuration changes across multiple clusters and efficiently patching and rebooting AKS nodes. Ideal for Day-2 operations, Ansible ensures seamless ongoing management without the complexity of infrastructure provisioning. However, for Infrastructure-as-Code (IaC) tasks, such as managing Azure resources, terraform remains the preferred tool. Leveraging Ansible alongside GitOps tools such as ArgoCD or Flux further enhances its utility in ensuring consistent, automated operations.

Scenario	Use Ansible?
Installing Fluentd, node-exporter, security agents	Yes
Dynamic config changes in multiple clusters	Yes
Patching and rebooting AKS nodes	Yes
Day-2 Ops (not IaC provisioning)	Ideal
Managing Azure Infrastructure	Use Terraform instead

Table 11.7: *Scenarios When to Use Ansible in Kubernetes Environment*

Ansible is especially effective in **post-deployment operations, security automation, and observability configuration**, especially when used alongside GitOps tools such as ArgoCD or Flux.

How to Automate AKS Configuration with Ansible?

Real-World Azure Use Case: Configure Fluentd on all AKS Nodes

Scenario: After provisioning AKS via Terraform, a DevOps team wants to deploy Fluentd on all nodes to forward logs to a centralized Elasticsearch instance. Instead of Helm or manual YAMLs, they opt to automate this using Ansible.

YAML + Inventory Lab

Step 1: `inventory.yaml` (Define AKS API endpoint or host group)

```
yaml

all:
  children:
    aks_nodes:
      hosts:
        node1.yourdomain.com:
        node2.yourdomain.com:
```

If targeting the API server instead of direct SSH, use the **`k8s`** module with kubeconfig.

Step 2: `fluentd_deploy.yml` (Ansible Playbook)

```
yaml

- name: Deploy Fluentd to AKS Nodes
  hosts: aks_nodes
  become: yes

  tasks:
    - name: Ensure Fluentd config directory exists
      file:
        path: /etc/fluentd
        state: directory
        mode: '0755'

    - name: Copy Fluentd config file
      copy:
        src: files/fluentd.conf
        dest: /etc/fluentd/fluentd.conf

    - name: Install Fluentd as Docker container
      shell: >
```

```
docker run -d --name fluentd
-v /etc/fluentd:/fluentd
-p 24224:24224
fluent/fluentd:v1.14-debian-1
```

Step 3: Run the Playbook

```
bash


ansible-playbook -i inventory.yaml fluentd_deploy.yml
```

This setup ensures all AKS nodes consistently receive the same logging configuration without having to write DaemonSet YAMLs manually.

Ansible Execution Model in Kubernetes Automation

Ansible is a powerful automation tool used extensively in infrastructure provisioning, configuration management, and orchestration. In the context of Kubernetes, Ansible can automate the setup, customization, and post-deployment operations of Kubernetes clusters using declarative playbooks. This execution model illustrates how Ansible integrates with Kubernetes environments to ensure consistent and repeatable cluster automation.

The following figure represents the Ansible Execution Model in Kubernetes Automation:

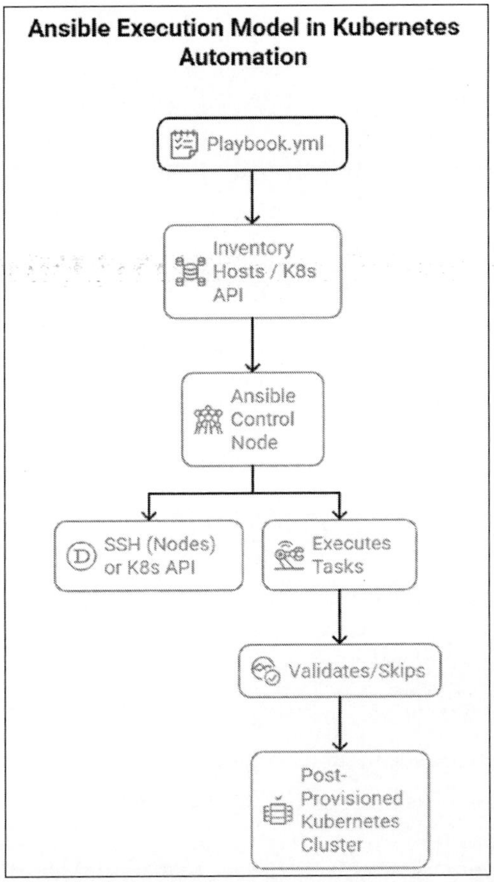

Figure 11.5: *Ansible Execution Model in Kubernetes Automation*

Explanation:

- Ansible reads from inventory and playbooks.
- Connects via SSH or kubeconfig to nodes or cluster.
- Applies tasks only when needed (idempotent).
- Excellent for Day-2 operations such as installing software, patching nodes, applying RBAC updates.

Step 1: Playbook Definition (`playbook.yml`)

The process begins with an Ansible Playbook file, written in YAML format. This playbook defines a series of declarative tasks and modules that describe the intended state of the infrastructure or application. It may include operations such as installing dependencies, configuring networking, setting up Kubernetes resources, or managing cluster security.

The playbook specifies:

- Target hosts or groups
- Task sequences
- Roles and modules to invoke
- Variables and conditions

This acts as the automation blueprint for Ansible to follow.

Step 2: Inventory Definition (Hosts or Kubernetes API)

Before executing the playbook, Ansible needs an inventory. Traditionally, this inventory is a list of target hosts defined in a static or dynamic inventory file. In Kubernetes automation, the inventory can be either:

- A list of node IPs or hostnames (for SSH-based access).
- A Kubernetes dynamic inventory that communicates directly with the Kubernetes API to manage cluster resources.

The inventory acts as a map, telling Ansible which systems to connect to and manage.

Step 3: Ansible Control Node

The control node is the machine where Ansible is installed and from which playbooks are executed. This node holds the playbooks, inventory definitions, custom modules, roles, and configuration files. It is responsible for:

- Parsing the playbook
- Connecting to the target nodes or Kubernetes API
- Executing tasks in order
- Capturing and returning output

Unlike other tools, Ansible does not require any agent installation on the target systems. It uses a push-based model via SSH or API calls.

Step 4: Connection and Task Execution

At this stage, the Ansible control node initiates execution by connecting to the defined targets.

- For traditional nodes (for example, virtual machines), Ansible uses SSH to connect and execute commands remotely.
- For Kubernetes-native workflows, Ansible can communicate directly with the Kubernetes API server using modules such as **`k8s`**, **`k8s_facts`**, or **`k8s_info`**.

The playbook tasks are executed sequentially or conditionally, depending on the structure of the playbook. Tasks might include operations such as applying YAML manifests, configuring RBAC, deploying Helm charts, or scaling pods.

Step 5: Validation and Conditional Execution

Ansible has built-in support for idempotency, meaning it checks whether a task has already achieved the desired state. If it has, the task is skipped. If not, the task is executed.

Additionally, validation steps can be embedded using conditional statements (**`when`**, **`failed_when`**) or through custom checks (such as validating if a service is running or a port is open). This ensures that automation is not only executed but also verified for correctness.

Step 6: Post-Provisioned Kubernetes Cluster

Once all tasks have successfully executed and passed validation, the result is a fully automated, post-provisioned Kubernetes environment. This may include:

- Bootstrapped cluster nodes
- Deployed networking plugins
- Installed monitoring and observability agents
- Configured storage classes and secrets
- Enforced security policies and role bindings

This cluster is now ready for application workloads, CI/CD integrations, or further automated operations such as scaling or disaster recovery.

The Ansible execution model for Kubernetes automation provides a reliable, agentless, and declarative way to manage complex Kubernetes workflows. By integrating directly with either the underlying infrastructure or the Kubernetes API, Ansible enables seamless automation of cluster lifecycle events. The combination of Playbooks, inventory, and validation mechanisms makes this model highly suitable for enterprise-grade Kubernetes deployments.

Example Role Structure for Kubernetes Setup

```
text

roles/
└── fluentd/
    ├── tasks/
    │   └── main.yml
    ├── templates/
    │   └── fluentd.conf.j2
    └── defaults/
        └── main.yml
```

Roles make your Ansible setup modular and reusable across different clusters or environments.

GitOps + Ansible Integration

Ansible can also be used in CI/CD pipelines with GitOps. For example:

- Triggered via GitHub Actions or Jenkins
- Pulls **`inventory + playbook`** from Git repo
- Runs **`ansible-playbook`** on AKS with updated role logic

Azure Reference Scenarios: In the context of Azure Kubernetes Service (AKS), Ansible offers robust automation capabilities for various critical tasks. For instance, deploying the Azure Monitor Agent can be seamlessly achieved using Ansible's Kubernetes module to interact with the AKS API. Ensuring security across the cluster is simplified by leveraging Kubernetes RBAC to enforce pod security policies, while KeyVault integration allows for efficient rotation of secrets within AKS clusters. Additionally, OS patching on VMSS-based AKS nodes is streamlined through Ansible's win_updates or Linux package management modules, complete with restart handlers, ensuring system integrity and compliance. These use cases exemplify how Ansible enhances operational efficiency and security in AKS environments.

Use Case	Ansible in AKS
Install Azure Monitor Agent	Use the `k8s` module to deploy via API
Set cluster-wide pod security policies	Apply RBAC using `k8s` and `template`
Rotate secrets across AKS + KeyVault	Integrate with `azure_rm_keyvaultsecret`
Patch OS on VMSS AKS Nodes	Use `win_updates` or `apt/yum` with restart handlers

Table 11.8: *Azure Scenarios When to Use Ansible in AKS*

Summary: Why Ansible Still Matters?

Even in Kubernetes-native environments, **Ansible fills the gap** where **Terraform and Helm fall short**. It provides:

- Fine-grained control for configuration and updates.
- Centralized automation without custom scripts.
- Day-2 operations standardization.

By combining Terraform (for infrastructure), Helm (for applications), and Ansible (for configuration), teams create a robust, automated, and reproducible Kubernetes platform – especially in Azure-focused enterprise environments.

Automating Multi-Cluster Environments

Why is Multi-Cluster Management Complex Without Automation?

As cloud-native workloads grow, organizations increasingly adopt multi-cluster Kubernetes architectures. This design is critical for:

- **Environment Isolation**: Separate dev, staging, UAT, and prod clusters reduce risk.
- **Disaster Recovery**: Replicating workloads across availability zones or regions.
- **Data Residency Compliance**: Clusters deployed in region-specific jurisdictions.
- **Latency Optimization**: Serving users from geographically closer data centers.

The challenge arises when engineering teams manually manage these clusters – configurations drift, policies become inconsistent, and deployment pipelines grow unmanageable.

Example Problem: A data platform team manages dev and prod clusters manually. Over time, inconsistent RBAC policies emerge, causing unexpected failures in production ETL jobs that do not occur in dev.

Without automation, multi-cluster maintenance is fragile, error-prone, and unsustainable at scale.

What are the Tools and Patterns for Automating Multi-Cluster Workflows?

To tame the complexity of multi-cluster environments, you must adopt **Infrastructure as Code (IaC)** and configuration orchestration. The tools of choice include:

Tool	Role in Automation
Terraform Workspaces	Maintain isolated cluster state per environment.

Helmfile/Helm	Template and sync workloads across clusters.
Ansible Dynamic Inventory	Discover, label, and configure multi-cluster nodes.
Flux/ArgoCD	GitOps-style config synchronization.

Table 11.9*: Tools for Automating Multi-Cluster Workflows*

These tools help standardize:

- Cluster creation and destruction
- Bootstrap workloads (metrics agents, ingress, logging)
- Multi-cluster configuration propagation
- Disaster recovery failover setups
- Policy and secrets management replication

When Should You Automate Multi-Cluster Deployments?

You should prioritize multi-cluster automation when:

- You run 2+ Kubernetes clusters in different regions or accounts.
- You deploy data pipelines in multiple environments (dev, QA, prod).
- Your organization has SLA targets for uptime or disaster recovery (DR) failover.
- You need to enforce baseline security, logging, and observability standards.
- You aim to reduce manual onboarding time for new clusters (example, PoC and onboarding new teams)

Case Study: A cloud analytics firm uses Terraform + Helmfile to bootstrap and replicate Spark + Kafka clusters across dev, QA, and prod AKS environments. Cluster readiness is reduced from 3 days to 30 minutes.

How Do You Implement Multi-Cluster Automation?

Here is a complete practical breakdown.

1. **Terraform for Cluster Provisioning (Azure AKS)**

   Each cluster is defined via isolated **Terraform workspaces** to track state per environment.

   Example: Terraform Workspace Structure

   ```
   bash

   $ tree environments/
   environments/
   ├── dev
   │   └── main.tf
   ├── qa
   │   └── main.tf
   └── prod
       └── main.tf
   ```

   Provision AKS with Workspace Context

   ```
   hcl

   provider "azurerm" {
     features = {}
   }
   ```

```
resource "azurerm_kubernetes_cluster" "aks_cluster" {
  name                = "aks-${terraform.workspace}"
  location            = "East US"
  resource_group_name = "rg-${terraform.workspace}"
  ...
}
bash

terraform workspace new prod
terraform init
terraform apply
```

2. **Helmfile to Sync App Charts across Clusters**

   Define environment-specific overrides using **`values.yaml`**.

```
helmfile.yaml

yaml

environments:
  prod:
    values:
    - values-prod.yaml
  dev:
    values:
    - values-dev.yaml

releases:
  - name: airflow
    namespace: data-pipelines
    chart: bitnami/airflow
    values:
    - ./environments/{{ .Environment.Name }}/airflow-values.yaml

bash

helmfile -e prod apply
```

   This deploys the same chart with different resources, credentials, and storage classes per cluster.

3. **Ansible for Cluster Bootstrapping (Post-Provisioning)**

   Use Ansible to install logging agents, monitoring tools, or RBAC policies across clusters.

   Inventory: Multi-cluster kubeconfig

```
ini

[aks_clusters]
dev_ansible_cluster ansible_host=dev.kubeconfig
prod_ansible_cluster ansible_host=prod.kubeconfig
```

   Playbook: install Fluent Bit

```
yaml

- name: Install fluent-bit in all clusters
  hosts: aks_clusters
  tasks:
    - name: Apply Fluent Bit Helm chart
```

```
      shell: |
        helm upgrade --install fluent-bit fluent/fluent-bit \
          --namespace logging --create-namespace \
          -f fluent-bit-values.yaml --kubeconfig={{ ansible_host }}
```

Best Practice: Use `ansible-vault` to secure secrets in playbooks.

4. **GitOps for Continuous Sync Across Clusters**

   GitOps tools such as ArgoCD or Flux can be configured to pull manifests from Git and apply changes automatically to each cluster.

   Example: ArgoCD Application Set per environment

```
yaml

apiVersion: argoproj.io/v1alpha1
kind: ApplicationSet
metadata:
  name: multi-cluster-sync
spec:
  generators:
    - list:
        elements:
          - cluster: dev
            url: https://kube.dev.example.com
          - cluster: prod
            url: https://kube.prod.example.com
  template:
    metadata:
      name: '{{cluster}}-airflow'
    spec:
      project: default
      source:
        repoURL: https://github.com/org/airflow-deployments
        path: '{{cluster}}'
        targetRevision: HEAD
      destination:
        server: '{{url}}'
        namespace: airflow
      syncPolicy:
        automated:
          prune: true
          selfHeal: true
```

5. **Multi-Cluster Automation Pipeline**

   The following figure represents the Multi-Cluster Automation Pipeline:

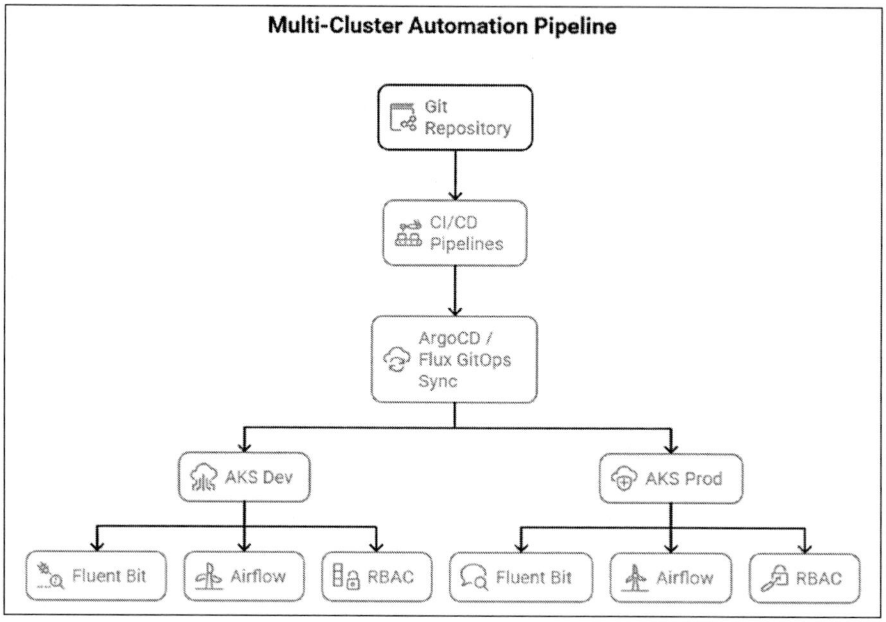

Figure 11.6: *Multi-Cluster Automation Pipeline*

Step-by-Step Explanation

In large-scale enterprise environments, it is common to maintain multiple Kubernetes clusters–such as dedicated clusters for development, staging, and production workloads. Managing infrastructure, deployments, and configurations across these clusters in a consistent and automated fashion is critical to ensure agility, security, and scalability. The Multi-Cluster Automation Pipeline offers a solution for precisely this need, using GitOps principles and modern CI/CD tooling.

This architecture enables declarative multi-cluster management using a single source of truth: a version-controlled Git repository. The pipeline ensures that any changes committed to the Git repository are automatically synced to the relevant clusters using GitOps tools such as ArgoCD or Flux.

Step 1: Git Repository as the Source of Truth

The foundation of the automation pipeline is a Git repository. This repository contains:

- Kubernetes manifests
- Helm charts
- Kustomize overlays
- RBAC configurations
- Application deployment specifications

All cluster configuration and application deployment logic are declared in Git. This makes every change traceable, auditable, and rollback-friendly.

Step 2: CI/CD Pipeline Integration

When a developer pushes code or configuration changes to the Git repository, it triggers a CI/CD pipeline. This pipeline is responsible for:

- Running tests and validations.
- Building and tagging container images.

- Pushing images to container registries.
- Updating Kubernetes manifest versions, image tags, or Helm values.

The CI/CD pipeline acts as the initial gatekeeper to ensure that all changes meet organizational standards before being rolled out.

Step 3: GitOps Sync with ArgoCD or Flux

Once the CI/CD pipeline completes successfully, GitOps tools such as ArgoCD or Flux come into play. These tools continuously monitor the Git repository for changes and synchronize the desired state defined in Git with the actual state of each Kubernetes cluster.

Each cluster is configured as a target in the GitOps controller, and sync policies define what should be applied, when, and with what rollback or drift detection strategies.

Step 4: Environment-Specific Target Clusters

The pipeline is designed to support multiple clusters–such as a development cluster (AKS Dev) and a production cluster (AKS Prod). These clusters are usually hosted in managed Kubernetes environments such as Azure Kubernetes Service (AKS), but the architecture is cloud-agnostic and applies to any Kubernetes environment.

Each cluster is associated with its own Git directory, branch, or overlay to separate configuration and deployment concerns between environments. This ensures isolation, yet consistency in structure.

Step 5: Component-Level Automation within Each Cluster

Within each cluster, specific components or workloads are deployed and managed through the GitOps sync mechanism. Common components include:

- **Fluent Bit:** This is a lightweight log collector that runs as a DaemonSet on every node. It gathers logs from application pods and forwards them to a centralized logging backend such as Elasticsearch or Azure Monitor.
- **Airflow:** A workflow orchestration engine used in data engineering and machine learning pipelines. It is deployed via Helm or manifests and can be version-controlled in Git for consistent automation.
- **RBAC:** Role-Based Access Control policies are defined and managed through YAML configurations. These YAMLs are applied to ensure that developers, applications, and automated agents only have the permissions they need–nothing more, nothing less.

These workloads are deployed independently to each cluster, allowing tailored automation per environment while ensuring the base framework remains consistent

Conclusion: The Multi-Cluster Automation Pipeline enables declarative, Git-centric management of Kubernetes environments at scale. It integrates the power of GitOps, CI/CD pipelines, and modern Kubernetes tools to automate everything from RBAC to observability and orchestration.

By adopting this model, organizations benefit from:

- Complete infrastructure as code
- Environment-specific automation
- Real-time configuration drift detection
- Secure and auditable operational practices

This pipeline serves as a robust foundation for implementing enterprise-grade Kubernetes automation with strong DevOps and GitOps alignment.

Real-World Use Case: Multi-Region Data Platform

A data engineering team deployed:

- AKS clusters in **East US**, **Central India**, and the **UK South**
- Spark + Kafka pipelines
- Azure Blob Storage for persistent volumes

Automation stack:

- Terraform (for AKS + VNet + ACR)
- Helmfile (for app deployments)
- Ansible (for cluster-wide Fluent Bit and Prometheus setup)
- ArgoCD (for GitOps sync across all clusters)

Outcome: Reduced platform provisioning time from days to <1 hour with zero manual errors.

Key Best Practices:

- Use **Terraform Workspaces** or S3 bucket-per-environment for isolated states.
- Tag clusters with labels for **dynamic GitOps ApplicationSet generation.**
- Integrate **Kubernetes Secrets encryption** for DR-safe configuration.
- Regularly validate cluster drift using **Terraform plan + Helm diff.**
- Keep Ansible playbooks **idempotent** and decoupled from app logic.

Automating multi-cluster environments is essential for cloud-scale data platforms and production-grade microservice architectures. Leveraging Terraform, Helmfile, Ansible, and GitOps enables organizations to build secure, repeatable, and auditable cluster lifecycle pipelines. This abstraction unlocks the ability to manage tens or hundreds of clusters with minimal manual effort, high resilience, and true DR readiness.

Integrating IaC with CI/CD Pipelines

Why is IaC Integration into CI/CD Critical?

Manual infrastructure provisioning is error-prone, slow, and non-reproducible – especially in modern DevOps environments where environments must be spun up, tested, validated, and torn down on demand. Infrastructure as Code (IaC) bridges this gap by making infrastructure declarative, version-controlled, and automatable. However, the real power unfolds when IaC tools are integrated directly into CI/CD pipelines.

Without IaC in CI/CD:

- DevOps workflows are limited to application layers.
- Infrastructure drift occurs across staging and prod.
- Rollbacks become harder due to inconsistent infra states.

What is IaC-Enabled CI/CD?

IaC-enabled CI/CD pipelines allow infrastructure provisioning and application deployment to happen in a unified flow. Tools such as:

- **Terraform:** Provision cloud infrastructure (example, AKS, VNETs, and NSGs).
- **Helm:** Deploy and upgrade Kubernetes applications.
- **Ansible:** Configure resources post-deployment (example, RBAC and agents).

- **GitHub Actions/Jenkins:** Automate the above in pipelines with approvals and validations.

This creates **fully declarative pipelines** that handle both infrastructure and application lifecycle.

When Should You Use IaC in Pipelines:

- Setting up ephemeral environments (QA, staging, review apps).
- Enforcing compliance and security gates via policy checks.
- Automating cloud-native provisioning (AKS clusters, managed identities, node pools).
- Performing controlled rollouts in regulated production environments.

How to Implement This?

Case Study: Azure DevOps Teams Automating Cluster + App Deployment

Scenario: A fintech platform uses AKS for multi-tenant applications and wants to automate:

- Cluster provisioning
- Ingress and DNS setup
- Application release using Helm

Solution Stack:

- **Terraform:** Azure AKS, VNET, node pools
- **Ansible:** Fluent bit and RBAC config post-deploy
- **Helm:** Multi-tenant Helm charts
- **GitHub Actions:** Pipeline orchestration with gates and approval jobs

Result: 3x faster environment setup, infra reproducibility, and compliant rollouts.

Lab: GitHub Actions with Terraform + Helm

Folder Structure:

```
.
├── .github
│   └── workflows
│       └── ci-infra-app.yaml
├── terraform
│   ├── main.tf
│   └── variables.tf
├── helm
│   └── myapp/
└── ansible
    └── post_config.yml
```

YAML Lab: GitHub Actions – IaC Pipeline

```yaml
yaml

# .github/workflows/ci-infra-app.yaml
name: AKS Infra + Helm Deploy

on:
  push:
    branches:
      - main

jobs:
  terraform:
```

```
    runs-on: ubuntu-latest
    steps:
    - name: Checkout code
      uses: actions/checkout@v3

    - name: Set up Terraform
      uses: hashicorp/setup-terraform@v2

    - name: Terraform Init
      run: terraform -chdir=terraform init

    - name: Terraform Plan
      run: terraform -chdir=terraform plan

    - name: Terraform Apply (Approval gated)
      if: github.ref == 'refs/heads/main'
      run: terraform -chdir=terraform apply -auto-approve

  helm:
    needs: terraform
    runs-on: ubuntu-latest
    steps:
    - name: Install Helm
      run: |
        curl https://raw.githubusercontent.com/helm/helm/master/scripts/
get-helm-3 | bash

    - name: Deploy App via Helm
      run: |
        helm upgrade --install myapp ./helm/myapp \
        --set image.tag=${{ github.sha }}

  ansible:
    needs: helm
    runs-on: ubuntu-latest
    steps:
    - name: Run Ansible Playbook
      uses: dawidd6/action-ansible-playbook@v2
      with:
        playbook: ansible/post_config.yml
```

Flow Diagram: IaC + CI/CD Pipeline (GitHub Actions on Azure AKS)

```
GitHub Commit → GitHub Actions
     │
     ├─ Terraform Plan → Apply → AKS Cluster + Node Pool
     │
     ├─ Helm Chart Deploy → MyApp Helm Release → AKS Namespace
     │
     └─ Ansible Playbook → Configure Logs, RBAC, Monitoring
```

Explanation:

- The workflow first provisions AKS resources using Terraform.
- Then, Helm charts install application workloads declaratively.
- Finally, Ansible agents configure critical services across the new cluster.
- This pipeline supports rollback by versioning Terraform state, Helm releases, and Ansible inventories.

Best Practices for IaC + CI/CD Pipelines (Azure AKS Context)

Best practices for Infrastructure as Code (IaC) and CI/CD pipelines in the Azure AKS context emphasize security, manageability, and observability. Utilizing Azure Storage with locking for Terraform state management ensures collaboration without conflicts. Role separation via Azure AD groups strengthens access control by managing permissions for Terraform and Helm. For secrets management, storing sensitive information in Azure Key Vault and integrating it through Terraform or GitHub Actions ensures robust security. Lastly, integrating Azure Monitor for tracking Terraform, Helm, and Ansible runs enhances observability, allowing for seamless monitoring and troubleshooting across the pipeline. These practices collectively streamline workflows while maintaining a secure and transparent infrastructure lifecycle.

Practice	Description
State Backend	Use Azure Storage with locking for Terraform state management.
Role Separation	Use Azure AD groups to manage TF/Helm permissions.
Secrets Management	Store secrets in Azure Key Vault; integrate via Terraform provider or GitHub Actions.
Observability	Monitor Terraform, Helm, and Ansible runs using Azure Monitor + logs export.

Table 11.10: *Best Practices for IaC and CI/CD Pipelines*

Integrating Infrastructure as Code into CI/CD pipelines automates not only application delivery but also the cloud infrastructure lifecycle. By combining Terraform, Helm, and Ansible into orchestrated workflows via GitHub Actions or Jenkins, organizations achieve greater velocity, repeatability, and compliance. Especially in Azure AKS environments, this fusion ensures resilient, traceable deployments of both platform and data-layer workloads.

Conclusion

Infrastructure as Code (IaC) has become the cornerstone of scalable, repeatable, and auditable Kubernetes operations. In this chapter, we explored how Helm simplifies Kubernetes deployments, Terraform provisions cloud-native infrastructure such as AKS on Azure, and Ansible automates post-provisioning configuration across clusters. By integrating these IaC tools into CI/CD pipelines, teams achieve true DevOps maturity - automating infrastructure provisioning, application deployment, and policy enforcement across multi-cluster environments. These automation patterns not only reduce operational toil but also improve consistency, reliability, and velocity in managing modern Kubernetes-based data platforms.

In the next chapter, we will explore cutting-edge advancements in the Kubernetes ecosystem from serverless Kubernetes and eBPF to WASM, AI workloads, and platform engineering. We will gain insights into how emerging trends are shaping the future of cloud-native architectures and their implications for engineers, architects, and enterprise platforms moving forward.

CHAPTER 12
Emerging Trends in Cloud-Native and Kubernetes

Introduction

Cloud-native technologies are evolving rapidly, and Kubernetes is at the forefront of this transformation. This chapter dives into how Kubernetes supports **AI/ML workflows**, facilitates **event-driven autoscaling** with **KEDA**, manages **serverless workloads**, and enables **edge computing** with tools such as **K3s** and **MicroK8s**. Additionally, we will explore **emerging runtimes** including **WebAssembly** and their integration with Kubernetes, providing a comprehensive overview of modern advancements in container orchestration.

Structure

In this chapter, we will cover the following topics:

- AI/ML Integration in Kubernetes
- Serverless Containers with KEDA and OpenFaaS
- Edge Computing with Kubernetes
- Future of Container Orchestration

Kubernetes and AI/ML Integration

In recent years, the convergence of AI/ML and cloud-native infrastructure has led enterprises to re-evaluate how they build and scale intelligent applications. Traditional ML systems often suffer from siloed environments, lack of reproducibility, and scalability limitations. As organizations transition toward MLOps practices, they need infrastructure that offers:

- Scalability for data and compute.
- Reproducible training environments.
- Integrated workflows for experimentation, training, and deployment.
- Automated resource management with GPUs/TPUs.
- Portability across hybrid and multi-cloud environments.

Kubernetes as a Solution

Kubernetes offers a unified control plane for managing containerized workloads, and this extends naturally to the AI/ML lifecycle. Here is why Kubernetes is preferred for AI/ML:

- **Elastic Scalability:** Horizontal Pod Autoscaling (HPA), Vertical Pod Autoscaling (VPA), and Cluster Autoscaler allow on-demand scaling.
- **GPU Scheduling:** Kubernetes supports NVIDIA device plugin and supports scheduling GPU-enabled pods for AI/ML workloads.
- **Multi-Tenancy and Isolation:** Namespaces, RBAC, and Network Policies isolate ML teams and pipelines.
- **Pipeline Automation:** ML pipelines can be defined as code (for example, with Kubeflow Pipelines), integrated into CI/CD.
- **Cloud-Agnostic Deployment:** Enables hybrid-cloud and multi-cloud ML strategies.
- **Integration with Azure AKS:** Azure Kubernetes Service simplifies provisioning GPU nodes, securing data with Azure Key Vault, and logging with Azure Monitor and Log Analytics.

Key Tools Powering This Shift

The core tools and frameworks that power this ecosystem are detailed in the following table:

Tool	Purpose	Azure Integration
Kubeflow	End-to-end ML lifecycle on Kubernetes	Deploy via Azure Marketplace or custom manifests
MLflow	Experiment tracking, model registry	Integrate with Azure ML for model versioning
KServe (formerly KFServing)	Model serving on Kubernetes	Runs on AKS; integrates with Azure Container Registry
Ray	Distributed computing for training/inference	Deploy Ray clusters on AKS for scalable distributed training

Table 12.1: *Core Tools and Frameworks in the Ecosystem*

Kubeflow

- Manages the complete ML lifecycle: Notebooks, Pipelines, Training, and Serving.
- Supports TensorFlow, PyTorch, XGBoost, and more.
- Runs within Kubernetes namespaces; each `user/team` gets isolated environments.

MLflow

- Tracks experiments with metrics, artifacts, and parameters.
- Can serve models using REST APIs via MLflow server.
- Azure supports MLflow integration with Azure ML backend store.

KServe

- Uses Knative to autoscale models on demand.
- Supports multiple ML frameworks (TensorFlow, PyTorch, ONNX, XGBoost).
- Provides prediction endpoints using Istio or Ambassador ingress.

Ray

- Python-based framework for distributed AI workloads (for example, reinforcement learning, tuning).

- Leverages Kubernetes to scale training jobs dynamically.
- Especially suited for complex parallel workloads such as hyperparameter tuning or data processing.

Kubernetes Use Cases: Training versus Inference

Training Workloads: Kubernetes emerges as a powerful backbone for orchestrating AI/ML training workloads, particularly when confronted with vast datasets, GPU-accelerated computation, and intricate preprocessing pipelines. Leveraging Azure Kubernetes Service (AKS) with GPU-enabled node pools - such as the NC and ND series - enables scalable distributed training while ensuring cost-efficiency. Persistent data access is seamlessly achieved through Azure Blob Storage mounted via the Blobfuse CSI driver. For robust experiment tracking and repeatability, tools such as MLflow and Kubeflow Pipelines integrate natively into this architecture, offering a reproducible and modular approach to machine learning lifecycle management.

Scenario	Training on Kubernetes
Large datasets (> GBs or TBs)	Use PVCs with distributed training
Need for GPU/TPU acceleration	Schedule GPU-enabled pods
Complex preprocessing pipelines	Use multi-step ML pipelines with Argo or Kubeflow
Experiment tracking	Integrate with MLflow or Kubeflow pipelines

Table 12.2: *Training Workloads*

Use AKS with GPU-enabled node pools (for example, NC, ND series in Azure) and integrate Azure Blob Storage as a persistent volume via Blobfuse CSI driver.

Inference Workloads: Kubernetes serves as an ideal runtime for production-grade inference workloads that demand high availability, version control, and elastic scalability. With KServe orchestrating autoscaled RESTful endpoints, models can be deployed with seamless canary routing to manage multiple versions concurrently. The KNative autoscaler dynamically adjusts compute resources based on real-time traffic, ensuring optimal performance and cost efficiency. For decentralized or edge deployments, Azure Arc combined with lightweight Kubernetes distributions such as K3s extends inference capabilities beyond the cloud, enabling consistent, scalable AI delivery across hybrid environments.

Scenario	Inference on Kubernetes
High-availability REST APIs	Use KServe + autoscaling
Need to serve multiple model versions	Use canary routing in Kserve
Scaling based on load	Use KNative autoscaler
Edge model serving	Use Azure Arc + K3s

Table 12.3: *Inference Workloads*

Use Kubernetes when the model needs to be served in production with high throughput and scale-out demands.

Architecting Distributed AI Workloads with GPUs, PVCs, and Auto-Scaling

Running machine learning workloads in a production-grade Kubernetes environment requires a structured approach to handle model training, deployment, scalability, and automation. The following architecture leverages Azure Kubernetes Service (AKS) as the foundational compute layer, integrated with Kubeflow Pipelines for orchestrating training workflows and KServe for scalable and efficient model inference. The solution also incorporates CI/CD pipelines, GPU acceleration, persistent volumes, and horizontal pod autoscaling to deliver a fully automated MLOps experience.

The following figure illustrates the **architecture for deploying AI/ML workloads on Azure AKS using KServe**, providing a comprehensive view of the integrated components:

- **GitHub/Azure DevOps** is the CI/CD source for pipeline triggers.
  - **Kubeflow Pipelines** orchestrate data preprocessing, model training, and validation.
  - **KServe** handles scalable and resilient model serving, using GPU-enabled inference nodes when required.
  - **PVCs** backed by **Azure Blob Storage** persist datasets and model artifacts across runs.
  - **Horizontal Pod Autoscaler** automatically scales the inference service based on CPU/GPU load or request rate.

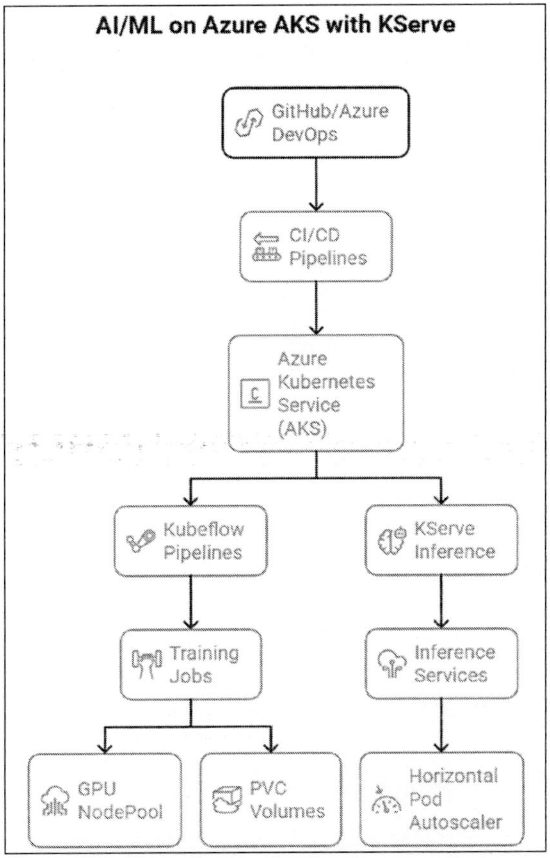

Figure 12.1: *AI/ML on Azure AKS with KServe*

Let us walk through this system step by step.

Step 1: Source Control and Automation Triggers (GitHub/Azure DevOps)

All ML code, training workflows, and deployment configurations are stored in a **Git repository** hosted on platforms such as GitHub or Azure DevOps. This acts as the single source of truth for model versioning, CI/CD triggers, and Infrastructure-as-Code (IaC) configurations.

Whenever a developer pushes code (for example, a new training pipeline or inference manifest), it triggers downstream automation through CI/CD pipelines.

Step 2: CI/CD Pipelines

Modern MLOps workflows rely heavily on automation. **CI/CD pipelines**, typically built using tools such as GitHub Actions or Azure Pipelines, serve several critical functions:

- Validate and lint Kubernetes manifests or Kubeflow pipeline specs.
- Build container images and push them to Azure Container Registry.
- Deploy training jobs or inference services to AKS.
- Run integration tests on endpoints after deployment.

The pipeline ensures reproducibility, consistency, and traceability across model lifecycle events.

Step 3: Azure Kubernetes Service (AKS)

AKS is the managed Kubernetes platform on Azure that serves as the control plane for running all ML workloads. It abstracts cluster provisioning, auto-scaling, patching, and node pool management.

This environment runs both the **training pipelines** and **inference services**, giving teams a unified platform to operationalize machine learning models at scale.

Step 4: Left Branch – Kubeflow Pipelines for Model Training

Kubeflow Pipelines

Kubeflow Pipelines provide a structured, reproducible, and versioned way to define training workflows using Python DSL or YAML. Each step in the pipeline (data preprocessing, model training, evaluation, and validation) is containerized and orchestrated as a Kubernetes pod.

Training Jobs

The output of the Kubeflow pipeline is the submission of a **training job**, typically using TensorFlow, PyTorch, or Scikit-learn. The training jobs run as pods and are scheduled onto specialized nodes if needed.

GPU Node Pools

If the training job requires heavy computation (such as, deep learning), the pod can be scheduled onto a **GPU-backed node pool**. These node pools are provisioned with NVIDIA GPUs and labeled accordingly. Kubernetes node selectors or tolerations ensure proper placement.

PVC Volumes

To persist datasets, models, or checkpoints, training jobs can mount **`PersistentVolumeClaims`** **(PVCs)** backed by Azure Disks or Azure Files. This storage allows model checkpoints to be reused, logs to be captured, or final models to be saved for deployment.

Step 5: Right Branch – KServe for Model Inference

KServe Inference

KServe is a Kubernetes-native serverless framework for serving ML models. It abstracts the complexity of deploying inference endpoints and supports advanced capabilities, such as autoscaling, request/response logging, model explain ability, and revision rollout.

KServe supports various runtimes such as TensorFlow Serving, TorchServe, ONNX Runtime, Scikit-Learn, and custom inference containers.

Inference Services

Each model is deployed as a **KServe InferenceService**. It wraps the model server in a Kubernetes Custom Resource Definition (CRD), managing the model's lifecycle declaratively.

Example CRD fields define:

- The model storage location (for example, Azure Blob, S3, PVC)
- Resource requests and limits
- Autoscaling and rollout policies

Horizontal Pod Autoscaler (HPA)

To maintain performance and cost-efficiency, **HPA** is configured for inference pods based on CPU, memory, or custom metrics such as requests per second or latency. This ensures that the inference service scales out during high traffic and scales down during low usage periods automatically.

Benefits of This Architecture

- **Modular Design:** Training and inference workflows are isolated but integrated via shared services and storage.
- **Scalability:** GPU acceleration for training and autoscaling for inference ensures optimal use of cloud resources.
- **Portability:** Based on open standards such as Kubeflow, KServe, and Kubernetes CRDs.
- **Security and Governance:** Integrated with Azure AD, RBAC, and network policies.
- **Automation:** GitOps-driven CI/CD ensures reproducibility, auditability, and rollback safety.

This architecture empowers machine learning teams to streamline experimentation, automate deployment, and monitor performance using Kubernetes-native tooling. It exemplifies best practices for MLOps on Azure AKS using modern open-source tools, and is adaptable to other cloud providers with minimal changes.

Case Study: Serving ML Models with KServe on Azure AKS

Objective

Serve a pre-trained image classification model (ResNet50) on Azure AKS using KServe with GPU acceleration and autoscaling.

Step-by-Step Implementation

1. **Provision AKS with GPU Nodes**

```
bash

az aks create \
  --resource-group ai-ml-rg \
  --name aks-mlcluster \
  --nodepool-name gpu \
  --node-vm-size Standard_NC6 \
  --node-count 2 \
  --enable-addons monitoring \
  --enable-managed-identity \
  --generate-ssh-keys
```

2. **Deploy KServe with GPU Support**

```
bash

kubectl apply -f https://github.com/kserve/kserve/releases/download/v0.11.0/
kserve.yaml
```

3. **Model Deployment YAML**

```
yaml

apiVersion: serving.kserve.io/v1beta1
kind: InferenceService
metadata:
  name: resnet50
  namespace: kubeflow-user
spec:
  predictor:
    containers:
      - name: kserve-container
        image: <youracr>.azurecr.io/resnet50:latest
        resources:
          limits:
            cpu: "1"
            memory: "2Gi"
            nvidia.com/gpu: 1
        ports:
          - containerPort: 8080
```

Make sure that GPU device plugin is deployed:

```
bash

kubectl apply -f https://raw.githubusercontent.com/NVIDIA/k8s-device-plugin/
v0.12.3/nvidia-device-plugin.yml
```

4. **Access the Inference Endpoint**
   - Expose the service via Istio Gateway or Azure Application Gateway Ingress.
   - Query using REST endpoint:

```
bash

curl -X POST <inference-endpoint>/v1/models/resnet50:predict -d @input.json
```

Best Practices

- Use AKS with GPU node pools for scalable and cost-efficient AI/ML workloads.
- Leverage PVCs with Azure Blob Storage to decouple compute from data.
- Adopt KServe for serving models with GPU and autoscaling support.
- Use Kubeflow Pipelines for end-to-end ML workflows with reproducibility.
- Enable autoscaling using HPA or KNative based on request throughput.

This architectural pattern enables enterprises to create highly scalable, cost-efficient, and production-ready AI/ML systems using Kubernetes in Azure.

Serverless Containers with KEDA and OpenFaaS

Kubernetes revolutionized container orchestration by automating deployment, scaling, and management of containerized applications. However, traditional Kubernetes workloads generally operate under an "always-on" paradigm, meaning pods are continuously running, consuming compute resources even when idle. This results in inefficient resource utilization and higher operational costs, especially for workloads characterized by unpredictable or bursty traffic patterns.

Serverless architecture on Kubernetes addresses this inefficiency by enabling **event-driven, scale-to-zero** workloads. In this model, containers (or functions) are instantiated only when triggered by an event—such as a message arriving on a queue or an HTTP request—and terminated when idle. This approach not only optimizes cost by eliminating resource waste but also simplifies application design by decoupling compute provisioning from workload demand.

Serverless on Kubernetes leverages the native platform's flexibility while adding dynamic autoscaling capabilities beyond CPU or memory metrics. This shift aligns perfectly with cloud-native goals of agility, scalability, and cost optimization. On Azure, combining Azure Kubernetes Service (AKS) with event-driven tools such as **KEDA** (Kubernetes Event-Driven Autoscaler) and **OpenFaaS** enables enterprises to build efficient, responsive, and maintainable serverless applications while retaining full control of their container infrastructure.

What KEDA and OpenFaaS do Differently than Standard Autoscaling

Kubernetes Horizontal Pod Autoscaler (HPA) Limitations

By default, Kubernetes provides Horizontal Pod Autoscaler (HPA), which scales pods based primarily on CPU and memory usage metrics. While suitable for many steady-state workloads, HPA does not natively support autoscaling based on **external event sources** such as message queues, streaming events, or custom application metrics without additional custom metrics adapters.

KEDA: Kubernetes Event-Driven Autoscaler

KEDA extends Kubernetes autoscaling capabilities by bridging external event sources with pod scaling decisions. It introduces a custom resource called ScaledObject, which defines triggers based on event metrics such as queue length, message lag, or custom Prometheus queries.

Unlike HPA, KEDA supports **scale-to-zero**, meaning pods are automatically terminated when no events are present, saving infrastructure costs. It supports over 60 event sources, including many Azure services:

- **Azure Service Bus** for messaging queues and topics.
- **Azure Event Hubs** for event streaming.
- **Azure Blob Storage** for file event triggers.
- **Prometheus** for custom metrics.
- Other popular sources: Kafka, RabbitMQ, Redis, AWS SQS, HTTP webhooks, and more.

KEDA operates by periodically polling the event source, and based on thresholds configured in the **ScaledObject**, it adjusts pod replicas dynamically.

OpenFaaS: Function-as-a-Service on Kubernetes

OpenFaaS is a framework designed to deploy serverless functions as containers on Kubernetes. It simplifies building and deploying individual functions with:

- Easy packaging of code in Docker containers.

- Automatic exposure of functions as REST endpoints.
- Integration with Prometheus metrics for scaling.
- Support for event-driven invocation and HTTP triggers.

While OpenFaaS provides a **function abstraction layer** over Kubernetes, it can be combined with KEDA to achieve **event-driven autoscaling**, allowing functions to scale from zero to many instances based on real-time demand.

Key Differentiators

Feature	Kubernetes HPA	KEDA	OpenFaaS
Scaling triggers	CPU/Memory	Event sources (queues, and more)	HTTP and event-based triggers
Scale-to-zero	No	Yes	Yes
Supported event sources	Limited (via custom metrics)	60+ including Azure services	Integrates with KEDA or Prometheus
Abstraction level	Pod-level	Pod-level	Function-level
Deployment scope	Native Kubernetes object	Custom Kubernetes object	Kubernetes + FaaS framework

Table 12.4: *Key Differentiators*

When to Adopt Event-Driven Containers for Cost-Efficient Workloads

Event-driven serverless containers on Kubernetes excel in scenarios where workloads are:

- **Intermittent or Bursty:** Traffic fluctuates unpredictably, with idle periods.
- **Triggered by External Events:** Messages, file uploads, or scheduled jobs.
- **Microservice or Function-Oriented:** Discrete units of work executed on demand.
- **Cost-Sensitive:** Infrastructure costs must be minimized by scaling to zero.
- **Highly Scalable:** Need to scale rapidly from zero to many instances during spikes.

Typical Use Cases

- Message queue processing (for example, processing orders, emails, or sensor data).
- Real-time data transformation in ETL pipelines.
- Machine learning inference triggered by events.
- Webhook event processing and API gateways.
- IoT device telemetry ingestion.
- Batch jobs and serverless cron jobs.

Azure Context

Azure provides managed event sources that integrate seamlessly with KEDA:

- **Azure Service Bus** queues and topics.
- **Azure Event Hubs** for telemetry streams.
- **Azure Blob Storage** event notifications.

Using AKS with KEDA, organizations can build **fully managed event-driven systems** that respond to Azure cloud-native events efficiently and cost-effectively.

Scale-to-Zero Pods with KEDA on Azure Kubernetes Service (AKS)

KEDA (Kubernetes-based Event-Driven Autoscaler) is a powerful open-source component that extends Kubernetes autoscaling capabilities by allowing workloads to scale based on external event sources such as message queues, databases, or cloud services. A particularly valuable use case of KEDA is its scale-to-zero capability–automatically scaling down pods to zero when no workload is present, and scaling them back up when activity resumes.

This is particularly beneficial for event-driven applications or intermittent workloads, such as background processors or job consumers. In the Azure ecosystem, KEDA integrates seamlessly with Azure Service Bus Queues, enabling cost-efficient, serverless-style Kubernetes deployments.

The following figure illustrates the architecture for implementing scale-to-zero, trigger-based Pods, detailing the components and YAML configuration necessary for achieving serverless container elasticity:

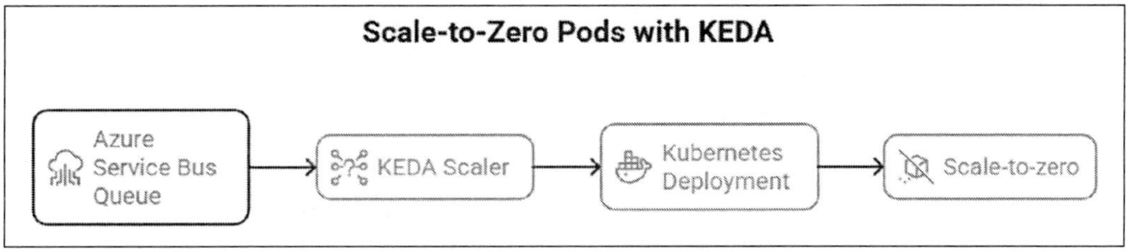

Figure 12.2: *Scale-to-Zero Pods with KEDA*

- **Event Source:** Azure Service Bus holds the messages to be processed.
- **KEDA:** Periodically queries queue length via its trigger.
- **Kubernetes Deployment:** Worker pods scale from zero upwards to process messages.
- **Scale-to-zero:** When no messages exist, pods terminate, avoiding charges.

Let us explore the components of the figure step by step.

Step 1: Azure Service Bus Queue

An **Azure Service Bus Queue** acts as a message broker that receives and stores events or jobs. These messages are often generated by upstream services or applications that decouple event generation from event processing. For example, an e-commerce platform might place order processing messages onto a Service Bus queue to be consumed by backend worker services.

In this figure, the queue is the **trigger** that determines whether the Kubernetes workload needs to be scaled up or can remain idle.

Step 2: KEDA Scaler

KEDA watches the Service Bus queue for activity. It is configured via a **ScaledObject** custom resource in Kubernetes, which defines the event source (Azure Service Bus), the polling interval, and the thresholds for scaling.

Key functions of the KEDA Scaler:

- Continuously monitors the queue length.
- Emits custom metrics into the Kubernetes Metrics Server.
- Dynamically modifies the number of replicas in the associated Deployment based on queue activity.

When KEDA detects that the queue length has gone above a certain threshold, it triggers a scale-up event. When the queue is empty for a defined cooldown period, it triggers a scale-down, even all the way to zero replicas.

Step 3: Kubernetes Deployment

This is the actual workload–a **Kubernetes Deployment** that defines the containerized application meant to process messages. It could be a background worker, event consumer, or any microservice responsible for executing a specific job.

KEDA hooks into this Deployment and modifies its replica count based on queue metrics.

Features of the Deployment:

- Specifies CPU, memory, and environment configurations.
- Initially deployed with zero replicas.
- Scaled up automatically when messages appear in the queue.

Step 4: Scale-to-Zero Behavior

When there is **no workload**, KEDA scales the deployment down to **zero pods**–this is known as "scale to zero." It ensures:

- Zero compute consumption (no pods = no node-level resource usage).
- Cost efficiency, especially in pay-per-use cloud environments.
- Efficient use of cluster capacity in multi-tenant or high-density environments.

When a new message is detected in the queue, KEDA immediately scales up the deployment to the desired number of replicas to process that workload.

Benefits of KEDA-based scaling:

- **Event-Driven Autoscaling:** Unlike traditional HPA that reacts to CPU or memory, KEDA reacts to *business events* such as messages or HTTP queue depth.
- **Cost Optimization:** Automatically reduces pod count to zero, saving on compute costs.
- **Serverless-Like Behavior:** KEDA gives Kubernetes workloads the elasticity of serverless computing without giving up Kubernetes primitives.
- **Seamless Azure Integration:** Works with Azure Service Bus, Azure Monitor, Event Hubs, and more.
- **Supports Multiple Triggers:** KEDA can be configured to listen to over 50 different event sources.

Real-World Example Use Case

Imagine a retail company running an image-processing service that processes user uploads via a queue. Instead of keeping pods running 24/7, they use KEDA to scale the image-processing pods to zero during off-hours. When new uploads arrive and messages appear in the queue, KEDA spins up just enough pods to handle the load. Once complete, the service scales back to zero–delivering a serverless, Kubernetes-native experience.

Conclusion: KEDA unlocks a new dimension of workload optimization on Kubernetes by combining reactive autoscaling with native platform controls. When used in conjunction with Azure services including Service Bus, it enables developers to build lean, reactive microservices architectures that scale precisely with demand–without manual intervention or idle compute.

YAML Example: Deploying KEDA-Driven Worker Pods on AKS

Step 1: Install KEDA on AKS

```
bash

kubectl apply -f https://github.com/kedacore/keda/releases/download/v2.13.0/
keda-2.13.0.yaml
```

Step 2: Kubernetes Deployment for Worker Pods

This deployment defines a worker app that processes messages from an Azure Service Bus queue:

```
yaml

apiVersion: apps/v1
kind: Deployment
metadata:
  name: azure-servicebus-worker
spec:
  replicas: 0 # start at zero replicas for scale-to-zero behavior
  selector:
    matchLabels:
      app: azure-worker
  template:
    metadata:
      labels:
        app: azure-worker
    spec:
      containers:
      - name: worker
        image: youracr.azurecr.io/azure-servicebus-worker:latest
        env:
        - name: SERVICE_BUS_CONNECTION_STRING
          valueFrom:
            secretKeyRef:
              name: servicebus-secret
              key: connectionString
        - name: QUEUE_NAME
          value: "my-queue"
```

Step 3: Define KEDA ScaledObject

This custom resource instructs KEDA to scale the deployment based on Azure Service Bus queue length.

```
yaml

apiVersion: keda.sh/v1alpha1
kind: ScaledObject
metadata:
  name: servicebus-scaledobject
  namespace: default
spec:
  scaleTargetRef:
    name: azure-servicebus-worker
  minReplicaCount: 0
  maxReplicaCount: 10
  triggers:
  - type: azure-servicebus
```

```
    metadata:
      queueName: "my-queue"
      connectionFromEnv: SERVICE_BUS_CONNECTION_STRING
      messageCount: "5" # threshold to scale up
```

Explanation

- The **worker deployment** starts with zero replicas, ensuring that no pods are running when there is no work.
- The **KEDA ScaledObject** monitors the Azure Service Bus queue length.
- When messages in the queue exceed 5, KEDA triggers Kubernetes to spin up worker pods.
- Pods process messages until the queue is drained, after which KEDA scales down pods back to zero.
- This approach ensures **optimal resource utilization and cost savings**.

Real-World Example: Scaling Python Functions on AKS with KEDA and RabbitMQ

In many event-driven architectures, RabbitMQ is a preferred message broker. Integrating KEDA with RabbitMQ enables automatic scaling of Python worker functions based on queue depth.

Python Worker Function Skeleton

```
python

import pika
import time
import os

def callback(ch, method, properties, body):
    print("Received message:", body.decode())
    # Simulate work
    time.sleep(2)
    ch.basic_ack(delivery_tag=method.delivery_tag)

connection = pika.BlockingConnection(pika.ConnectionParameters('rabbitmq'))
channel = connection.channel()
channel.queue_declare(queue='task-queue')

channel.basic_consume(queue='task-queue', on_message_callback=callback)

print('Waiting for messages...')
channel.start_consuming()
```

Deploy this worker in a container and use a KEDA ScaledObject (similar to the previous YAML) to auto-scale based on the task-queue length.

Additional Azure Integrations

- **Blob Storage Triggers**: KEDA supports scaling based on new blob uploads.
- **Event Hubs**: Perfect for telemetry ingestion pipelines.
- **Azure Monitor**: Custom metrics can be used for advanced scaling scenarios.

Serverless containers on Kubernetes redefine application deployment by enabling **event-driven, cost-efficient, and scalable workloads**. Tools such as **KEDA** extend Kubernetes autoscaling beyond CPU/memory, reacting directly to business-relevant events such as queue depth or message count. **OpenFaaS** complements this by abstracting functions as lightweight containers that can be dynamically triggered.

On Azure, the seamless integration between AKS, KEDA, and Azure-native event sources allows Cloud Engineers and Architects to build reactive, scalable, and economical systems without sacrificing control or flexibility. The practical YAML examples and architecture patterns provide a clear blueprint to implement these solutions in production.

Edge Computing with Kubernetes

Why Edge Use Cases Require Decentralized, Lightweight Clusters

Modern enterprise applications are evolving to meet the needs of real-time responsiveness, low-latency processing, and localized computing. In domains such as **retail, manufacturing, smart cities, and autonomous vehicles**, a significant volume of data is generated at the edge—closer to the source—rather than in centralized cloud regions. Transferring this data back to centralized cloud clusters for processing introduces unacceptable **latency, bandwidth costs, and reliability risks**.

Edge computing aims to **bring compute and storage closer to the data source**, enabling near-instant decision-making. Kubernetes, with its powerful orchestration capabilities, is now being extended to the edge to orchestrate workloads running across hundreds or thousands of distributed sites. However, traditional Kubernetes distributions are too heavyweight for resource-constrained edge devices. This led to the rise of **lightweight Kubernetes distributions** (for example, K3s, MicroK8s) and **multi-cluster orchestration platforms** such as **Azure Arc**, which enable centralized management of fleets of edge clusters.

Deploying Kubernetes at the edge helps organizations:

- Reduce cloud data transfer and processing costs.
- Comply with data locality and privacy regulations.
- Deliver ultra-low-latency services (for example, real-time analytics or AI at edge).
- Increase system resilience in disconnected or intermittently connected environments.

Tools for Edge (K3s, MicroK8s, Azure Arc)

Several tools are designed specifically for deploying, orchestrating, and managing Kubernetes workloads in edge environments. The following table provides a comparison of leading solutions:

Tool	Description	Ideal Use Case
K3s	Lightweight CNCF-certified Kubernetes distribution by Rancher (<100MB binary, single binary)	IoT gateways, edge servers with minimal resources
MicroK8s	Lightweight Kubernetes by Canonical with snap install and offline mode	Developer workstations, lab environments, edge clusters
Azure Arc	Azure-native control plane to manage on-prem and edge clusters centrally	Hybrid cloud management, policy-driven governance

***Table 12.5:** Tools for Edge*

Key Capabilities of Azure Arc for Edge:

- Register and manage **K3s or any CNCF-certified Kubernetes cluster** in Azure.
- Enable **GitOps-based configuration management** with Azure Policy.
- Integrate edge clusters with **Azure Monitor**, **Defender for Kubernetes**, and **Azure Key Vault**.
- Use Azure Arc as a control plane while running workloads at the edge (on-premise, factory floor, and more).

Centralized Management of Edge Clusters Using Azure Arc

As enterprises extend their cloud-native infrastructure beyond traditional data centers and into remote or disconnected environments - such as retail stores, manufacturing plants, or IoT installations-centralized control becomes critical. **Azure Arc** provides a unified control plane for managing Kubernetes clusters, virtual machines, and applications running at the edge.

Figure 12.3 illustrates how Azure Arc enables **secure, policy-driven, and observable management** of edge Kubernetes clusters using lightweight distributions like **K3s** or **MicroK8s (MK8s):**

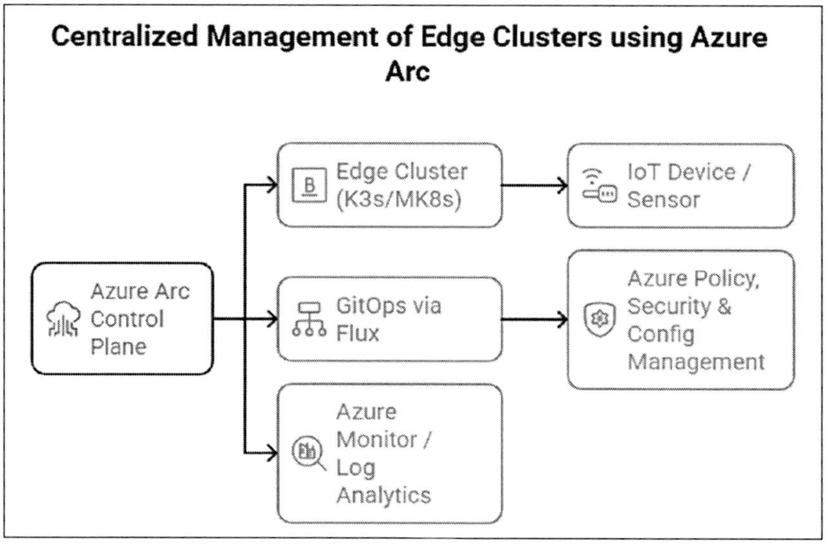

***Figure 12.3**: Centralized Management of Edge Clusters Using Azure Arc*

Let us walk through each component of the flow, highlighting the roles and interactions across the edge-to-cloud control spectrum.

Azure Arc Control Plane

The central component is the **Azure Arc control plane**, which acts as the single source of truth for fleet-wide governance. It runs in Azure and connects to hybrid or edge environments through secure agents and APIs.

Key functions:

- Registers edge Kubernetes clusters with Azure Resource Manager (ARM).
- Synchronizes GitOps configurations.
- Applies centralized policies, security rules, and RBAC.
- Enables telemetry, monitoring, and update visibility.

This control plane decouples Kubernetes management from physical location, enabling cloud-like control over remote infrastructure.

Edge Cluster (K3s / MicroK8s)

The **Edge Cluster** represents a lightweight Kubernetes distribution deployed at a remote site, such as a retail branch, warehouse, or manufacturing facility. Popular choices include:

- **K3s**: Optimized for small footprint and limited resources.
- **MicroK8s (MK8s)**: Modular and suitable for IoT, testing, or constrained environments.

These clusters host edge applications such as video analytics, real-time inventory tracking, or telemetry processors. Azure Arc enables onboarding of these clusters into Azure without needing them to be Azure-native.

These edge clusters:

- Operate independently when offline.
- Sync with the Azure control plane when connected.
- Interact with local devices such as sensors and gateways.

IoT Device / Sensor Integration

Edge clusters often interface with physical **IoT devices or sensors**. Examples include:

- Barcode scanners in retail stores
- Temperature sensors in warehouses
- CNC machines in factories

The Kubernetes cluster receives, processes, or relays data from these devices using containerized workloads. Azure Arc does not manage the devices directly but allows the **edge applications** managing those devices to be controlled via GitOps and policy.

GitOps via Flux

Azure Arc supports **GitOps** deployments using Flux. GitOps is a modern deployment approach that treats Git as the source of truth for application and infrastructure state.

How it works:

- Flux is deployed on the edge cluster via Azure Arc.
- It monitors a Git repository for changes (for example, Helm charts, YAML manifests).
- When changes are detected, it automatically applies them to the cluster.
- Supports rollback, version history, and auditability.

This ensures **declarative, consistent, and automated delivery** of configurations across multiple edge sites without needing to SSH into remote nodes or manually push updates.

Azure Policy, Security, and Configuration Management

One of the biggest challenges in edge environments is **compliance and security at scale**. Azure Arc allows cloud-native governance tooling to be extended to edge clusters.

Features include:

- Enforcing **Azure Policies** such as allowed container registries or namespace restrictions.
- Running **security baselines** (for example, CIS benchmarks).
- Integrating with **Azure Defender for Containers** for threat detection.
- Applying **Configuration Management** across distributed clusters using Azure Policy + Guest Configuration.

This standardizes governance across heterogeneous environments, making edge as secure as cloud.

Azure Monitor / Log Analytics

Azure Arc also integrates edge clusters with **Azure Monitor** and **Log Analytics**, enabling observability of workloads running far from core data centers.

Capabilities include:

- Collecting performance metrics (CPU, memory, pod status).
- Logging Kubernetes events, system logs, and container logs.
- Visualizing trends in the Azure Portal.
- Sending alerts for node failure, pod crashes, or anomalous behavior.

This is particularly useful for edge scenarios where manual log collection is infeasible and real-time insight is needed for fleet-wide health monitoring.

Practical Example: Edge Cluster in a Retail Store

Let us imagine a large retailer that deploys K3s clusters to 1,000 stores across regions. Each cluster runs a set of applications that manage point-of-sale data, inventory sensors, and digital signage. Using Azure Arc:

- The head office centrally pushes updates via GitOps.
- Policy ensures that only the approved workloads run.
- Logs and alerts from all stores are visible in a unified dashboard.
- Edge clusters can function even if disconnected temporarily, then resync when back online.

This architecture enables **autonomous edge operations with centralized control**, ideal for retail, manufacturing, oil and gas, and logistics.

Figure 12.3 elegantly captures how Azure Arc transforms edge Kubernetes management:

- Central control plane brings consistency and security.
- Lightweight edge runtimes like K3s/MK8s are perfect for remote environments.
- GitOps provides hands-free configuration management.
- Azure Monitor and Policy ensure compliance and insight.

By bridging cloud-native tooling with edge-native deployments, Azure Arc enables scalable, secure, and automated edge computing at enterprise scale.

When to Deploy Apps Across Cloud-Edge Environments

Edge computing is not suitable for every workload. The decision to deploy workloads to the edge versus centralized cloud should be based on **data sensitivity, latency requirements, network conditions, and processing scale**.

Scenario	**Recommended Target**
Low latency analytics (<10ms)	Edge (K3s with GPUs)
Autonomous retail kiosks or POS	Edge (K3s + Azure Arc)
Batch analytics or training models	Cloud (AKS + GPUs)
Offline or intermittent connectivity	Edge
Central policy, compliance management	Azure Arc

Table 12.6: *Apps across Edge versus Centralized Cloud*

Example: A large retail chain collects customer footfall data through in-store video feeds. Edge devices preprocess this data to extract anonymized heatmaps and only transmit summaries to the cloud for historical analysis.

How to Automate Edge Rollouts and Central Monitoring

Automating edge application delivery is essential when managing thousands of edge sites. This is achieved using **GitOps**, lightweight CI/CD pipelines, and monitoring agents connected to Azure.

Key Design Practices:

- **GitOps-Based Edge Rollout:**
  - Use **Flux** (built into Azure Arc) to push configurations from a Git repo.
  - Applications are deployed as Helm charts or Kustomize overlays.
- **Centralized Monitoring with Azure Monitor + Arc Agent:**
  - Each edge cluster installs the Azure Monitor agent.
  - Logs and metrics are streamed to Log Analytics in Azure for central observability.
- **Declarative Policy Management:**
  - Azure Policy for Kubernetes (via Azure Arc) ensures that every edge cluster complies with security, naming, and resource usage policies.

Hands-on Lab: Deploying a Data Pipeline to K3s Edge Cluster with Azure Arc

This lab demonstrates how to deploy a simulated IoT data collector application to a K3s edge cluster registered with Azure Arc.

Prerequisites

- Azure subscription
- K3s cluster (on VM or Raspberry Pi)
- Azure CLI, Helm, Git installed

Step 1: Register the Cluster with Azure Arc

```
bash

az connectedk8s connect --name edge-retail-cluster \
  --resource-group edge-k8s-rg \
  --location eastus
```

Step 2: Install Flux for GitOps-Based Deployments

```
bash

az k8s-configuration flux create \
  --resource-group edge-k8s-rg \
  --cluster-name edge-retail-cluster \
  --name edge-config \
  --namespace edge-iot \
  --cluster-type connectedClusters \
  --scope cluster \
  --url https://github.com/myorg/iot-pipelines \
  --branch main \
  --sync-interval 5m \
  --kustomization name=iot-deploy path=./manifests prune=true
```

Step 3: Sample YAML (IoT App Deployment)

```
yaml

apiVersion: apps/v1
kind: Deployment
```

```
metadata:
  name: iot-sensor-app
  namespace: edge-iot
spec:
  replicas: 1
  selector:
    matchLabels:
      app: iot-sensor
  template:
    metadata:
      labels:
        app: iot-sensor
    spec:
      containers:
      - name: sensor
        image: myregistry.azurecr.io/iot-sensor:latest
        env:
        - name: SENSOR_TYPE
          value: "temperature"
        ports:
        - containerPort: 8080
---
apiVersion: v1
kind: Service
metadata:
  name: iot-sensor-service
  namespace: edge-iot
spec:
  type: ClusterIP
  selector:
    app: iot-sensor
  ports:
  - port: 80
    targetPort: 8080
```

Step 4: Monitoring and Logs

Enable Azure Monitor via:

```
bash

az k8s-extension create \
  --name azuremonitor-containers \
  --extension-type Microsoft.AzureMonitor.Containers \
  --cluster-type connectedClusters \
  --cluster-name edge-retail-cluster \
  --resource-group edge-k8s-rg
```

This will enable log collection from pods and send it to Azure Log Analytics.

Case Study: Retail Edge Data Processing with Azure Arc + K3s

Context: A multinational retailer wants to enable real-time demand forecasting and anomaly detection at each of its 500 stores.

Architecture:

- K3s cluster deployed at each store on a mini-server.
- Each store cluster is registered to Azure Arc.

- IoT camera data is preprocessed locally using OpenCV, and ML models (TinyML) run in the cluster.
- Summarized results (for example, people count, aisle traffic) are sent to Azure for aggregation.
- Azure Monitor collects metrics, logs; Azure Policy ensures security compliance.

Outcomes:

- Achieved sub-50ms decision latency at the store level.
- Reduced cloud egress costs by over 70%.
- Central team can push updates, patches, and ML models via GitOps.

Future of Container Orchestration

Why the Kubernetes Ecosystem is Evolving Beyond Orchestration

While Kubernetes has become the industry-standard platform for container orchestration, its scope is rapidly extending beyond simply managing pods and services. Enterprises today demand **developer self-service**, **zero-trust security models**, **deep observability**, and **composable platforms**. These requirements are pushing Kubernetes into a broader ecosystem where it is no longer just a scheduler but a **platform foundation**.

Modern applications are **polyglot, distributed, and dynamic**, spanning runtimes such as containers, functions, and WebAssembly (WASM). These workloads demand fine-grained networking, low-latency security enforcement, and multi-environment policy control–all areas where traditional Kubernetes alone falls short.

As a result, the Kubernetes landscape is evolving toward:

- Programmable infrastructure (eBPF, service meshes).
- Runtime diversity (WASM, microVMs, serverless).
- Policy-driven automation (OPA, Kyverno).
- Self-service internal developer platforms (IDPs) aligned with platform engineering practices.

This evolution transforms Kubernetes into the **control plane of modern cloud-native platforms**, extending its reach to edge, hybrid, and multi-cloud environments while introducing **declarative governance and dynamic runtime optimization**.

Emerging Trends: eBPF, WASM, Cilium, Platform Engineering

Let us unpack the major trends reshaping the container orchestration landscape.

eBPF (Extended Berkeley Packet Filter)

eBPF is a Linux kernel technology that allows sandboxed programs to run in the kernel space. Tools such as **Cilium** use eBPF to deliver advanced networking, observability, and security without modifying the kernel.

- Eliminates sidecar proxies for observability and security.
- Enables low-overhead network visibility and policy enforcement.
- Powers zero-trust and real-time telemetry at the kernel level.

Example: Using Cilium with Azure Kubernetes Service (AKS) to enforce L3-L7 network policies and monitor service-to-service communication without deploying Envoy sidecars.

WASM (WebAssembly)

WebAssembly is a portable binary instruction format designed for high-performance execution. WASM is gaining traction for running **sandboxed workloads** inside Kubernetes due to its fast startup times, low memory usage, and strong isolation.

- Useful for running serverless functions or compute-intensive plugins.
- Emerging runtimes such as **wasmtime**, **Spin**, and **Krustlet** integrate WASM into K8s.
- WASM can run securely even on edge nodes with limited resources.

Example: A serverless WASM function executes a fraud detection rule in <10ms at an edge cluster, deployed using Krustlet on AKS with Azure Arc.

Cilium

Cilium, built on eBPF, replaces traditional kube-proxy and enables:

- L3/L7-aware network policies.
- Transparent encryption (IPSec/WireGuard).
- Native service mesh mode (without sidecars).
- Built-in Hubble observability.

In AKS, Cilium is available via Azure's **BYOCNI (Bring Your Own CNI)** model.

Platform Engineering

Rather than building infrastructure ad hoc, organizations are moving toward **productizing their internal platforms**. Platform Engineering focuses on:

- Building **Internal Developer Platforms (IDPs)**.
- Providing golden paths, templates, and abstractions.
- Automating onboarding, deployment, and monitoring.

Tools such as **Backstage**, **Crossplane**, and **Port** are often integrated with Kubernetes-based platforms to build these IDPs. Azure DevOps, GitHub Actions, and Azure Service Catalogs complement this model by enabling controlled self-service workflows.

Adopting Next-Gen Paradigms for Security, Observability, and Performance

The decision to adopt these emerging paradigms depends on the scale, complexity, and maturity of your cloud-native ecosystem.

Use Case	**Recommended Technology**
Multi-team platform with reusable infrastructure	Platform Engineering with Backstage
Advanced network policy and visibility	Cilium with eBPF
Low-latency serverless and multi-runtime support	WASM with Krustlet or Spin
Secure, declarative access control and policy	OPA/Gatekeeper or Kyverno
Cloud-native multi-runtime application stack	Combine AKS + WASM + eBPF-based CNI

Table 12.7: *Adoption of Emerging Paradigms- Use Cases*

Example: A fintech company with strict security requirements moves from Envoy sidecars to Cilium with eBPF on Azure Kubernetes Service. They gain 30% performance improvement and adopt OPA for dynamic runtime policies across multiple clusters.

Architecting for Multi-Runtime, Zero-Trust, and Policy-as-Code Futures

To future-proof Kubernetes platforms, architecture must support the following principles:

Multi-Runtime Architecture

Support containers, WASM modules, and serverless functions within a unified control plane.

Azure Example:

- AKS as the base control plane.
- Integrate WASM via **Krustelet nodes**.
- Use **Azure Container Apps** for serverless runtimes.

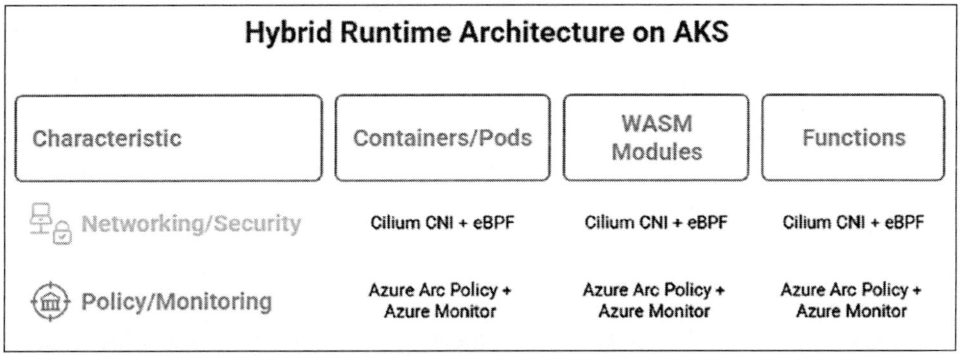

***Figure 12.4**: Hybrid Runtime Architecture on AKS*

Explanation- Hybrid Runtime Architecture on AKS:

As Kubernetes continues to evolve as the universal control plane for cloud-native workloads, modern clusters are no longer limited to just container-based applications. Emerging technologies such as WebAssembly (WASM) and serverless functions are being integrated alongside traditional workloads. Azure Kubernetes Service (AKS) offers an ideal platform to run these hybrid runtime environments securely, observably, and at scale.

This architecture demonstrates how containers, WASM modules, and functions can coexist and interoperate within a single AKS environment, powered by modern networking (eBPF), observability (Azure Monitor), and policy governance (Azure Arc).

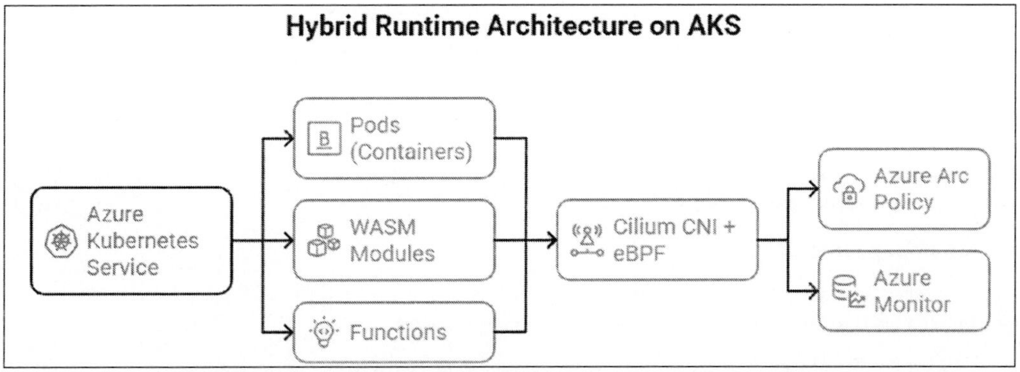

***Figure 12.5**: Hybrid Runtime Architecture on Azure Kubernetes Service (AKS)*

Step-by-Step Breakdown of the Architecture

1. **Azure Kubernetes Service (AKS)**

AKS serves as the orchestrated environment that provides:

- Managed Kubernetes control plane
- Cluster autoscaling and node pool management
- Integrated Azure identity and security

It acts as the foundation for hosting a diverse set of runtime workloads in a unified ecosystem.

Hybrid Workload Runtimes

AKS is extended to support **three distinct runtime types**, making it hybrid:

- **Pods (Traditional Containers)**
    - These are standard OCI containers (Docker or containerd) that run microservices, APIs, databases, and more.
    - Pods are deployed via Deployments, StatefulSets, or Jobs, and managed natively by Kubernetes.
- **WASM Modules**
    - WebAssembly (WASM) workloads are compiled from languages such as Rust, Go, or C++ and offer a lightweight, secure execution model.
    - WASM modules can run inside Kubernetes using runtimes such as WasmEdge, Wasmtime, or Spin, and are ideal for fast-startup microservices, plugin systems, and edge computing.
- **Functions**
    - Functions (often associated with serverless models) run as stateless, event-driven workloads.
    - AKS can host **Azure Functions** using the KEDA scaler and Kubernetes-based function runtimes, enabling integration with event sources such as Service Bus, Kafka, or HTTP.

These three workloads—containers, WASM, and serverless functions—are all orchestrated within the same AKS cluster, offering **runtime flexibility** without fragmenting infrastructure.

Cilium CNI and eBPF

To secure and observe these mixed workloads at the networking level, AKS integrates **Cilium** as the **Container Network Interface (CNI)**. Cilium uses **eBPF (Extended Berkeley Packet Filter)** to:

- Perform fine-grained network policy enforcement (for example, L7 HTTP rules).
- Provide real-time observability into service communication.
- Apply identity-based policies, independent of IP addressing.
- Reduce overhead compared to traditional iptables-based models.

eBPF runs directly in the Linux kernel, making it highly performant and scalable for complex runtime environments.

This ensures that even lightweight WASM modules and functions are subject to the same secure, observable networking layer as containers.

Azure Arc Policy Integration

AKS can be **attached to Azure Arc**, enabling GitOps-driven and declarative policy enforcement, even across hybrid and multi-cloud environments. With Azure Arc:

- **Policy definitions** (for example, deny-privileged-containers, restrict image registries) are applied at cluster or namespace level.

- **WASM workloads** and functions can be subjected to policy compliance just like traditional pods.
- Enables centralized control for DevSecOps governance.

This integration is crucial in a hybrid runtime model to ensure **uniform compliance**, regardless of the runtime type.

Azure Monitor for Observability

All runtime types emit metrics and logs—containers via stdout/stderr, WASM via instrumented observability modules, and functions via bindings and events.

Azure Monitor ingests:

- Prometheus metrics (via OpenTelemetry, kube-state-metrics)
- Container logs (via Fluent Bit or Log Analytics Agent)
- Distributed traces (via OpenTelemetry or Dapr instrumentation)

This allows operators to:

- Track application health,
- Correlate failures across different runtime types,
- Set up alerting and dashboards in Azure Portal or Grafana.

Unified observability ensures that debugging, monitoring, and performance optimization are **consistent across workloads**.

Summary: Why Hybrid Runtime Matters

This hybrid runtime architecture reflects the **future of Kubernetes workloads**:

- **Containers** provide stable, scalable, and widely adopted application packaging.
- **WASM** introduces fast, secure, lightweight compute ideal for edge, plugin, and performance-critical tasks.
- **Functions** enable event-driven architecture with elastic scaling and operational simplicity.

AKS becomes a **unified control and execution plane**, supporting these diverse runtimes under common layers of networking, security, policy, and observability.

Practical Use Case Example

A fintech company deploys a fraud detection pipeline:

- Core data analysis workloads run in **containers.**
- Lightweight event processing plugins run in **WASM modules** for faster startup and sandboxing.
- Notification handlers are written as **functions** triggered by message queues.

All workloads:

- Are subject to Cilium eBPF network policies.
- Are monitored by Azure Monitor.
- Comply with centralized GitOps-based Azure Arc policies.

This real-world alignment showcases the power of **hybrid runtime architecture** in production-grade Kubernetes environments.

Zero-Trust Networking with eBPF

Replace TLS-based mesh proxies with eBPF-powered Cilium mesh.

- Enforce per-service identity.

- Encrypt communication at the kernel level.
- Log flows via Hubble without sidecars.

Policy as Code

Integrate runtime policy enforcement with GitOps using tools, such as:

- **OPA/Gatekeeper** for RBAC and access policy.
- **Kyverno** for resource mutation/validation.
- **Azure Policy** for cluster-wide governance.

Example OPA Policy to Block Privileged Containers:

```
package kubernetes.admission

deny[msg] {
  input.request.kind.kind == "Pod"
  input.request.object.spec.containers[_].securityContext.privileged == true
  msg := "Privileged containers are not allowed."
}
```

Developer Self-Service via Internal Platforms

- Expose golden paths using Azure DevOps pipelines or GitHub Actions.
- Enable developers to deploy predefined Helm charts via Backstage UI.
- Use Crossplane to offer infrastructure resources as CRDs.

Strategic Outlook: Role of Kubernetes in Platform-as-a-Product Mindset

Kubernetes is no longer just a cluster orchestrator–it is the **foundation of internal cloud platforms**. In the **platform-as-a-product** mindset:

- The platform team treats infrastructure as a product with SLAs and feedback loops.
- Developers consume self-service workflows, not YAML files.
- Platform maturity is measured by velocity, reliability, and compliance.

Key Principles:

- Treat the platform as an evolving software product.
- Abstract complexity behind APIs and UI portals.
- Empower teams without compromising governance.

Azure-Driven Model:

- AKS + Azure Arc for control and governance.
- Azure Policy + Monitor for compliance.
- GitOps + DevOps pipelines for lifecycle automation.
- Backstage or Azure Service Catalog for self-service.

Case Study: Platform Engineering with Kubernetes + Cilium on AKS

Industry: Enterprise SaaS

Challenge: The engineering team needed fine-grained observability, zero-trust networking, and a self-service platform for over 100 microservices.

Solution:

- Deployed AKS with **BYOCNI** using Cilium for eBPF-based networking.
- Enabled GitOps-based rollout using Flux and Azure Arc.
- Used **OPA** for real-time policy enforcement.
- Built an internal developer platform with **Backstage**, exposing golden paths backed by Helm charts and Azure Pipelines.

Outcomes:

- Reduced MTTR by 40% due to eBPF-based observability.
- Achieved full PCI-DSS compliance using policy-as-code.
- Cut onboarding time for new apps by 60%.

Career Path and Certifications for Kubernetes Professionals

In today's rapidly shifting cloud-native landscape, Kubernetes has emerged not just as a platform, but as a de facto operating system for modern infrastructure. This shift has redefined the expectations from engineers and architects alike. Certifications validate not only one's theoretical understanding but also the hands-on expertise required to operate Kubernetes in real-world production environments.

For Cloud Engineers, DevOps Engineers, and Cloud Architects, holding a Kubernetes certification serves multiple functions:

- **Professional credibility** in cross-functional and cross-cloud teams.
- **Organizational trust**, especially when managing sensitive deployments such as financial, healthcare, or multi-tenant workloads.
- **Demonstrable expertise** in complex topics such as GitOps, security, observability, and CI/CD automation within Kubernetes-based systems.
- **Career acceleration** into senior or strategic roles such as Platform Engineer, Site Reliability Engineer (SRE), or Cloud Solution Architect.

Within regulated Azure enterprise environments, certified Kubernetes professionals are often key decision-makers in infrastructure governance, compliance alignment (for example, Azure Policy + Azure Defender for Kubernetes), and automation scaling.

What Certifications to Pursue (CKA, CKAD, CKS, KCNA)

The Cloud Native Computing Foundation (CNCF) offers four critical Kubernetes certifications that cover progressive learning and specialization tracks:

- **KCNA (Kubernetes and Cloud Native Associate)**
    - o **Audience**: Entry-level engineers, students, or professionals transitioning into cloud-native.
    - o **Focus**: Cloud-native principles, architecture, container orchestration basics, and ecosystem tools.
    - o **Value**: Provides foundational fluency before tackling CKA or CKAD.
- **CKA (Certified Kubernetes Administrator)**
    - o **Audience**: DevOps engineers, cloud administrators, SREs.
    - o **Focus**: Cluster administration, scheduling, storage, networking, and troubleshooting.

- **Azure Alignment**: Skills map directly to AKS (Azure Kubernetes Service), ARM templates, Azure Monitor, and Azure Load Balancer configurations.

- **CKAD (Certified Kubernetes Application Developer)**
  - **Audience**: Software engineers, backend developers, data pipeline engineers.
  - **Focus**: Pod design, configuration, observability, and application lifecycle.
  - **Azure Alignment**: Relevant for AKS-based app development with Azure DevOps or GitHub Actions pipelines.
- **CKS (Certified Kubernetes Security Specialist)**
  - **Audience**: Security engineers, cloud architects, platform engineers.
  - **Focus**: Secure cluster configurations, RBAC, network policies, and supply chain security.
  - **Azure Alignment**: Maps closely to Azure Policy, Azure Defender for Containers, and Microsoft Entra ID (Azure AD) RBAC integration.

The Certification Ladder Diagram is illustrated in the following figure:

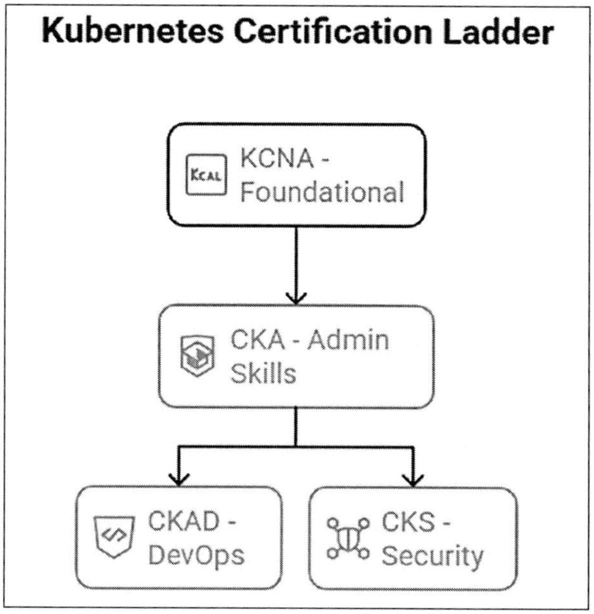

Figure 12.6: *Kubernetes Certification Ladder*

When and How to Plan Certification + Hands-on Preparation

Certifications should be pursued in a phased, purpose-driven manner - depending on your career intent, domain maturity, and current technical footprint. The following matrix provides practical guidance:

Role	Recommended Start	Timeline	Tools for Hands-on Labs
Cloud/DevOps Engineer	KCNA → CKA	3–6 months	Azure AKS, K3d, Kind, kubeadm, Terraform
Software Engineer	KCNA → CKAD	3–5 months	Minikube, AKS Dev Spaces, Helm, Skaffold

Security Architect	CKA → CKS	4-8 months	Azure Defender, Kyverno, Gatekeeper, OPA
Data/ML Engineer	KCNA → CKAD/CKA	4-6 months	Kubeflow, Ray, Azure ML, PVC, CSI drivers

Table 12.8: *Certification Planning and Phases*

Practical Tip:

Use **Azure AKS free tier clusters** with GPU or standard node pools to create realistic practice environments. Integrate Azure Monitor for observability and deploy real CI/CD pipelines using GitHub Actions or Azure DevOps for authentic workloads.

How to Grow from Engineer to Architect or Platform Owner

Achieving Kubernetes certification is only the beginning. The real evolution comes from applying that knowledge to production-grade architecture decisions. This shift requires transitioning from *task execution* to *platform thinking*—designing systems that abstract complexity for broader teams.

Core Growth Vectors

- **Contribute to Internal Developer Platforms (IDP):** Use tools such as Backstage, Crossplane, or Azure Arc to expose reusable Kubernetes infrastructure components.
- **Participate in Governance and Policy-as-Code:** Work with Azure Policy, Open Policy Agent (OPA), and Gatekeeper to define guardrails and enforce multi-tenant security.
- **Adopt Multi-Cloud or Hybrid Strategies:** Use Azure Arc for Kubernetes to manage edge, on-prem, and multi-cloud clusters through a unified control plane.
- **Evangelize GitOps and Platform Engineering:** Drive enterprise-level automation using FluxCD, ArgoCD, Terraform, and Helm in an Azure-native environment.

Career Transition path

Engineer → Senior Engineer → Platform Engineer → Solution Architect → Platform Owner

- **Engineer**: Manages deployments and YAML manifests.
- **Platform Engineer**: Automates lifecycle, enables dev teams, and integrates with Azure services.
- **Platform Owner**: Aligns platform strategy with business outcomes, SLAs, and compliance.

Roadmap: Continuous Learning Paths and Open Source Contributions

Learning Paths: Becoming a recognized Kubernetes expert requires continuous investment in both learning and community involvement.

Pathway	Tools and Skills	Azure Relevance
GitOps	FluxCD, ArgoCD, Azure DevOps	GitOps in AKS, Azure Repos
Observability	Prometheus, Grafana, Azure Monitor	Custom dashboards for AKS and Application Insights
Security and Governance	OPA, Kyverno, Azure Defender	Azure Policy, K8s Threat Detection
Platform Engineering	Backstage, Crossplane, Helm	Azure Service Operator (ASO) for Kubernetes

Table 12.9: *Learning Path*

Open-Source Contributions

Contribute to CNCF projects such as:

- **KEDA:** Event-driven autoscaling
- **Flux:** GitOps delivery
- **Dapr:** Distributed application runtime
- **OpenFaaS:** Serverless on Kubernetes

Even minor documentation updates or bug fixes are highly valued and demonstrate initiative.

Case Study: Building a Platform Engineer Career in Azure Kubernetes

Scenario: A DevOps Engineer at a fintech company running Azure-native workloads decides to transition into a Platform Architect role.

Actions:

- Completes **CKA + CKS** within 6-12 months.
- Builds a GitOps-based CI/CD pipeline on AKS using **FluxCD + Terraform + Azure Key Vault**.
- Implements **OPA Gatekeeper** to restrict privileged workloads.
- Creates self-service deployment templates for internal teams using **Backstage + Helm charts**.
- Submits PRs to Azure/AKS GitHub samples and earns CNCF contributor badge.

Outcome: Within a year, the engineer becomes a Platform Engineering Lead and is involved in shaping the company's compliance and developer enablement strategy.

Conclusion

As Kubernetes continues to evolve beyond orchestration into a platform engineering foundation, professionals must stay ahead of emerging paradigms such as AI/ML integration, serverless containers, edge computing, and next-gen technologies such as eBPF and WASM. This chapter unpacked how tools including KEDA, Azure Arc, and Kubernetes-native security frameworks reshape operational models and career trajectories. With cloud-native infrastructure becoming more dynamic and decentralized, mastering these innovations is no longer optional – it is essential for building future-proof platforms on Azure and beyond.

In the next chapter, we will dive deep into advanced Kubernetes concepts that are crucial for running production-grade, distributed systems. We will explore the inner workings of StatefulSets for managing persistent applications, advanced scheduling techniques for workload placement, and strategies for operating across multiple clusters with reliability and scale. With practical examples and Azure-native references, this chapter will sharpen your architecture and operational mastery in complex Kubernetes environments.

CHAPTER 13

Advanced K8s - StatefulSets and Multi-Cluster Management

Introduction

As Kubernetes environments evolve, particularly in large-scale deployments, they become increasingly complex. This chapter dives into how Kubernetes handles stateful applications with StatefulSets, implements fine-grained resource scheduling strategies, and efficiently manages multi-cluster environments to achieve scalability, resilience, and high availability in modern enterprise systems.

Structure

In this chapter, we will cover the following topics:

- Stateful Applications with StatefulSets
- Kubernetes Scheduling and Resource Management
- Multi-Cluster Federation and Hybrid Cloud Management
- Real-World Use Cases and Best Practices
- Considerations for Data Engineers and Architects

Stateful Applications with StatefulSets

Kubernetes was originally designed to handle stateless applications – those that do not retain user or transactional data between sessions – making it ideal for web frontends, RESTful services, and API gateways. However, running **stateful applications**, such as relational databases, message brokers, and distributed file systems, introduces unique challenges including:

- **Persistent State**: Databases and queues maintain critical state – for instance, a PostgreSQL database stores user data and Kafka retains message offsets. These must persist beyond the life cycle of individual pods.
- **Stable Network Identity**: Clustering and replication often require stable DNS names or peer identities (for example, `cassandra-0`, `kafka-1`).
- **Persistent Storage**: Applications must retain access to their underlying storage volumes even after being terminated or rescheduled.

- **Order-sensitive Lifecycle**: Systems such as ZooKeeper or etcd rely on an ordered startup and shutdown to maintain quorum integrity.

Traditional Kubernetes controllers such as **Deployments** and **ReplicaSets** are insufficient for these needs as they treat pods as interchangeable and ephemeral. **StatefulSets** were introduced to address this limitation.

An Overview of StatefulSet

A **StatefulSet** is a specialized Kubernetes controller that manages the deployment and scaling of stateful applications. It provides:

- **Stable Pod Identity**: Pods are named deterministically (`pod-0`, `pod-1`, and more), which is essential for intra-cluster discovery.
- **Sticky Storage**: Each pod is associated with a `PersistentVolumeClaim` (PVC) that survives pod termination and is reattached upon restart.
- **Ordered Lifecycle Management**: Pods are started, stopped, and updated in a controlled sequence.
- **Headless Services**: Enable DNS-based service discovery (for example, `db-0.mydb headless.svc.cluster.local`).

These features make StatefulSets the right choice for workloads such as PostgreSQL clusters, Kafka brokers, and Cassandra rings.

Managing Distributed Databases with StatefulSets on Kubernetes

PostgreSQL Cluster on AKS (Azure Kubernetes Service)

- **Use Case:** High-availability PostgreSQL with failover and replication (for example, Patroni-managed).
- **AKS Considerations:**
  - Leverage Azure Managed Disks for PVCs.
  - Use a **Headless Service** for DNS-based peer resolution.
  - Implement custom Kubernetes operators such as **Zalando Postgres Operator** for auto-recovery and health checks.
  - Deploy in availability zones for high resilience.

Cassandra Cluster on AKS

- **Use Case:** Horizontal scalability and fault-tolerant writes for IoT or big data workloads.
- **Design Notes:**
  - Each node must have a unique identity and persistent volume.
  - Use **anti-affinity rules** to spread nodes across AKS worker nodes.
  - Favor **Azure Premium SSDs** for low-latency reads/writes.
  - Integrate with **Prometheus** for health and ring visibility.

Kafka Brokers on AKS

- **Use Case:** Event-driven architecture with stream processing.
- **Design Requirements:**

- Maintain broker ID and partition logs via stateful volumes.
- Coordinate with external Zookeeper or use KRaft (Kafka's native consensus engine).
- Persistent disk is required for log durability between restarts.
- Use a headless service for broker-to-broker communication.

Using Volume Persistence and Dynamic Provisioning for StatefulSets

StatefulSets are designed for applications that require stable, persistent storage. Ensuring that data remains intact across pod restarts or rescheduling events is crucial for stateful workloads. This is where volume persistence and dynamic provisioning come into play.

Persistent Volume Claims Per Pod

Each pod in a StatefulSet receives its **own** PVC. Kubernetes ensures volume rebinding if a pod restarts. This guarantees no data loss during rescheduling or crash recovery.

Azure-AKS Volume Provisioning with StorageClass

In Azure, volume provisioning is handled dynamically using **StorageClasses** backed by Azure Managed Disks.

```
yaml

apiVersion: storage.k8s.io/v1
kind: StorageClass
metadata:
  name: managed-premium
provisioner: disk.csi.azure.com
parameters:
  skuName: Premium_LRS
reclaimPolicy: Retain
volumeBindingMode: WaitForFirstConsumer
```

- **`skuName: Premium_LRS`** ensures performance-grade SSDs.
- **`reclaimPolicy: Retain`** protects against unintentional volume deletion.
- **`volumeBindingMode: WaitForFirstConsumer`** ensures that the disk is provisioned only when scheduled, improving placement accuracy.

Architecting Stateful Applications with StatefulSets - Azure Reference

This section presents an Azure-focused architectural perspective on deploying and operating stateful workloads using Kubernetes StatefulSets. It highlights platform-specific design considerations, storage choices, networking patterns, and operational best practices when running stateful systems on Azure Kubernetes Service (AKS).

Architectural Flow Diagram

This diagram illustrates how Kubernetes StatefulSets manage stateful pods on Azure Kubernetes Service (AKS), where each pod maintains a stable identity and is bound to a dedicated Azure Managed Disk through a `PersistentVolumeClaim`.

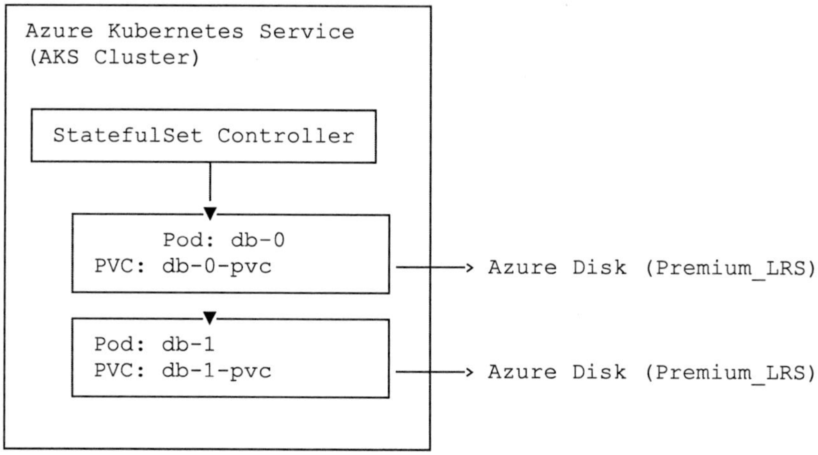

***Figure* 13.1:** *Azure AKS Statefulset Architecture with Persistent Volumes*

Architectural Highlights

- **Stateful Pods:** Each pod has a unique hostname (**`db-0`**, **`db-1`**) and a dedicated volume.
- **Persistent Disks:** Azure Premium SSDs provide low-latency IOPS and are retained upon pod deletion.
- **Headless Services:** DNS resolution supports internal communication for consensus or clustering.
- **StorageClass Automation:** Ensures Azure-native provisioning and retention of volumes aligned with StatefulSet semantics.

Architecting Stateful Applications with StatefulSets on Azure AKS

Modern cloud-native platforms often rely on **stateless microservices** for scalability and resilience. However, many mission-critical applications—such as databases, distributed caches, and message brokers—require stable network identity, persistent storage, and ordered deployment. Kubernetes addresses these needs using **StatefulSets**, a controller specifically designed to orchestrate **stateful workloads**.

This section explores how Azure Kubernetes Service (AKS) supports stateful applications through StatefulSets, using **Azure Disks** for persistence and leveraging **StorageClasses** for automated volume management.

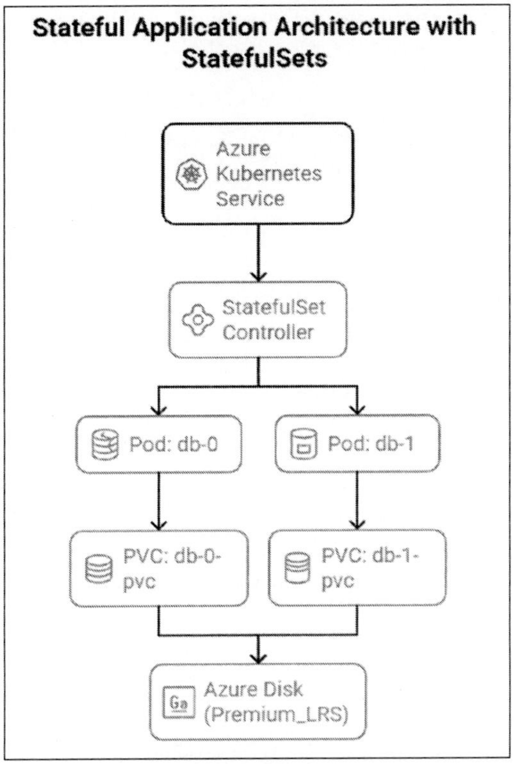

Figure 13.2: *Stateful Application Architecture with StatefulSets*

Step-by-Step Architecture Breakdown

1. **Azure Kubernetes Service (AKS)**

AKS provides the underlying infrastructure for managing containerized workloads. In this scenario, it acts as the platform on which the StatefulSet is deployed. AKS abstracts the complexity of cluster provisioning, scaling, networking, and integration with Azure-native storage systems.

2. **StatefulSet Controller**

The StatefulSet controller is a Kubernetes workload API object that:

- Manages **ordered** deployment and scaling of pods.
- Guarantees **stable, unique network identities** (such as, `db-0`, `db-1`).
- Maintains a **one-to-one mapping** between a pod and a persistent volume claim (PVC).
- Enforces **pod re-creation** in the same order after failures or restarts.

In our architecture, the StatefulSet controller is responsible for deploying two pods: `db-0` and `db-1`.

3. **Stateful Pods: `db-0` and `db-1`**

Unlike stateless Deployments, each pod in a StatefulSet:

- Has a consistent DNS name: for example, `db-0.myservice.namespace.svc.cluster.local`.
- Is assigned a **persistent identity** that does not change, even when the pod is rescheduled.
- Starts and stops **in order** based on ordinal indices (important for consensus protocols like Raft or Paxos).

In this example, two pods are created (**`db-0`**, **`db-1`**), ideal for distributed databases such as Cassandra, MongoDB, or etcd.

4. **`PersistentVolumeClaims` (PVCs)**

Each pod has a dedicated Persistent Volume Claim:

- **`db-0`** is bound to **`db-0-pvc`**
- **`db-1`** is bound to **`db-1-pvc`**

This mapping is **non-interchangeable**. Even if the pod is deleted and recreated, Kubernetes ensures it **rebinds to the same PVC**, preserving state and application continuity.

PVCs are provisioned dynamically based on the **StorageClass** associated with the StatefulSet.

5. **Azure Disks (`Premium_LRS`)**

PVCs in AKS are typically backed by Azure-managed storage. In this case, we use:

- **Azure Premium Managed Disks (`Premium_LRS`)** – which offer:
  - High IOPS (input/output operations per second)
  - Low latency
  - Data durability guarantees with Locally Redundant Storage (LRS)

These disks:

- Are attached to the node where the pod runs.
- Retain data even when pods are terminated or moved.
- Can only be mounted to one node at a time (ReadWriteOnce).

This makes them well-suited for primary database workloads that require strong data consistency and performance.

Supporting Concepts (Not shown but essential):

a. **Headless Services**

   A StatefulSet is typically paired with a **Headless Service** (**`clusterIP: None`**) that allows each pod to be accessed directly using DNS. This is essential for:

   - Internal service discovery
   - Inter-pod communication in clustered databases

b. **`StorageClass` Configuration**

   The underlying volumes are dynamically provisioned via Kubernetes **`StorageClass`** objects. A StorageClass in AKS may look like:

```
yaml

kind: StorageClass
apiVersion: storage.k8s.io/v1
metadata:
  name: premium-managed
provisioner: kubernetes.io/azure-disk
parameters:
  storageaccounttype: Premium_LRS
reclaimPolicy: Retain
```

The **`Retain`** policy ensures that volumes are **not deleted** when PVCs are deleted – useful in disaster recovery and manual reattachment scenarios.

Summary: Why Use StatefulSets?

StatefulSets are essential for building reliable, distributed applications that require:

- **Consistent identity** and **ordering guarantees.**
- **Dedicated storage** that survives restarts.
- Seamless support for **Azure-native disks.**
- Integration with **Kubernetes DNS**, **StorageClasses**, and **monitoring tools.**

In the AKS context, StatefulSets align well with Azure's managed disk offerings, enabling **production-grade persistence** without third-party storage layers.

Real-World Use Case Example

Scenario: A financial institution runs a PostgreSQL-based microservice with leader-follower clustering.

How this architecture helps:

- StatefulSet ensures that predictable pod names for internal PostgreSQL replication (`pg-0`, `pg-1`).
- Azure Disks retain WAL logs and tables across rolling updates.
- Headless services simplify HAProxy-based routing.

This level of orchestration ensures high availability, recoverability, and performance for stateful applications in production.

Hands-On YAML Lab: PostgreSQL StatefulSet Deployment in Azure AKS

Step 1: Define the StorageClass

```
yaml

apiVersion: storage.k8s.io/v1
kind: StorageClass
metadata:
  name: managed-premium
provisioner: disk.csi.azure.com
parameters:
  skuName: Premium_LRS
reclaimPolicy: Retain
volumeBindingMode: WaitForFirstConsumer
```

Step 2: Create a Headless Service

```
yaml

apiVersion: v1
kind: Service
metadata:
  name: postgres-headless
spec:
  clusterIP: None
  selector:
    app: postgres
  ports:
    - port: 5432
      name: postgres
```

Step 3: Deploy the StatefulSet

```
yaml

apiVersion: apps/v1
kind: StatefulSet
metadata:
  name: postgres
spec:
  serviceName: postgres-headless
  replicas: 3
  selector:
    matchLabels:
      app: postgres
  template:
    metadata:
      labels:
        app: postgres
    spec:
      containers:
      - name: postgres
        image: postgres:13
        ports:
        - containerPort: 5432
        volumeMounts:
        - name: postgres-data
          mountPath: /var/lib/postgresql/data
        env:
        - name: POSTGRES_PASSWORD
          value: "examplepassword"
  volumeClaimTemplates:
  - metadata:
      name: postgres-data
    spec:
      accessModes: [ "ReadWriteOnce" ]
      storageClassName: managed-premium
      resources:
        requests:
          storage: 10Gi
```

Case Study: Cassandra Cluster on AKS for IoT Analytics

Scenario: A retail company implements a real-time IoT analytics platform to process telemetry from edge devices.

Architecture:

- **StatefulSet**: Cassandra deployed with 5 replicas for high availability.
- **Azure Disks**: Premium SSDs used for storage; one per pod.
- **Pod Anti-Affinity**: Ensures that each pod runs on separate nodes to prevent single-point failure.
- **Monitoring**: Integrated with Prometheus and Grafana using Cassandra-exporter.
- **DNS & Discovery**: Headless service used for inter-node communication and gossip protocol.

Outcome: The setup allows for consistent high-throughput ingestion, replication across zones, and seamless recovery from node failures.

Key Takeaways:

- Use **StatefulSets** for workloads needing identity, persistence, and ordered lifecycle management.
- Azure Managed Disks and StorageClasses provide durable, dynamic provisioning suited for AKS.
- Design for high availability using **anti-affinity rules**, **zonal awareness**, and **operators**.
- Ideal use cases: PostgreSQL clusters, Kafka brokers, Cassandra rings, Redis with persistence.
- Always test failover and backup scenarios to validate data durability and availability.

Kubernetes Scheduling and Resource Management

Kubernetes scheduling and resource management are essential components for optimizing how workloads run on your cluster. The scheduler is responsible for placing pods onto nodes based on resource requirements, availability, and constraints. Effective scheduling ensures that workloads are distributed efficiently, with high availability and minimal resource contention.

Kubernetes resource management goes hand-in-hand with scheduling by controlling how resources (CPU, memory, storage, and so on) are allocated and utilized within the cluster. With features such as resource requests and limits, Kubernetes helps ensure that pods have enough resources to function correctly while preventing over-utilization or under-utilization of the cluster's capacity.

Importance of Kubernetes Scheduling and Resource Management

Kubernetes provides a powerful scheduling mechanism to determine how and where Pods are placed within a cluster. While default behavior is sufficient for many stateless workloads, production-grade systems often demand more precise control:

- Some workloads require specific hardware configurations (for example, GPU for AI/ML, NVMe SSD for fast I/O).
- High-availability setups demand spreading workloads across zones or failure domains.
- Stateful and mission-critical workloads need graceful handling during node drain, upgrade, or failure.
- Large multi-tenant clusters must balance workloads to avoid resource starvation or contention.

In enterprise environments such as **Azure Kubernetes Service (AKS)**, understanding and applying these mechanisms is essential for maximizing uptime, ensuring security, and achieving cost-efficiency.

Kubernetes Scheduling and Resource Management Entailed Processes

Let us break down the key features available in Kubernetes for workload placement and optimization:

1. **Advanced Scheduling Policies**
    - **Node Affinity and Anti-Affinity:** Allows Pods to be scheduled based on node labels.

- **Pod Affinity/Anti-Affinity:** Controls co-location or separation of Pods based on label selectors.
- **Topology Spread Constraints:** Ensures workload distribution across zones/nodes.

2. **Taints and Tolerations**
   - **Taints:** Applied to nodes to repel Pods unless Pods explicitly tolerate them.
   - **Tolerations:** Let Pods run on tainted nodes, often used for dedicated or GPU nodes.
3. **Pod Disruption Budgets (PDB)**
   - Define acceptable levels of voluntary disruptions (for example, upgrades, maintenance) to ensure minimum availability of replicas.
4. **Resource Requests and Limits**
   - Allow specifying CPU and memory boundaries:
     - `requests`: Minimum resource guarantee.
     - `limits`: Maximum allowed resource consumption.
   - Enable the **Kubernetes scheduler** to make optimal placement decisions.

Using These Techniques in Real-World Azure AKS Clusters

The following table details real-world use cases on an AKS cluster, outlining the corresponding benefits for each scenario:

Use Case	Recommended Feature	Benefit
Distribute stateful replicas across zones	Pod anti-affinity, zone topology keys	High availability
Schedule GPU workloads for ML training	Node affinity + taints/ tolerations	Hardware targeting
Ensure 80% of app replicas remain during maintenance	Pod Disruption Budget	Controlled disruptions
Prevent overprovisioning and cost overruns	CPU/memory limits	Budget enforcement
Reserve resources for critical apps	CPU/memory requests	Stability for key services

Table 13.1: *AKS Cluster Real-World Use Case and Benefits*

These patterns are particularly critical in Azure AKS clusters operating under scale, budget constraints, or regulatory SLAs.

Implementing Scheduling and Resource Management – Azure AKS Practical Guide

Node Affinity and Anti-Affinity in Azure AKS

YAML Example: Enforcing Node Affinity

```
yaml

apiVersion: v1
kind: Pod
metadata:
  name: gpu-ml-inference
spec:
  affinity:
```

```
    nodeAffinity:
      requiredDuringSchedulingIgnoredDuringExecution:
        nodeSelectorTerms:
        - matchExpressions:
          - key: accelerator
            operator: In
            values:
            - nvidia-gpu
  containers:
  - name: model
    image: myregistry.azurecr.io/ml-inference:latest
    resources:
      requests:
        cpu: "2"
        memory: "4Gi"
```

Explanation:

- This Pod will only be scheduled to a node labeled with **`accelerator=nvidia-gpu`**, typically done for AKS nodes with GPU SKUs (for example, NC series).
- Helps isolate high-performance AI workloads to GPU-enabled nodes only.

Taints and Tolerations in Azure AKS

YAML: Defining a GPU Node Taint

```
bash

az aks nodepool update \
  --resource-group myrg \
  --cluster-name myaks \
  --name gpupool \
  --node-taints accelerator=nvidia-gpu:NoSchedule
```

YAML: Pod with Matching Toleration

```
yaml

tolerations:
- key: "accelerator"
  operator: "Equal"
  value: "nvidia-gpu"
  effect: "NoSchedule"
```

Explanation:

- Taints on GPU nodes prevent general workloads from landing there.
- Tolerations on AI/ML Pods allow only the right workload to bypass the taint.

Pod Disruption Budgets (PDB)

YAML: Ensuring Availability during Maintenance

```
yaml

apiVersion: policy/v1
kind: PodDisruptionBudget
metadata:
  name: kafka-pdb
spec:
  minAvailable: 2
```

```
    selector:
      matchLabels:
        app: kafka
```

Explanation:

- Guarantees that at least 2 Kafka brokers remain available during voluntary node disruptions.
- Azure AKS upgrades or node repairs respect this configuration to maintain service continuity.

Resource Requests and Limits

YAML: Defining Resource Boundaries

```
yaml

resources:
  requests:
    memory: "1Gi"
    cpu: "500m"
  limits:
    memory: "2Gi"
    cpu: "1"
```

Explanation:

- The scheduler uses requests to determine if a node can handle this Pod.
- The Pod is throttled at limits, preventing resource hogging and promoting fair usage.

Architectural Flow

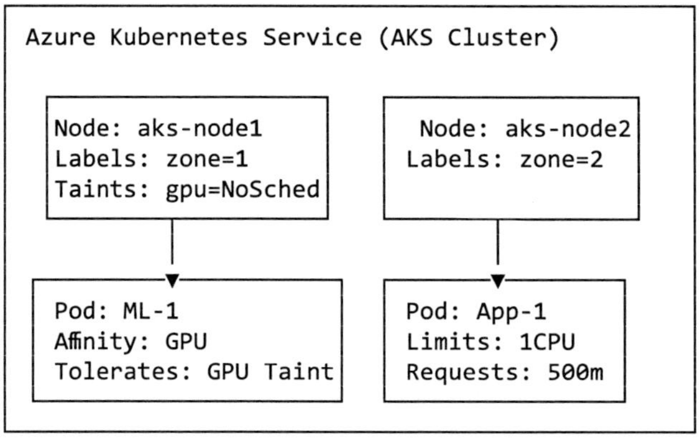

Figure 13.3: *Azure AKS Scheduling with Node Affinity, Taints and Resource Constraints*

Explanation:

ML workloads are scheduled onto GPU-enabled nodes using node affinity and taint tolerations, while general application workloads rely on resource requests and limits to prevent contention. Pod Disruption Budgets (PDBs) ensure workload resilience during node maintenance, upgrades, or failures.

Hands-On YAML Lab: Resilient Microservices with Scheduling Controls

Scenario: Run a scalable microservice app that should:

- Run across multiple zones.

- Not run on GPU nodes.
- Handle AKS upgrades, without dropping below 50% availability.

Step 1: Define Node Anti-Affinity

```
yaml

affinity:
  podAntiAffinity:
    requiredDuringSchedulingIgnoredDuringExecution:
    - labelSelector:
        matchExpressions:
        - key: app
          operator: In
          values:
          - myapp
      topologyKey: "kubernetes.io/hostname"
```

Step 2: Apply Pod Disruption Budget

```
yaml

apiVersion: policy/v1
kind: PodDisruptionBudget
metadata:
  name: myapp-pdb
spec:
  minAvailable: 3
  selector:
    matchLabels:
      app: myapp
```

Case Study: Optimizing AI Inference on Azure AKS

Industry Use Case: A software architect at a fintech company is deploying multiple AI inference services for fraud detection across Europe.

Challenge:

- Avoid overloading nodes.
- Ensure low-latency GPU inference for real-time transactions.
- Minimize disruptions during AKS upgrades.

Solution:

- Created a GPU-enabled node pool with **`accelerator=nvidia-gpu`** taint.
- Used node affinity and tolerations for inference pods only.
- Set **`PodDisruptionBudgets`** to keep at least 80% of inference capacity active.
- Enforced strict resource limits to prevent memory overruns from large models.

Outcome:

- Achieved 99.99% uptime with no dropped inference calls during upgrades.
- Azure cost savings by preventing unintentional overuse of GPU nodes.

Key Takeaways:

- **Use Node Affinity** to target specific hardware or failure zones.

- **Apply Taints and Tolerations** to isolate dedicated workloads (for example, GPU, high-memory).
- **Set Pod Disruption Budgets** to preserve workload availability during AKS upgrades or maintenance.
- **Always define Resource Requests and Limits** to guide the scheduler and control resource usage.
- In Azure AKS, leverage **zonal topology**, **premium nodes**, and **node pools** with custom labels to maximize performance, resilience, and efficiency.

Multi-Cluster Federation and Hybrid Cloud Management

As organizations scale their Kubernetes environments across multiple clusters, whether on-premises, in the cloud, or across various regions, managing these clusters as a unified system becomes a complex but critical task. Multi-cluster federation and hybrid cloud management are key strategies to address these challenges and ensure high availability, load balancing, and resilience in distributed environments.

Importance of Multi-Cluster Federation and Hybrid Cloud Management

In modern enterprise environments, organizations are expanding beyond single Kubernetes clusters to support geographically distributed applications, regulatory compliance, disaster recovery, hybrid cloud deployments, and high availability across zones or regions. The traditional single-cluster setup, though manageable for small to mid-sized applications, falls short in scenarios requiring:

- **Data Locality and Compliance:** Regulatory frameworks such as GDPR or HIPAA may mandate local data processing.
- **Disaster Recovery:** Having workloads across multiple clusters in different regions minimizes downtime during outages.
- **Scalability and Segmentation:** Teams can independently manage workloads across development, staging, and production clusters.
- **Hybrid Architecture:** Combining on-premise Kubernetes with cloud (for example, Azure Kubernetes Service) is becoming increasingly common for cost, control, and legacy integration.

To address these requirements, Kubernetes Federation and multi-cluster management solutions offer a unified way to manage multiple clusters at scale.

Understanding Multi-Cluster Federation and Hybrid Cloud

This section introduces the core concepts and tooling required to manage workloads across multiple Kubernetes clusters and hybrid cloud environments. It explains how federation, centralized management platforms, and cross-cluster networking enable consistency, scalability, and resilience in enterprise Kubernetes deployments.

Kubernetes Federation (KubeFed)

KubeFed is an upstream Kubernetes project that enables you to manage multiple clusters as a single logical cluster. Federation helps in:

- Propagating resources (Deployments, Services) across clusters.
- Synchronizing configurations automatically.
- Defining placement rules and overrides per cluster.

Multi-Cluster Management

This involves tools and practices to view, manage, and operate several Kubernetes clusters together, including:

- **Azure Arc for Kubernetes:** Extend Azure control plane to on-prem or other cloud-hosted clusters.
- **Rancher, Anthos, Red Hat ACM:** Enterprise-grade tools for hybrid cluster control.
- **Cluster API (CAPI):** Declarative way to manage cluster lifecycle.

Hybrid Cloud Kubernetes Connectivity

Hybrid deployments require secure and performant connectivity between clusters:

- **VPN, Azure ExpressRoute:** Private networking between on-prem and Azure.
- **Service mesh extensions** such as Istio, Linkerd for multi-cluster routing.
- **Network policies, DNS federation**, and ingress routing must be aligned across clusters.

Workload Synchronization

Workload synchronization ensures consistency in:

- Deployment manifests
- Secrets and ConfigMaps
- Auto-scaling policies
- Horizontal Pod Autoscalers (HPAs) that span multiple clusters.

Using Federation and Multi-Cluster Patterns

This section summarizes common enterprise-grade federation and multi-cluster deployment patterns used to improve availability, governance, and disaster recovery. The following table maps real-world use cases to recommended solutions and highlights the key benefits of each approach.

Use Case	Solution	Benefits
Active-active deployments across regions	KubeFed + Azure Traffic Manager	Fault tolerance, latency optimization
Centralized governance of edge/ on-prem clusters	Azure Arc-enabled Kubernetes	Policy compliance, visibility
Disaster recovery across multiple zones	Federated Deployments with priority failover	RTO and RPO optimization
Isolated team workloads with shared control plane	Rancher or Anthos	Governance with autonomy

Table 13.2: *Multi-Cluster Patterns and Federation Use Cases*

Implementing Federation and Hybrid Kubernetes in Azure

Step 1: Register On-Prem Clusters to Azure Arc

```
az connectedk8s connect \
  --name onprem-cluster \
  --resource-group arc-k8s-rg
```

Explanation: This command registers a non-Azure Kubernetes cluster (for example, bare-metal or OpenShift) to the Azure control plane, enabling monitoring, policy control, and governance through Azure.

Step 2: Deploy KubeFed Control Plane (Optional)

```
kubectl create ns kube-federation-system
helm repo add kubefed-charts https://kubefed.github.io/charts
helm install kubefed kubefed-charts/kubefed \
  --namespace kube-federation-system
```

Explanation: This deploys the Kubernetes Federation control plane in one cluster which acts as the control hub. Other clusters are registered as members.

Step 3: Federate a Deployment Across Clusters

```
apiVersion: types.kubefed.io/v1beta1
kind: FederatedDeployment
metadata:
  name: analytics-api
  namespace: default
spec:
  template:
    spec:
      replicas: 2
      containers:
      - name: api
        image: myacr.azurecr.io/analytics:v1
  placement:
    clusters:
    - name: aks-central
    - name: aks-east
```

Explanation: This resource ensures that the same deployment runs in both `aks-central` and `aks-east` clusters.

Step 4: Implement Cross-Cluster Load Balancing with Azure Traffic Manager

Use Azure Traffic Manager to route traffic to the closest healthy cluster.

```
az network traffic-manager profile create \
  --name multi-region-api \
  --resource-group k8s-global-rg \
  --routing-method Priority \
  --unique-dns-name my-multi-api \
  --ttl 30 \
  --protocol HTTP \
  --port 80 \
  --path "/health"
```

Explanation: Azure Traffic Manager handles DNS-based routing and failover to active clusters.

Azure Hybrid Kubernetes Federation

The following figure illustrates the workflow of the Azure Hybrid Kubernetes Federation:

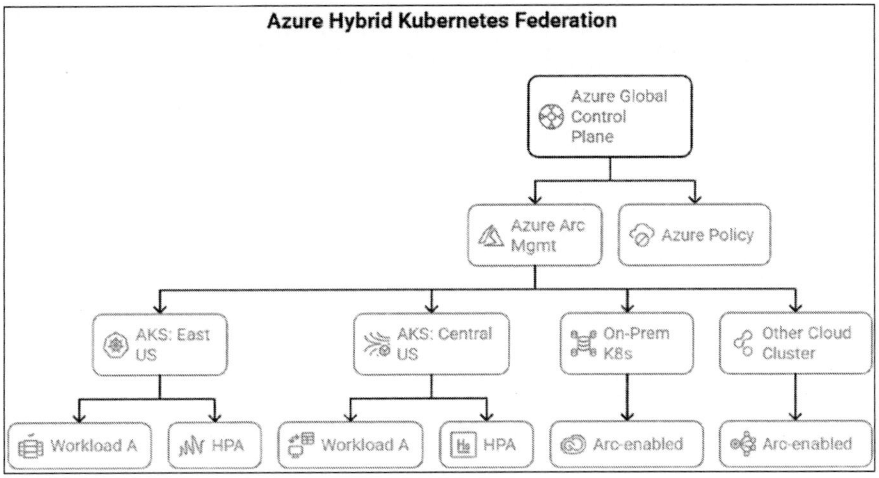

***Figure 13.4**: Azure Hybrid Kubernetes Federation*

A short interpretation of the figure is as follows:

- Azure Arc provides a unified control plane.
- Federated workloads are deployed consistently across AKS East, AKS Central, and On-prem clusters.
- (Not shown but essential): Azure Traffic Manager can route requests to any of these clusters based on health and location.

Case Study: Multi-Cluster Deployment for a Global Fintech Firm

Background: A global fintech enterprise needs to maintain ultra-low latency APIs across EMEA and North America while ensuring resilience against cloud region failures.

Challenges:

- Guarantee service availability even during regional outages.
- Comply with data residency rules (for example, financial data processed within EU).
- Manage multiple clusters centrally while allowing localized updates.

Solution:

- Deployed three clusters: AKS (Germany), AKS (US East), and On-prem EU cluster (Arc-enabled).
- Used KubeFed to synchronize APIs across all clusters.
- Deployed Azure Traffic Manager with geolocation routing.
- Implemented cluster-specific ConfigMap overrides for regional settings.

Result:

- Achieved <100ms latency for EU and US clients.
- Maintained 99.999% availability during a simulated regional outage.
- Simplified governance through Azure Policy and Arc.

YAML Lab: Syncing ConfigMaps Across Clusters

Federated ConfigMap Definition

```
apiVersion: types.kubefed.io/v1beta1
kind: FederatedConfigMap
metadata:
  name: env-settings
  namespace: default
spec:
  template:
    data:
      ENV: "production"
      REGION: "auto"
  placement:
    clusters:
    - name: aks-east
    - name: onprem-eu
  overrides:
    - clusterName: onprem-eu
      clusterOverrides:
      - path: "/data/REGION"
        value: "eu"
    - clusterName: aks-east
      clusterOverrides:
      - path: "/data/REGION"
        value: "us"
```

Explanation: This configuration ensures each cluster gets environment-specific values while maintaining centralized control.

Real-World Use Cases and Best Practices

Managing real-world Kubernetes deployments across regions is crucial for the following reasons:

- **Scalability and Performance Requirements:** As modern enterprise applications scale globally, a single Kubernetes cluster in one region can become a bottleneck. Running clusters across multiple Azure regions ensures lower latency, geo-redundancy, and data sovereignty.
- **Compliance and Regulatory Boundaries:** Enterprises dealing with PII (Personally Identifiable Information) or sensitive customer data are often mandated by regional compliance (such as GDPR, HIPAA) to store and process data within specific geographical boundaries.
- **Resilience and High Availability:** Single-region failure can cause downtime. Multi-region Kubernetes deployment with failover strategies ensures business continuity.
- **Distributed Data Pipelines and Event-Driven Architectures:** Real-time analytics, machine learning workflows, and batch data processing pipelines often span multiple cloud regions and demand stateful and stateless workloads to coexist seamlessly.

What is Involved in Optimizing Multi-Region and Stateful Workload Pipelines

Multi-region workloads and stateful pipelines involve managing orchestration, storage, network, security, and observability at scale. Key components include:

- **Multi-cluster orchestration tools** such as Azure Arc, KubeFed, and Cluster API.
- **Cross-region storage replication** using Azure Disk Replication and Azure NetApp Files.
- **Event queues** (for example, Azure Event Hubs, Kafka) for decoupling producers and consumers.

- **Stateful processing frameworks** such as Apache Flink, Spark Structured Streaming running in AKS with StatefulSets.

Example Scenario:

A retail analytics company runs a distributed data pipeline processing transactions from Europe, Asia, and North America. The pipeline:

- Uses AKS clusters in three Azure regions.
- Writes raw events to Kafka using StatefulSets.
- Processes in-region events with Flink.
- Replicates result sets to a centralized PostgreSQL (Citus) cluster in West Europe.

When to Use Multi-Region Patterns and What to Watch Out For

Scenario	When to Use	Risks to Mitigate
Real-time analytics for multiple geographies	Use distributed clusters for compliance and low latency	Network partitioning, data consistency
HA databases such as PostgreSQL, Cassandra	Use StatefulSets with volume replication and operator support	Storage replication lag, failover time
Application resiliency	Use AKS with Azure Front Door for global routing	DNS propagation, failover configuration

Table 13.3: *Multi-Region Patterns and Scenarios*

Best Practices Include:

- Always use headless services for StatefulSet communication.
- Prefer zone-redundant AKS node pools.
- Use CSI snapshot capabilities for backup.
- Monitor metrics per region with Prometheus + Thanos.

How to Architect and Troubleshoot Multi-Region AKS Applications

Architectural Flow: Multi-Region Analytics with Stateful AKS Clusters

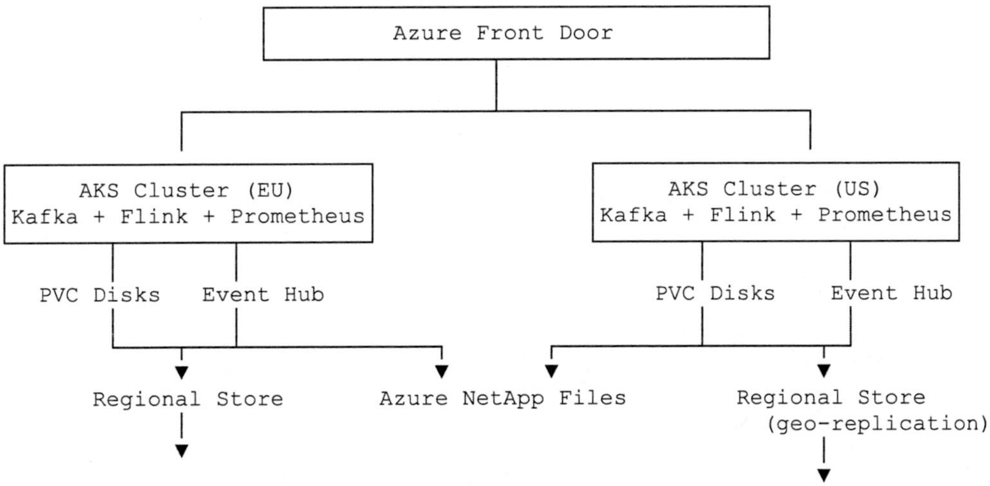

Figure 13.5: *Central PostgreSQL Cluster (AKS - West Europe)*

Explanation:

- **Azure Front Door** routes traffic to the nearest AKS cluster.
- Each cluster has its own Kafka and Flink StatefulSet pipeline, Prometheus for observability.
- Persistent Volumes use Azure Disk or Azure NetApp Files with geo-replication enabled.
- Central PostgreSQL stores processed results and synchronizes data via pipelines or replication.

Hands-On YAML Lab: Regional Kafka Cluster with StatefulSet

Step 1: Define Azure Premium StorageClass

```
apiVersion: storage.k8s.io/v1
kind: StorageClass
metadata:
  name: managed-premium
provisioner: disk.csi.azure.com
parameters:
  skuName: Premium_LRS
reclaimPolicy: Retain
volumeBindingMode: WaitForFirstConsumer
```

Step 2: Headless Service for Kafka

```
apiVersion: v1
kind: Service
metadata:
  name: kafka-headless
spec:
  clusterIP: None
  selector:
    app: kafka
  ports:
    - name: kafka
      port: 9092
```

Step 3: StatefulSet for Kafka Brokers

```
apiVersion: apps/v1
kind: StatefulSet
metadata:
  name: kafka
spec:
  serviceName: kafka-headless
  replicas: 3
  selector:
    matchLabels:
      app: kafka
  template:
    metadata:
      labels:
        app: kafka
    spec:
      containers:
      - name: kafka
        image: bitnami/kafka:latest
        ports:
```

```
          - containerPort: 9092
          volumeMounts:
          - name: kafka-storage
            mountPath: /bitnami/kafka
  volumeClaimTemplates:
  - metadata:
      name: kafka-storage
    spec:
      accessModes: ["ReadWriteOnce"]
      storageClassName: managed-premium
      resources:
        requests:
          storage: 20Gi
```

Case Study: Multi-Region Fraud Detection Platform on Azure AKS

Background: A financial services provider must detect fraudulent transactions in near real-time across continents.

Solution Design:

- Azure Front Door directs clients to the nearest AKS region (for example, Singapore, Frankfurt, Virginia).
- Each region runs:
  - Kafka for ingesting transactions.
  - Apache Flink for detecting fraud patterns.
  - StatefulSet with PVC on Premium SSD.
- Detected fraud events are pushed to Azure Event Hub (central).
- Central team runs batch training jobs with Azure ML + AKS in West Europe.
- Monitoring: Prometheus with Thanos and Grafana federated view.

Impact:

- Reduced fraud detection time from minutes to sub-seconds.
- Maintained compliance with data residency regulations.
- Achieved 99.99% SLA using regional failover.

Key Takeaways for Multi-Region and Real-World Kubernetes Patterns

- Architect clusters with region-level failover, localized processing, and central aggregation.
- Use StatefulSets for all stateful stream processors and message brokers.
- Azure tools like Azure Arc, Azure Front Door, and Azure Monitor are crucial in federated operations.
- Use persistent disks with geo-replication for reliable state management.
- Prioritize observability and cross-region alerting via federated Prometheus/Grafana.
- Monitor not only workloads but also inter-cluster latency, disk I/O, and Kafka lag.

Considerations for Data Engineers and Architects in Kubernetes

For data engineers and architects, Kubernetes offers a robust platform to deploy and manage stateful workloads such as databases, message brokers, and ETL pipelines. Kubernetes helps streamline the orchestration of these complex, distributed systems, making it easier to handle large-scale data processing, real-time analytics, and AI/ML workloads. This section will explore how Kubernetes empowers data engineers and architects to manage distributed data systems efficiently, optimize resources, and design scalable architectures for hybrid and multi-cluster environments.

Why: Addressing the Unique Needs of Data Workloads in Kubernetes

Traditional Kubernetes workloads are designed with stateless microservices in mind. However, Data Engineers and Architects deal with deeply stateful systems—databases, message queues, stream processors, and machine learning pipelines—that require persistent storage, deterministic scheduling, and high network throughput.

In this section, we focus on how Kubernetes can be effectively leveraged by data-centric roles to:

- Deploy stateful, distributed data platforms (Kafka, Cassandra, PostgreSQL).
- Tune and optimize resource allocation for real-time ETL and AI/ML workflows.
- Architect hybrid and multi-cluster environments for large-scale data processing.
- Achieve performance, scalability, and resiliency using Azure-native integrations.

Key Components of Data-Centric Kubernetes Architectures

- **Stateful Workloads with StatefulSets**

  Use Cases:

  - **Kafka:** Distributed event streaming with durable log storage.
  - **Cassandra:** Highly available, decentralized NoSQL database.
  - **PostgreSQL:** Reliable relational database with failover clustering.

  Why StatefulSets:

  - Enforces pod identity (example, kafka-0, kafka-1).
  - Maintains persistent volume claims even after restarts.
  - Ensures ordered deployment which is critical for quorum-based systems.

- **Kubernetes Resource Management for Data Pipelines**

  ETL Pipelines:

  - **Input:** Kafka, Azure Event Hub.
  - **Processing:** Apache Flink, Spark Operator.
  - **Output:** Blob storage, PostgreSQL, Data Lake.

  AI/ML Workloads:

  - Training and inference on GPU-enabled nodes using Kubeflow or Azure ML with AKS integration.
  - Tuned CPU/memory/GPU requests and limits for performance consistency.

- **Multi-Cluster Design for Distributed Processing**

  Hybrid Architectures:

  - On-prem clusters (Minikube, MicroK8s, VMware Tanzu) bridged with AKS using Azure Arc.

- Data locality via node affinity and topology spread constraints.

Federated Data Pipelines:

- Kafka MirrorMaker2 for replicating topics across AKS clusters.
- Cassandra multi-datacenter replication with rack-aware placement.

Real-World Scenarios Demanding These Approaches

Scenario 1: Streaming ETL with Kafka and Spark on AKS

- Event data ingested via Kafka StatefulSet.
- Apache Spark operator processes and transforms data in micro-batches.
- Output pushed to Azure Data Lake.

Scenario 2: AI/ML Model Training with Resource-Optimized Scheduling

- ML training jobs submitted via Kubeflow Pipelines.
- Scheduled on GPU-enabled AKS node pools using nodeSelector and resource limits.
- Realtime model feedback sent to PostgreSQL backend.

Scenario 3: Hybrid Data Processing in Federated Environments

- Cassandra clusters span on-prem and Azure.
- AKS clusters replicate data using inter-cluster networking over Azure VNet Peering.

Practical Implementation Using Azure Kubernetes Service (AKS)

This section demonstrates a practical hybrid multi-cluster implementation using Azure Kubernetes Service (AKS), showing how stateful data platforms and streaming systems can be integrated across on-premises and Azure environments for resilience, scalability, and data consistency.

Architectural Flow Diagram

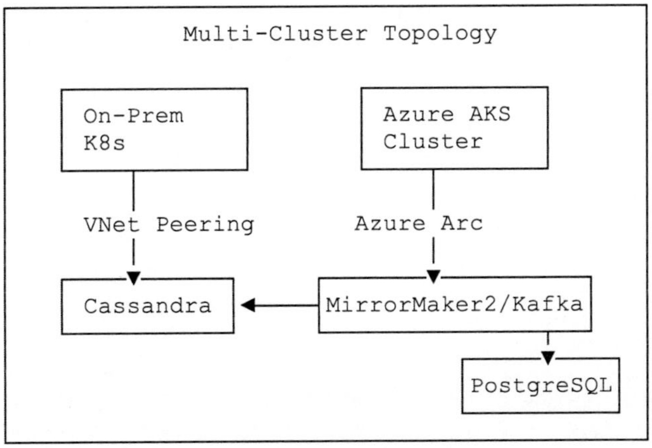

Figure 13.6: *Hybrid Multi-Cluster Architecture on AKS Using Azure Arc*

Explanation:

- Cassandra is replicated across clusters using rack-aware topology.
- Kafka topics are mirrored from on-prem to AKS for stream redundancy.

- PostgreSQL persists the analytical results on AKS.
- AKS uses Azure Premium Disks for durable storage.

YAML Lab: Deploying Cassandra for IoT Data Processing

Step 1: StorageClass for Cassandra Disks

```
apiVersion: storage.k8s.io/v1
kind: StorageClass
metadata:
  name: cassandra-premium
provisioner: disk.csi.azure.com
parameters:
  skuName: Premium_LRS
reclaimPolicy: Retain
volumeBindingMode: WaitForFirstConsumer
```

Step 2: Cassandra Headless Service

```
apiVersion: v1
kind: Service
metadata:
  name: cassandra-headless
spec:
  clusterIP: None
  selector:
    app: cassandra
  ports:
  - port: 9042
    name: cql
```

Step 3: Cassandra StatefulSet

```
apiVersion: apps/v1
kind: StatefulSet
metadata:
  name: cassandra
spec:
  serviceName: cassandra-headless
  replicas: 3
  selector:
    matchLabels:
      app: cassandra
  template:
    metadata:
      labels:
        app: cassandra
    spec:
      containers:
      - name: cassandra
        image: cassandra:4.0
        ports:
        - containerPort: 9042
        volumeMounts:
        - name: cassandra-data
          mountPath: /var/lib/cassandra
  volumeClaimTemplates:
```

```
  - metadata:
      name: cassandra-data
    spec:
      accessModes: ["ReadWriteOnce"]
      storageClassName: cassandra-premium
      resources:
        requests:
          storage: 20Gi
```

Case Study: AI/ML Pipeline Scaling with Azure AKS

Industry: Financial Services

Problem: A bank needed to retrain fraud detection models daily using millions of transactions from distributed Kafka topics.

Solution:

- Kafka on AKS with persistent volumes.
- Spark MLlib jobs submitted via K8s Spark Operator.
- GPU-enabled node pools used for heavy training with nvidia.com/gpu resource requests.
- PostgreSQL used for storing model results and metadata.

Benefits:

- Dynamic scheduling allowed full node utilization.
- Multi-cluster design provided redundancy across Azure regions.
- Training times reduced by 35% using GPU workloads.

Conclusion

In this chapter, we explored the advanced capabilities of Kubernetes essential for running modern enterprise-grade applications. We began with **StatefulSets** for managing persistent workloads such as PostgreSQL, Kafka, and Cassandra, followed by **intelligent scheduling and resource optimization** using node affinity, taints, tolerations, and resource limits. We then examined **multi-cluster federation and hybrid cloud strategies**, enabling seamless workload portability between Azure and on-prem environments. Through real-world use cases and best practices, we highlighted how to handle stateful data pipelines, troubleshoot multi-cluster environments, and scale applications efficiently. Finally, we tailored the key insights for **Data Engineers and Architects**, bridging Kubernetes with real-time data processing, AI/ML workloads, and distributed cloud-native designs. Together, these topics equip architects and engineers with the tools to design resilient, scalable, and production-ready Kubernetes platforms on Azure and beyond.

Index

D

E

F

G

H

L

M

N

O

P

R

W

Y